Tübinger Platon-Tage

4

Platon und die Seele
Plato and the Soul

edited by

Klaus Corcilius
Irmgard Männlein
Samuel Meister

Mohr Siebeck

Klaus Corcilius, born 1966; 2006 PhD, Humboldt University, Berlin; 2009–2011 Junior Professor of Ancient Philosophy at the University of Hamburg; 2011–2016 Associate Professor, Department of Philosophy, University of California at Berkeley; Full Professor of Philosophy, Faculty of Philosophy, Department Philosophy at the University of Tübingen.
orcid.org/0000-0003-2777-6848

Irmgard Männlein, born 1970; 2000 PhD, University of Würzburg; 2005 Habilitation; Full Professor of Classics / Greek Philology, Faculty of Philosophy, Department for Classical Studies at the University of Tübingen.
orcid.org/0000-0003-0250-5427

Samuel Meister, born 1990; 2020 PhD, Brown University; 2023 research associate at the University of Tübingen; Assistant Professor of Ancient Philosophy at the University of Geneva.
orcid.org/0000-0001-7991-1824

Funded by
the European Union

European Research Council
Established by the European Commission

Funded by the European Union. Views and opinions expressed are however those of the author(s) only and do not necessarily reflect those of the European Union or the European Research Council Executive Agency. Neither the European Union nor the granting authority can be held responsible for them. This work is supported by ERC grant TIDA, 101053296.

ISBN 978-3-16-200505-2 / eISBN 978-3-16-200506-9
DOI 10.1628/978-3-16-200506-9

ISSN 2629-3978 / eISSN 2629-3986 (Tübinger Platon-Tage)

The Deutsche Nationalbibliothek lists this publication in the Deutsche Nationalbibliographie; detailed bibliographic data is available on the Internet at *https://dnb.dnb.de*.

Printed on non-aging paper.

Mohr Siebeck GmbH & Co. KG, Wilhelmstraße 18, 72074 Tübingen, Germany
www.mohrsiebeck.com, info@mohrsiebeck.com

Vorwort zur Reihe „Tübinger Platon-Tage"

Die „Tübinger Platon-Tage", die seit 2008 alle zwei Jahre stattfinden, sind internationale und interdisziplinäre Tagungen zu großen Themen der Platon-Forschung und der Forschung zum Platonismus. Grundlegend ist dabei die Idee, die lange Tübinger Platon-Tradition im In- und Ausland neu zu beleben, sowie neue Impulse methodischer und inhaltlicher Art aus der aktuellen Platon- und Platonismus-Forschung zu präsentieren und zu diskutieren. Die „Tübinger Platon-Tage" sind ein lebendiges Kooperationsprojekt zwischen dem Philologischen Seminar und dem Philosophischen Seminar.

Die Themen der jeweiligen Tagungen und der daraus hervorgehenden Tagungsbände orientieren sich vornehmlich an zentralen philologischen und philosophischen Fragestellungen zu Platons Dialogen und seiner Philosophie, aber auch an Themen der Rezeption und Transformierung sowie Neumodellierung platonischer Philosophie in Kaiserzeit und Spätantike.

Die TeilnehmerInnen sind ausgewiesene ExpertInnen, aber auch jüngere einschlägige WissenschaftlerInnen aus dem In- und Ausland. Uns ist wichtig, hier fortgeschrittenen Studierenden, Doktoranden und Post-Docs die Gelegenheit zu geben, ihre Forschungen zu Platon und Platonismus vor führenden Fachleuten zu präsentieren.

Die ReihenherausgeberInnen

Foreword to the Series "Tübinger Platon-Tage"

The "Tübinger Platon-Tage", which have been held every two years since 2008, are international and interdisciplinary conferences on major research topics in Plato and in Platonism. The fundamental idea is to revive the long tradition of Tübingen Plato studies, both in Germany and abroad, and to present and discuss new methodological and content-related impulses from current research on Plato and Platonism. The "Tübinger Platon-Tage" are a lively collaborative project between the Department of Classics and the Department of Philosophy of the University of Tübingen.

The topics of the conferences and the resulting proceedings are primarily oriented toward philological and philosophical questions concerning Plato's dialogues and his philosophy, but also toward topics of reception, transformation, and remodeling of Platonic philosophy in the imperial period and late antiquity.

The participants are renowned experts, but also younger scholars from Germany and abroad. We place great importance on giving advanced students, doctoral candidates, and postdocs the opportunity to present their research on Plato and Platonism to leading experts.

The series editors

Vorwort

Der vorliegende Band umfasst die Beiträge der „Tübinger Platon-Tage“ aus dem Jahr 2024, die vom 11. bis 13. April in den Räumen des Philologischen Seminars in Tübingen stattfanden. Das Thema dieser internationalen und interdisziplinären Tagung war „Platon und die Seele.“

Die Vorbereitung zum Satz hat Frau Dr. Laura Bottenberg (Philologisches Seminar) übernommen, der für Ihre Mühen unser herzlicher Dank sicher ist. Herrn Andreas Kindler (Philosophisches Seminar) sei ebenfalls für die Erstellung der Indices herzlich gedankt.

Ebenso sind wir Herrn Tobias Stäbler sowie Herrn Markus Kirchner vom Mohr Siebeck Verlag für ihre sachkundigen und stets konstruktiven Hilfestellungen bei der Vorbereitung zum Druck zu großem Dank verpflichtet.

Schließlich bedanken wir uns herzlich für die großzügige finanzielle Unterstützung sowohl der Tagung als auch des Tagungsbandes durch den ERC 2021 Advanced Grant: Text and Idea of Aristotle's Science of Living Things (Akronym: TIDA).

Tübingen, im Januar 2026

Klaus Corcilius
Irmgard Männlein
Samuel Meister

Foreword

This volume contains the contributions to the 'Tübingen Platon-Tage' held in April 2024 at the Philological Seminar in Tübingen. The theme of this international and interdisciplinary conference was 'Plato and the Soul.'

Dr. Laura Bottenberg (Philological Seminar) was responsible for preparing the text, and we would like to express our sincere thanks to her for her efforts. We would also like to thank Mr. Andreas Kindler (Philosophical Seminar) for compiling the indices.

We are also very grateful to Tobias Stäbler and Markus Kirchner from Mohr Siebeck for their expert and consistently constructive assistance in preparing the proceedings for printing.

Finally, we would like to express our sincere gratitude for the generous financial support provided by the ERC 2021 Advanced Grant: Text and Idea of Aristotle's Science of Living Things (acronym: TIDA) for both the conference and the conference proceedings.

Tübingen, January 2026

Klaus Corcilius
Irmgard Männlein
Samuel Meister

Table of Contents

Platon und die Seele: Einleitung

Klaus Corcilius und Samuel Meister

Platon gilt vielen als ‚Begründer' der Psychologie. Mit dieser Aussage ist dann aber häufig nicht viel mehr gemeint, als dass Platon als erster ausdrücklich die Seele zum Thema der Diskussion gemacht, und in seinen Schriften mehr oder weniger ausführlich verschiedene Ansichten über die Natur und Beschaffenheit der Seele zur Sprache gebracht hat. Und die Seele hat in der Tat eine durchgehend wichtige, und vielleicht auch fundamentale Bedeutung in Platons Werk. Das Problem ist nur, dass Platon in seinem Werk der Seele sehr unterschiedliche Funktionen und Bedeutungen zuspricht. Erschwerend kommt hinzu, dass er auf ganz unterschiedlichen Ebenen von der Seele spricht, nämlich teils von der Seele des menschlichen Individuums und teils von der Seele des Alls, der Weltseele. Wie diese verschiedenen Bedeutungen, Funktionen und Ebenen miteinander zusammenhängen, ist eine schwierige, und bis heute durchaus nicht zufriedenstellend beantwortete Frage. Zwar bieten die späteren Systeme der Platoniker Antworten, was aber Platon selber betrifft, so beschränken sich die Ausleger in ihren Darstellungen üblicherweise damit, verschiedene Funktionen und Kontexte zu unterscheiden, in denen bei Platon von der Seele die Rede ist, ohne die Frage nach deren Zusammenhang systematisch zu beantworten. Ein Prinzip der Gliederung ist dabei die allgemein akzeptierte Einteilung nach Schaffensperioden in frühe, mittlere und Spätdialoge, oder – feinteiliger – nach Dialogen, während noch andere sich in ihren Darstellungen auf einzelne, als besonders wichtig herausgestellte Aspekte der platonischen Seelenlehre beschränken.[1] Im günstigsten Fall ergibt sich daraus ein mosaikähnliches Bild. Hier und da tauchen verschiedene Teile und Fragmente einer einheitlichen Seelenlehre auf, von denen dann zwar nicht klar ist, ob sie ein einheitliches Lehrgebäude ergeben, von denen aber auch nicht ausgeschlossen wird, dass eventuell ein tieferer systematischer Zusammenhang besteht. Dies mag philosophisch zwar nicht sehr befriedigend sein, wirkt aber gerade aufgrund seines Mangels an systematischer Vollständigkeit umso anregender auf das eigene

[1] Beispielhaft genannt seien hier Peter M. Steiner, *Die Psyche bei Platon*, Göttingen 1992, sowie Hendrik Lorenz, "Plato on the Soul", in: G. Fine (Hg.), *Oxford Handbook on Plato*, Oxford 2008, 243–266.

Nachdenken über die Seele. Man wird wohl nicht ganz fehlgehen, wenn man die anregende Wirkung als von Platon beabsichtigt versteht.

Grob betrachtet lassen sich drei Hauptfunktionen und Kontexte der Rede von der Seele bei Platon unterscheiden: (i) Seele als Prinzip von Bewegung und Lebendig-Sein, (ii) Seele als Erkenntnis- und Strebesubjekt, (iii) Seele als moralischer Akteur, der gut oder schlecht sein, bzw. werden, kann. Was (iii) betrifft, so lässt sich vielleicht sagen, dass in diesen Kontexten von der Seele als Person die Rede ist, und dass (ii) und (iii) zusammengenommen ungefähr so etwas wie das Gebiet der Psychologie im engeren Sinne abdecken. Wie (ii) und (iii) zusammenhängen, wird deutlich, wenn wir uns die berühmte Seelenteilungslehre in der *Politeia* vergegenwärtigen. Man kann Platon dort kurz gesagt so verstehen, dass eine *menschliche Person* zu sein heißt, eine aus drei motivationalen Antrieben bestehendes Aggregat zu sein, nämlich aus den drei sogenannten ‚Teilen der Seele' Begierde, *Thymos* und rationale Strebung, wobei jeder dieser Teile seiner jeweils eigenen Güterklasse als Gegenstand zugeordnet ist (körperliche Güter für die Begierde, soziale Güter für den Thymos und rational Gutes für die rationale Strebung). Eine *moralische Person* zu sein, konstituiert sich dann dadurch, dass diese drei Seelenteile in einer gewissen hierarchischen Ordnung stehen: Die moralisch gute Person bzw. der gute ‚Charakter' konstituiert sich dadurch, dass die rationale Strebung über die anderen Strebearten herrscht. In diesem Fall ist man letztlich durch das Wissen vom rational Guten motiviert. Ist der *Thymos* die herrschende Motivationsform, ist man durch Ehre und soziale Anerkennung als höchste Güter motiviert, wobei die Rationalität dann gleichsam in den Dienst einer nicht-rationalen Strebeform tritt. Herrscht schließlich die Begierde, so sind beide übrige Strebearten dem Streben nach körperlicher Lust unterworfen. Diese, vom moralischen Standpunkt suboptimalen Herrschaftsverhältnisse konstituieren dann moralisch minder gute, oder gar moralisch schlechte Personen bzw. Charaktere. Die Rede von den Seelenteilen und die auf ihrer Konzeption basierende Moralpsychologie taucht in Platons Dialogen immer wieder auf,[2] und es ist vielleicht nicht zu viel gesagt, wenn man diese als Platons hauptsächlichen Beitrag zur

[2] Außerhalb der *Politeia* wird dies im *Phaidros*, im *Timaios* und in den *Gesetzen* am deutlichsten, aber auch im *Phaidon* und im *Gorgias* lassen sich deutliche Spuren aufweisen. Zur Seelenteilungslehre bei Platon, s. Andreas Graeser, *Probleme der platonischen Seelenteilungslehre*, Zetemata 47, München 1969; generell in der Philosophie der Antike bis zu Galen, s. Klaus Corcilius, „Faculties: Ancient Debates", in: C. Mercer / D. Perler (Hgg.), *Oxford Philosophical Concepts ‚Faculty'*, Oxford 2015, 19–58; speziell in Platons *Politeia*, s. Christopher Shields, „Plato's Divided Soul", in: , Mark L. McPherran (Hg.), *Plato's Republic: A Critical Guide*, Cambridge 2010, 147–70. Für eine philosophische Verteidigung der Dreiteilung der Seele s. Myles Burnyeat, „The Truth of Tripartition", *Proceedings of the Aristotelian Society* 106 (2006), 1–23. Zum Verhältnis der Seelenteilungslehre zu Platons Moralpsychologie s. Hendrik Lorenz, *The Brute Within*, Oxford 2006; Rachana Kamtekar, *Plato's Moral Psychology*, Oxford 2018.

‚Psychologie' betrachtet. Allerdings ist hier gleich die wichtige Einschränkung geltend zu machen, dass die einzigen Stellen in Platons Werk, in denen er sie förmlich zu definieren scheint, die Seele als Selbstbeweger, der Ursprung aller anderen Bewegungen darstellt, also im Sinne von (i) fassen.[3] Die Rede von der Seele im Sinne von (ii) und (iii) scheint allerdings wohl relativ nahe am damaligen allgemeinen Sprachgebrauch, wo wir es auch mit der Seele als Subjekt mentaler Episoden zu tun haben. Dieser Gebrauch von ‚Seele' ist dem heutigen Gebrauch nicht ganz fremd, wenn auch der im Grunde nicht weniger problematische Ausdruck ‚Geist' der Sache vom philosophischen Sprachgebrauch her der Sache näher zu kommen scheint.

Dieser Band, der auf die *Tübinger Platon-Tage* vom 11. bis 13. April 2024 zurückgeht, hat zum Ziel, auf gebündelte Weise einige Themen der platonischen Seelenlehre, vor allem in dem gerade beschriebenen engeren Sinn von (ii) und (iii) aufzuarbeiten. Ergänzt werden diese Beiträge durch allgemeinere zur Konzeption der Seele bei Platon und in der Alten Akademie.

Ein Thema, das sich durch viele Beiträge zu (ii) und (iii) zieht, ist das Verhältnis von Körper und Seele in der Erklärung psychologischer Phänomene. Um ein Beispiel herauszugreifen: im berühmten letzten Argument des ersten Teiles des *Theaitetos* (184b–186e), wo die Definition von Wissen als Wahrnehmung endgültig widerlegt wird, scheint Sokrates zwischen einer Beschreibung der Wahrnehmung als passiver körperlicher Affektion und als aktiven Vorgangs der Seele zu schwanken. Deshalb stellt sich die Frage, inwiefern die Wahrnehmung an dieser Stelle ein Phänomen ist, zu dessen Erklärung man sowohl auf die körperliche Affektion als auch auf die Aktivität der Seele verweisen muss. Ähnliches gilt etwa für die Erklärung von Wahrnehmung, Erinnerung und Begierde im *Philebos* (33c–35d) oder die platonische Theorie der Vorstellung (*phantasia*) im *Sophistes*.

Auch wenn man von der radikalen These, dass für Platon der Körper mit einigen dieser Phänomene gar nichts zu tun habe, absieht, gibt es eine Reihe philosophisch unterschiedlicher Interpretationsmöglichkeiten. Man könnte zum Beispiel den Verweis auf den körperlichen Prozess als Teil der Definition der psychologischen Phänomene betrachten oder aber nur als Vorbedingung für ein psychologisches Phänomen, die nicht selbst in der Definition erwähnt wird. Im ersten Fall wären zumindest einige psychologische Phänomene für Platon essentiell körperlich, während im zweiten Fall für dieselben Phänomene das Gegenteil gelten würde: sie wären essentiell rein seelisch. Eine weiterführende Frage wäre zudem, ob Platon eine einheitliche Theorie aller dieser

[3] *Phdr.* 245, *Lg.* 896. Die verschiedenen Diskussionen der Weltseele in Platons Werk beinhalten (i) und in den *Gesetzen* und im *Timaios* auch (ii) und (iii), wobei (iii) im *Timaios* höchstens angedeutet wird. Die Erwähnung der Weltseele im *Politikos* hat ihre eigenen Schwierigkeiten, auf die wir hier nicht eingehen können.

psychologischen Phänomene vertritt oder bei verschiedenen Phänomenen zu unterschiedlichen Schlüssen kommt.

Kurzum, ein Themenkomplex der platonischen Psychologie kann um die Frage angeordnet werden, ob Phänomene wie die Wahrnehmung oder die Begierde der Seele und dem Körper „gemeinsam" (κοινῇ) zukommen (*Philebos* 34a3–5). Bei der Antwort geht es aber nicht nur um ein Ja oder Nein, sondern auch darum, was denn dieses Ja oder Nein impliziert, das heißt, auf welche Weise die einschlägigen Phänomene dem Körper und der Seele gemeinsam sind und auf welche Weise nicht. Dabei ist insbesondere die Unterscheidung zwischen der Ursache der Phänomene und notwendigen Bedingungen für ihre Entstehung wichtig: Ist die Seele allein die Ursache oder das Prinzip der Wahrnehmung oder Begierde oder sind sowohl Seele als auch Körper Ursachen, womöglich auf unterschiedliche Art?

Sowohl *Mary Louise Gill* als auch *Béatrice Lienemann* greifen diese Frage in Bezug auf die Wahrnehmung auf. Gemäß Gill lassen sich im *Theaitetos* zwei Phasen der Wahrnehmung unterscheiden, wobei die erste, rein physiologische und für den Wahrnehmenden passive Phase eine zweite Phase auslöst, in der die Seele die externe Affektion aktiv wahrnimmt. Lienemann hingegen argumentiert, dass nicht nur im *Theaitetos*, sondern auch im *Philebos* die Wahrnehmung passiv, und erst das Denken der Seele ein aktiver Vorgang sei, sie betont aber gleichzeitig auch die Unabdingbarkeit der Wahrnehmung als Vorbedingung für gewisse Arten des Wissens.

Andere Beiträge drehen sich um die Lust, Begierde und Vorstellung. *Georgia Mouroutsou* beleuchtet das Verhältnis der dialektischen Behandlung der Lust im *Philebos* mit der physiologischen im *Timaios* und untersucht, inwiefern diese vereinbar sind. *Samuel Meister* widmet sich der Analyse der Begierde im *Philebos*. Er argumentiert, dass die Definition der Begierde den Körper zwar nicht erwähnt, man auf diesen aber zur Erklärung des Auftretens einzelner Episoden von Begierde nicht verzichten kann. *Fiona Leigh* wiederum bespricht das Thema der Vorstellung (*phantasia)* im *Sophistes*, welche sie als durch Wahrnehmung verursachte Meinung versteht, die uns besonders anfällig für sophistische Argumente macht.

Mit dem Thema der Seele und Körper gemeinsamen Phänomene ist eine weitere Frage nach dem Status der Seele als Prinzip verknüpft: *Wovon* ist sie Prinzip? Bis jetzt haben wir von „psychologischen" oder „geistigen" Phänomenen im Sinne von (ii) und (iii) gesprochen. Aber man könnte diese Wortwahl für unglücklich halten und darauf pochen, stattdessen von „biologischen" Phänomenen zu sprechen. Die Seele wäre also ein Prinzip biologischer Prozesse als Bewegungsursache im Sinne von (i), worunter dann auch die (menschliche) Wahrnehmung oder Begierde fallen würden, aber nur neben vielen anderen Phänomenen, welche allgemein alle Lebewesen (*zōia*) betreffen. Die platonische Psychologie im engeren Sinn müsste dann im Rahmen der platonischen Biologie verstanden werden, nicht als eigene Spezialdisziplin, und die Seele müsste auch in ihrer Rolle als Prinzip von Phänomenen wie der Wahrnehmung oder Begierde allgemeiner als Lebensprinzip aufgefasst werden. Zu klären wäre dann das Verhältnis von (i) zu (ii) und (iii). Wie verhält sich die Rolle der Seele als selbstbewegendes Prinzip aller anderen Bewegungen zu den im engeren Sinne seelisch-geistigen und moralischen Funktionen der Seele? Wie genau haben wir die Aussage, dass die Seele das Lebensprinzip von Organismen ist, zu verstehen?

Andrea Falcon nimmt sich dieser Frage im Rahmen des *Timaios* an. Dabei vertritt er die Ansicht, dass bei Platon die Seele eine beschränktere explanatorische Rolle innehat als bei Aristoteles, da Phänomene wie die Atmung nicht unter Bezugnahme auf die Seele erklärt werden (während Aristoteles mithilfe des seelischen Nährungsvermögens genau dies zu leisten versucht). *Riccardo Chiaradonna* und *Peter Oxenknecht* behandeln beide die Aussage im letzten Argument für die Unsterblichkeit der Seele im *Phaidon*, dass die Seele das Leben „bringe". Auf Grundlage einer Analyse der Relation der Eponymie (der gemäß etwas, das an einer Form von Gegenteilen wie dem Großen oder Kleinen teilhat, den Namen dieser Form trägt), argumentiert Chiaradonna, dass die Seele als Prinzip des Lebens selbst nicht essenziell, sondern nur notwendigerweise lebendig ist. Oxenknecht wiederum versucht zu zeigen, dass die Seele ein Lebewesen belebt, indem sie ein Teil von ihm ist.

Die Seele, insbesondere die rationale Seele, ist bei Platon aber auch noch auf andere Weise Prinzip: als Herrscherin und Ordnerin des körperlichen Lebewesens sowie seiner Dispositionen und der Prozesse, in denen der Körper auf irgendeine Weise involviert ist, d.h. als Herrscherin über das, was Körper und Seele gemeinsam zu sein scheint. Als Prinzip in diesem Sinn ist die Seele nicht nur dafür verantwortlich, dass die relevanten Prozesse sich überhaupt ereignen, sondern auch dafür, von welcher Art sie sind, zum Beispiel welche Strebungen entstehen und sich durchsetzen. Wie diese beiden Rollen der Seele als Prinzip – die allgemeine biologische Rolle und ihre ordnende Rolle – zusammenspielen, ist durchaus nicht offensichtlich. Die doppelte Rolle der Seele als Prinzip legt aber nahe, dass sich die Seele als Erkenntnis- und Strebesubjekt nach (ii) nicht ohne weiteres von der Moralpsychologie (iii) abgrenzen lässt: was uns (biologisch) als Menschen bestimmt, scheint zugleich das zu sein, was es uns erlaubt, gute Menschen zu sein.

Dieser Gedanke kommt in den Beiträgen von *Jan Szaif* und *Klaus Corcilius* zu tragen. Szaif lenkt unsere Aufmerksamkeit auf eine wenig beachtete Stelle im *Philebos* (64b), wo Sokrates sein Argument mit einer „körperlosen Ordnung *(kosmos)* des beseelten Körpers" vergleicht. Szaif zufolge weist der Vergleich darauf hin, dass der Diskurs über das Gute im *Philebos* den idealen rationalen Zustand der Seele vorwegnimmt. Corcilius beschäftigt sich demgegenüber mit der Frage, wie unter Zugrundelegung der im *Timaios* beschriebenen *conditio humana* die menschliche Seele trotz ihres Eingeschlossenseins im Körper zur wahren Erkenntnis der Welt außerhalb ihrer selbst gelangen kann. Er argumentiert, dass die Seele des Menschen im Gegensatz zur Weltseele nur über Wahrnehmungsdaten zu einer solchen wahren Erkenntnis gelangen kann.

Bis jetzt haben wir das Verhältnis von Seele und Körper in der Erklärung von Phänomenen wie der Wahrnehmung (ii) sowie den Status der Seele als Bewegungs- (i) und als ordnendes Moralprinzip (iii) erwähnt. Aber dadurch, dass die Seele Prinzip eines körperlichen Lebewesens ist und die Phänomene, die sie erklärt, zumindest zum Teil mit dem Körper zu tun haben, stellt sich für (ii) und (iii) umgekehrt auch die Frage nach dem Einfluss des Körpers auf die Seele, insbesondere auf die ihr typische Aktivität des Denkens. Denn das menschliche Denken scheint abhängig von der Wahrnehmung, sodass unser Zugang zur Welt auch im Denken nicht von Prozessen, die den Körper involvieren, unabhängig zu sein scheint. Auf diese Weise stellt sich also einmal mehr die Frage nach dem Verhältnis zwischen Körper und Seele, sogar in einem Bereich, von dem man vielleicht hätte vermuten können, dass der Körper keine Rolle spielt, nämlich demjenigen des Denkens. Wenn es eine übergeordnete Tendenz dieses Bandes gibt, dann sicherlich dahingehend, dass man das Thema „Platon und die Seele“ nicht ohne das Thema „Platon und der Körper“ behandeln kann.

Die Frage nach dem Verhältnis von Körper und Seele lässt sich aber noch allgemeiner stellen, nämlich nicht nur auf einzelne Funktionen der Lebewesen bezogen, sondern auf die Wirkung der Seele auf die wahrnehmbare Welt insgesamt. Insbesondere die Rolle mathematischer Proportionen in der Konstruktion der Weltseele im *Timaios* (34b–36d) wirft die Frage auf, wie eine Seele – sei es die Weltseele oder die Seele eines einzelnen Lebewesens – überhaupt Ursache von Phänomenen in der wahrnehmbaren, veränderbaren Welt sein kann. Hier ist das Problem nicht so sehr, wie Körper und Seele an der Erklärung eines bestimmten Prozesses in der wahrnehmbaren Welt, wie etwa der Veränderung, beteiligt sind, sondern wie die Seele überhaupt an einer solchen Erklärung teilhaben kann, geschweige denn diese Erklärung hauptsächlich oder gar vollständig ausmachen. *Thomas Johansen* möchte in seinem Aufsatz zeigen, wie im *Timaios* die mathematischen Proportionen der Seele in der *chōra* oder dem „Behälter“ Bewegung auslösen, sodass nach Platon mathematische Entitäten zumindest Teil der Erklärung von Bewegung und Veränderung sein können.

Susanna Kinzig und *Christoph Poetsch* besprechen dasselbe Thema in Bezug auf Platons Nachfolger in der Alten Akademie. Kinzig unterzieht die Testimonia, in denen Xenokrates die berüchtigte Definition der Seele als selbstbewegende Zahl zugeschrieben wird, einer eingehenden Analyse, um nicht nur die Bedeutung der Definition selbst, sondern auch die Motivation für die Definition und ihren historischen Hintergrund insbesondere im *Timaios* zu prüfen. Auf allgemeinere Weise bespricht Poetsch die Konzeptionen der Seele in der Alten Akademie, wobei er weitreichende strukturelle Ähnlichkeiten feststellt.

Man könnte nun versucht sein, die Frage nach dem Verhältnis der (mathematischen) Seele zur wahrnehmbaren Welt als Verallgemeinerung der Frage nach dem Zusammenhang von Seele und Körper von einzelnen Lebewesen zu behandeln. Auf gewisse Weise scheint dies gerechtfertigt, besonders wenn es um die Seele als ordnendes Prinzip des Lebewesens oder der Welt als ganzer geht. Was aber die Erklärung spezifischer Phänomene wie der Wahrnehmung betrifft, kann das Problem des Verhältnisses von Körper und Seele unabhängig von der mathematischen Konstruktion der Seele betrachtet werden. Denn unabhängig davon, wie die Seele konstruiert ist, kann man sich die Frage stellen, inwiefern die Seele oder Körper bei Lebewesen gewisse psychologischen – oder biologischen – Tatsachen erklärt. Obwohl man also alle hier erwähnten Themenkomplexe grob unter der Überschrift „Leib und Seele“ aufführen könnte, sollte man die spezifischen psychologischen oder biologischen Fragestellungen nicht von Problemen, die von der mathematischen Konstruktion der Seele herrühren, abhängig machen.

Diese Unterscheidung hilft dabei, die zwiespältige Antwort auf Platons Psychologie, die wir bei Aristoteles finden, zu erklären. Denn einerseits hat er für den Gedanken, dass die Seele als mathematische Entität psychologische Phänomene erklären könnte, wenig übrig, wie sich zum Beispiel an seiner schroffen Behandlung der xenokrateischen Definition der Seele als selbstbewegende Zahl zeigt (*De anima* I.2, 405a28–30). Aber andererseits scheint er die Fragestellung nach dem Zusammenspiel von Körper und Seele in der Erklärung von Phänomenen, die dem Körper und der Seele gemeinsam sind, besonders in *Parva Naturalia* in etwa so aufzugreifen, wie wir sie bei Platon finden. Dies bedeutet natürlich nicht, dass er zu denselben Ergebnissen kommt wie Platon, aber dennoch zeigt es – und dies ist vielleicht eine zweite übergeordnete Konklusion dieses Bandes –, dass die Problemlage, mit der Aristoteles sich auseinandersetzt, stark von Platon geprägt ist, und zwar nicht nur was den Status der Seele betrifft, sondern auch bezüglich des Beitrags des Körpers zur Erklärung seelischer Phänomene.

Plato and the Soul: Introduction

Klaus Corcilius and Samuel Meister

Plato is often considered the 'founder' of psychology. But this claim tends to mean little more than that Plato was the first to explicitly discuss the soul while expressing various views about its nature and constitution. Indeed, the soul plays an important, perhaps even fundamental role in Plato's writings. However, the functions and roles he ascribes to the soul vary greatly. Furthermore, Plato speaks of the soul at different levels, namely, both as the soul of the individual human being and as the world soul. It thus remains a difficult question how these functions, roles, and levels hang together. For whereas the systems of later Platonists offer some answers, interpreters of Plato usually restrict themselves to distinguishing the different functions and contexts of the soul in Plato's writings without responding to the question of their systematic connection. One organisational principle they assume is the widely accepted division of Plato's works into early, middle, and late dialogues (or more finely, into individual dialogues). Meanwhile, other scholars focus on certain aspects of the Platonic account of the soul that they consider especially important.[1] At best, the resulting overall picture resembles a mosaic. In the scholarly literature parts and fragments of a unified account of the soul emerge, but it is neither clear whether they constitute a single theory, nor whether such a systematic connection can be ruled out. While this may not be philosophically satisfying, the lack of systematic completion does nevertheless stimulate one's own reflections on the soul. Plato may very well have intended precisely this effect.

We can distinguish roughly three functions or contexts in which Plato speaks of the soul: (i) the soul as the principle of motion and life, (ii) the soul as subject of cognition and desire, (iii) the soul as a moral agent that may be or become good or bad. Concerning (iii), one might say that the soul is, or comes close to, being conceived of as a person, while (ii) and (iii) jointly roughly comprise the area of psychology in a narrower sense. How (ii) and (iii) relate becomes clear when we consider the famous doctrine of the division of the soul in the *Republic*. In the *Republic*, Plato can be understood in a nutshell as

---

[1] Examples include Peter M. Steiner, *Die Psyche bei Platon*, Göttingen, 1992, and Hendrik Lorenz, "Plato on the soul", in: G. Fine (ed.), *Oxford Handbook on Plato*, Oxford 2008, 243–266.

claiming that being a *human person* means being an aggregate of three motivational drives, the three so-called 'parts of the soul': appetitive desire, *thymos* and rational desire, each of which is assigned to a class of goods as their objects (roughly, bodily goods, social goods, and the rationally good). A *moral person* is then constituted by the hierarchical order in which these three parts of the soul are arranged: The morally good person or 'character' is the person in which rational desire rules over her other types of desire. In this case, the person is ultimately motivated by her grasp of the rational good. If *thymos* is the dominant form of desire, one is motivated by honour and social recognition as the highest goods, whereby rationality becomes subservient to a non-rational form of desire. Finally, if appetitive desire prevails, the other two types of desire are subordinated to the pursuit of physical pleasure. These latter two kinds of power relations are suboptimal from a moral point of view. They constitute morally inferior or even morally bad persons (viz. characters). This is a substantial and very powerful theory of personhood that lies at the heart of Plato's moral psychology. It may not be an overstatement to say that this theory is Plato's major contribution to 'psychology'. And the fact that the discussion of the parts of the soul and the moral psychology based on that discussion appear repeatedly in Plato's dialogues seems to conform that.[2] That said, the only passages in which Plato seems to formally define the soul characterize it not as an aggregate of soul parts but as a radically spontaneous self-mover that sets other things in motion. Plato's formal attempts to define the soul, then, offer an understanding of the soul not in terms of (ii) and (iii) but in terms of (i).[3] On the other hand, talk of the soul in accordance with (ii) and (iii) seems close to common usage at the time, where it connotes, among other things, being the subject of mental episodes. This usage of the word 'soul' is not entirely alien to us nowadays, even though the contemporary philosophical term 'mind', though hardly less problematic, might better capture what is at stake.

---

[2] Besides the *Republic*, this is clearest in the *Phaedrus*, in the *Timaeus*, and in the *Laws*, but there are traces of it also in the *Phaedo* and the *Gorgias*. For the theory of the divided soul in Plato, see Andreas Graeser, *Probleme der platonischen Seelenteilungslehre*. Zetemata 47, München, 1969; in ancient philosophy up to Galen, see Klaus Corcilius, "Faculties: Ancient Debates", in: C. Mercer / D. Perler (eds.), *Oxford Philosophical Concepts 'Faculty'*, Oxford 2015, 19-58; specifically for Plato's *Republic*, see Christopher Shields, "Plato's Divided Soul", in: Mark L. McPherran (ed.), *Plato's Republic: A Critical Guide*, Cambridge 2010, 147–70. For a philosophical defense of the tripartition of the soul see Myles Burnyeat, "The Truth of Tripartition", *Proceedings of the Aristotelian Society* 106 (2006), 1–23. For the import of the divided soul for Plato's moral psychology, see Hendrik Lorenz, *The Brute Within*, Oxford 2006; Rachana Kamtekar, *Plato's Moral Psychology*, Oxford 2018.

[3] *Phdr*. 245, *Lg*. 896. The different discussions of the world soul in Plato involve (i) and, in the *Laws* and in the *Timaeus*, also (ii) and (iii), although (iii) is at most alluded to in the *Timaeus*. The mention of the world soul in the *Statesman* raises difficulties of its own that we cannot address here.

Originating in the *Tübinger Platon-Tage* on the 11th to 13th of April 2024, the goal of this volume is to address some topics from Plato's psychology, especially in the narrower senses of (ii) and (iii). These contributions are complemented with some more general treatments of the conception of soul in Plato and the Old Academy.

Many contributions concerning (ii) and (iii) touch on the relation between body and soul in the explanation of psychological phenomena. To give just one example, in the famous last argument of the first part of the *Theaetetus* (184b–86e), where the definition of knowledge as perception is finally refuted, Socrates seems to vacillate between a description of perception as a passive bodily affection and as an active process of the soul. Hence, one should ask to what extent perception is here a phenomenon that must be explained with reference to both the bodily affection and the activity of the soul. Similar points hold, for example, for Plato's accounts of perception, memory, and desire in the *Philebus* (33c–35d) or his treatment of imagination (*phantasia*) in the *Sophist*.

Even if one sets aside the radical thesis that, for Plato, the body does not have anything to do with these phenomena at all, there are several philosophical and interpretive options. One could, for instance, treat the reference to the bodily process involved in a psychological phenomenon either as part of its definition or alternatively as expressing only a necessary condition for the psychological phenomenon that does not enter the definition. In the first case, the phenomenon in question would be essentially bodily, whereas in the second case, its essence would remain purely 'psychological' (i.e., pertain only to the soul). A further question is whether Plato advocates a unified theory of all these psychological phenomena or whether he arrives at different conclusions for different phenomena.

In short, then, one set of topics in Plato's psychology may be grouped around the question whether phenomena like perception or desire belong "commonly" (κοινῇ) to body and soul (*Philebos* 34a3–5). This question goes beyond a mere Yes or No but explores the details of the ways in which the relevant phenomena are common to body and soul and in the ways in which they are not. The distinction between cause and necessary condition is especially important: is the soul alone the cause or principle of perception or desire, or are both body and soul causes, possibly in different ways?

Both *Mary Louise Gill* and *Béatrice Lienemann* address this cluster of issues concerning perception. According to Gill, we can distinguish two phases of perception in the *Theaetetus* where the first phase, which is purely physiological and (for the perceiver) passive, triggers a second phase in which the soul actively notices the external affections. Lienemann, on the other hand, argues that perception is passive and thinking is the active process not only in the *Theaetetus* but also in the *Philebus*. But she also emphasizes that perception is an indispensable precondition for certain kinds of knowledge.

Other contributions focus on pleasure, desire, and imagination. *Georgia Mouroutsou* discusses the relation between the dialectical treatment of pleasure in the *Philebus* with the physiological treatment in the *Timaeus* and examines whether they are compatible with each other. *Samuel Meister* addresses the analysis of desire in the *Philebus* and argues that, although the definition of desire does not mention the body, one must take the body into consideration to explain occurrences of episodes of desire. Finally, *Fiona Leigh* discusses the topic of imagination (*phantasia*) in the *Sophist*, which she understands as perceptually caused opinion that makes us especially vulnerable to sophistic arguments.

A further question is linked to the phenomena that are common to both body and soul: *what* is the soul a principle of? So far, we have spoken of 'psychological' or 'mental' phenomena in the sense of (ii) and (iii), but this terminological choice might be unfortunate; instead, one might insist on speaking of 'biological' phenomena. Thus, the soul would be a principle of motion somewhat along the lines of (i), under which perception and desire could be subsumed, but only alongside a variety of phenomena that generally concern living things (*zōia*). One would then have to understand Platonic psychology (in the narrow sense) within the framework of Platonic biology and not as a separate specialized discipline. To understand the soul in its role as a principle of phenomena like perception and desire, we would first have to consider it more generally as a principle of life. The relation, then, between (i), (ii), and (iii) requires further examination. How is the role of the soul as a self-moving principle of the motion of other things related to its psychological-mental and moral functions? And how exactly are we to understand the claim that the soul is the principle of the life of organisms?

Andrea Falcon deals with the latter question in the context of the *Timaeus*. He defends the view that, in Plato, the soul has a more restricted explanatory role than in Aristotle because phenomena like breathing are explained without reference to the soul (whereas Aristotle tries to furnish such an explanation by means of the soul's nutritive capacity). *Riccardo Chiaradonna* and *Peter Oxenknecht* both discuss the claim in the final argument for the immortality of the soul in the *Phaedo* that the soul 'brings' life. On the basis of an analysis of the relation of eponymy (according to which something that partakes of a form of opposites, such as the great or the small, acquires the name of this form), Chiaradonna argues that the soul as a principle of life is not itself essentially alive but only necessarily alive. Oxenknecht, on the other hand, tries to show that the soul renders an organism alive by being a part of it.

But for Plato, the soul, and especially the rational soul, is a principle in another way as well. It is the ruler and controller of corporeal living things and their dispositions and processes which involve the body; that is, it is the ruler of everything that seems common to body and soul. As a principle in this sense, the soul is responsible not only for the fact that the relevant processes occur at all but also for the fact that they are the kinds of processes they are, for example, which kinds of desires come about and prevail. How these two roles of the soul as a principle – the general biological role and the controlling role – fit together is by no means obvious. But the soul's dual role as a principle suggests that the role of soul as a subject of cognition and desire, as in (ii), cannot easily be delimited from moral psychology (iii): it would seem that what determines us (biologically) as humans is at the same time what allows us to be good human beings.

This thought comes to bear in the contributions by *Jan Szaif* and *Klaus Corcilius*. Szaif draws our attention to a little-discussed passage in the *Philebus* (64b) where Socrates compares his argument to a 'bodiless order (*kosmos*) of the ensouled body'. According to Szaif, the comparison suggests that the discourse about the good in the *Philebus* prefigures the ideal rational state of the soul. Corcilius, on the other hand, addresses the question how, on the basis of the scenario in the *Timaeus*, the human soul can reach true knowledge of the outside world despite its confinement in a body. He argues that for Plato the human soul, unlike the world soul, can achieve such true knowledge only on the basis of perceptual data.

So far, we have mentioned the relation between soul and body in the explanation of phenomena like perception (ii) as well as the status of the soul as a principle of motion (i) and an ordering moral principle (iii). But given that the soul is a principle of a corporeal living thing, one may raise the converse question with regard to both (ii) and (iii), namely, how the body influences the soul, especially its characteristic activity of thinking. Human thinking seems to depend on perception such that, even in thinking, our access to the world does not appear independent of processes that involve the body. Once again, we face the question as to the relation between body and soul, even in the case of thinking where one might have expected that the body has no role to play. If there is an overarching tendency in this volume, it is surely to the conclusion that one cannot treat the topic 'Plato and the Soul' without the topic 'Plato and the Body'.

But the question as to the relation between soul and body can also be raised in a more general manner, not concerning the particular functions of living things but rather concerning the effect of the soul on the perceptible world as a whole. The role of mathematical proportions in the construction of the world soul in the *Timaeus* (34b–36d) raises the question of how the soul – be it the world soul or the soul of a particular living thing – can be a cause of phenomena in the perceptible, changeable world. Here the question is not about explaining some process in the perceptible world in which body and soul are involved but rather about how the soul can take part in such an explanation at all, let alone constitute it primarily or entirely. In his essay, *Thomas Johansen* wants to show how in the *Timaeus*, the mathematical proportions of the soul provoke motion in the *chōra* or 'receptacle' such that, for Plato, mathematical entities can form part of the explanation of motion and change.

Susanna Kinzig and *Christoph Poetsch* discuss the same topic with a view to Plato's successors in the Old Academy. Kinzig scrutinizes with great care the testimonies that attribute to Xenocrates the notorious definition of the soul as self-moving number and examines not only the meaning of the definition itself but also its motivation and its historical background, particularly in the *Timaeus*. Poetsch, in turn, looks at the conceptions of the soul in the Old Academy in a more general way registering far-reaching similarities between them.

One might be tempted to treat the question of the relation between the (mathematical) soul and the perceptible world as a generalization of the question about the connection between the soul and body of an individual living being. In some sense, this seems justified, especially insofar as we inquire into the soul as a ruling principle, either of particular living things or the world as a whole. But regarding the explanation of specific phenomena such as perception, the problem of the connection between soul and body can be addressed independently of the mathematical construction of the soul. For independently of how the soul is constructed, one can ask to what extent soul and body explain certain psychological – or biological – phenomena. Hence, although one may roughly subsume all the themes mentioned under the heading 'body and soul', one should not make the specific psychological and biological questions depend on problems that derive from the mathematical construction of the soul.

This distinction helps us explain the conflicted response to Plato's psychology that we find in Aristotle. On the one hand, he has little sympathy for the thought that the soul as a mathematical entity could explain psychological phenomena, as we can see from his impatient treatment of the Xenocratean definition of the soul as a self-moving number (*De anima* I 2, 405a28–30). But on the other hand, and especially in the *Parva Naturalia*, he seems to take up the question of the interplay between body and soul in the explanation of phenomena that are common to both in roughly the same way we find in Plato. This does not, of course, imply that Aristotle reaches the same results as Plato, but it does show – and this points to a second overarching conclusion of this volume – that the problems Aristotle faces are heavily influenced by the way in which Plato raised them, not only concerning the soul but also concerning the contribution of the body to the explanation of psychological phenomena.

Plato on Perception and Judgment: *Theaetetus* 184–186

Mary Louise Gill

Twice in *Theaetetus* Part I Socrates rejects Theaetetus' proposal (151e1–3) that knowledge is perception. This chapter focuses on Socrates' second refutation at 184–186. In both refutations he insists that what counts as knowledge must satisfy two criteria: 1) be of what-is (being) (τοῦ ὄντος) and 2) be without falsehood (ἀψευδές), that is, true (first refutation: 152c5–6; second: 186c7–d1; 186d3–5; 186e4–5). The Final Argument excludes perception as knowledge precisely on the grounds that perception cannot grasp being and so cannot attain truth.

Scholars have debated the nature of being (οὐσία), introduced in the Final Argument as one of the common objects (κοινά), along with difference and sameness, oneness and number, unlikeness and likeness and others, which Socrates claims perception cannot grasp. This is not the occasion for me to defend a view of being but I will simply note the following:[1] Socrates speaks of the being *of* the objects perceived, the difference *between* a color and a sound, the sameness *of* each *to* itself, and so on: we think something *about both* (περὶ ἀμφοτέρων) (185a4–b9). The common objects are thus introduced as *attributes* of sensible objects. Moreover, being – a single Platonic form – can function in two ways, first, as a stand-alone attribute (185a8–9): you think about a sound and a color "that they both *are*/*exist*" (ὅτι ἀμφοτέρω ἐστόν: Classical Greek has no separate verb "to exist"); and second as a link connecting a subject to its further attributes, as in: "You are beautiful, Theaetetus" (Καλὸς γὰρ εἶ, ὦ Θεαίτητε) (185e3). In saying that one form of being operates in more than one way, I am echoing Lesley Brown, who argues that the verb "to be" is complete but expects a further completion.[2] If X *is*/exists, then X *is something or other* – has some feature.

Whether being is a stand-alone property of X or connects X to further properties it has, the combination of subject and simple or compound attribute yields the content of a *judgment*, a subject–predicate complex, which can be

[1] I argue in detail for my view of Plato on being in Gill, *Philosophos*, esp. chs. 2 and 5.
[2] Brown, "Being in the *Sophist*".

true or *false*.[3] Socrates connects being to truth in the Final Argument of *Theaetetus* Part I via judgment. Notably, the Final Argument never uses the noun δόξα in its discussion of judgment but marks off from perception an activity of the soul through itself, which Part II identifies at the outset as judgment (δοξάζειν, δόξα) (187a8, b4–6). Instead, Socrates says that the soul *thinks* (διανοῇ) or *grasps* (λαμβάνει, ἅψασθαι), or *considers* (ἐπισκοπεῖν/σκοπεῖσθαι), or *decides* (κρίνειν) things.[4] In this contribution I will argue that the soul must act through itself in making the simplest perceptual judgments, for instance, that *this* (surface I touch) *is hard*. Even at this basic level the soul must grasp being and can be mistaken.

I will also argue that perception is an unstructured act but consists of two distinct phases: Phase one, from the perspective of the perceiver, is a passive physiological process in which an external perceptible object initiates a series of motions inward through a sense organ to the soul. The culmination of this physiological process triggers phase two, an active psychic act of noticing the external affection that originated the causal chain through the body.

At the end of my contribution, I will appeal to the Wax Block in Part II to argue that when the soul judges, it matches an external πάθος perceived to an internal πάθημα stamped on memory during the first phase of perception, a πάθημα which is enhanced by further perceptions. The imprint, which Socrates compares to the stamp of a signet ring, is both a representation of the external πάθος (or complex object) perceived and a capacity to recognize that and similar πάθη or objects when perceived again.[5]

I will make my case by going, mostly sequentially, through 184–186.

1. The Soul and the Senses

At the beginning of the Final Argument Socrates makes several proposals about perception that Theaetetus readily accepts. Theaetetus should not think of the sense organs as though they were a band of warriors stationed in a wooden horse, each operating as an independent agent housed in a senseless shell (184d1–6). Instead, human and nonhuman perceivers see *with* the soul (τῇ ψυχῇ: instrumental dative) and *through* (διά) the eyes and hear *with* the soul

[3] Plato sorts out this topic in the *Sophist* in his discussion of true and false statements.

[4] He also speaks of the soul comparing and making calculations.

[5] In this contribution I do not discuss how Plato's Socrates moves from a narrow conception of perception restricted to proper objects (sight of colors, hearing of sounds, etc.) in 184–186 to an expansive conception of perception in 191–196 allowing it to grasp ordinary objects such as Theaetetus and Theodorus. On this topic, see the excellent paper by Schroeder, "Plato on Object Perception". I thank Lea Schroeder for sharing with me an advance copy of her paper.

through the ears (184b7–d5). Myles Burnyeat has argued that what we perceive *with* – the soul – is the perceiving subject in all acts of perception and coordinates the five senses. What we perceive *through* – the senses (and organs) – are the soul's means of gaining access to sensible qualities outside the soul.[6] While I agree with Burnyeat that the soul is the chief instrument of perception, the end of the passage tells against the soul being the subject of all our perceiving.[7] At 186d2–6 Socrates identifies perception as παθήματα traveling through the body to the soul. The soul is not the subject of that process, but its beneficiary, stimulated to act by the information the senses provide. The soul uses the senses, not by looking out through them like telescopes, but by collecting information they transmit inward and then actively responding to it. Socrates alludes to the soul's active role when he says: "I want to know if it is with some part of ourselves that we *reach* (ἐφικνούμεθα) whites and blacks through the eyes" (184d7–e1). Since the soul is the subject only of phase two of perception, we should read the dative as we read the dative in Aristotle's *De Anima* I 4:[8]

> Indeed, to say that the soul is angry would be like someone saying that the soul weaves or builds; in fact, it is surely better not to say that the soul pities or learns or thinks, but that the person does so *with the soul* (τῇ ψυχῇ: instrumental dative). (408b11–15)

If we read the *Theaetetus* as Aristotle recommends, the soul and the sense organs are both instruments of perception but in different ways. *We* (animals) perceive, and we do so *through* (διά) the sense organs which transmit

---

[6] Burnyeat, "Plato on the Grammar of Perceiving", §§1–3. I have also profited from reading an unpublished paper by Justin Broackes, "Plato and the Grammar of Perception".

[7] In Gill, *Philosophos,* 109–110, I agreed with Burnyeat's proposal and argued that the goings-on in the sense organs were not themselves seeing or hearing, but the proximate (material and efficient) causes of those acts of the soul. But Socrates calls those goings-on at the end of the passage "perceptions". So here I modify my earlier position. Sarah Broadie suggested to me that the dative could be locative ("in the soul"). A locative dative would avoid the appearance that the soul is a mere instrument as opposed to the subject of all perceiving, but a locative dative in prose tends to be restricted to proper names, e.g., *Athēnēsi* ("at Athens"): Smyth, *Greek Grammar,* §1534.

[8] Cf. Cherniss, *Aristotle's Criticism of Plato and the Academy*, 402–403 fn. 327. Burnyeat, "Plato on the Grammar of Perceiving", 38–39 fn. 28, dismisses Cherniss's view as "definitely wrong". Says Burnyeat: "Aristotle, I take it, is opposing the suggestion that the subject of consciousness can be anything but the man himself: a separate subject within him – let it be as single as you like – will not do." Of course, Aristotle disagrees with Plato that the soul is a self-mover – for Aristotle the soul is a first unmoved mover – but what he goes on to say sounds strikingly like the Platonic view I defend later in this contribution. After claiming that the reason why it is better not to say that the soul is angry but that the person is angry *with* their soul is not because there is motion in the soul (as Plato thinks), "but because motion sometimes reaches as far as the soul, and sometimes proceeds from it. For instance, perception [starts] from particulars, whereas recollection [starts] from the soul" (408b15–18).

information to the soul, and we do so *with* the soul (τῇ ψυχῇ) once it receives that information. The soul actively uses the sense organs but is the passive recipient of the information they provide.

Socrates says that we perceive through the bodily organs (184c5–9), such as eyes and ears, and also through the capacities (δυνάμεις) of those organs, such as sight and hearing. He uses the "through" idiom in the capacities sense when he presses Theaetetus to agree to another proposal about perception, that what we perceive though one sense modality we cannot perceive through another:

> Do you wish to agree that the things which you perceive through one capacity (δι' ἑτέρας δυνάμεως), it is impossible to perceive through another [capacity], for instance, what you perceive through hearing [it is impossible to perceive] through sight, or what you perceive through sight [it is impossible to perceive] through hearing? – Yes, how could I not admit that? (184e8–185a3)

While each sense is restricted to its own proper objects, the senses converge on the soul which grasps the full array of sensible qualities, combines them, and makes judgments about them.[9]

2. Judgment and the Common Features

Take two sensible qualities (185a8–b6), an instance of the color red (grasped through sight) and an instance of the sound C# (grasped through hearing).[10] Theaetetus agrees that we can think various things about red and C# – that they both are, that each is different from the other and the same as itself, that together they are two and each is one. Theaetetus hesitates when Socrates asks about likeness and unlikeness, and he responds with an uncertain "Perhaps" ("Ισως) (185a4–b6). Socrates wants to know through what instrument (διὰ τίνος) Theaetetus grasps all those common features about red and C# (185b7–9).

[9] Burnyeat, "Plato on the Grammar of Perceiving", 47–48; cf. *The Theaetetus of Plato*, 56–57, thinks that Plato adopts a stronger principle than he needs by ignoring what Aristotle calls the common sensibles, such as shape, size, change and rest, perceived by more than one sense (Aristotle, *De An.* II 6, 418a16–20). Yet Plato seems to have a point in that when we perceive shape through sight, we perceive its visible aspects (its look), whereas when we perceive shape through touch, we perceive its tangible aspects (its feel). Cf. the similar treatment of sight and hearing at *R.* V, 477c1–d6 – there, too, different sense capacities are set over different objects. Putting visible, audible, and tangible aspects together will (for Plato) require more than sense perception. Heitsch, *Überlegungen Platons im Theaetet,* 99–100 discusses the soul's use of the common features to synthesize the evidence of the senses into whole objects. For a defense of Plato's principle different from my own, see Modrak, "Perception and Judgement in the *Theaetetus*", §1.

[10] I agree with Burnyeat, "Plato on the Grammar of Perceiving", 48 fn. 55, that in this section Plato is talking about instances of qualities rather than types of qualities.

To clarify what he means and to settle Theaetetus' doubts, Socrates gives him an odd example. We shall go through the passage in two main chunks:

> *Through* what do you think all those things [being, difference, sameness, twoness, oneness, unlikeness, likeness] about the two of them [red and C#]? For you are not able to grasp the common feature about them (τὸ κοινόν…περὶ αὐτῶν) *through* hearing or *through* sight. Moreover, the following too is a proof (τεκμήριον) of what we are saying: If it were possible to consider (σκέψασθαι) whether both [red and C#] are salty or not (ἐστὸν ἁλμυρὼ ἢ οὔ), you would be able to say *with* what (ᾧ) you will consider them, and this is evidently neither sight nor hearing, but something else. – Yes, of course, it's the capacity *through* the tongue (ἥ γε διὰ τῆς γλώττης δύναμις). (185b7–c2)

Many commentators think that Socrates is sloppy when he says that Theaetetus would readily be able to say *with* what he would consider whether red and C# are salty or not, because he adds that this is evidently neither sight nor hearing, and Theaetetus replies "the capacity through the tongue", an answer Socrates approves (185c3). On this view, Socrates should have used the "through" idiom rather than the instrumental dative at 185c1, because he is saying that Theaetetus can readily tell him through what he will examine whether red and C# are salty or not, and that is the capacity through the tongue, namely taste.[11] But surely Socrates does not blur the grammatical distinction he has just introduced and on whose precise use he insisted (184d7–e3).[12] He speaks very precisely.[13] Socrates says that it is easy to say *with* what we address the question

---

[11] E.g., Burnyeat, "Plato on the Grammar of Perceiving", 42, 48–49, Kanayama, "Perceiving, Considering, and Attaining Being", 39–40, Bostock, *Plato's Theaetetus,* 111, 121 fn. 35, though cf. fn. 36, and Lorenz, *The Brute Within,* 78–79. Cooper, "Plato on Sense-Perception and Knowledge", 131–132, and Modrak, "Perception and Judgement in the *Theaetetus*", 42–43, 52 fn. 4, do not mention the sloppiness, but they evidently interpret "with" at 185c1 as "through".

[12] Getting the right interpretation of this passage is important because it has been taken as evidence that the senses can make simple perceptual judgments in labeling the content of perception. Cooper (1970: 132) finds two distinct views of perception in the Final Argument and takes the present passage as evidence for labeling. Cf. Modrak (1981: 42–48). Fine (2017) discusses grades of perception stated by Descartes: (1) the immediate stimulation of the bodily organs by external objects; (2) all the immediate effects produced in the mind, effects including perceptions; and (3) judgments about things around us. She argues that perception in *Tht.* 184–186 falls at grade (2), which she interprets in the Platonic context as essentially involving the soul and consisting of sensory states that have representational but non-conceptual content. In my view, perception in *Tht.* 184–186 includes both grade (1) and grade (2) as phases of a single process, though I restrict grade (2) to active noticing. I take the passage to make a twofold distinction between *perception* (including grades (1) and (2)) and *judgment* (grade 3), including perceptual judgment but also higher-level judgments.

[13] Sedley, *The Midwife of Platonism,* 106–107 fn. 29, is the only author I know of who rejects the idea that Socrates is being careless here, but he thinks that Socrates now proposes that if (counterfactually) we could determine whether red and C# are salty or not, taste would take over from the soul the unifying role of judging agent. I do not think that this can be

about the saltiness of red and C#. That answer is easy, because Theaetetus and Socrates have already agreed that we perceive all that we perceive *with* the soul (184d1–6), not the separate senses (185c1–2).

To Socrates' easy question, "*With* what do we answer the question about the saltiness [of red and C#]?" Theaetetus replies "the capacity through the tongue" (ἥ γε διὰ τῆς γλώττης δύναμις) (185c3). His answer is ambiguous, because "capacity" could refer to either of two things: (1) the soul, the capacity engaged in perception and judgment, which operates through the tongue in perceiving saltiness; or (2) taste, the capacity of the tongue in tasting. If Theaetetus means the second, he has misunderstood Socrates' question, for Socrates' question was not "*through* what do you perceive saltiness?" but "*with* what do you perceive saltiness?"

Whatever Theaetetus thinks he is saying, Socrates takes him to have answered the easy question he explicitly asked and to have answered it correctly: the capacity which uses information conveyed through the tongue is the soul. The soul is that *with* which we would perform the task. In returning to the hard question ("what do we perceive *through*?"), Socrates picks up on Theaetetus' use of the word δύναμις and disambiguates the answer so that it comes out correct:

> Well said. And then *the capacity through what* [instrument] (ἡ δὲ δὴ διὰ τίνος δύναμις) clarifies to you that which is common both to everything and these [red and C#], to which you apply the words "is" and "is not", and what we asked about them just now [viz. "are they both salty or not?"]? For all these, what sorts of instruments will you assign *through* which *the perceiving part of us* perceives (αἰσθάνεται ἡμῶν τὸ αἰσθανόμενον) each of them? (185b7–c8)

Socrates refers to the same capacity he took Theaetetus to refer to, namely the capacity with which we consider the being, not-being, difference and sameness, likeness and unlikeness of two sensible qualities, and that is the capacity he characterizes at the end of the passage as "the perceiving part of us", namely the soul. That is what we perceive *with.* He then re-asks the hard question: "*through* what" does that capacity (the soul) consider the question?

And now Theaetetus, having first made sure that he has understood the question and that Socrates is talking about being, not-being, sameness, difference, and other common features (185c9–d2), restates the question: "[Y]ou are asking *through* what [instrument] of those in the body we perceive [being, not-being, likeness, unlikeness, etc.] *with* the soul (τῇ ψυχῇ)" (185d2–3). This time Theaetetus responds to the question unambiguously – indeed, he corrects Socrates' use of "perceives" at 185c8 – there is no special instrument (ὄργανον ἴδιον) in this case, "but the soul (ἡ ψυχή) appears to me to consider (ἐπισκοπεῖν) the common features of everything *itself through itself* (αὐτὴ δι'

right, given what Socrates previously said about the correct use of the "with" idiom: we do all our perceiving *with* the soul.

αὐτῆς)" (185d6–e2). Socrates applauds Theaetetus and thanks him for saving him a lot of trouble (185e3–9).

To sum up: Socrates introduces the hypothetical example to demonstrate his previous claim that we cannot grasp the common features through sight or through hearing, and his example implicitly invokes all the common features just enumerated: In order to determine whether red and C# are salty or not (ἐστὸν ἁλμυρὼ ἢ οὔ), one must first identify, in at least a preliminary way, what each of them is (namely, red or C#) and determine that they are different from each other and the same as themselves, that both together are two and each is one. Furthermore, in deciding whether they are salty or not, one must also determine whether they are like or unlike each other in being or not being salty (185a8–b5). The odd illustration focuses on the common features likeness and unlikeness, because Theaetetus began to hesitate when Socrates first mentioned them (185b6). Socrates has asked him to take two token sensible qualities and to say whether they are salty or not. The answer is problematic, since red and C# have no flavor at all, but the peculiarity of the example is precisely the point. This is a thought experiment, something the soul will have to consider through itself. Socrates would approve an answer one must arrive at through reflection: red and C#, though different from each other in being red and C#, are *like* each other in *not being salty*.[14]

The need for the soul to engage in reflection and judgment using evidence of the senses is easier to grasp in the complicated illustration than in simple cases, such as judging this hard thing I touch to be hard or this red thing I see to be red. The next part of the Final Argument reveals that Theaetetus has grasped Socrates' point for the κοινά but becomes confused as soon as Socrates asks him about more familiar attributes, such as beauty and ugliness, goodness and badness, and sensible qualities, such as hardness and softness.

3. Judgment and Ordinary Attributes

I have so far argued that the soul must act on its own to determine whether two sensible qualities such as red and C# are salty or not, but how much can perception do without such intervention? What is the lowest level at which the

---

[14] Cf. *Prm.* 147c1–8. In Gill, *Philosophos*, ch. 5 §4 and §6, I discuss Plato's theory of negation and falsehood, and attribute to him a view typically known as the Incompatibility range interpretation, e.g., by Brown, "The *Sophist* on Statements, Predication, and Falsehood". I called it the "Incompatibility set" interpretation of negation to allow for groups that fall under a wider kind, such as animals or shapes that do not compose a range. According to this view the true statement "red and C# are not salty" might be taken to imply that they have some other flavor instead, but I think that it need not have that implication. See Gill, *Philosophos*, ch. 5 fn. 70.

soul must intervene and act through itself? Can the soul grasp a single instance of a quality, say hardness, and identify it as hard through touch, or must the soul act through itself even at this fundamental level? I will argue that the soul must act on its own even in the simplest perceptual judgments. Though I am by no means alone in that conclusion, I differ from others in my reconstruction of the upcoming argument establishing it.[15]

In the next stretch of text (185e3–186a8), Socrates invites Theaetetus to assign various sorts of properties either to the class of things the soul grasps through itself or to the class it grasps through one of the senses. Here he moves beyond the features common to everything and asks about aesthetic and moral values and then about sensible qualities. Theaetetus has just announced that the soul considers the common features of everything through itself, and Socrates cheers, using a phrase that will prove significant a few lines later: "You are beautiful (Καλὸς γὰρ εἶ), Theaetetus, and not ugly, as Theodorus said, for a man who speaks beautifully is beautiful and good!" (185e3–5). Then he repeats the distinction Theaetetus has just recognized, that the soul considers some things through itself and perceives others through the capacities of the body (185e6–7). Socrates asks Theaetetus to decide in which of the two groups he puts the being (τὴν οὐσίαν) that accompanies everything (186a2–3). Theaetetus replies that being is among the things the soul grasps by itself, and similarly likeness and unlikeness and sameness and difference (186a4–8).

Then Socrates asks: "What about beautiful and ugly, good and bad?" (Τί δέ; καλὸν καὶ αἰσχρὸν καὶ ἀγαθὸν καὶ κακόν;) (186a9), to which Theaetetus replies:

> In fact it seems to me that in these cases especially the soul considers their being (τούτων…τὴν οὐσίαν) in relation to each other (πρὸς ἄλληλα), calculating within itself the past and present in relation to the future. (186a10–b1)

"Hold on!" (Ἔχε δή) Socrates interjects (186b2).[16] He stops Theaetetus because the boy missed the point of the question, which was not: "Through what instrument does the soul grasp the being of the beautiful and the being of the ugly in relation to each other?" but "Through what instrument does the soul grasp the beauty and/or ugliness *of Theaetetus*?" picking up the adjectives from his exclamation a few lines before: "You are beautiful (Καλὸς γὰρ εἶ),

[15] See McDowell, *Plato: Theaetetus*, 190–193, and Lorenz, *The Brute Within,* 56 and ch. 6, esp. 83–91.

[16] Contrast Levett–Burnyeat's translation in Burnyeat, *The Theaetetus of Plato*: "Slow down", which suggests that Theaetetus jumped too quickly to the conclusion. For interpretations of "Hold on!" different from my own, see McDowell, *Plato: Theaetetus,* 190, Kanayama, "Perceiving, Considering, and Attaining Being", 77–78, Bostock, *Plato's Theaetetus,* 122–123, and Lorenz, *The Brute Within*, 86 fn. 41.

Theaetetus, and not ugly!"[17] Theaetetus correctly answered the questions about the common features, but as soon as Socrates takes a step beyond them to more familiar attributes such as beauty and ugliness, which the common feature being links to the subject Theaetetus, the boy becomes confused and takes him to be asking about the being of those features.[18] Socrates wants to know whether the soul grasps the beauty of Theaetetus – an *attribute* of his – through itself or through the senses.

Since Theaetetus missed the force of the question and answered a question Socrates later says can be answered only with difficulty and after much schooling (186b11–c6), Socrates goes back to the distinction already agreed on, between sensible qualities perceived with the soul through the senses, and the common features grasped with the soul through itself:

> Hold on! Wouldn't you say that through touch (διὰ τῆς ἐπαφῆς) it [the soul] will perceive (αἰσθήσεται) the hardness of the hard (τοῦ μὲν σκληροῦ τὴν σκληρότητα), and likewise the softness of the soft (τοῦ μαλακοῦ τὴν μαλακότητα)? – Yes. – But with respect at least to their being (τὴν δέ γε οὐσίαν) – that they both are (ὅτι ἐστόν) – and the opposition between them, and again the being of that opposition, the soul itself, rising up (ἐπανιοῦσα) and comparing them to each other, attempts to decide (κρίνειν) for us. – Of course. (186b2–10)

Precisely what Theaetetus agrees to about perception in the first part of the passage seems initially underdetermined. The question might allow the soul, operating through the senses, to make simple perceptual judgments about sensible things, and if so, the soul, acting though touch, could identify the hardness of the hard as hard and the softness of the soft as soft.[19] That reading seems to me mistaken, however, because Socrates uses the verb αἰσθήσεται, forms of which he uses fairly consistently when he speaks of perception. The first part of our passage describes what I will later identify as phase two of perception, the soul actively *noticing* the hardness of the hard conveyed to it through touch without yet identifying that hardness as hard.[20]

---

[17] Bostock, *Plato's Theaetetus,* 122 fn. 37, wonders why Socrates introduces the question "What about beautiful and ugly, good and bad" with adjectives instead of abstract nouns or adjectives plus definite articles. As I say in my main text, Socrates picks up the predicates in "You are beautiful, Theaetetus…" and is asking about the beauty *of* Theaetetus, not about beauty in its own right. Cf. Cooper, "Plato on Sense-Perception and Knowledge", 137, and Lorenz, *The Brute Within,* 85–86.

[18] McDowell, *Plato: Theaetetus*, 190, thinks that Theaetetus' answer about beauty and ugliness has some merit because they are features of objects of more than one sense.

[19] The Greek in "the hard" (and "the soft") is ambiguous between "the hard thing" (say a stone) or "hardness" (a tangible quality). In either case Socrates is talking about the hardness or softness of some external object, and at this point nothing turns on which sort of entity is at issue (whether sensible quality or thing that has that quality).

[20] Cooper, "Plato on Sense-Perception and Knowledge", 130–131, entertains but rejects this interpretation.

The second part of the passage presents the activities of the soul on its own as distinct from its perception through touch.[21] We decide about the being of the hard and the soft, that they are, the opposition between them, and the being of that opposition with the soul through itself. Only now at step one of this series does the soul judge *that* both the hardness of the hard and the softness of the soft *are* (ὅτι ἐστόν).[22] This perceptual judgment already requires the soul to act on its own to identify the being of the hard and soft, *that* they both *are* (one hard, the other soft). This is the first step toward determining the opposition between hardness and softness and the being of that opposition.[23] This process leaves room for progressively higher order judgments, as the next passage (186b11-c6) will make clear when it distinguishes affections infants and animals can perceive as soon as they are born, and calculations about being and benefit, which require much effort and education.

4. The Two Phases of Perception

Socrates finally corrects Theaetetus' hasty conclusion about beautiful and ugly (186a10–b1):

So human beings and animals as soon as they are born can by nature straightaway perceive those affections (παθήματα) that extend through the body to the soul, but calculations about them (τὰ δὲ περὶ τούτων ἀναλογίσματα) in relation to *being* and *benefit* (πρός τε οὐσίαν καὶ ὠφέλειαν) come to those to whom they come, only in time as a result of much trouble and education. – Absolutely. (186b11–c6)

Notice that Socrates uses forms of the word παθήματα here and again a few lines later:

So knowledge is not in the affections (Ἐν μὲν ἄρα τοῖς παθήμασιν οὐκ ἔνι ἐπιστήμη), but in our reasoning about them (ἐν δὲ τῷ περὶ ἐκείνων συλλογισμῷ). For here, as it seems, it is

---

[21] The contrast is marked by the μέν…δέ construction at 186b2 and b6.

[22] Previously (Gill, *Philosophos,* 115–116 and fn. 39) I accepted McDowell's, *Plato: Theaetetus,* 69, 191, translation of ὅτι ἐστόν as "what they are", instead of the more usual translation: "that they are". I now think the more usual translation is correct, given textual evidence earlier in the section. At 185a8–9 Socrates says: "First, about a sound and about a color (περὶ δὴ φωνῆς καὶ περὶ χρόας), don't you think this same thing about both (περὶ ἀμφοτέρων), *that they both are* (ὅτι ἀμφοτέρω ἐστόν)?" ὅτι is used repeatedly in the lines that follow. "So, too, *that* each is different from the other (ὅτι ἑκάτερον ἑκατέρου μὲν ἕτερον), and the same as itself (ἑαυτῷ δὲ ταὐτόν)?" (185a11–12). "And further *that* both are two (ὅτι ἀμφοτέρω δύο), and each one?" (185b2). The current passage foresees higher level questions, including questions about essence, but those are not explicitly the issue here.

[23] Lorenz, *The Brute Within,* 86–87 and fn. 44, discusses the third step – grasping the being of the opposition (between hardness and softness) – and he, too, appears to envisage something less than the investigation of essence.

possible to grasp *being* and *truth* (οὐσίας…καὶ ἀληθείας), but impossible there. – Apparently. (186d2–6)

Although Socrates does not call the affections "perception" in this passage, he goes on to give examples – seeing, hearing, smelling, feeling cold and feeling warm – and asks Theaetetus what he calls them, prompting the boy to call them perceiving (186d10–e1). Then Socrates himself calls them all together perception, an identification Theaetetus confirms (186e2–3).

In his claim about infants and animals (186b11–c2) the παθήματα (affections) are not perception (or at any rate not the whole of it), because Socrates treats them grammatically as the objects of perception.[24] He says that the παθήματα extend through the body to the soul. They travel from outside in. Given that he later calls them perceptions, I take the παθήματα to constitute the passive first phase of perception, initiating a second phase in which the soul uses the evidence received through the senses.[25]

A passage on perception in the *Timaeus* fleshes out the picture. Timaeus gives a detailed account of the mechanics of sense perception, sense organs, and sensible qualities – flavors, smells, sounds, colors, tangible qualities – and claims that these external πάθη are transmitted through the body by means of a series of motions – parts affecting other parts in the same way as they were affected – until they reach the soul (τὸ φρόνιμον) and "announce" (ἐξαγγείλῃ)

---

[24] This passage has encouraged some scholars, e.g., Crombie, *An Examination of Plato's Doctrines II,* 26, and Bostock, *Plato's Theaetetus,* 117–118, to propose that Plato had a representationalist theory of perception, according to which we perceive the inner παθήματα that reach the soul, and on the basis of them make inferences about the external world. McDowell, *Plato: Theaetetus,* 69, 111, translates the line in a different way, with the result that the παθήματα are features of external objects, such as the hardness of a stone. This construal has the consequence that the word παθήματα has a different meaning here from its meaning a few lines later at 186d2. I follow most commentators in taking the affections in both passages to be the inner motions that reach the soul, but I argue below that the object of perception is indeed the external object, not the inner affection that reaches the soul. For this sort of view, see also Burnyeat, "Plato on the Grammar of Perceiving", 42–43 and fn. 39.

[25] The mention of infants and animals excludes from perception any judgment requiring the possession of language: As noted above (fn. 12), Cooper, "Plato on Sense-Perception and Knowledge", 132, favors an interpretation of perception that includes labeling the data of sense with elementary color, taste, etc., descriptions, and claims that there is evidence in the Final Argument for two distinct notions of perception, of which one is mere discrimination without the application of concepts, and that is what we have here. Kanayama, "Perceiving, Considering and Attaining Being", 31, 47–48, thinks that for Plato perception includes non-conceptual discrimination, which he calls "implicit judgment", and that animals as well as human infants have that capacity. This may well be the correct view about perception, and there is a lively debate about non-conceptual content – e.g., Fodor ("The Revenge of the Given") and Heck ("Are there Different Kinds of Content?") – but I doubt that Plato had that view of perception.

the capacity (τὴν δύναμιν) of that which produced them (τοῦ ποιήσαντος) (*Ti.* 64b3–6).[26] In light of this passage, there is some material-efficient causal story to tell about the transmission of an external πάθος through the body to the soul, according to which the innermost link "announces" the πάθος that started the chain. A completed chain "gives rise" to the second phase of perception by stimulating the soul to perceive the external πάθος that originated the series.

An earlier passage in *Theaetetus* 184–186, mentioned above, speaks of the soul actively reaching out to sensible qualities.[27] In saying why he insists on precision in the use of the "with" and "through" idioms, Socrates announces:

> I want to know if it is with some same part of ourselves that we *reach* (ἐφικνούμεθα) whites and blacks through the eyes, and in turn [reach] other [perceptual qualities] through other [organs]. (184d7–e2)

On the interpretation I am defending, the soul reaches outward not by peering outward through the eyes, but rather by depending on the eyes to convey information inward.[28] If the information arrives, the final affection in the series spurs the soul to notice the color of something outside itself.[29]

The *Philebus* contains a passage like the one about infants and animals in the *Theaetetus*, and here Socrates speaks of perception as *noticing*:

> Assume that among the various affections (παθημάτων) of our body, some are extinguished in the body before they reach the soul, leaving it [the soul] unaffected (ἀπαθῆ), while others go (ἰόντα) through both [body and soul] and provoke as it were an upheaval (ὥσπερ σεισμὸν ἐντιθέντα) both proper and common to each. – Let it be assumed. – Will we speak correctly, if we say that the soul fails to notice (λανθάνειν) the ones that do not go through both, but notices (μὴ λανθάνειν) those that go through both? – Of course. (*Phlb.* 33d2–e1)

This passage does not mention an external πάθος that initiates a chain through the body, but it indicates the direction of travel, through the body to the soul. Affections that reach the soul prompt the soul's perception ("provoke as it were an upheaval"), so that the soul notices the affection that sparked the series and fails to notice those that set up truncated chains.

Although perception includes two phases, phase two is a simple unstructured act in which the soul notices some perceptual quality outside itself. Any

---

[26] The theory of perception in the *Timaeus* is discussed by Silverman, "Plato on Perception and the 'Commons'", 149–158. See also Johansen, *Plato's Natural Philosophy,* ch. 8, esp. 170–171.

[27] Cf. Burnyeat, "Plato on the Grammar of Perceiving", 42–43.

[28] Burnyeat, "Plato on the Grammar of Perceiving", 40–43, presents evidence of the spatial use of *dia* ("through") in perceptual contexts, and most of the evidence he cites indicates travel of sensible qualities inward through the sense organs – e.g., music pours through the ears as through a funnel (*R.* III, 411a5–6) – though there is also some evidence of the soul peering outward through the organs as through the bars of a prison cell (*Phd.* 82d9–83b4).

[29] Cf. Burnyeat, "Plato on the Grammar of Perceiving", 43.

attribution of being, on the other hand, whether the identification of a quality perceived as red or salty, hard or soft, or any higher-level ascription, requires the soul to compare what it perceives now with earlier perceptions of that sort of thing stored in its memory. That act leaves room for mistakes. Attaining truth in perceptual contexts demands two acts, first a perception of something (in two steps), and then a judgment about what is perceived. Even a claim as simple as "this is red" requires the soul operating through sight to notice something visible (the referent of "this"), and then, operating through itself, to identify that correctly or incorrectly as red.

5. Impressions in Perception and Judgment

Part II of the *Theaetetus* considers the proposal that knowledge is true judgment and for the most part ignores the insights about perception and judgment in the Final Argument of Part I – that is, until Socrates offers the Wax Block model to explain how false judgment is possible (191a8–195b8). That discussion in turn adds a dimension to the treatment of perception and judgment in 184–186 by emphasizing the role of impressions (σημεῖα).[30]

Socrates compares the soul to a lump of wax, which takes impressions as it were from signet rings, and in this way learns from its perceptual experience. A person remembers and knows things of which the soul has taken an impression but forgets those whose impression becomes obliterated (191c8–e1). The wax can be of various consistencies, better or worse able to record and preserve impressions, and the condition of the wax accounts, at least in part, for variations in the clarity, depth, and longevity of the impressions (194a6–195a9).[31] An impression of something enables a person to recognize that thing when they encounter it again – for instance, someone might have impressions of both Theaetetus and Theodorus from previous perceptual encounters, see Theaetetus in the distance, and either match the present perception to the right impression or to the wrong one (193b9–d2).

An impression (σημεῖον) can be clear and deep or unclear and without depth. Depending on the quality of the impression, we are more likely or less likely to fit the present perception to the correct imprint. Since impressions can differ in their clarity, the quality of the impression contributes to the accuracy of our identifications, along with the quality of the wax and other perceptual conditions.

---

30 This section relies heavily on Gill, *Philosophos*, 122–123.

31 In envisaging a role for the quality of the wax in concept formation, I differ from Woolf, "The Shaggy Soul Story", esp. 597–598, who thinks the quality of the wax and of the representations is irrelevant to the main thesis Socrates develops.

Connecting the Wax Block image with the treatment of perception in 184–186 allows us to conclude that an impression results from a series of affections (παθήματα) that reach the soul through the body, combined with others over time into a relatively lasting representation of an external quality or object.[32] The impression gains depth and clarity and becomes enduring through repeated encounters with qualitatively similar things or with different aspects of the same thing. The soul uses the impression to identify and re-identify what it perceives.

An impression serves two functions:[33] it *represents* something perceived, and the representation resembles the perceptible object to a greater or lesser degree (like the stamp of a signet ring); it equips its possessor to recognize the object again on future encounters and is thus a *capacity for recognition.* I call the impression a capacity and not merely a representation, because the impression stores within itself a history of past encounters and anticipates future ones. The impression is intrinsically relational: it is about the perceptible object and stores information from a person's previous encounters with it, and when stimulated by a new encounter the impression enables the judger to recognize that object again.

On this interpretation, the impression plays a complex causal role in perception and judgment and in linking them together. In perception affections (παθήματα) reach the soul through the senses and stimulate it to notice the external object that produced them. The perception in turn stimulates the soul to match what it has noticed to a stored impression. The impression serves as a capacity for recognition by linking perception to judgment, enabling the soul to re-identify something it perceives as something it perceived before. This

[32] Socrates says that we take impressions of everything we *wish* (βουλήθωμεν) to remember among the things we have seen, heard, or thought of ourselves, and this suggests that the soul actively memorizes things perceived that it wants to remember, with the unfortunate consequence that animals and infants will not develop impressions simply as a matter of course. Lorenz, *The Brute Within,* argues that Aristotle's conception of impressions and memory is indebted to the Wax Block image in the *Theaetetus* but points to this passage as indicating two significant differences between Plato's and Aristotle's views, one of which is the generation of impressions (Lorenz, *The Brute Within*, 161–162 fn. 34). In my view the phrase need not be taken literally, since it comes up as part of Socrates' elaborate metaphor of taking stamps from signet rings, but I think the word is important for Plato. Perhaps at the outset children and animals develop impressions automatically, but at some stage of development the soul learns to pay attention to some things and to ignore others, and then develops impressions from those things it attends to.

[33] Woolf, "The Shaggy Soul Story", 588, also speaks of two aspects of the impression, and we coincide on the first. The second he mentions is permanence, or at least a degree thereof. He thinks this permanence endows us with a capacity, whereas I regard the impression itself (which has some degree of permanence) as a capacity.

causal role is conceptually distinct from the content of the representation itself, though capacity and content characterize the same impression.[34]

Bibliography

Bostock, David, *Plato's Theaetetus*, Oxford 1988.

Broackes, Justin, "Plato and the Grammar of Perception", Unpublished typescript.

Brown, Lesley, "Being in the *Sophist*: A Syntactical Inquiry", *Oxford Studies in Ancient Philosophy* 4 (1986), 49–70.

–, "The *Sophist* on Statements, Predication, and Falsehood", in: Gail Fine (ed.), *The Oxford Handbook of Plato*, Oxford ²2019, 437–462.

Burnyeat, Myles F., "Plato on the Grammar of Perceiving", *Classical Quarterly* 26 (1976), 29–51.

–, *The Theaetetus of Plato*. M. J. Levett (trans.), revised by Myles F. Burnyeat, Indianapolis, Ind. 1990.

Cherniss, Harold, *Aristotle's Criticism of Plato and the Academy*, Baltimore, Md. 1944.

Cooper, John M., "Plato on Sense-Perception and Knowledge (*Theae.* 184–186)", *Phronesis* 15 (1970), 123–146. Reprinted in John M. Cooper, *Knowledge, Nature, and the Good: Essays in Ancient Philosophy*, Princeton, N. J. 2004.

Crombie, Ian M., *An Examination of Plato's Doctrines*, Vol. 2: *Plato on Knowledge and Reality*, London 1963.

Fine, Gail, "Plato on the Grades of Perception: *Theaetetus* 184–186 and the *Phaedo*", *Oxford Studies in Ancient Philosophy* 53 (2017), 65–110.

Fodor, Jerry, "The Revenge of the Given", in: Brian P. McGlaughlin / Jonathan Cohen (eds.), *Contemporary Debates in Philosophy of Mind*, Malden, Mass. / London 2007, 105–116.

Gill, Mary L., *Philosophos: Plato's Missing Dialogue*, Oxford 2012.

Heck, Richard G. Jr., "Are there Different Kinds of Content?", in: Brian P. McGlaughlin / Jonathan Cohen (eds.), *Contemporary Debates in Philosophy of Mind*, Malden, Mass. / London 2007, 117–138.

Heitsch, Ernst, *Überlegungen Platons im Theaetet*, Mainz / Stuttgart 1988.

Johansen, Thomas K., *Plato's Natural Philosophy: A Study of the Timaeus-Critias*, Cambridge 2004.

Kanayama, Yasuhira Y., "Perceiving, Considering, and Attaining Being (*Theaetetus* 184–186)", *Oxford Studies in Ancient Philosophy* 5 (1987), 29–81.

Lorenz, Hendrik, *The Brute Within: Appetitive Desire in Plato and Aristotle*, Oxford 2006.

McDowell, John, *Plato: Theaetetus*, Oxford 1973.

Modrak, Deborah K., "Perception and Judgment in the *Theaetetus*", *Phronesis* 26 (1981), 35–54.

[34] I gave a version of this contribution as a paper at the Platon-Tage on "Plato and the Soul" in Tübingen. I thank my hosts, Klaus Corcilius, Irmgard Männlein, and Samuel Meister for their hospitality and my audience for the valuable discussion. I also thank the participants in my *Theaetetus* seminar at Brown in the spring 2026 for their helpful questions and comments.

Schroeder, Lea, "Plato on Object Perception (*Theaetetus* 184–187 and 191–196)", in: *Journal of the History of Philosophy*. Volume 63/2 (2025), 165-189.

Sedley, David N., *The Midwife of Platonism: Text and Subtext in Plato's* Theaetetus, Oxford 2004.

Silverman, Allan, "Plato on Perception and the 'Commons'", *Classical Quarterly* N.S. 40 (1990), 148–175.

Smyth, Herbert W., *Greek Grammar*, Cambridge, Mass. 1956.

Woolf, Raphael, "The Shaggy Soul Story: How not to Read the Wax Tablet Model in the *Theaetetus*", *Philosophy and Phenomenological Research* 69 (2004), 573–604.

Plato on the Role of Perception in the Acquisition of Knowledge

Béatrice Lienemann

Plato is well-known for opposing knowledge (*epistêmê*) and belief (*doxa*). Some have interpreted the contrast as pinning Plato down to a "Two-World"-Epistemology.[1] According to this theory, the realm of knowledge (the Forms) and the realm of belief (the perceptual world) are completely disjoint with the consequence that there is neither belief of Forms nor knowledge of perceptible objects. I do not intend to enter the discussion about the plausibility of the "Two-World" Epistemology here. My aim is more limited, although it may have implications for the persuasiveness of the Two-World-Epistemology.

There are mainly two hypotheses for which I would like to argue. First, I will argue for a more generous understanding of knowledge in Plato which includes a "dynamic" conception of the relation between knowledge and belief. This dynamism is in contrast to the static conception, as held by the "two worlds" theory. Second, I will argue that sense perception can play a crucial role in the acquisition of certain kinds of knowledge, in particular human cognition of the perceptible realm. It also functions as an impetus and enabling condition in the process of attaining knowledge of Forms. I will discuss passages from four dialogues in order to show that sense perception, along with memory, not only plays a negative role of offering deceptive impressions but also serves constructive ends by motivating us to improve our cognitive grasp and by enabling us to access the perceptible realm. The passages are taken from dialogues that were written at different stages of Plato's life, thus providing a relatively broad framework. This may suggest a possible development in Plato's thinking, but this will not be my main concern.

---

[1] The most recent advocate of this position is Jessica Moss, going against the majority of recent scholarship and instead drawing on ancient receptions of Plato (Moss, *Plato's Epistemology*).

1. Plato as an 'Empiricist'?

I would like to begin my discussion by juxtaposing a passage from Aristotle's *Posterior Analytics* with a passage from Socrates' so-called autobiography in Plato's *Phaedo*. In the final chapter of the *Posterior Analytics* (II 19), which closely mirrors an account given in *Metaphysics* I 1,[2] Aristotle describes original prior knowledge and the successive steps by which first principles become known:[3]

> And so from perception there arises memory, as we say, and from memory (when it occurs often in connection with the same thing) experience; for many memories form a single experience. And from experience, or [rather] from the entire universal that has come to rest in the soul (the one apart from the many, whatever is one and the same in all those things), [there arises] a principle of craft and scientific knowledge – of craft if it concerns what comes to be, of scientific knowledge if it concerns what is. (*APo.* 100a3–9; translation Bronstein)[4]

This is one of probably three allusions to Plato that Aristotle makes in the last chapter of the *Posterior Analytics*.[5] It concerns our ability to reach universals based on sense perception. Aristotle here identifies four stages prior to the highest form of knowing, *nous*. He calls these preceding steps a "principle (*archê*) of craft (*technê*) and scientific knowledge (*epistêmê*)". The first stage is perception from which, when stored in the mind, memories arise. When many

---

[2] *Metaph.* I 1, 980a27–b21 and 980b25–981a3: "By nature animals are born with the faculty of sensation, and from sensation memory is not produced in some of them, though it is produced in others. [...] The animals other than man live by appearances and memories, and have but little of connected experience; but the human race lives also by art and reasonings. And from memory experience is produced in men; for many memories of the same thing produce finally the capacity for a single experience. Experience seems to be very similar to science and art, but really science and art come to men through experience."

[3] In my reading of the last chapter, I try to remain neutral with respect to whether Aristotle's project in II 19 is an inquiry into original prior knowledge or into the method by which we gain knowledge of first principles. In my eyes, the chapter deals with both issues, although it starts with the question of original prior knowledge, namely perception. For discussion, cf. Bronstein, *Aristotle on Knowledge and Learning*. Bronstein criticizes Barnes, for instance, on this issue; cf. Barnes, *Aristotle. Posterior Analytics*.

[4] Ἐκ μὲν οὖν αἰσθήσεως γίνεται μνήμη, ὥσπερ λέγομεν, ἐκ δὲ μνήμης πολλάκις τοῦ αὐτοῦ γινομένης ἐμπειρία· αἱ γὰρ πολλαὶ μνῆμαι τῷ ἀριθμῷ ἐμπειρία μία ἐστίν. ἐκ δ' ἐμπειρίας ἢ ἐκ παντὸς ἠρεμήσαντος τοῦ καθόλου ἐν τῇ ψυχῇ, τοῦ ἑνὸς παρὰ τὰ πολλά, ὃ ἂν ἐν ἅπασιν ἓν ἐνῇ ἐκείνοις τὸ αὐτό, τέχνης ἀρχὴ καὶ ἐπιστήμης, ἐὰν μὲν περὶ γένεσιν, τέχνης, ἐὰν περὶ τὸ ὄν, ἐπιστήμης.

[5] Peter Adamson explores the Platonic background of *APo.* II 19 and pins down three allusions to Plato. The first allusion addresses the so-called "*Meno* Paradox" regarding how learning or inquiry is possible. The second concerns Aristotle's description of our ability to reach universals based on sense perception. The third reference, proposed by Adamson, is Aristotle's appeal to *nous* as the highest form of cognition, a kind of knowledge that is superior to *epistêmê*. Cf. Adamson, "*Posterior Analytics* 2.19".

memories are repeated, a single experience (*empeiria*) ensues. In the fourth stage, an entire universal (*pantos katholou*), which "has come to rest in the soul", is grasped. This entire universal is not itself a first principle; it is rather a "preliminary account" (Bronstein), which is required for scientific inquiry in the form of demonstrative syllogisms.

This passage bears a striking resemblance to Socrates' report concerning his early engagement with natural philosophy in the *Phaedo*:[6]

> Do we think with our blood, or air, or fire, or none of these, and does the brain provide our senses of hearing and seeing and smell, from which come memory and belief, and from memory and belief which has come to rest, arises knowledge? (*Phd.* 96b3–9; translation Grube. In: Cooper 1997).[7]

Comparing the passages from the *Phaedo* and the *Posterior Analytics*, there are striking similarities in their descriptions of the stages prior to the highest form of knowing – *epistêmê* for Plato, and *nous* for Aristotle. In both passages, perception (*aisthêsis*) is recognised as a starting point in the acquisition of further cognition. Plato has Socrates further specify hearing, seeing and smelling as three kinds of perception. Aristotle, in turn, states just before the quoted passage that perception is an "innate discriminatory capacity" that is not specific to rational animals but belongs to *all* animals.[8] Furthermore, memory (*mnêmê*) is not unique to humans either, as some animals also have the ability to store perceptions, which, according to Aristotle, allows us to ascribe *gnôsis* to them.[9] Significantly,

---

[6] Cf. Barnes, *Early Greek Philosophy*, 259: "The source of B.19 is to be found in Plato (i.e. *Phaedo* 96b and *Phaedrus* 249b)".

[7] Καὶ πότερον τὸ αἷμά ἐστιν ᾧ φρονοῦμεν, ἢ ὁ ἀὴρ ἢ τὸ πῦρ; ἢ τούτων μὲν οὐδέν, ὁ δ' ἐγκέφαλός ἐστιν ὁ τὰς αἰσθήσεις παρέχων τοῦ ἀκούειν καὶ ὁρᾶν καὶ ὀσφραίνεσθαι, ἐκ τούτων δὲ γίγνοιτο μνήμη καὶ δόξα, ἐκ δὲ μνήμης καὶ δόξης λαβούσης τὸ ἠρεμεῖν, κατὰ ταῦτα γίγνεσθαι ἐπιστήμην;

[8] *APo.* II 19, 99b32–100a3: "We must therefore possess some sort of capacity, but not one that will be more valuable than these states in respect of exactness. And this is clearly true of all animals: they have an innate discriminatory capacity, which is called perception. Given that the capacity to perceive is present in [them], some animals retain what they have perceived, and others do not. Those [animals] that do not [retain it] have no knowledge (*gnôsis*) when they are not perceiving (either in general or about the things they do not [retain]). But those [animals] that do [retain what they have perceived] still have [it] in their soul even after perceiving. When many such things are [retained] there is then a further difference: some animals come to have reason (*logos*) from retention of such things, and others not."

[9] Note that the term *gnôsis* covers a wide range of cognitive states in Aristotle, from "our perceptual awareness of sensible particulars to our intellectual grasp (i.e. *nous*) of necessary and eternal first principles" (Bronstein, *Aristotle on Knowledge and Learning*, 16–17). Yet, here, I take it, Aristotle uses *gnôsis* not in this wide sense as a term for the genus of cognition in general (with *epistêmê* [scientific knowledge] as a species), but in a more restricted sense, as referring to a cognitive state that is different from and at a lower level than *epistêmê* (*epistasthai*).

Aristotle remarks that the faculty that gives us knowledge of first principles (i.e. "these states", referring to "instances of knowing more exact than demonstration", 99b27: ἀκριβεστέρας ἔχοντας γνώσεις ἀποδείζεως) is a "less valuable" (*mê timiôtera*) faculty that belongs even to the lowliest animals.

Both passages mention memory (*mnêmê*), which arises from perception, as the second stage in the ascent to knowledge. Furthermore, both Plato and Aristotle invoke the image of something's "com[ing] to rest" (*hêremein*) in the soul. Plato mentions memory and belief coming to rest. According to Aristotle, it is the entire universal that comes to rest in the soul (*êremêsantos*). Moreover, Aris-totle seems to refer implicitly to Plato when he uses the phrase "the one apart from the many" (*henos para ta polla*), which clearly hints at Plato's description of Forms as being "one over many" (*hen epi polla*).[10]

There are different opinions when it comes to interpreting these remarkable similarities between the two passages. Peter Adamson reads Aristotle's allusion as an *ad hominem* polemic against Plato, arguing that Aristotle "is deliberately exploiting a Platonic resource to answer a Platonic question, even though it was not so exploited by Plato himself". This interpretation is based on the fact that Aristotle refers in the same passage to a possible answer to how we can acquire knowledge of first principles, namely insofar as we already possess such knowledge from birth without being aware of it, which he summarily dismisses by saying that "it is strange" (*atopon*). It is tempting to associate the rejected solution with Plato's theory of recollection according to which we had actual knowledge of the Forms prior to being born – knowledge which must be recovered by recollection over the course of life because it has been forgotten. Aristotle may seem to be echoing the description found in the autobiography in the *Phaedo*, because he himself does indeed adopt the solution found in the *Phaedo*, while seeming to assume that Plato denied this (in his eyes) more promising and convincing 'empiricist' answer in favour of the recollection account.[11]

[10] Although there are also differences between the two passages, most are insignificant and may be merely contextual. Plato, for example, only mentions belief, alongside memory, while Aristotle leaves out belief but mentions experience (*empeireia*), which is apparently equivalent to "entire universal" – which arises from repeated memories. Further, Plato mentions as a final stage only knowledge, whereas Aristotle refers to craft (*technê*) and knowledge (*epistêmê*). One might suspect that Aristotle at first omits *doxa*, only to replace it – or bring it on board again – shortly afterwards with *technê*.

[11] I use the anachronistic terms "empiricist" or "empiricism" here in a broad and loose way, namely in the sense that knowledge is acquired somehow by means of the senses – in other words not completely independently of the senses as, e.g., through contemplation, intuition or thinking. Whether and, if so, to what extent a form of empiricism can be attributed to Aristotle is controversial. A proponent of such a position is Gasser-Wingate (cf. Gasser-Wingate, *Aristotle's Empiricism*). For a critical stance on this debate, see the review of Gasser-Wingate's book by Falcon (cf. Falcon, Review of "Gasser-Wingate, Marc,

My intention is to question this interpretation – not so much in terms of whether it is a correct reading of the passage but in terms of the more general question whether (and to what extent) Aristotle may have been wrong to deny that Plato held a more empiricist view of the acquisition of knowledge (involving the cognitive factors mentioned in the autobiography). For this purpose, I discuss four passages from four different dialogues which together suggest that sense perception, although potentially impeding the progress of knowledge by offering deceptive impressions, can also play a constructive part in motivating us to improve our cognitive grasp, in pushing the process of cognition forward, and even in gaining access to knowledge of the perceptual realm.

2. The *Phaedo*: Sense Perception as a Necessary Means in the Acquisition of Knowledge of the Forms?

The first example occurs in the passage containing the recollection argument in the *Phaedo*, which is supposed to show the prenatal existence of the soul. Here, Socrates gives a new explanation of the doctrine of recollection with which we are already familiar from the *Meno*. He discusses the example of knowledge of the Equal and how it is evoked by the perception of certain instances, i.e. equal sticks or stones. Here Socrates asks: "Wherefrom have we acquired the knowledge of the Equal itself?" (*Phd.* 74b4). In response, he points out, on four occasions, that it is the sight of equal and unequal things which first moves us to reflect on the Equal and Equality itself, and to wonder whether it is the same as or different from the equal things. Socrates repeats many times that in the search for knowledge, perception (here always sight) or affection (*paschomen* in 74d4 and *peponthamen* in 74e6) always takes place first, and then thinking is engaged, prompted by the puzzling information gained by perception:

> [Socrates:] "But it is definitely from equal things, though they are different from the Equal, that you have derived and grasped the knowledge of equality?" – "Very true, Socrates." [...] "As long as the sight of one thing makes you think of another, whether it be similar or dissimilar, this must of necessity be recollection?" – "Quite so." [...] [Socrates:] "Whenever someone, on seeing something, realises that that which he now sees wants to be like some other reality but falls short and cannot be like that other since it is inferior, do we agree that the one who thinks this must have prior knowledge of that to which he says it is like, but deficiently so?" – "Necessarily." (*Phd.* 74c7–e4)

Thus, the passage containing the recollection argument supports an interpretation of the connection between perception and thinking (*ennoein*) according to which perception functions as a necessary catalyst for thinking by triggering recollection, which can eventually lead to knowledge. The analysis of the

Aristotle's Empiricism"). In this context, there is no space or need to go into this question in depth. By using the term loosely, I remain neutral on this controversy.

necessary link between perception and reason culminates with Socrates saying that our conception of the Equal "derives from seeing or touching or some other sense perception, and *cannot come into our mind in any other way*, for all these senses are the same" [my emphasis].[12] Here, Socrates wholeheartedly – and in contrast to the apology at the outset in the *Phaedo* – appreciates the role that the senses play in attaining knowledge. Thus, according to the argument, sense perception – seeing equal or unequal objects – seems to play a necessary role in eventually acquiring knowledge of the Equal and the Unequal.

Commentators often focus on the difference between perception and thought when discussing the recollection argument: perception, which is directed towards sensible objects, is not a reliable source of knowledge because sensible objects provide changing and puzzling information; by contrast, only Forms provide reliable and stable evidence. However, the argument can also be read as acknowledging the productive connection between perception and reason; without the countervailing information that perception supplies, reason would lack the motivation and the impetus to contribute to clarification and, eventually, to knowledge.

Nevertheless, we must also bear in mind the limitations of the argument. First, even if perception is necessary for acquiring knowledge of the Equal, this does not mean that perception is necessary for knowledge of *every* kind of object, i.e. for every Form. Second, the argument does not show that sense perception is *sufficient* for knowledge of the Equal. Third, although his appreciation of sense perception puts Plato closer to Aristotle in that perception constitutes a first stage on the way to knowledge, it is crucial to note that what sense perception enables is different in each account. For Aristotle, perception results in memory (*mnêmê*) and, ultimately, experience (*empeiria*), whereas for Plato, according to the argument in the *Phaedo*, it allows for recollection (*anamnêsis*) of the Forms that we once knew but have forgotten.[13]

---

[12] *Phd.* 74e9–75a8: Ἀναγκαῖον ἄρα ἡμᾶς προειδέναι τὸ ἴσον πρὸ ἐκείνου τοῦ χρόνου ὅτε τὸ πρῶτον ἰδόντες τὰ ἴσα ἐνενοήσαμεν ὅτι ὀρέγεται μὲν πάντα ταῦτα εἶναι οἷον τὸ ἴσον, ἔχει δὲ ἐνδεεστέρως. – Ἔστι ταῦτα. – Ἀλλὰ μὴν καὶ τόδε ὁμολογοῦμεν, μὴ ἄλλοθεν αὐτὸ ἐννενοηκέναι μηδὲ δυνατὸν εἶναι ἐννοῆσαι ἀλλ' ἢ ἐκ τοῦ ἰδεῖν ἢ ἅψασθαι ἢ ἔκ τινος ἄλλης τῶν αἰσθήσεων· ταὐτὸν δὲ πάντα ταῦτα λέγω.

[13] Both Plato and Aristotle are fully aware of this difference, and both distinguish terminologically between memory and recollection. Plato distinguishes memory from recollection in that memory can take the form of a persisting memory of a previous experience, whereas recollection is characterized as the recovery of some experience or knowledge after a period of absence. Aristotle discusses the difference between memory and recollection in the treatise *On Memory* at the beginning of the second chapter: "recollection is neither the recovery nor the acquisition of memory. For when someone first learns or experiences something, he does not recover any memory, since none has preceded" (451a20–23, translation Sorabji). The idea is that recollection is a recovery of certain experiences that were previously absent, whereas memory can directly derive from an experience without any absence. Another difference for Aristotle is that memory belongs essentially to

3. The *Republic* VII: Objects of Perception that Do and Do not Summon the Understanding (*noein*)

The second example, the so-called "finger passage", occurs in book VII of the *Republic* (523a5–525a3), where we find a specific treatment of sense perception (*aisthêsis*) as a cognitively relevant event.

In this part of the argument, Socrates introduces a distinction between two sorts of sensations: those that do not summon understanding, because the findings of sense perception are sufficiently determined and the judgment of sense perception alone is adequate (523b1–2: ὡς ἱκανῶς ὑπὸ τῆς αἰσθήσεως κρινόμενα), and those where the findings of sense perception do not produce anything "sound"[14] or "healthy" (οὐδὲν ὑγιὲς)[15] and which encourage us to reflect further and develop understanding. Here is the first part of the distinction:

Soc.: The ones [i.e. sensations] that do not summon the understanding are all those that do not go off into opposite sensations at the same time. But the ones that do go off in that way I call *summoners* – when sense perception does not manifest (reveal) (δηλοῖ) one thing any more than its opposite (μὴδεν μᾶλλον τοῦτο ἢ τὸ ἔναντίον), no matter whether the object striking the senses is near at hand or far away. You will understand my meaning better if I put it this way: These, we say, are three fingers – the smallest, the second, and the middle finger. [...] Each of them [*sc.* fingers] equally appears as a finger, regardless of whether it is seen from the middle or from one side, be it pale or dark, thick or thin, or so on, for in all cases, an ordinary soul is not compelled to ask the understanding what a finger is, for never has sight indicated that the finger is simultaneously [a finger and] the contrary. (*R.* VII 7, 523b9–c5 and c10–d6; my emphasis)[16]

---

phantasia and is therefore present also in non-human animals (*On Memory* 449b28–30). Recollection, by contrast, occurs only in humans because, on his view, it is a sort of reasoning (453a7–10).

[14] In Stoic logic "ὑγιὲς" is used with the meaning "sound".

[15] *R.* VII 7, 523a10–b4: Socrates: "I will point out, then, if you can grasp it, that some sense perceptions don't summon the thought to look into them, because the judgment of sense perception is itself adequate, while others encourage it in every way to look into them, because sense perception seems to produce no healthy result."

δείκνυμι δή, εἶπον, εἰ καθορᾷς, τὰ μὲν ἐν ταῖς αἰσθήσεσιν οὐ παρακαλοῦντα τὴν νοήσιν εἰς ἐπίσκειψιν, ὡς ἱκανῶς ὑπὸ τῆς αἰσθήσεως κρινόμενα, τὰ δέ παντάπασι διακελευόμενα ἐκείνην ἐπισκέψασθαι, ὡς τῆς αἰσθήσεως οὐδὲν ὑγιὲς ποιούσης.

[16] *R.* VII 7, 523b9–c5 and c10–d6: Τὰ μὲν οὐ παρακαλοῦντα, ἦ δ` ἐγώ, ὅσα μὴ ἐκβαίνει εἰς ἐναντίαν αἴσθησιν ἅμα· τὰ δ` ἐκβαίνοντα ὡς παρακαλοῦντα τίθημι, ἐπειδὰν ἡ αἴσθησις μηδὲν μᾶλλον τοῦτο ἢ τὸ ἐναντίον δηλοῖ, εἴτ` ἐγγύθεν προσπίπτουσα εἴτε πόρρωθεν. ὧδε δὲ ἃ λέγω· σαφέστερον εἴσῃ. οὗτοί φαμεν τρεῖς ἂν εἶει δάκτυλοι, ὅ τε σμικρότατος καὶ ὁ δεύτερος καὶ ὁ μέσος. [...] – δάκτυλος μὲν αὐτῶν φαίνεται ὁμοίως ἕκαστος, καὶ ταύτῃ γε οὐδὲν διαφέρει, ἐάντε ἐν μέσῳ ὁρᾶται ἐάντ` ἐπ` ἐσχατῳ, ἐάντε λευκὸς ἐάντε μέλας, ἐάντε παχὺς ἐάντε λεπτός, καὶ πᾶν ὅτι τοοιοῦτον. ἐν πᾶσι γὰρ τούτοις οὐκ ἀναγκάζεται τῶν πολλῶν ἡ ψυχὴ τὴν νοήσιν ἐπερέσθαι τί ποτ` ἐστὶ δάκτυλος· οὐδαμοῦ γὰρ ἡ ὄψις αὐτῇ ἅμα ἐσήμηνεν τὸν δάκτυλον τοὐναντίον ἢ δάκτυλον εἶναι.

Here, Socrates introduces objects of sense perception that do not compel the soul to ask what they are and that therefore do not summon understanding (παρακαλοῦντα τὴν νοήσιν). These are things that do not have an opposite and therefore do not give rise to opposite impressions simultaneously. Because of this, they do not force the soul to examine things further, since they offer clear evidence, i.e. they by themselves manifest or reveal (δηλοῖ) what they are. A finger, for example, has no opposite, and in seeking to gain an adequate understanding of what a finger is, it is irrelevant which finger – whether the thumb or the index finger – we perceive. In the case of things without contrariety, it is unlikely, according to Socrates, that perception "would summon or awaken understanding" since this is unnecessary, as we grasp what a finger is based solely on our sense perception of it.

There are a few striking things about this description of sensory perception. First, *aisthêsis* is itself described as a discriminatory activity (κρινόμενα) which, on its own, forms a judgment (κρίσις) about what an object is. Furthermore, sense perception alone is credited with showing or revealing (δηλοῖ) that an object is something (a finger) by using the notions of sameness and contrariety (μὴδεν μᾶλλον τοῦτο ἢ τὸ ἔναντίον). I take it that this sort of perceptual judgment is not one that presupposes a general concept or "any universal comprehension"[17] of a thing (finger), but one that involves only a kind of preliminary account of what a finger is (obtained through repeated perceptions). In any case, the judgmental operation of sense perception is described along the same lines as the typical processes of *doxa*, since the determination carried out by *aisthêsis* takes a propositional structure in associating a predicate ("being a finger") with a subject.[18] The *doxa*-like nature of sense perception persists when Socrates goes on to describe the controversial case, namely objects of sense perception that *do* summon understanding because they give rise to opposite impressions:

> [Socrates:] "But what about the largeness and smallness of fingers? Does sight perceive them adequately? Does it make no difference to it whether the finger is in the middle or at the end? And is it the same with the sense of touch, as regards thickness and thinness, hardness and softness? And do the other senses reveal such things clearly and adequately? Does not each of them rather do the following: First of all, the sensation presiding over hardness would also necessarily preside over softness, and report (παραγγέλλει) to the soul that it has apparently perceived the same thing as both hard and soft?" […] – [Socates:] "And is it not necessary that in such cases the soul is puzzled as to what this sense signifies (σημαίνει) with hardness, when it declares (λέγει) that the same thing is also soft, or what it signifies (σημαίνει) with the light and the heavy, when it declares that the heavy is light, or the light heavy?" (*R.* VII 7, 523e1–524a3)[19]

---

[17] Trivellizzi, *Disentangling Belief.*

[18] Cf. Trivellizzi, *Disentangling Belief.*

[19] *R.* VII 7, 523e1–524a3: Τί δε δή; τὸ μέγεθος αὐτῶν καὶ τὴν σμικρότητα ἡ ὄψις ἆρα ἱκανῶς ὁρᾶ, καὶ οὐδὲν αὐτῇ διαφέρει ἐν μέσῳ τινὰ αὐτῶν κεῖσθαι ἢ ἐπ` ἐσχάτῳ; καὶ ὡσαύτως παχός καὶ λεπτότητα ἢ μαλακότητα καὶ σκληρότητα ἡ ἀφή; καὶ αἱ ἄλλαι αἰσθήσιεις ἆρ` οὐκ

Sensations that do summon understanding are characterised as having opposites. When we look at a finger, what we see allows us to say that it is large (in comparison to the little finger, for instance), but also that it is small (in comparison to the arm). Here, the senses give rise to contradictory impressions, and it turns out that we cannot adequately grasp what largeness or smallness is solely on the basis of sense perception. The same applies to all senses equally: touching a piece of wood can give the impression of its being hard (in comparison to grass) and of its being soft (in comparison to a rock) at the same time. As long as the soul relies only on the results delivered by the senses, it cannot resolve the puzzle of contradictions in perception; it is therefore compelled to reflect on these "strange reports" in order to dissolve its contradictory findings and to determine what the real nature of largeness and smallness (and the other pairs of opposites) is. Thus, the soul begins to calculate and strive for understanding so as to eventually gain an adequate grasp of such things, i.e. knowledge.

Again, what is striking in the description of the workings of the senses in the controversial case is the *doxa*-like character of sense perception. In the case of contradictory sensations, perception alone is unable to fully determine a perceived object because it is unable to determine which of two opposites applies to it – e.g. whether the finger is large or small. This is what sense perception "reports" (παραγγέλλει τῇ ψυχῇ ὡς) to the soul in controversial cases. Subsequently, the soul is compelled to ask itself what sense perception "signifies" (σημαίνει) with largeness and smallness when it "declares" (λέγει) that the finger is both large and small. It is at least remarkable that Socrates is using a vocabulary that is appropriate to describing the processes of *doxa* to describe the workings of sense perception, suggesting that the discriminative activities of the senses mimic linguistic processes, or perhaps work analogously.

Finally, when perception alone is no longer sufficient to decide on conflicting impressions, this eventually leads the soul to go beyond perceptual inputs and to start inquiring into general concepts or properties. To do this, the soul needs a "further criterion of discrimination" which is not available to sense perception but must be grasped by understanding:[20]

ἐνδεῶς τὰ τοιαῦτα δηλοῦσιν; ἢ ὧδε ποιεῖ ἑκάστη αὐτῶν· πρῶτον μὲν ἡ ἐπὶ τῷ σκληρῷ τεταγμένη αἴσθησις ἠνάγκασται καὶ ἐπὶ τῷ μαλακῷ τετάχθαι, καὶ <u>παραγγέλλει τῇ ψυχῇ ὡς</u> ταὐτὸν σκληρόν τε καὶ μαλακὸν αἰσθανομένη; – Οὐκοῦν, ἦν δ` ἐγώ, ἀναγκαῖον ἐν τοῖς τοιούτοις αὖ τὴν ψυχὴν ἀπορεῖν τί ποτε σημαίνει αὕτη ἡ αἴσθησις τὸ σκληρόν, εἴπερ τὸ αὐτὸ καὶ μαλακὸν λέγει, καὶ ἡ τοῦ κούφου καὶ ἡ τοῦ βαρέος, τί τὸ κοῦφον καὶ βαρύ, εἰ τό τε βαρὺ κοῦφον καὶ το κοῦφον βαρὺ σημαίνει;

[20] The transition between perceptions objects that the senses alone can judge and those in which the soul is led to move beyond sensory inputs is also discussed by Vogt (Vogt, "Belief and Truth in the *Republic*", 65). She proposes an interpretation according to which belief (*doxa*) and knowledge can have the same objects even within the framework of a Two-World Theory; for this purpose, she distinguishes between beliefs with and without knowledge, the second are beliefs about intelligible objects but without knowledge due to lack of a full grasp

> If the one is adequately caught by itself by sight or some other sensation, it would not lead to the being, as we said for the case of the finger; instead, if some opposite of it [*sc.* the perceived object] is always simultaneously perceived, so that nothing appears one more than also the opposite, [the soul] would then need a further criterion of discrimination (τοῦ ἐπικρινοῦντος), and would be forced to ask itself and start an inquiry, by waking reflection in itself, and ask what on earth the one in itself is. (*R.* VII 524d9–525a1)[21]

In sum, what seems to be important about this whole passage is that here, too, the description of perception can be interpreted in different ways. In one way, the juxtaposition of the two types of sensations hints at the unreliability of sense perception. If we were to confine ourselves to the senses, we would be unable to resolve puzzling sensations and to determine whether the finger is large or small, or, more generally, what largeness and smallness are. Thus, in order to gain a cognitive grasp of general, abstract notions, we need a reliable and invariable foundation such as the Forms. Yet on the other hand, one can just as well evaluate the role of sense perception in a much more positive and charitable light. First, sense perception plays a constructive role on the way to knowledge; if we were not confused by the ambiguous and contradictory findings of perception, the soul would have no reason or motivation to engage in thinking or to further examine the nature of largeness and smallness. Second, perception is even ascribed a discriminatory capacity whose workings are analogous to those of *doxa* in performing determining judgments with a propositional structure.[22]

We will see in the next section that the nature of sense perception seems to be narrowed down in subsequent dialogues, such as the *Theaetetus* and the *Philebus*, and, as a result, is more clearly differentiated from the operations of *doxa.*

4. The *Theaetetus*: The Interdependence of Perception and Reasoning

The third passage is a famous passage from the *Theaetetus*, where the qualities that are not specific to a single sense (or indeed to any sense at all) are at stake, namely the so-called "commons" or "common concepts" (*koina*), such as being,

---

of the corresponding form. On the same topic see also Patterson, *Image and Reality in Plato's Metaphysics*, 103–106.

[21] *R.* VII 524d9–525a1: εἰ μὲν ἱκανῶς αὐτὶ καθ' αὑτὸ ὁρᾶται ἢ ἄλλῃ τινὶ αἰσθήσει λαμβάνεται τὸ ἕν, οὐκ ἂν ὁλκὸν εἴη ἐπὶ τὴν οὐσίαν, ὥσπερ ἐπὶ τοῦ δακτύλου ἐλέγομεν· εἰ δ' ἀεί τι αὐτῷ ἅμα ὁρᾶται ἐναντίωμα, ὥστε μηδὲν μᾶλλον ἓν ἢ καὶ τοὐναντίον φαίνεσθαι, τοῦ ἐπικρινοῦντος δὴ δέοι ἂν ἤδη καὶ ἀναγκάζοιτ' ἂν ἐν αὐτῷ ψυχὴ ἀπορεῖν καὶ ζητεῖν, κινοῦσα ἐν ἑαυτῇ τὴν ἔννοιαν, καὶ ἀνερτᾶν τί ποτέ ἐστιν αὐτὸ τὸ ἕν.

[22] It could be argued against this interpretation that the propositional description of sense perception is merely metaphorical. However, the *doxa*-like description of the working of perception is very striking and precise that there is much to suggest that Plato used it deliberately and intentionally.

sameness, and difference. The passage is important for my purposes because the description of the processes of sense perception (αἴσθησις) differs from that provided in the *Republic* to the extent that it significantly restricts the function and scope of αἴσθησις.

The *koina* passage is the final step in the refutation of the first definition of knowledge, according to which "knowledge is perception". It starts at 184b4 and ends at 187a1, with the refutation of this first hypothesis.[23] In the context of this passage, Socrates distinguishes between what we perceive *by virtue of* the soul (expressed by the instrumental dative, e.g. "ᾧ") and what we perceive *through* the bodily sense organs (expressed by the preposition "δία", followed by the genitive). He starts by explaining in more detail what we perceive through the bodily organs, and how it is we do so. Here, αἴσθησις is clearly restricted to the five canonical senses and their specific sensory organs. We see, for example, the black and white *through* our eyes (ὄμμασι), and we hear the high and low *through* our ears (ὠσίν). Theaetetus agrees that "the things through which [we] perceive hot and hard and light and sweet [...] are all parts of the body". This shows that αἴσθησις is now reduced to a form of bodily registration. In addition, Socrates holds that there are specific sets of simple perceptual qualities, such as colours or sounds, which are apprehended through a specific sense and a specific bodily organ: colours through sight (δι' ὄψεως) and the eyes (δι' ὀφθαλμῶν), sounds through hearing (δι' ἀκοῆς) and the ears (δι' ὤτων). This point goes hand in hand with the further assumption that each sense has its own proper set of sensory qualities that are inaccessible to all other senses and sense organs. In other words, any sort of crosswise apprehension of perceptual qualities is impossible:[24]

> [Socrates:] "Would you agree that what you apprehend through the one organ you cannot also perceive through another? For instance, that what [you perceive] through sight [you cannot perceive] through hearing, and what through hearing not through sight? [...] But if you thought something about both things [i.e. colour and sound], you could not achieve this either through the former organ or through the latter, nor, in turn, could you perceive both of them through either of the abovementioned organs." (*Tht.* 184e7–185a6)

If we compare the description of perception developed thus far with the finger passage from the *Republic*, these last two aspects seem to align with the treatment in the *Republic* insofar as it also contains the assumption that each sense has its own sets of specific sensory qualities – hardness and softness for touch, smallness and largeness for sight – and nothing that is said in the *Republic* contradicts the inaccessibility thesis, even if it is not explicitly stated. This may be an unne-cessary strong (and perhaps implausible) premise, since there are certainly sensible qualities which can be perceived by more than one single sense and which are nonetheless perceptive through the senses and not with the soul,

---

[23] *Tht.* 184b4–185c3.

[24] Hendrik Lorenz calls these sensory qualities that are accessible to only one single sense and sense organ "special sensibles" (Lorenz, *The Brute Within*).

i.e. by an independent activity of the soul. Be that as it may, what is remarkable is that sense perception is credited with many more capacities in the *Republic* than it is in the *Theaetetus*, as will soon become clear.

In the next step, Socrates begins to introduce thought (διάνοια) as a cognitive capacity that is distinct from sense perception. He asks Theaetetus: "But if you thought (διανοῇ) something about both things [i.e. colour and sound], you could not achieve this either through the former organ or through the latter, nor, in turn, could you perceive both of them through either of the abovementioned organs" (*Tht.* 185a4–6). The difference between perceiving (αἰσθάνεσθαι) and thinking (διανοεῖσθαι) is not based on different classes of objects (sensible and intelligible), because both are said to be directed at colours and sounds. What distinguishes the faculties is their specific take on their objects. As Socrates asks, "[…] about sound and colour do you not think just this, in the first place, about both, namely that they both *are*?" (*Tht.* 185a8–9; my emphasis). Whereas the senses apply only and exclusively to their specific perceptual qualities, there are other features to which no sense or sense organ gives us access. These are the so-called "commons" or common features (*koina*), such as being and not-being, and these are accessed only through thought.

Subsequently, Socrates introduces a whole series of further examples of *koina*, such as unity, likeness and unlikeness, oddness and evenness, identity and difference, as well as beautiful and ugly, good and bad.[25] When Socrates asks Theaetetus to explain how these common features are revealed to us if not by any "special instrument" (*organon idion*), i.e. by any bodily sense, Theaetetus answers:[26] "[…] I would not be able to tell, except that it seems to me that there is no such organ proper to these determinations [i.e. those that are 'thought

---

[25] I cannot enter the discussion about the question whether the *koina* are an allusion or even an equivalent for the Platonic Forms. The identification of *koina* with Forms has been defended by Cornford, pointing to the striking correspondence between the *koina* and the Forms discussed in the *Parmenides* (Cornford, *Plato's Theory of Knowledge*). Dorothea Frede also recognizes an allusion to the Forms which lays the ground for arguing for a non-aporetic end of the dialogue (Frede, "The Soul's Silent Dialogue"). I confine myself to proposing an understanding of the *koina* as e.g. Sedley has suggested, according to which all the *koina* are general, abstract predicates or concepts that are "suitable objects of dialectical rather than empirical investigation" (Sedley, *The Midwife of Platonism*, 107).

[26] *Tht.* 185c3–d6: [Socrates:] "Good. Now through what does the power (*dynamis*) function which reveals to you what is common (*koinon*) in the case both of all things and of these two – I mean that which you express by the words 'is' and 'is not' and the other things mentioned in our questions about them just now? What kind of instruments (*organa*) will you assign for all these? Through what does that which is percipient in us perceive (*aisthanetai*) all of them? – [Theaetetus:] You mean being and not-being, likeness and unlikeness, same and different; also one, and any other number applied to them. And obviously too your question is about odd and even, and all that is involved with these attributes; and you want to know through what bodily instruments we perceive all these with the soul. – [Socrates:] You follow me exceedingly well, Theaetetus."

about'] as there is one for those [i.e. the perceptual ones]; rather, it seems to me that the soul investigates the common determinations (κοινά) in all things through itself (δι' αὐτῆς)." Socrates applauds Theaetetus' insight that there are some things that the soul considers through itself (δι' αὐτῆς), alongside others that the soul considers through the body (διὰ τοῦ σώματος) (*Tht.* 185e6–8).[27]

Having distinguished simple perceptual qualities and common determinations, Socrates goes on to examine further the process of dianoetic thinking that the soul carries out through itself. Theaetetus suggests the following as a way of characterising the process of *dianoia*: in thinking, the soul explores the "mutual relations" (πρὸς ἄλληλα) between opposite perceptual qualities ("compares them with each other"), such as identical and different, or beautiful and ugly, "by comparatively reckoning in itself the past and present things with respect to the future" (186a11–b1: ἀναλογιζομένη ἐν ἑαυτῇ τὰ γεγονότα καὶ τὰ παρόντα πρὸς τὰ μέλλοντα).[28] Socrates picks up on this and emphasises the point again. While the soul perceives the hardness of the hard thing and the softness of the soft thing through the bodily sense of touch, "the being and the fact that both [i.e. hardness and softness] are, as well as the contrariety between the two of them and the being of the contrariety, it is *the soul itself* that, going back to and comparing one against the other perceptions (ἐπανιοῦσα καὶ συμβάλλουσα πρὸς ἄλληλα), makes the discernment (κρίνειν)" (*Tht.* 186b2–9).[29]

If we compare the account of the workings of αἰσθῆσις in the finger passages in the *Republic* with the *koina* passage in the *Theaetetus*, some interesting differences emerge. In the *Theaetetus*, we find a clear division of tasks between perception and thinking (*dianoia*). In perceiving, the soul receives, through the different sense organs, specific isolated perceptual inputs. When perceiving, the soul only records and registers isolated sensory inputs coming from the body. In thinking, by contrast, the soul actively reacts to these sensory inputs by comparing the isolated bits of data and applying to them the common determinations. This contrast is clearly spelled out by Socrates in the following passage:

> Thus, some things, it is possible for humans and animals to perceive them immediately as they are born; and these are all the affections (παθήματα) that reach the soul through the body (διὰ τοῦ σώματος); on the contrary, the comparisons between instances of them (τὰ δὲ τούτων

---

[27] *Tht.* 185e6–8: [...] εἰ φαίνεταί σοι τὰ μὲν αὐτὴ δι' αὑτῆς ἡ ψυχὴ ἐπισκοπεῖν, τὰ δὲ διὰ τῶν τοῦ σώματος δυνάμεων.

[28] Note that this phrase may hint at the intermediate role that memory plays in the process of acquiring knowledge which is also referred to in the autobiography in the *Phaedo* and which will be analyzed in more detail in the *Philebus* (as we will see below).

[29] *Tht.* 186b2–9: Ἔχε δή· ἄλλο τι τοῦ μὲν σκληροῦ τὴν σκληρότητα διὰ τῆς ἐπαφῆς αἰσθήσεται, καὶ τοῦ μαλακοῦ τὴν μαλακότητα ὡσαύτως; – Ναί. – Τὴν δέ γε οὐσίαν καὶ ὅτι ἐστὸν καὶ τὴν ἐναντιότητα πρὸς ἀλλήλω καὶ τὴν οὐσίαν αὖ τῆς ἐναντιότητος αὐτὴ ἡ ψυχὴ ἐπανιοῦσα καὶ συμβάλλουσα πρὸς ἄλληλα κρίνειν πειρᾶται ἡμῖν.

ἀναλογίσματα) as regards being and usefulness come about (in those in which they come about) with some difficulty and in time, through many activities and education." (*Tht.* 186b11–c5)[30]

What seems important about this passage is that although it discusses some of the same examples of perception (e.g. hardness and softness) that we find in the finger passage of the *Republic*, the process of perception in the *Theaetetus* is intriguingly presented in a different way. First, as in the last chapter of the *Posterior Analytics*, perception is described here as a faculty that belongs to all living beings, both rational and non-rational, from birth on – recall that Aristotle speaks of an "innate discriminatory capacity". In both places, perception is presented as a necessary prerequisite for attaining further knowledge.

Second, calling sense perceptions affections, παθήματα, suggests that perception is a passive process – perception as the passive capacity to receive and record sensory inputs. Thinking, by contrast, is an active counterpart to this receptive faculty that is able to work on the received inputs by applying common determinations to them in order to reach comparative insights about the nature of objects beyond simple perceptual qualities. In a classic paper, Michael Frede refers to this passage to argue that perception is presented here as "a purely passive affection" of the soul that merely consists in perceiving a perceptual quality, e.g. the colour red, and not, strictly speaking, that *A* is *F* – that the apple is red.[31] This seems to me to be exactly right. The same point is addressed by Lorenz from a different angle.[32]

Lorenz raises the question what Theaetetus has in mind in speaking of the soul considering the being of such things as goodness or badness, or beauty and ugliness (186a7). According to Lorenz, Theaetetus must have in mind two different uses of "being" by describing the soul's examination of the "being" that good and bad things have in comparison to one another: either it is a *complemented use* such as "x *is* F" or "the soup *is* salty", where the general term ("salty") completes the verb "being" (the copula), or it is an *uncomplemented use* when the verb "being" needs no complement ("being" in the existential sense). In other words, the verb "being" can be used either to express something's having being (uncomplemented use) or something's being something or other (complemented use).

What is important now, according to Lorenz, is that for both uses an independent activity of the soul is needed. An independent activity of the soul is clearly required for the attribution of being or not-being (in the uncomplemented sense) to things beyond sense perception because no sense has access to being or

[30] *Tht.* 186b11–c5: Οὐκοῦν τὰ μὲν εὐθὺς γενομένοις πάρεστι φύσει αἰσθάνεσθαι ἀνθρώποις τε καὶ θηρίοις, ὅσα διὰ τοῦ σώματος παθήματα ἐπὶ τὴν ψυχὴν τείνει· τὰ δὲ τούτων ἀναλογίσματα πρός τε οὐσίαν καὶ ὠφέλειαν μόγις καὶ ἐν χρόνῳ διὰ πολλῶν πραγάτων καὶ παιδείας παραγίγνεται οἷς ἂν καὶ παραγίγνεται.

[31] Frede, "Observations on Perception in Plato's Later Dialogues".

[32] Lorenz, *The Brute Within*, chap. 6.

not-being. But this activity is also required even for the application of perceptual predicates to sensible objects in the complemented sense. It belongs to the soul to raise and settle questions of whether something bears a common feature such as being different or being like another object; and even to raise the question whether something is salty or hard requires that the independent activity of the soul is involved because applying a perceptual predicate to a sensible object goes beyond the capacity of sense perception and necessarily involves a reference to being (expressing something's being something).

I agree with substantial parts of Lorenz' analysis, above all insofar as the *koina* passage serves Socrates to show that sense perception plays merely a subordinate role in belief formation – in fact, according to Lorenz' interpretation, sense perception plays no role at all in belief formation. This it is an important departure from how perception is described in the *Republic*. There, perception is characterised not only as a passive cognitive capacity that is responsible for recording sensory inputs but as a discriminatory activity that is able to form judgments. Reducing αἴσθησις to a passive affection of the body has an interesting consequence: it reduces our susceptibility to perceptual errors and turns perception into a less suspicious cognitive capacity. In addition, perception is disentangled from thinking, since it is by thinking that the soul can compare sensory inputs by itself by applying the common determinations to perceptual information. While perception provides the necessary input, it is the function of thinking to work on this raw material in order to organise the isolated affections and to form a judgment about what an object is.

This striking redistribution of tasks between perception and thinking can also be observed in linguistic terms. Unlike in the *Republic,* the verb "αἰσθάνεσθαι" is used with a direct object, i.e. with an accusative: "[…] will the hardness of the hard thing be perceived in any way other than through touch, as well as the softness of the soft? (Ἔχε δή· ἄλλο τι τοῦ μὲν σκληροῦ <u>τὴν σκληρότητα</u> διὰ τῆς ἐπαφῆς αἰσθήσεται, καὶ τοῦ μαλακοῦ <u>τὴν μαλακότητα</u> ὡσαύτως;)" (*Tht.* 186b2–4).[33] Thus, we do not perceive that *x* is *F* (hard); we merely perceive *F* (hardness or the colour red), without any mention of a subject to which the property belongs.[34] In the *Republic*, by contrast, perception takes, as we have seen, a propositional structure in associating a predicate with a subject, expressed by a that-clause using "παραγγέλλει … ὡς" (cf. *R.* 524a2–3: παραγγέλλει τῇ ψυχῇ ὡς ταὐτὸν σκληρόν τε καὶ μαλακὸν αἰσθανομένη). What is more, perception arrives at its discriminative judgement by using the notions of sameness and difference.

[33] See also: 184d4–5; 184e3–6; 184e8–185e2; 186b11–c2.

[34] A similar non-propositional interpretation of this passage is held, e.g., by Silverman (Silverman, "Plato on Perception and 'Commons'", esp. 161–162). He draws a distinction between 'percepts' and 'concepts' – percepts being the non-conceptual constituents of perceptions (such as my red impression), and concepts, conceptual in nature, being potential constituents of many beliefs.

In the *Theaetetus*, sameness and difference are among the *koina*, and these common determinations are introduced as inaccessible to perception. Here it is the task of διάνοια to apply the *koina* to the perceptual information that the soul receives through the body. This is also reflected in language: that the soul attributes a common determination to a subject is captured by using "περί" with the genitive, for example in the question "[...] about sound and colour do you think just this, in the first place, about both (περὶ ἀμφοτέρων), namely that they both are?" (185a7–8)[35] and the claim "neither through hearing nor through sight is it possible to grasp the common determinations about them (περὶ αὐτῶν)" (185b7).[36] The activity of the soul thereby bridges the gap between perceiving a collection of isolated sensory qualities and grasping an object to which these qualities belong.

To be clear, in the passage from the *Theaetetus* considered above, the restriction of sense perception amounts to a refutation of the first hypothesis. Only those cognitive activities by which we grasp being are conducive to truth; perception that does not grasp being cannot be knowledge, since knowledge implies truth. Nevertheless, I think it is also possible to infer a constructive role for perception in the acquisition of knowledge from this passage – and here my interpretation differs from Lorenz'. His reading downplays the necessary and constructive role that sense perception still has in the acquisition of certain forms of cognition. Admittedly Lorenz grants perception the function of awareness and a cognitive role below belief and reason. But it is important, I think, to stress what this means: without perceptual awareness of sensible objects, we would lack access to the sensible world. Even if the realm of sense perception is not the realm of true being, cognizing the sensible world still plays an important role in a complete grasp of what is and what is not.

One difference between the discussions in the *Republic* and the *Theaetetus* consists in the fact that the latter enables us to acknowledge the role of sense perception for certain forms of cognition and it allows us to value the necessary contribution of perception more adequately. After all, the modification and limitation of the function and scope of perception brings with it a sharpening of its responsibilities. By removing the discriminatory activity from sense perception, it is reduced to a passive affection that is less susceptible to error and misunderstanding. At the same time, perception still operates as an indispensable receptor for perceptual information, without which thought would lack the necessary material to apply common determinations and, ultimately, to form judgments about a subject's properties.

---

[35] *Tht.* 185a7–8: περὶ δὴ φωνῆς καὶ περὶ χρόας πρῶτον μὲν αὐτὸ τοῦτο περὶ ἀμφοτέρων ἦ διανοῇ, ὅτι ἀμφοτέρω ἐστόν;

[36] *Tht.* 185b7: Οὔτε γὰρ δι' ἀκοῆς οὔτε δι' ὄψεως οἷόν τε τὸ κοινὸν λαμβάνειν περὶ αὐτῶν. See also: 185a8–9; 185b7; 185e1–2; 186d2–3.

5. The *Philebus*

In the *Philebus*, we find a short but very illuminating passage on the psychology underlying the second Form of pleasure and pain, i.e. the one which only belongs to the soul (33c5–6). Socrates treats on less than two pages perception, memory and recollection, and their interrelationship. Although we find here perhaps the most elaborate treatment of memory in Plato, one might be disappointed by this foray into philosophical psychology because Socrates says just enough to advance the discussion at stake (i.e. the contest between knowledge and pleasure about the good life) and leaves many important issues unresolved. In the remainder of this text, I will only emphasise a few points from this treatment which are relevant for the preceding discussion.[37]

Socrates turns his attention to memory since he characterizes the second Form of pleasure as "having come to be entirely because of memory (*dia mnêmês*)". Memory has already been introduced at the very beginning of the dialogue, namely as the most surprising entry on the list of intelligent states or activities that are better than pleasure:

> [Socrates:] "Philebus holds that what is good for all creatures is to enjoy themselves, to be pleased and delighted, and whatever else goes together with that kind of thing. We contend that not these, but knowing (*phronein*), understanding (*noein*), and remembering (*memnêsthai*), and what belongs to them (*syngenê*), right opinion (*doxa orthês*) and true calculations (*alêtheis logismous*), are better than pleasure and more agreeable to all who can attain them; those who can, get the maximum benefit possible from having them, both those now alive and future generations." (*Phlb.* 11b3–c2)

The present treatment of memory is also meant to show how pleasure is tied to these intelligent contestants. Memory needs to be determined because of its connection to pleasure. Perception has to be dealt with because memory will be identified as "preserving *aisthêsis*". The foray into psychology therefore starts with a brief discussion of perception (*aisthêsis*).

Socrates begins his discussion of perception by distinguishing between two kinds of bodily affections (*pathêmata*): those that happen only to our body and do not reach the soul, leaving the soul unaffected, as well as those that jointly affect body and soul by going through both of them (body and soul) and introducing a sort of shock (*seismos*) "that is peculiar to each but also common to both of them" (33d4–6). Socrates further specifies perception by looking at it from the perspective of the soul. Affections that only penetrate the body escape the soul's notice, whereas affections that happen to body and soul together do not escape the soul's notice. He further insists that the soul's lack of notice should not be understood as obliviousness of something we are not currently

---

[37] For the following, I generally agree with the decisive reading of the passage put forward by Verity Harte in her (unpublished) commentary on the *Philebus* [unpublished manuscript].

remembering. For obliviousness is the loss of memory, and one cannot forget something one never had in the first place. He therefore coins the term "*anaisthêsis*" (nonperception or absence of perception) for the case when the soul remains unaffected by the shock peculiar to the body and is not aware of anything.[38]

Socrates continues to describe perception (*aisthêsis*) as a type of movement (*kinêsis*) which happens when body and soul are affected together (*koinêi*) in a single affection (*pathei*) and, as a result, are moved in common (*koinêi*). Perception is thus identified with a movement that soul and body undergo in common, brought about by affections in which body and soul are involved in common. This characterization highlights the passivity of perception because the movement that soul and body undergo together is a *passive* movement brought about by a joint affection:

Socrates: "But when the soul and the body come in common to be involved in a single affection (*pathei*) and are moved in common, we would not speak out of turn in, correspondingly, naming this *movement* '*aisthêsis*' (perception)." – "You are right." – "And so we know by now what we mean by perception?" – "Certainly." (*Phlb.* 34a3–5)

The passage therefore provides evidence for the assumption (defended by e.g. M. Frede) that Plato narrows down sense perception in the later dialogues by conceiving of it as a purely passive phenomenon.

That the passivity of perception is the crucial element in its characterization becomes clear when it comes to the contrast with memory (*mnêmê*). Memory is described in even less words than perception, in only one sentence and without any preamble, being ultimately defied as the "preserving of perception" (*sôteria tês aisthêsis*). Describing memory as a *sôteria* suggests that memory is identified as an activity, the activity of preserving perception.[39] This is in contrast to the passive movement of perception. The perception which is preserved by memory seems to be not the *act* of perception, the perceiving, but the *result* of perception, the *aisthêta*, because memory does not keep the perceiving going, but captures

[38] *Phlb.* 33d2–34a2: [Socrates:] "You must realize that some of the various affections of the body are extinguished within the body before they reach the soul, leaving it unaffected. Others penetrate through both body and soul and provoke a kind of shock that is peculiar to each but also common to both of them." – "I realize that." – "Are we fully justified if we claim that the soul remains oblivious of those affections that do not penetrate both, while it is not oblivious of those that penetrate both?" – "Of course are we justified." – But you must not so misunderstand me as to suppose I meant that this 'obliviousness' gave rise to any kind of forgetting. Forgetting is rather the loss of memory, but in the case in question here no memory has yet arisen. It would be absurd to say that there could be the process of losing something that neither is nor was in existence, wouldn't it?" – "Quite definitely." – "You only have to make some change in names, then." – "How so?" – "Instead of saying that the soul is oblivious when it remains unaffected by the disturbances of the body, now change the name of what you so far called obliviousness to that of *nonperception*." – "I understand."

[39] Here I adopt Verity Harte's interpretation on this passage.

the things perceived: "Then in saying that memory (*mnêmê*) is preserving of *aisthêsis* (perception), someone would speak correctly, in my opinion, at least." – "Rightly so." (*Phlb.* 34a10–11)

After offering this very short description of memory, Socrates addresses the question of what distinguishes memory from recollection (*anamnêsis*):

> *Socrates:* "And do we not hold that recollection differs from memory?" – "Perhaps." – "Does not their difference lie in this?" – "In what?" "Do we not call it 'recollection' when the soul recalls as much as possible by itself, without the aid of the body, what she had once experienced together with the body? Or how would you put it?" – "I quite agree." "But on the other hand, when, after losing memory whether of perception or in turn of something learnt (*mathêma*), the soul calls up this memory for itself, we also call all these are recollections and memories." (*Phlb.* 34b2–8)

The explanation of the difference is again very short, and, in addition, it contains a textual problem. The textual problem is whether to retain, emend or delete the manuscript reading "and memories" at the end of the passage. Besides, it is not obvious how the first and the second description of recollection relate to each other. One may argue that two types of recollections are introduced. I assume, however, that a single phenomenon is dealt with by two supplementary descriptions. In the first description, it does not become clear what distinguishes memory and recollection because recollection is characterized in the same way as memory before: recollecting is an activity which the soul performs by itself, without the aid of the body, and it is associated with perceiving, i.e. with the perceptions that the soul received together with the body. The ability of recollecting depends on the preserving activity of memory in order to retrieve preserved perceptions. The second description is more specific about what is retrieved in recollection. Two things are mentioned which can be recollected after losing memory: perception (*aisthêsis*) and things learnt (*mathêmata*). This shows two points. First, recollection takes place when a memory gets lost, i.e. after a certain time of absence of an occurrent memory. Second, the objects of the act of recollecting are things perceived *or* things learnt. Again, it must be the *results* of acts of perceiving or learning and not the respective activities. Associating recollecting with learning is familiar from the discussion of recollection in the *Phaedo* or the *Meno*. But by mentioning recollection of a *mathêma* alongside with recollection of perception, it becomes clear that recollection is not equated here with learning and is not confined to Forms as its objects. Recollection, just like remembering, therefore plays an important role for accessing and grasping the sensual world. Both are identified as activities of the soul, through which the soul by itself reacts to bodily affections. Further, the investigation of memory and recollection – in the context of the treatment of the second form of pleasure – picks up the temporal structure of human living because they function as ne-cessary factors for future-oriented attitudes such as expecting and anticipating and post-oriented attitudes.

6. Conclusion

To conclude, I would like to mention three questions that arise from the argumentation but cannot be tackled in this article. When comparing the above passages, the question arises as to how the example of the finger from the *Republic* may be assessed in the light of the new distribution of tasks in the *Theaetetus*. As the finger is a complex object that bundles various properties, it does not seem to be accessible (as a whole) to any of the senses. Instead of being an item that perception alone can tackle, it now seems to be an object of thought, to be dealt with by reasoning and comparison.

A second issue which remains to discuss in more detail is the relation of my considerations to the question of the scope of the Forms. One could make the following assumption: the fact that perception alone is adequate for grasping something entails that no corresponding Form is needed. This would point to an interesting development regarding the scope of the hypothesis of the Forms, namely towards the assumption that secondary qualities do not require Forms because they can be grasped by perception alone.

To end with an even greater speculation, the argument presented here could relate to the question of what makes a good definition. Supposing that secondary qualities such as colours do not require corresponding Forms to exist and to be what they are, this could imply that Plato leaves open the possibility that a different kind of definition, not relying on Forms and their connections, is also appropriate under certain (empirical) conditions. In the *Meno*, Socrates seeks to give an example of a good definition and to do so describes what colour is by giving an empirical definition: "Colour is an effluence from surfaces, commensurate with sight, and so perceptible" (*Men.* 76d4–5). My suggestion is that in empirical cases such as these, grasping through perception is adequate and sufficient to attain perceptual knowledge, and this goes hand in hand with the appropriateness of empirical causal definitions in these cases.

Bibliography

Adamson, Peter, "*Posterior Analytics* 2.19: a dialogue with Plato?", *Bulletin of the Institute of Classical Studies* 54 (2011), 1–19.

Barnes, Jonathan, *Aristotle. Posterior Analytics. Translated with a commentary*, Oxford [2]1993.

–, *Early Greek Philosophy*, New York 2002 [[1]1987].

Bronstein, David, 2016, *Aristotle on Knowledge and Learning. The* Posterior Analytics, Oxford 2016.

Cooper, John (ed.), *Plato. Complete Works*, 1997.

Cornford, Francis, *Plato's Theory of Knowledge*, London 1935.

Falcon, Andrea, Review of "Gasser-Wingate, Marc, *Aristotle's Empiricism*, Oxford 2021", *Gnomon* 96/3 (2024), 219–223.

Frede, Dorothea, "The Soul's Silent Dialogue. A Non-Aporetic Reading of the *Theaetetus*", *Proceedings of the Cambridge Philological Society* 35/215 (1989), 20–49.

Frede, Michael, "Observations on Perception in Plato's Later Dialogues", in: id. (ed.), *Essays in Ancient Philosophy,* Oxford, 3–8.

Gasser-Wingate, Marc, *Aristotle's Empiricism*, Oxford 2021.

Harte, Verity, *Commentary on the* Philebus, unpublished manuscript.

Lorenz, Hendrik, *The Brute Within: Appetitive Desire in Plato and Aristotle*, Oxford 2006.

Moss, Jessica, *Plato's Epistemology. Being and Seeming*, Oxford 2021.

Patterson, Robert, *Image and Reality in Plato's* Metaphysics, Indianapolis 1985.

Platonis Opera, Tetralogiae V–VII, rec. Burnet, Oxford 1903.

Platonis Opera, Tetralogiae I–II, rec. E. A. Duke, W. F. Hicken, W. S. M. Nicoll, D. B. Robinson et J. C. G. Strachan, Oxford 1995.

Ross, W.D., *Aristotle. Analytica Priora and Posteriora*, Oxford 1964.

Sedley, David, *The Midwife of Platonism. The Text and Subtext in Plato's* Theaetetus, Oxford 2011.

Silverman, Allan, "Plato on Perception and 'Commons'", *The Classical Quarterly* 40/1 (1990), 148–175.

Trivellizzi, Lara, *Disentangling Belief, Sense-Perception and Appearance Plato's Epistemology of Perceptibles in the Later Dialogues*, Basel / Berlin, 2025.

Vogt, Katja Maria, "Belief and Truth in the *Republic*", in: ead. (ed.), *Belief and Truth. A Skeptic Reading of Plato*, Oxford 2014, 51–70.

Analysis of Pleasure: From a Twofold Dialectic on Pleasure in the *Philebus* to a Reading Exercise Framed by the Absence of this Dialectic in the *Timaeus*[1]

Georgia Mouroutsou

This paper focuses on Plato's analysis of pleasure in the *Philebus* and the *Timaeus* 64a–65b. It first outlines key elements in the *Philebus*, before turning to the shorter *Timaeus* passage to present a reading exercise that aims to explain the divergences in the analysis of pleasure: in the *Timaeus*, the *Philebus*' account of pleasure and the classification of pleasures mixed and unmixed with pain, labelled as impure and pure respectively, do not emerge explicitly, due to a different agenda, as will become clear in what follows.

The *Philebus* offers a twofold dialectic approach to the topic of pleasure. In Plato, "dialectic"[2] refers either to discursive dialogue or to dialectic as metaphysics, which involves a range of methods and topics of study, including hypothesis, definition, and division. Although the *Philebus* has been widely analyzed, the two aspects investigated in this paper have not drawn sustained attention: first, the non-therapeutic nature of the dialogue between Socrates and Protarchus – "dialectic" in the first sense – in which this dialogue differs from exchanges between Socrates and Protagoras, the fictive masses, and Callicles has not been discussed at all to my knowledge; and second, the division of pleasure into mixed and unmixed types within the dialectic conducted in the dialogue, with "dialectic" understood here in the metaphysical sense, has not yet been significantly analyzed in terms of its essential function.

The *Timaeus* passage lacks both kinds of dialectic identified in the *Philebus*. This paper shows that the *Timaeus* offers a physiological, rather than dialectical, analysis of pleasure, relying neither on dialogue nor on

[1] The translations of the *Philebus* and the *Timaeus* are Frede's and Zeyl's respectively, with adaptations.

[2] The notion of "dialectic" appears in the following phrases: "the dialectical method" (ἡ διαλεκτικὴ μέθοδος, *R.* 511b), "the undertaking of dialectic" (ἡ πραγματεία τοῦ διαλέγεσθαι, *Th.* 161e), "the art concerning discussions" (ἡ περὶ τοὺς λόγους τέχνη, *Phd.* 90b) "the method of the discussion" (ἡ μέθοδος τῶν λόγων, *Sph.* 227a), "the science of dialectic" (ἡ ἐπιστήμη τοῦ διαλέγεσθαι, *R.* 511c), "the power of dialectic" (ἡ δύναμις τοῦ διαλέγεσθαι, *R.* 511b, 532d, 533a, 537d; *Parm.* 135c, *Phil.* 573).

metaphysical inquiry into pleasure. Despite the vast amount of literature on pleasure in Plato, the *Timaeus* passage has not received specific attention,[3] and the contrast be-tween the dialectical approach in the *Philebus* and the physiological approach in the *Timaeus* has not been studied. The only analysis of the *Timaeus* passage[4] considers it a continuation of the metaphysical dialectic of the *Philebus*, which resorts to questions and answers to investigate types of pleasure. This paper resists the temptation to use the *Philebus* as a Procrustean bed for the *Timaeus*, although both perspectives – dialectical and physiological – rely on a concept-tion of pleasure as the perceived restoration of natural equilibrium, and, as such, do not offer two distinct accounts of pleasure, a dialectical and a physical one.[5]

Moreover, this paper suggests that, although there is no explicit dialogue with Presocratic thinkers, the *Timaeus* passage provides Plato's responses to questions some Presocratics had addressed regarding pleasure and pain: Are all perceptions pleasant? Are they all painful? Plato, through Timaeus, answers that they are not, and explains why.

Platonic dialectic remains a challenge; its meaning shifts across dialogues[6] and eludes a straightforward analysis by philosophers. While the concept of Platonic dialectic as metaphysics is difficult to grasp, dialogue is often dismissed as superficial, a mere dramatic form, beneath which lies the philosophical content worthy of investigation. And yet Plato's conception of philosophy is fundamentally dialogical. In the *Philebus*, the dialogue mainly takes place between Socrates and the hedonists; this paper also examines the conception of pleasure developed in dialogue with both Protarchus and the Presocratics.

On account of his choice of the dialogical method, Plato sometimes appears dangerously close to the very interlocutors that he critiques – whether hedonists or Presocratic theorists, as ancient and modern interpretations show. As for us,

---

[3] David Sedley ("The *Timaeus* as Vehicle for Platonic Doctrine") addresses the "physiological perspective" of the *Timaeus* most effectively, and explains the discrepancies between dialogues as systematically supporting Plato's cosmogony in the Timaean context. He suggests that both the content and the manner of exposition of metaphysical doctrines (e.g., the role of forms as paradigms, forms of natural species, the "two-worlds" thesis), the dialectical method of collection and division, the tripartite soul, the doctrine of recollection, and the cognitive defects of sense-perception have a specifically cosmogonical context and "explicit cosmological content" (67), but "not divorced from ethics and metaphysics" (59) conducted elsewhere. Sedley does not consider the treatment of pleasure. The "physiological focus" of the *Timaeus* is analyzed below.

[4] Wolfsdorf, "Timaeus' Explanation of Sense-Perceptual Pleasure".

[5] For the dialectical and physical perspectives providing different accounts of an emotion, see Aristotle, *De Anima* I 1, 403a29–b1, on anger, rather than pleasure. Aristotle diverges from Plato in his understanding of the scope, nature, and objects of physics and dialectic.

[6] See Robinson, *Plato's Earlier Dialectic*, 70: "The fact is that the word 'dialectic' had a strong tendency in Plato to mean 'the ideal method, *whatever that may be*'."

when we ignore dialogue and the importance of its role in philosophical investigation, we impoverish our understanding of Plato.

1. The *Philebus*: Restoring a Dialectical Reading but Which Dialectic, Exactly?

This study relies on the hermeneutical presupposition that the *Philebus* represents the culmination of Plato's inquiry into pleasure; this standpoint informs our analysis of other dialogues. However, this does not imply that the *Philebus* offers Plato's definitive, most authoritative conception of pleasure, because this topic is discussed further in the *Timaeus* and in the *Laws*. Nor should the *Philebus* be treated as the standard to which all Platonic analyses of pleasure must conform, as it does not constitute a complete analysis of pleasure.

The dialogue is the culmination in Plato's twofold investigation of pleasure: his critique of different types of hedonists for whom pleasure is the only or highest good goes hand-in-hand with his critique of pleasure in a range of dialogues, including *Protagoras*, *Gorgias*, *Phaedo*, and the *Republic*.[7] The two Platonic meanings of Platonic "dialectic" and the two aspects of his investigation converge in the *Philebus*, where the art of dialectic is deployed in interpersonal dialogue with Protarchus and, occasionally, with Philebus who represent the view that pleasure is the only good. This dialogue relies on rules and presuppositions to progress toward the attainment of truth and knowledge about the notion of pleasure and its value in human life. Socrates leads the discussion; as such, the *Philebus* stands out among the later dialogues in which Socrates, although engaged, is not depicted by Plato in this role.[8] At the same time, dialectic, in a variety of occurrences, refers to the Platonic metaphysical theories and methods applied to the topic under investigation – here, pleasure.

Although pleasure is our primary focus, it is not the sole concern of the *Philebus*: the central theme is a debate weighing the roles of intelligence and pleasure in human happiness. The interlocutors are striving to define the human good and to determine what disposition of the soul – pleasure or intelligence – is best suited to the provision of true happiness (11d3–6). Pleasure receives the most attention, because it has not been conclusively analyzed in the Platonic

---

[7] This analysis of the *Philebus* focuses on the non-therapeutic nature of the dialectic with Protarchus and on the essential dependence of pleasure on its relationship with pain. No research has been conducted on these points; to maintain focus and avoid long digressions, existing interpretations will be discussed only when required for the purpose of the argument.

[8] In the *Sophist,* the *Statesman*, and the *Timaeus*, Socrates is present and states the topic of the discussion; he is not present in the *Laws*. On "Socrates' return", see Frede, "The Hedonist's Conversion".

corpus; in that respect, the *Republic* paves the way for the *Philebus*. In the critical examination of pleasure, distinctions are drawn between better and worse pleasures (31b–52c), and between different kinds of knowledge (55c–59d).

The Non-Therapeutic Character of Dialectic as Interpersonal Dialogue in the Philebus

This study cannot focus on the investigation of pleasure in the dialogue without highlighting that while the *Philebus* explicitly examines pleasure, knowledge, and associated views, it does not examine Protarchus' soul – at least, not primarily or in the same way as the souls of Protagoras or Callicles are examined elsewhere. Indeed, in the *Philebus*, the dialectician – Socrates – never asks Protarchus whether he personally subscribes to the views that he advances at each stage of the discussion, whereas this fundamental principle of the dialectic of examination (*elenchus*) is applied in the discussions with the hedonists in the *Protagoras* and *Gorgias*. Although the examination in the *Philebus* remains interpersonal, it lacks the personal character derived from the principle of commitment.

Even in the sole elenctic section of the *Philebus*, 20–22, a discussion of the choice of the best possible human life, Protarchus is not explicitly asked to express his own opinion nor whether he commits to the views that he articulates. Rather, he represents all human beings in their pursuit of the human good and whatever pertains to it. To justify the absence of the principle of commitment in the dramatic context, Plato introduces (11a–c) the character of Protarchus as a substitute for Philebus: he inherits Philebus' doctrine after the latter's withdrawal from the conversation. As such, he is free to argue for or against this doctrine regardless of his own beliefs, and yet he reveals himself as a hedonist during the examination of the life of pleasure (21a–d), despite having entered the discussion as merely a representative of the Philebean standpoint.[9] Not only does he concede that he would be utterly satisfied with nothing but the greatest pleasures in his life (21a8–13), but he also repeatedly states, throughout the dialogue, that all pleasures are true – until Socrates ultimately persuades him of his error.

The dialogue in question is thus conducted between Socrates and a hedonist, albeit of a different type from that of the masses, of Protagoras and the sophists, and of Callicles; this results in a different type of dialectic. The absence of the personal *elenchus* also deprives the dialogue of the therapeutic function identifiable in the *Protagoras* and *Gorgias*. Indeed, in the *Philebus*, Socrates does not attempt a therapy of cognitive nature, through which he would bring his

[9] For a detailed analysis of these lines, see Mouroutsou, "Choosing a Life and Rejecting a Thoughtless Life in *Philebus* 20–22".

interlocutors to the next stages of knowledge and of self-knowledge by tailoring the dialectic to their individual, psychological, and ethical situations. Rather, he avoids any psychotherapeutic attempt and does not venture into Callicles' narcissistic thoughts to expose the roots of this pathological understanding of pleasure; nor does he endeavor to guide Protagoras toward acknowledgeing his unconscious, or concealed, core belief that pleasure is the only good.[10]

The dialogue with the hedonist Protarchus does not aim to reveal the underlying roots of his hedonism, nor to disclose the origin of his views. One might counter that Socrates does not feel compelled to undertake the therapeutic process because Protarchus' character is much more stable than that of a narcissist. Although this is true, he is not asked to account, for instance, for his simplistic theory that "pleasure is simple and as such always true". Plato does not digress into the reasons underlying this view, be they metaphysical or otherwise, but rather follows his agenda for the dialogue.[11]

Thus, the dialectic with the hedonist Protarchus in the *Philebus* is "depersonalized" and lacks the therapeutic character adapted to the individual,[12] but it remains educational. Despite the collaborative spirit of the inquiry, Protarchus is subjected to a considerable number of Platonic lessons on ontology that he is only just able to comprehend. In this dramatic context, removing the therapeutic character of the dialectic is a means for Plato to facilitate this rigorous educational agenda. The *Philebus* reflects and celebrates the discussions, teachings, and debates about pleasure that took place in the Academy in its contemporary context. It also conveys Plato's celebration of his own literary

---

[10] *The Therapeutic Nature of Dialectic: Plato and the Hedonists in the Protagoras and the Gorgias* (manuscript nearing completion) contains a thorough analysis of the therapeutic dialectic, in its cognitive character specifically, in the relevant passages of the *Protagoras* and the *Gorgias*.

[11] Although Plato often seeks to elevate his interlocutors and uncover metaphysical truths beyond their comprehension (as with the materialists in the *Sophist*), he chooses not to analyze Protarchus' views of pleasure. The simplicity-of-pleasure view could rely on the argument that the category of "truth" is irrelevant, either because a relativist grounds pleasure – as one's experience of being pleased – as always true to oneself, or because a metaphysician acquainted with simple entities rejects bivalence in the case of pleasure and regards it as a simple entity that one either possesses and truthfully reports, or does not possess and about which one neither speaks truth nor falsehood.

[12] And yet the ethical aspect is not irrelevant; rather, the views are examined more independently from the interlocutor than in the *Gorgias* and *Protagoras*. Louis-André Dorion ("Aristotle's Definition of Elenchus"), sagaciously demonstrates the depersonalization of the Aristotelian *elenchus* using the definition given in the *Sophist* (230b–d), but does not mention the *Philebus* beyond identifying early signs of Aristotelian depersonalization in Protarchus' defense of a thesis that is not his own, among other instances in later dialogues. He does not address the therapeutic aspect of Plato's elenctic dialectic either.

and pedagogical achievements, and provides ample instruction both to the overburdened Protarchus, and to us.[13]

Dialectic as Metaphysics of Pleasure in the Philebus*: The Model of Restoration and the Fundamental Distinction between Pure and Impure Pleasures*

The challenging opening sections of the dialogue present the dialectic of unity and multiplicity of forms (16b–20c). This dialectic provides a foundation for the fourfold classification of all that exists – (1) the unlimited, (2) the limit, (3) the mixture of the limit and the unlimited, and (4) intelligence as the cause of a good mixture (23b–30d, including the cosmological digression) – as well as for the subsequent dialectic of pleasure. This framework presents an assessment of the respective merits of pleasure and intelligence for creating a good human life. Intelligence is deemed the most valuable aspect, while pleasure takes but third place: second place is awarded to the life that blends pleasure with intelligence, because pleasure, in itself, is unlimited, and can be assimilated with goodness only occasionally. Socrates then presents the most comprehensive analysis of pleasure found in Plato's works (31b–53c).

This paper does not attempt to summarize the complexities inherent to Platonic dialectic as metaphysics in general and the metaphysics of pleasure in particular, nor to examine their potential interconnection, or lack thereof, in the dialogue. To support the argument, it will be more profitable to introduce the theoretical model of restoration, which serves as a framework for understanding both pleasure and pain, in their bodily manifestations specifically. Although this model is not presented as a definition, it is used throughout the dia-logue to account for pleasure. Furthermore, dialectic as metaphysics here deals with the method of division as regards pleasure; the present analysis will show that the distinction between "pure" pleasures, which are free from pain, and "impure" pleasures, which are mixed with pain, is fundamental in the *Philebus*, although the dialogue also envisages other distinctions – a large part of it is devoted to persuading Protarchus that false pleasures are as real as true ones. Accordingly, the paper will provide textual evidence that the distinction bet-ween mixed and unmixed pleasure is a primary, though not reductive, distinct-ion.

[13] Whether there is room to accommodate two types of elenctic (see Szaif, "Philosophical Paideia in Plato's *Sophist*") – one pertaining to the interlocutors and the other to the theses – falls outside the scope of this paper. Instead, I seek to elucidate a point that has not been addressed in existing interpretations of the *Philebus*, namely that it does not merely present a strict separation of the scope of elenctic of theses and persons; rather the dialectic with Protarchus lacks the (psycho)therapeutic dimension found in the elenctic engagements with Callicles and Protagoras.

The Restorative Model

To analyze bodily pleasures, Socrates introduces the model of restoration, according to which a disturbed natural state can be restored to equilibrium;[14] for instance, eating when hungry, or drinking when thirsty both provide pleasure, because these actions reestablish a natural balance that had been disrupted:

> [...] And the coagulation of the fluids against the animal's nature through freezing is pain; while the process of their dissolution or redistribution toward nature is pleasure [ἡ κατὰ φύσιν ὁδὸς ἡδονή]. To cut matters short, see whether the following account seems acceptable to you. When the form of the natural state of a living organism, a state constituted of limit and unlimited, as I explained before [reference to the third kind of mixture, including harmony and health as mentioned], is destroyed, this destruction is pain, while the return toward its own nature [τὴν δ' εἰς τὴν αὑτῶν οὐσίαν ὁδόν], this general restoration, is pleasure. (32a6–b4)

Here, pleasure is presented as the process of restoration; pain, of disintegration. This will be refined later in the discussion: pleasure and pain are not all suchlike processes (themselves), but rather the perception of suchlike processes (42d5–43c7). Conceptualizing pleasure and pain in these terms promotes the understanding of how they function as opposites: they are experienced as opposites because they accompany opposing processes of which we are aware.[15]

The Primary Distinction Between Mixed Pleasures and Pleasures Unmixed with Pain

Socrates does not begin the analysis of pleasure by establishing a straightforward distinction between mixed and unmixed pleasures. His field of investigation is broader, and a prominent concern is to distinguish between true and false pleasures – Protarchus vehemently rejects the concept of false pleasure. Moreover, Socrates' intention is not to present his points, including this distinction,

---

[14] Socrates analyzes the healthy ordinary bodily restorations (πρόχειροι, 45a4) with the aid of this model. It seems to be of use for pleasure in general, with the *caveat* that not all pleasures are restorations of a natural equilibrium: the pleasures of itching and scratching and the malicious pleasure of the comedy are certainly not restorations of a *natural* equilibrium.

[15] Pleasures and pains are characterized as opposites at 33b8–9 and 41d1–3. In the first passage, Protarchus refers to being in pain as the opposite of feeling pleasure; the gods do not experience these affective processes. In the second passage, pains and pleasures linked to bodily disturbances, and to the soul's anticipation of them, are called opposites. They are perceived by the soul simultaneously: while this does result in opposite (pleasant and painful) perceptions, the grammar does not allow 'opposite perceptions' as a translation (τούτων in τούτων ἐναντίων οὐσῶν refers to λύπας τε καὶ ἡδονάς); *pace* Frede's translation (1993).

by lecturing his audience, because the context is not that of Plato's Academy. Rather, he is engaging in a dialogue with the hedonist Protarchus, to whom he seeks to convey the multiplicity, inner complexity, and varying value of pleasures in accordance with their diverse objects. That said, a careful reading of 31b2–53c3 reveals that the distinction between mixed and unmixed pleasures is Plato's focal point: there, Socrates establishes this distinction gradually and systematically and refers to it explicitly in three pivotal instances, as he identifies the pleasures that he has analyzed as those mixed with pain.

Socrates first addresses the pleasures and pains associated with bodily processes (31b1–32b7), before directing the focus onto the pleasures and pains present within the soul, given that they are related to the bodily states previously mentioned (32d9–36c2). For instance, when one experiences the pain of hunger, the soul yearns for satisfaction, and past pleasurable experiences lead to the anticipation of pleasure – one anticipates the resolution of hunger in the hopeful expectation of a future meal. However, this interplay of pains and pleasures will be characterized formally as "mixed pleasures" only later in the dialogue.

The discussion then famously turns to the consideration of four types of false pleasures (36c3–50e4). Protarchus strongly resists the notion of false propositional pleasures (36c3–41a4), but he seems to accept Socrates' suggestion that false pleasures result from the overestimation or underestimation of pleasures (41a5–42c4), or from a conceptual misunderstanding that equates pleasure with the absence of pain (42c5–44d6). The fourth category of false pleasure is identified as the mixture of pleasure and pain (44d7–50e4): in the conclusion to this section, Socrates categorizes the pleasures under discussion as being "mixed with pain". The possibility of the combination of pleasure and pain resulting in falsehood is considered, and the pleasures deemed greatest in intensity and quantity provide the model for the investigation. Socrates refers explicitly to the distinction between mixed and unmixed pleasures at 46b8–c4, 47c1–d3, and at 50d, just before the introduction of the concept of pure pleasures. He establishes a threefold classification in these three passages:

> There are mixtures that have their origin in the body and are confined to the body [a]; then, there are mixtures of the soul itself in the soul [b]. But then we will also find mixtures of pleasures and pains in both soul and body, and at one time the combination of both will be called pleasure; at other times it will be called pain [c]. (46b8–c4)

In this first passage, Socrates identifies three sources for the mixture of pleasure and pain: within bodily processes [a], in emotional experiences not causally dependent on current bodily states [b], and in the combination of bodily processes with opposing states of the soul [c].

The second passage conveys the same threefold distinction between pleasures mixed with pain. It refers explicitly to the earlier discussion, but it does not include the pleasures confined to the soul itself:

Yes, as far as concerns the pleasures that arise in the external and internal affections of the body that are mutually interconnected, Protarchus [a]. But take now the cases where the soul's contributions are opposed to the body's: when there is pain over and against pleasures, or pleasure against pain, both are finally joined in a mixed state [b]. We have talked about them earlier and agreed that in these cases it is the deprivation that gives rise to the desire for replenishment, and while the expectation is pleasant, the deprivation itself is painful. When we discussed this, we did not make any special mention, as we do now, of the fact that, in the vast number of cases where soul and body are not in agreement, the final result is a single mixture that combines pleasure and pain. (47c1–d3)

Socrates then focuses on the final category of mixed pleasures (47d5–50e4), which encompasses a wide range of emotional pleasures, such as those caused by love or anger. These are intrinsically tied to pain, and are not directly triggered by current or former bodily processes, although this does not preclude their coexistence with bodily processes, such as those taking place when one is in love, or during an outburst of anger. Here, the dialectical analysis of pleasure is not concerned with its physiological aspects. Plato's nuanced demonstration reveals that pain underlies pleasure, even when one believes that one is experiencing emotional pleasure devoid of any emotional pain. For example, anger involves the pain of having suffered injustice mixed with the anticipated pleasure of revenge, while seemingly innocent comic amusement can be intertwined with resentment.

In his final mention of the threefold distinction between mixed pleasures, Socrates ensures that it is firmly embedded in Protarchus' understanding and memory – and ours:

[...] once the main point was understood that there exists the possibility, for the body without the soul, for the soul without the body, and for both of them in a joint affection, to contain a mixture of pleasure and pain. (50d3–6)

After this investigation of mixed pleasures, Socrates expresses the necessity to turn to their opposites, namely the unmixed, or pure, pleasures. Throughout this analysis, Plato explicitly presents this distinction as being the most significant. Therefore, it is also the most fundamental distinction when it comes to dialectic as a metaphysics of pleasure, which is here focused on division as the dialectical method of relevance. The conception according to which impure pleasures are mixed with pain and pure pleasures are free from pain rests on the underlying premise that the essence of both kinds of pleasure is defined by their relationship to pain.

The passages quoted above provided textual evidence of the importance of this division throughout the analysis of pleasure. The second kind of falsehood, according to which false estimations of the quantity of pleasure result from the interdependence with pain, provides further justification. To explain how this falsehood occurs, Plato resorts to the example of bodily affections co-occurring with the soul's desire for the opposite state; this example pertains to the second type of mixed pleasures, although it is not yet labeled as such. In such cases, the opposite, simultaneously occurring pains and pleasures can be identified as pairs in which one element takes place in the soul, while the other originates in the body (41d1–3). Because they are opposite – this has been demonstrated earlier in the *Philebus* and is here taken for granted – it is presupposed that they can both be measured on the same scale. Such measurements are more accurate when pleasures are compared with pleasures, and pains with pains (41e). Errors may occur, because these pleasures and pains may appear greater or smaller than what they really are, depending on their immediacy or remoteness in time: pleasures and pains seem greater in the moment in which they occur than they do when they are relegated to the remote future (this is an example of our bias toward things that are temporally closer to us). The perception of pleasures or pains tends to be inflated by the immediacy of experience, because they seem, in the moment, to form one's entire reality and only truth. This inflation affects judgments about the nature and value of the current pleasure or pain, and of the object that causes it.[16]

The quantity and value of pleasures might also be influenced by the juxtaposition of pleasures with pains. Judgments that merely rely on comparative measurement can be influenced by the pleasures and pains taken as pairs, depending on their immediacy or remoteness in time:

> But now these [pleasures and pains] themselves change because they are looked at from close up or far away each time and, when simultaneously put side by side, pleasures seem greater compared to what is painful [αἱ μὲν ἡδοναὶ παρὰ τὸ λυπηρόν] and more intense, and pains the opposite because of their being inside pleasures. (*Phil.* 42b)[17]

Although the concept of mixed pleasures has not yet been introduced, Plato here explains how any mixed pleasure may become distorted, inflated, or deflated. For instance, the immediate, pleasant expectation of a future meal can be intensified by extreme hunger and may cause much more intense past pains to fade as the current situation influences our measurement. The bias toward past pains minimizes or discounts them.

The primacy of the division is also highlighted by the introduction of pure pleasures as the opposites of impure ones – the final type of false pleasures analyzed by Socrates. Protarchus calls this newly introduced category of pleasures 'true', and Socrates does not correct him (51b1–2). The choice of this qualification by Protarchus may be elucidated by considering the opposition of the pure pleasures to the two types of false pleasures mentioned by Socrates at 51a5–9: the first type encompasses apparent, but false, pleasures, stemming

[16] In *Phaedo* 83c–d, Socrates describes the judgment according to which the thing that causes the current bodily pleasure or pain is the clearest and most real thing as "the greatest and most extreme evil"; it has been affected by the intensity of the present bodily pleasure or pain.

[17] See also 41d1–2 and 47a1. Aubry, "*Nicomachean Ethics* VII 14, (1154a22–b34)", 243–244, notices the *Philebus* parallel in *EN* 1154a29–31.

from the erroneous conception of pleasure as the absence of pain (the third kind of falsehood). The second type is pleasure mixed with its opposite, pain, and therefore not real pleasure (belonging to the fourth kind of falsehood, i.e., pleasure mixed with degrees of pain). On the contrary, pure pleasures are true (i.e., real and unadulterated).

All forms of impure pleasure are restorations from a perceived lack; therefore, they are intrinsically linked to pain. Present or past pain affecting either body or soul is involved in all possible combinations. Whenever a lack, and therefore pain, is felt, the possibility of intensification and inflation arises and may turn to immoderacy when a natural equilibrium or a virtuous character are not involved. Plato's pure pleasures originate from sensations caused by a beautiful object, and from the process of learning: the sudden experience of the delightful smell of roses, of a patch of white color, of shapes constructed by compass, rule, and square. Intelligible objects are also an adequate source of pure intellectual pleasure, when one is attaining knowledge in the final stages of learning. Beside the nature of their specific sources,[18] these pleasures are characterized by their independence from any preexisting, felt, and therefore painful, lack.[19] As such, they are not linked to a desire to remedy the lack, as is the case when one craves for a good meal when hungry, or attempts to end a painful itch by scratching. Pure pleasures are not cessations of preexisting, opposite pains and, for this very reason, they are free from pain. Being unmixed with pain *in their nature*, they are also *necessarily* not mixed with pain in what they are. As such, the pleasures described in the following examples are not pure pleasures: the intellectual pleasure that arises when a successful moment in one's learning process provides an opportunity to increase one's number of publications corresponds to the cessation of the pain caused by the perceived lack. Similarly, the pleasure experienced when one perceives a perfume that reveals that a beloved person is present involves the pain arising from lacking the other person's presence.

In cases of a felt lack, pleasure ceases the opposite pain arising due to that lack whereas with unfelt lacks, pleasure is not the cessation of an opposite pain. In both cases, though, pleasure is understood as fundamentally contingent upon its relationship to pain. This is not surprising against the background of the restorative model presented in the *Philebus*: pleasure is either mixed with pain or free from it.

---

[18] See Warren, "Truth, Beauty, Purity, and Pleasure: *Philebus* 50e–53c".

[19] I have analyzed this point in Mouroutsou, "Placing Pure Pleasures Beyond the Chain of Hunger"; and in "Plato's *Phaedo*: Are the Philosophers' Pleasures of Learning Pure?", by the same author.

2. The *Timaeus*' Physiological Focus as a Specific Ontology of Bodies

The *Timaeus* lacks many of the dialectical aspects found in other Platonic works; indeed, it is not a dialogue but rather a succession of monologues. The passage under investigation in this paper belongs to a single, lengthy monologue by Timaeus, rather than the usual back-and-forth exchange. Critias' preceding account follows the same format. Although Plato continued to value interpersonal dialogue in his later works, he chose not to apply this form to the *Timaeus*.[20]

This analysis will follow the present focus on dialectic as applied to the analysis of pleasure in the *Philebus*. In the monological Timaean account, there is, unsurprisingly, no dialogue with hedonists either: no hedonist is present in the dramatic context, nor are any fictive hedonists invited to join – the only two scenarios deployed in other dialogues. The negative point is restricted to dialogue with hedonists as we will see in the sequence. The dialectic as metaphysics of pleasure is absent from the *Timaeus* too, given that Timaeus is not interested in analyzing the nature of pleasure, drawing distinctions between types of pleasure, or offering a definition against the background of Platonic metaphysics of unity and multiplicity.

The topic of pleasure and pain is developed at 64a1–65b3. For the reasons delineated above, this section is non-dialectical. Still, this new perspective offers a unique and positive contribution to the investigation into pleasure, which does not rely on the imposition of dialectic as metaphysics, nor on seeking to define and categorize types of pleasure. Finally, notwithstanding the absence of an explicit dialogical format, this section of the *Timaeus* is shaped by a dialectical aspect of relevance – dialectic as dialogue.

The passage belongs to the second part of the Timaean monologue (46c7–68d7), which centers on the auxiliary causes in the pre-cosmic and cosmic phases. These causes belong to one of the two types of causes identified by Timaeus in his narrative of the creation of the world, and are used as the basis for the tripartite structure of his monologue. The first part (27d5–47e2) focuses on reason, the divine cause responsible for the creation of the world, the aim

[20] For two distinct but compatible analyses of Plato's choice to have Timaeus deliver a long speech rather than engage in dialogue with others, see Johansen, *Plato's Natural Philosophy*; Szlezák, "Gespräche unter Ungleichen"; and Szlezák, *Das Bild des Dialektikers in Platons späten Dialogen*, 218–235. Johansen suggests that the structure of the speech reflects the world's order, while Szlezák argues that presenting two intellectual equals discussing the most elevated topics (*Tim.* 28c, 48c, 53d) would contradict the *Phaedrus*' critique of writing, which excludes such topics from publication. These explanations are compatible if we accept that Platonic physics relies on Platonic metaphysics more robustly than Aristotle's does, and that part of Platonic metaphysics is beyond the scope of the *Timaeus*.

of which is to bring about the best purpose. The second part (46c7–68d7) turns to the auxiliary causes as the material – recalcitrant in its pre-cosmic state – out of which the divine demiurge creates the world. The co-operation between reason and material causes shapes the narrative in the third part of the monologue after 68e1.[21]

The auxiliary causes (τὰ συναίτια, 46c7), "make things cold or hot, compact or disperse them and produce all sorts of similar effects" (46d2–3). The causes identified here as auxiliary are productive causes: τὸ αἴτιον is τὸ ποιοῦν, or τὸ ἀπεργαζόμενον (46d3), that is, an active, productive power – δύναμις τοῦ ποιεῖν, in Plato's terminology.[22] Plato also explains what things (τὰ ὄντα, 46d5) act as such causes and adds that this type of causality manifests itself in the realm of bodies, bodies ensouled in the physical world. Because bodies are therefore the object of the δυνάμεις and are influenced by them, the causes must be material causes. In his later works, Plato translates body and soul into different forms of motion; indeed, Timaeus, unsurprisingly, turns to the consideration of motions in the present passage. He refers to bodies moved by other bodies and necessitating other bodies to acquire motion, although he does not distinguish here the characteristics of the motion of bodies: they can be moved only by external forces and are deprived of the capacity to move themselves. This contrasts with the soul, which has the ability to move itself (46e1–2). Platonic physics treats bodies as powers to move and be moved by one another, and, as such, is an ontology pertaining to a specific realm rather than a general ontology concerned with all beings.[23]

I call the focus on the powers of bodies and their inherent causality prevalent in the second part of the *Timaeus* a "focus on physiology à la specific ontology of bodies". This significantly qualifies the scope of the physiological focus in the Timaean account of pleasure[24] by adding a secondary focus in Timaeus'

---

[21] The *Philebus* follows a similar structure: after an extended examination of pleasure (31b–55b), followed by a less detailed discussion of arts and sciences as domains of knowledge (55c–59d), Socrates explores the contribution of these essential elements to the optimal mixture required for the good life (59e–64b).

[22] See 64b6, τοῦ ποιήσαντος τὴν δύναμιν.

[23] The *dunamis*-ontology of bodies as formulated in the *Timaeus* specifies the criterion of "a power to act or be acted upon" (*Soph.* 247d8-e4) for the specific realm of bodies. A dunamis-ontology of all beings as general ontology, including bodies, souls and forms has been argued for by Mouroutsou, *Die Metapher der Mischung*, chapter 2, with discussion of ontology in the context. The specific ontology of bodies also accords with the ontological analysis of body and soul as different motions in *Laws X* (see Mouroutsou, "Die Frage nach der schlechten Seele in dem zehnten Buch von *Nomoi*"). On motion in later dialogues, see Skemp, *The Theory of Motion in Plato's Later Dialogues*). On the notion of ontology involved in the *Timaeus*, consider Mouroutsou, "Plato in Search of a Language Without Particulars", and "Sarah Broadie, Nature and Divinity in Plato's *Timaeus*, Cambridge 2012".

[24] The understanding of the "physiological perspective" by Sedley, "The Timaeus as Vehicle for Platonic Doctrine", embraces physics, cosmogony, and cosmology in the entire

investigation of Platonic physics. More significantly, a "focus on physiology as a specific ontology of bodies" underscores the essential blend of physiology with the Platonic ontology of beings as powers to act or be acted on applied to the realm of bodies.

Timaeus introduces the topics of pleasure and pain as follows:

> The most important point that remains concerning the affections common to the whole body [that is, those that have the power to affect any part of the body via the sense of touch], pertains to the explanation of the pleasant and the painful [affections] *in* what we have described [the tactile affections] and *in* all that registers sensations through the bodily parts [the localized pleasures and pains, related to specific sense organs: eyes, ears, tongue and nose], sensations which are simultaneously accompanied by pains and pleasures in those parts. (64a2–6)

Lines 61c3–68d7 explain the perceptible properties of the four primary bodies of fire, air, water, and earth, and of their compounds. Lines 64a2–65b3 account for the manner in which the power of these bodies to cause pleasure and pain asserts itself, is transmitted, and becomes manifest in human beings. It arises either from tactile perceptions received through any part of our flesh, or any other perceptions originating from the four senses, and localized in the respective sense organs. Whereas the four pairs of hot and cold, hard and soft, heavy and light, and smooth and rough are exclusively tactile qualities, all perceptible objects may be pleasant or painful; all objects of touch, sight, hearing, taste, and smell can cause pleasure or pain. Timaeus analyses the pleasant and painful qualities of the compounds and their resulting affections, before turning to localized perceptions. The special, mediating character of pleasure and pain is highlighted by Timaeus' choice to address and analyze these topics in the midst of his considerations on the tactile, as well as all other localized perceptions: pleasure and pain offer a wider range of perceptions than the objects usually identified as affecting the five senses and, moreover, they encompass them all: tactile impressions, various families of tastes, smells, and sounds, and multiple forms of light and color.[25]

---

dialogue. To my knowledge, the distinction between the physiological and dialectical accounts — in particular, the dialectical component as reconstructed against the background of the *Philebus* — has not been explicitly foregrounded, although the physiological and psychological aspects have been acknowledged as complementary: psychic affections are given either a physiological description or a psychological explanation – the latter couched in phenomenal and intentional language. See Russell, *Plato on Pleasure and the Good Life*, 229–238, and Wolfsdorf "Timaeus' Explanation of Sense–Perceptual Pleasure"; they both agree that the psychological description plays but a small part in the *Timaeus* and that the distinction between physiology and psychology is not clear.

[25] Contrary to *Th.* 156b, pleasure and pain are not subsumed under sense-perception in the *Timaeus*: that all perceptible objects can cause pleasure or pain does not necessarily imply that pleasure and pain are sense-perceptions. The possibility that they are analyzed

To conduct this reading exercise of the *Timaeus* passage successfully, it is necessary to consider the scope of pleasure and pain and what expectations might consequently be raised in the current investigation. While the pleasure considered here encompasses the potential of all five senses, its origin remains firmly rooted in perceptible content. As such, it is a pleasure arising from immediate sense-perception (i.e., from sensory engagement). Therefore, the pleasures of recollection or anticipation of that same perceptible content, and intellectual pleasures whose source is not a present, perceptible element, are beyond the scope of this investigation (e.g., the pleasure of doing math, or the pleasure taken in the assumption that one is contemplating a painting by Da Vinci). All aesthetic pleasures, however, are not necessarily excluded: one may derive pleasure from hearing a pleasant note in a symphony or from admiring a pleasant painting. It is therefore possible to investigate the physical conditions for the emergence of those pleasures – our focal concern – and to leave aside their intellectual element or aesthetic-making factor.

While the present analysis focuses on pleasures originating from perceptible content, it is emphatically not interested in differentiating between lower- or higher-complexity bodily pleasures, nor indeed in drawing any distinction at all, be it between types of pleasures of perception, or between pleasures of perception and other forms of pleasure such as intellectual pleasures, for instance. Dividing the notion of pleasure into different kinds, and ascribing value to them, are tasks of dialectic that are not included in the present analysis. The focus here is solely on pleasures arising from perceptible content, in accordance with the physiological perspective introduced above.[26]

While an imaginative reader could suggest that a general inquiry into pleasure centered on the pleasures of perception might be applicable to all kinds of pleasure, there is no textual evidence to support this approach. On the contrary, the specificity of the physiological account of pleasure is reinforced, because it is not introduced as a general account of pleasure and pain, couched in terms of τὸ αἴτιον τῆς ἡδονῆς καὶ τῆς λύπης. Instead, the inquiry seeks to identify what makes perceptible bodies and bodily compounds pleasant or painful to beings equipped with sense-perception (τὸ τῶν ἡδέων καὶ τῶν

together with sense-perceptions because they may accompany them is not acknowledged by Frede, *Philebus*, 34. That said, the text itself is not entirely clear.

[26] I disagree with David Wolfsdorf (*Pleasure in Ancient Greek Philosophy*, 53), who claims that the *Timaeus* passage suggests a distinction between sense-perceptual and non-sense-perceptual bodily pleasures. Indeed, this passage contains no hint of a dialectic of pleasure as metaphysics (with a focus on division) to distinguish pleasures. While it is tempting to consider fine nuances, there is little to suggest that pleasures such as thirst, hunger, and sex are not sense-perceptual – given that Plato does not even mention these pleasures. Discussions of Platonic pleasure may be enriched by careful consideration of scope and methodology, as well as of what might reasonably be expected, before arriving at interpretive conclusions, which might then be clearly indicated as such.

ἀλγεινῶν αἴτιον); indeed, perceptible bodies have the power (δύναμις τοῦ ποιεῖν) to elicit pleasure and pain in beings that can be so affected.[27]

The *Philebus* investigates, and accounts for, those things that make a good human life. Pleasure and intelligence are assessed as potential efficient causes, but pleasure is assigned the lesser role of material cause: it is a component of a good life, but it is not the factor from which the goodness originates. This investigation of pleasure and causality is not the same as that conducted in the *Timaeus*. Although the *Philebus* relies on the distinction between what causes pleasure (τὸ ἡδύ) and the pleasure itself derived from the pleasant objects (ἡδονή), its primary concern is not the identification of what causes pleasure.

And yet, the question of why pleasant things cause pleasure is raised, and even embedded in the causal framework of the *Philebus*. First, Socrates seeks to identify where in the four ontological kinds (unlimited, limit, mixture, and cause) pleasure and pain are located, and what sort of affection causes them to arise whenever they arise (διὰ τί πάθος γίγνεσθον ὁπόταν γίγνεσθον, 31b3–4). He identifies one type of pleasure as the result of the restoration of a disturbed natural equilibrium (ἐν τούτοις τοῖς πάθεσιν, 32b7). A second type of pleasure – the anticipatory pleasure, mixed with pain – is experienced through these physical, past and present, affections. Indeed, all of the pleasures analyzed in the dialogue – apart from those affecting the soul in itself, such as anger and love – pertain to physical affections (κατὰ τὸ τούτων τῶν παθημάτων, 32b9–c1; τούτων τῶν παθημάτων, 36c3). Socrates also addresses the anticipation of pleasures and pains: only significant physical changes, able to affect both body and soul, and therefore perception, are pleasant or painful, as discussed earlier (33d). Most of the small or moderate physical changes remain imperceptible (42d–43c). Socrates shows no interest in a subtle analysis of the physical conditions for pleasure beyond laying the foundations for the discussion of the third kind of false pleasure, namely, the absence of pain: although it is a neutral state, it is mistaken for pleasure (42c5–44d6).

The *Timaeus* posits that perceived affections of the body provide a necessary condition for pleasant and painful affects. Therefore, Timaeus first explains how perceived affections emerge, unlike those that remain unperceived (αἰσθητόν / ἀναίσθητον πάθημα, 64a6–7): the latter are not transmitted further in the body or do not reach the soul (64a6–c7). Timaeus then explains, in more detail than in the *Philebus*, the process of perception, with its accompanying pleasures and pains, in the context of the physical παθήματα, whose subject is the body. The physiological mechanics as a specific ontology of bodies complements the analysis of sense-perception as "soul and the body being jointly affected and moved by one and the same affection" (*Philebus* 34a), in

[27] Our focus is τὸ αἰσθητικόν πάθημα (61d), a perceptible property/quality/affection, rather than a property existing independently in the bodies.

contrast to the absence of sensation (ἀναισθησία), which leaves the soul unaffected by the body's disturbances (*Philebus* 33e).

When even a minor disturbance affects that which is easily moved by nature, it spreads all around, with some parts causing affections to others in the same way they were affected, until they reach the soul and report the power of the producer [μέχριπερ ἂν ἐπὶ τὸ φρόνιμον ἐλθόντα ἐξαγγείλῃ τοῦ ποιήσαντος τὴν δύναμιν]. (*Ti.* 64b3–6)

Effective transmission is guaranteed by the most mobile elemental bodies of fire and air, whereas earth-compounds (as in bone and hair) are the most difficult to move and do not easily transfer motion. Although Timaeus does not reveal the contents of the transmission, what is registered in the soul must be the perceived quality, produced by the object and experienced by the receiving agent; for example, we might consider redness, high pitch, or hardness but also, as Timaeus later explains, the pleasure or pain potentially arising from those sensations.[28]

After analyzing sense-perception as a necessary condition for pleasure arising from perceptible content, Timaeus turns to pleasure and pain and introduces the central notion of natural state:

This, then, is what we should understand about pleasure and pain: a violent affection that happens suddenly and disturbs the natural state is painful, while the affection that equally suddenly restores the natural state is pleasant. (*Ti.* 64c7–d3)

Later, in his explanation of decay and of natural death, Timaeus reasserts the connections of the essential natural state with pleasure, and of the unnatural state with pain: "All that is against the natural state (παρὰ φύσιν) is painful, while all that occurs according to nature (τὸ δ' ᾗ πέφυκεν γιγνόμενον) is pleasant." (81e1–2) – here, he refers to any physical change *related to* the natural or unnatural state being perceived. This repetition of what had been explained at 64c7–d3 confirms that the notions of the natural state of the body and of the bodily organs, and of the restoration and deterioration of this state, are central to the Timaean account of pleasure, as they were in the *Philebus*. The physical mechanism of sense-perception plays a crucial role only insofar as sense-perception is a necessary condition for pleasure and pain to arise from perceptible content. As such, Timaeus proposes a more nuanced range of physical presuppositions of pleasure and pain than that of the *Philebus*, by considering the oppositions between mild and violent affections, or between gradual and sudden ones. His interest lies in listing the necessary conditions for pleasure and pain to arise from perceptible content.

---

[28] See 60a8–b2 where two powers or capacities (δυνάμεις) are attributed to honey: the ability to relax (διαχυτικόν) the taste passages of the mouth, and, as a result (ταύτῃ τῇ δυνάμει, 60b1–2), the power to produce sweetness (γλυκύτητα παρεχόμενον). The perceiving soul registers the honey's sweetness, but not the underlying cause producing that sweetness. See Johansen, *Plato's Natural Philosophy*, 170–171.

Once extreme cases – such as sudden bursts of intense light or uncomfortably loud sounds – are set aside, Timaeus considers the phenomenon of perceptual experiences that are neither pleasurable nor painful, such as the full and vivid acts of seeing and hearing (64d3–e4). His analysis implicitly suggests that perception alone is a necessary but insufficient condition for eliciting pleasure and pain. He concludes by revisiting the experiences of pleasure and pain, with particular focus on the combination of pleasant restoration with neutral deterioration of the natural state, as well as its opposite – painful deterioration with neutral restoration:

> Bodies consisting of larger parts, on the other hand [in contrast to the extremely fine and mobile particles composing the visual ray], hardly give way to what acts upon them. They pass on the motions they receive to the entire body, and so they do get pleasures and pains – pains when they are alienated from their natural condition and pleasures when they are once again restored to it [ἀλλοτριούμενα μὲν λύπας, καθιστάμενα δὲ εἰς τὸ αὐτὸ πάλιν ἡδονάς]. All those bodies which experience only gradual departures from their normal state or gradual depletions [ἀποχωρήσεις ἑαυτῶν καὶ κενώσεις] but whose replenishments are sudden and on a large scale are perceptive of their replenishment but not of their depletion [κενώσεως μὲν ἀναίσθητα, πληρώσεως δὲ αἰσθητικά], and hence they provide the mortal part of the soul with very substantial pleasures but no pains. This is clear in the case of fragrances. But all those bodies whose alienations are sudden [ἀπαλλοτριοῦται ἀθρόα] while their restorations to the former states of themselves are gradual and difficult [κατὰ σμικρὰ δὲ μόγις τε εἰς ταὐτὸν πάλιν ἑαυτοῖς], produce results that are entirely contrary to those mentioned just before. Again, this is manifest in the case of burns or cuts in the body. (*Ti.* 64e4–65b3)

This is a significant passage for the purpose of the present study. It does not offer an alternative definition of pleasure because Timaeus is not interested in Platonic dialectic nor in its search for definitions – such as that exemplified in the *Sophist* and in the *Statesman*. The essential distinction between mixed and unmixed pleasures, drawn in the *Philebus* as the culmination of Plato's dialectic of pleasure, and anticipated by *Republic* 584b–c, is unsurprisingly also absent from the *Timaeus*. In the *Republic*, Socrates uses the example of pure pleasures of smell (which "suddenly become very intense without being preceded by pain, and when they cease, they leave no pain behind") to support the argument that pleasure is not always a cessation of a preceding pain, but he mentions pure pain too. This corresponds to the Timaean references to the pleasures of smell and to the pain of bodily burns and cuts at 65a–b respectively. Although neither is qualified as pure in this passage, they are so nonetheless.

Thus, all Platonic texts considered here posit a notion of pleasure as the perceived restoration of a natural state; this includes the pleasures that are labeled, sometimes explicitly, as pure pleasures (or pains) caused by perceptible content. This model of restoration also underlies the conception of pleasures that do not equate to the cessation of pain.[29]

An additional insight may be drawn from the Timaean context. Although it includes no dialectic as interpersonal dialogue with hedonists, Timaeus is indeed engaging in an implicit dialectic with other interlocutors. He seems to be concerned with understanding why it is that not all perceptions are either pleasant or painful, although he does not asks this question explicitly, nor was it raised by Socrates in the *Philebus*. The problem can be reconstructed as threefold in nature: Why aren't all perceptions pleasant? Why aren't all perceptions painful? And why are some perceptions neither pleasant nor painful? Plato resorts to the character of Timaeus to engage in dialogue with the Presocratic physiologists on the topic of pleasure and pain, and to offer his own, more plausible, explanation.

Although evidence of the understanding and conception of pleasure and pain by Plato's predecessors is scarce, Theophrastus mentions Anaxagoras and Empedocles in his *De Sensibus*, where he reports on and criticizes the explanations of pleasure and pain provided by the pre-Aristotelian theories of perception. They follow a symmetrical structure: Empedocles explains perception as being caused by likes, and although he understands pleasure and pain as perceptions or its concomitants, he explains pleasure as being caused by likes and pain as being caused by opposites. Theophrastus points that this obvious inconsistency may be solved either by denying that all perception is caused by likes, or by rejecting the conception of pain as a perception (*DS* 16). Claiming that all perceptions are pleasant would also solve the inconsistency, but this is counter-intuitive and inconsistent. As for Anaxagoras, he explains perceptions as being caused by opposites, and Theophrastus ascribes to him the equally unreceivable thesis according to which all perceptions are painful (*DS* 17).[30]

---

[29] Although I disagree with Frede in several instances in Mouroutsou, *Die Metapher der Mischung*, and Mouroutsou, "Placing Pure Pleasures Beyond the Chain of Hunger", I concur fully with her assertion that the remedial model of restoration is the only valid framework for the understanding of pleasure in Plato. For a study of the fine dialectic between Plato and Aristotle on the model of restoration, and on the characteristics of mixed and unmixed pleasures drawn from Plato in Aristotle's theory of pleasure, see Corcilius, *Streben und Bewegen: Aristoteles' Theorie der animalischen Ortsbewegung*, 65–102, and "Aristotle's Definition of non-Rational Pleasure". See also Corcilius/Gregoric, "Aristotle's Model of Animal Motion".

[30] Aspasius' Commentary on Aristotle's *Nicomachean Ethics* 1154b6–15 supports the Anaxagorean thesis that all perceptions are painful, and Aristotle has Anaxagoras in mind when referring to "physiologists" *ad loc.* See Warren, "Anaxagoras on Perception, Pleasure, and Pain" for the reconstruction of dialectic in reports on pleasure and pain in Anaxagoras, and Baltussen, *Theophrastus against the Presocratics and Plato* on the Peripatetic dialectic in *DS*.

Other comparable, existing theories of pleasure and pain failed to explain adequately why some perceptions are pleasant, and others, painful. Against their background, Plato not only addresses the fact that not all perceptions are either pleasant or painful but also explains why this is the case by providing the necessary conditions for the emergence of pleasure. Even when presented in a monologue rather than in a dialogue, as in the *Timaeus*, Plato's conception of philosophy remains fundamentally dialectical.

This analysis has examined two aspects of the dialectic on pleasure in the *Philebus* and has also established physiology as the relevant framework for the analysis in the *Timaeus*. Beyond contributing to the elucidation of each dialogue, this investigation has shown that Platonic philosophy may only be adequately understood if the underlying questions, and, where appropriate, their interlocutors, are identified in each context.

Bibliography

Aubry, Gwenaëlle, "Nicomachean Ethics VII.14, (1154a22-b34): The Pain of the Living and Divine Pleasure", in: Carlo Natali (ed.), *Aristotle*: Nicomachean Ethics, *Book* VII. *Symposium Aristotelicum*, Oxford 2009, 237–263.

Baltussen, Han, *Theophrastus against the Presocratics and Plato: Peripatetic Dialectic in the* De sensibus, Boston 2000.

Broadie, Sarah, *Nature and Divinity in Plato's* Timaeus, Cambridge 2012.

Corcilius, Klaus, *Streben und Bewegen*: *Aristoteles' Theorie der animalischen Ortsbewegung*, Berlin / New York 2008.

–, "Aristotle's Definition of non-Rational Pleasure and Pain and Desire", in: Jon Miller (ed.), *Aristotle's* Nicomachean Ethics. *A Critical Guide*, Cambridge 2011, 117–190.

Corcilius, Klaus/Gregoric, Pavel, "Aristotle's Model of Animal Motion", *Phronesis* 58 (2013), 52–97.

Cornford, Francis, *Plato's Cosmology. The* Timaeus *of Plato*, Indianapolis, Ind. / Cambridge 1937.

Dorion, Louis-André, "Aristotle's Definition of Elenchus in the Light of Plato's *Sophist*". in: Jakob Fink (ed.), *The Development of Dialectic from Plato to Aristotle*, Cambridge 2012, 251–269.

Frede, Dorothea, "Rumpelstiltskin's Pleasures: True and False Pleasures in Plato's *Philebus*", *Phronesis* 30 (1985), 151–180.

–, *Philebus*, Indianapolis, Ind. / Cambridge 1993.

–, "Mixed Feelings in Aristotle's *Rhetoric*", in: Amélie Rorty (ed.), *Essays on Aristotle's* Rhetoric, Berkeley / Los Angeles / London 1996, 258–285.

–, "The Hedonist's Conversion: The Role of Socrates in the *Philebus*", in: Christopher Gill / Mary Margaret McCabe (eds.), *Form and Argument in Late Plato*, Oxford 1996, 213–248.

–, *Platon*. Philebos, Göttingen 1997.

–, "Pleasure and Pain in Aristotle's *Ethics*", in: Richard Kraut (ed.), *The Blackwell Guide to Aristotle's* Nicomachean Ethics, Oxford 2006, 255–275.

–, "*Nicomachean Ethics* VII.11–12: Pleasure", in: Carlo Natali (ed.), *Aristotle*: Nicomachean Ethics, *Book* VII. *Symposium Aristotelicum*, Oxford 2009, 183–207.

Johansen, Thomas, *Plato's Natural Philosophy. A Study of the* Timaeus–Critias. Cambridge 2004.

Mouroutsou, Georgia, *Die Metapher der Mischung in den platonischen Dialogen Sophistes und Philebos*, Sankt Augustin 2010.

–, "Die Frage nach der schlechten Seele in dem zehnten Buch von Nomoi: Versuch einer Entmythologisierung", in: Dietmar von Koch / Irmgard Männlein-Robert / Niels Weidtmann (eds.), *Platon über das Göttliche*, Tübingen 2010, 139–173.

–, "Sarah Broadie, Nature and Divinity in Plato's *Timaeus*, Cambridge 2012", *Ancient Philosophy* 34 (2014), 207–216.

–, "Placing Pure Pleasures Beyond the Chain of Hunger: Plato's Quest for Paradigmatic Pleasures in the *Philebus*", in: Jakub Jirsa / Filip Karfík / Štěpán Špinka (eds.), *Plato's* Philebus, Prague 2016, 130–156.

–, "Plato in Search of a Language Without Particulars: *Timaeus* 49a6–50a4 in a New Light", *Philosophical Inquiry* 43 (2019), 240–276.

–, "Plato's *Phaedo*: Are the Philosophers' Pleasures of Learning Pure?", *Classical Quarterly* 69 (2019), 566–584.

–, "Choosing a Life and Rejecting a Thoughtless Life in *Philebus* 20–22", *Ancient Philosophy* 41 (2021), 393–412.

Robinson, Richard, *Plato's Earlier Dialectic*, Oxford ²1953.

Russell, Daniel, *Plato on Pleasure and the Good Life*, Oxford 2005.

Sedley, David, "The *Timaeus* as Vehicle for Platonic Doctrine", *Oxford Studies in Ancient Philosophy* 56 (2019), 45–71.

Skemp, Joseph, *The Theory of Motion in Plato's Later Dialogues*, Amsterdam 1967.

Szaif, Jan, "Philosophical Paideia in Plato's *Sophist*", in: *Philosophical Proceedings of the Symposium Platonicum* XIII. *Plato's* Sophist, forthcoming.

Szlezák, Thomas, "Gespräche unter Ungleichen", in: Gottfried Gabriel/Christiane Schildknecht (eds.), *Literarische Formen der Philosophie*, Stuttgart 1990, 40–61.

–, *Das Bild des Dialektikers in Platons späten Dialogen*, Berlin / New York 2004.

Warren, James, "Anaxagoras on Perception, Pleasure, and Pain", *Oxford Studies in Ancient Philosophy* 33 (2008), 19–54.

–, *The Pleasures of Reason in Plato, Aristotle, and the Hellenistic Hedonists*, Cambridge 2014.

–, "Truth, Beauty, Purity, and Pleasure: *Philebus* 50e–53c", in: Panos Dimas / Russell Jones / Gabriel Lear (eds.), *Plato's* Philebus: *A Philosophical Discussion*, Oxford 2019, 184–201.

Wolfsdorf, David, *Pleasure in Ancient Greek Philosophy*, Cambridge 2013.

–, "Timaeus' Explanation of Sense-Perceptual Pleasure", *Journal of Hellenic Studies* 134 (2014), 120–135.

Zeyl, Donald, *Plato.* Timaeus. Indianapolis, Ind. 2000.

Plato's Account of Desire in the *Philebus*

Samuel Meister

In a comparatively short section of the *Philebus* (34c10–35d7), Plato has Socrates develop an account of desire (ἐπιθυμία). The section follows on a discussion of memory and perception and is part of a first step towards Socrates' analysis of (the life of) pleasure. But despite recent progress,[1] the Phileban account of desire remains understudied. In particular, although Socrates clearly aims at a definition of desire, no clear view of the correct formulation of this definition has emerged, let alone any consensus surrounding it. This is unfortunate because it leaves the key philosophical question about desire in the *Philebus* elusive: whether desire is purely psychological, as scholars have maintained traditionally, or whether it is (essentially) psychophysical, as Carpenter and Harte have argued more recently.[2] Furthermore, without a good grasp of the definition of desire, we cannot assess the often-noted similarities or dissimilarities between the Phileban account and Aristotle's treatment of affections of the soul in *De anima*. In this paper, then, I will first reconstruct Socrates' argument concerning desire in the *Philebus* and then glean his definition of desire from it. I will argue that this definition does not contain any reference to body, and that therefore, desire is not (essentially) psychophysical. But I will also argue that the body plays a crucial role in Socrates' discussion of desire as the cause of the occurrence of desires. I will close with a verdict on the comparison with Aristotle: although certain parts of the Phileban account of desire can be appropriated by Aristotle, especially the thought that its "principle" (ἀρχή) belongs to the soul, the primary outcome is disagreement. For Aristotle not only rejects the Phileban view that the soul is the subject of

---

[1] See especially Amber Carpenter, "What Is Peculiar to Plato's and Aristotle's Psychologies? What Is Common to Them Both?", in: Verity Harte, Mary Margaret McCabe, Robert William Sharples, and Anne Sheppard (Hg.), *Aristotle and the Stoics Reading Plato* (*BICS* Supplements, Vol. 107), London 2010, 21–44; Verity Harte, "Desire, Memory, and the Authority of Soul: Plato, *Philebus* 35c–d", *Oxford Studies in Ancient Philosophy* 46 (2014), 33–72; Satoshi Ogihara, "The Independence of the Soul from the Body", in: Panos Dimas, Russell Jones, and Gabriel Richardson Lear (Hg.), *Plato's* Philebus: *A Philosophical Discussion*, Oxford 2019, 106–123.

[2] Carpenter, "Plato's and Aristotle's Psychologies"; Harte, "Desire".

desire, but he also thinks that desire is (essentially) psychophysical, contrary to the account offered by Socrates.

1. The Desire Argument

Socrates initiates the discussion of desire (ἐπιθυμία) with two questions (34d2–3): what is desire (τί ποτ' ἔστι) and where does it come about (ποῦ γίγνεται)? The answer to the second question seems to be that desire is "of the soul" (35d1–3), although what exactly this implies is less clear. The first question calls for a definition of desire,[3] but Socrates does not give an obvious canonical statement of this definition. In the next section, I will argue that the definition turns out to be that desire is a rush (ὁρμή) of the soul of an animal towards an affection opposite to its present affection. But before we can get to this stage, we have to understand the argument from which the definition emerges, including the conclusion that desire is "of the soul". Following Harte, I call this argument the "Desire Argument".

As a preliminary to the desire argument, Socrates and Protarchus agree that thirst and hunger are desires.[4] The argument then proceeds with the example of thirst but generalizes to (bodily) desire more broadly.[5] The drift of the argument is the following.[6] Thirst is a desire for fullness (πλήρωσις) with drink (34d–35a2) which arises when one is empty (34e11).[7] Thus, someone who is thirsty

[3] This seems clear from the τί ἐστι question as well as Socrates' question, "having looked to what self-same thing (πρὸς τί ποτε ἄρα ταὐτὸν βλέψαντες) could we call these things that differ so much by one name?" (34e3–4).

[4] Previously, hunger and thirst were classified as pains (31e3–32a5). Some desires, then, seem to be pains. One might conclude that desire is (a kind of) pain (Dorothea Frede, *Plato* Philebus, Indianapolis / Cambridge 1993, 35 fn. 2; Dorothea Frede, *Platon* Philebos, Göttingen 1997, 235; Harte, "Desire", 37). But it has also been argued that pain merely "triggers" desire (Ogihara, "Independence", 118–119), or even that hunger and thirst are not desires but "provoke" desires (Maurizio Migliori, *L'uomo fra piacere, intelligenza e Bene*, Milano 1993, 203). I will remain neutral on whether (all) desires are pains.

[5] As we will see below, Harte argues that the desire argument should apply to non-bodily desires, too, but I am sceptical of this extension.

[6] Cf. Matthew Evans, "Plato and the Meaning of Pain", *Apeiron* 40 (2007), 86–7; Harte, "Desire", 41; Ogihara, "Independence", 119.

[7] I tend to agree with Sylvain Delcomminette, *Le* Philèbe *de Platon : Introduction à l'agathologie platonicienne*, Leiden / Boston 2006, 331–333 that states, not processes, are involved. In particular, *pace* Frede (*Philebus*, 36; *Philebos*, 44–45), the thirsty person does presumably not become empty but *is* empty (κενοῦται, 34a11), and similarly κένωσις at 35b4 refers to emptiness, not the process of becoming (cf. Mehmet Erginel, "Plato on Pleasures Mixed with Pains: An Asymmetrical Account", *Oxford Studies in Ancient Philosophy* 56 (2019), 109–110). If this is right, it is natural to take πλήρωσις, too, to refer to the state of fullness rather than the process of filling or being filled. Even πληροῦσθαι at 35a4, then, can

"desires the opposites of what he is undergoing (πάσχει); for being empty, he covets being full (πληροῦσθαι)" (35a3–4). Hence, "some part of the one who is thirsty" (τι τῶν τοῦ διψῶντος) must "touch upon" (ἐφάπτεσθαι) fullness (35b6–7). But the body cannot touch upon fullness because it is empty (35b9). Instead, it must be the soul that touches upon fullness, and it does so by memory (35b11–c1). Therefore, we conclude first that desire is not "of body" (35c6–7), and secondly that desire is "of soul" (35d1–3).

There are three crucial junctures in the argument. The first is the inference from the claim that the thirsty person *desires* fullness to the claim that a part of his must *touch upon* fullness. How are we to understand the language of "touching upon" fullness? Here, the remark that a thirsty person could touch upon fullness by perception or memory (35a6–7) helps.[8] Touching upon fullness, then, need not be, or even imply, being or becoming physically full but can be a relation that we might call "mental", such as remembering. But to desire fullness is not the same as to touch upon fullness. For example, to remember being full with coffee is a distinct (type of) mental episode from desiring to be full with coffee. Socrates' point, then, is presumably that making some sort of contact, which may be mental, with fullness is a necessary condition on the desire for fullness.

The second juncture is the claim that, since the body is empty, it cannot touch upon fullness. The relevant passage reads as follows (S=Socrates, P=Protarchus):[9]

S: But surely, we say that someone who desires desires something.
P: What else?
S: Hence, he does not desire that which he is undergoing. For he is thirsty, and this is emptiness; but he desires fullness.
P: Yes.
S: But somehow some part of the one who is thirsty (τι τῶν τοῦ διψῶντος) is surely touching upon fullness.
P: Necessarily.
S: But it is impossible that it is the body; for it is presumably empty.

---

be taken to refer to the state of being full. Note also the explicit mention of "states" (ἑξέων) at 41c6 where Socrates says that the soul desires "the states opposite of the body". For the opposite view that desire is for processes, see, e.g., J. M. Lee, "*Philebus*, 35a6–10", *Phronesis* 11 (1966), 32. One could also hold a mixed view on which κενοῦται refers to being empty and πληροῦσθαι to becoming full (Ogihara, "Independence", 119 fn. 37 and fn. 38). My argument will not depend on this decision.

[8] According to the usual interpretation of this passage, Socrates asks whether a person who is empty "for the first time" (τὸ πρῶτον, 35a6) could touch upon fullness either by perception or memory (35a6–8). Delcomminette, *Agathologie*, 333–334 defends an alternative reading on which the passage concerns a *state* that is empty "to begin with" (τὸ πρῶτον). For the relevance of the passage for the desire argument, see Lee, "*Philebus* 35a6–10".

[9] All translations are mine.

P: Yes.
S: It remains, then, that the soul touches upon fullness, and it is clear that it does so by memory; for by what else could it touch upon it?
P: Surely by nothing else. (35b1–c2)

The crucial preliminary question is what it would be for the body to touch upon fullness. In light of the remark that a thirsty person could touch upon fullness by perception or memory (35a6–7), one might conclude that the body would have to touch upon fullness by perception or by memory. But this move threatens to trivialize Socrates' argument. For now, it seems to rest on the stipulation that touching upon must be a sort of *mental* contact. It follows that the body cannot touch upon fullness – but this is simply because it cannot touch upon *anything* (and regardless of whether it is empty or not). In response, Harte and Ogihara claim that, while the body does not have memory, it has perception.[10] This seems to save the argument if we add that for the body to perceive fullness entails its being full. For now, it is indeed because the body is empty that it cannot perceive fullness. But I am sceptical of this move. For just before discussing desire, Socrates argued that perception involves *both* body and soul (34a3–5), and surely this rules out that the body *by itself* could perceive anything. Hence, it remains the case that, if touching upon fullness requires memory or perception, the body (by itself) can in principle not touch upon anything.

Instead, it seems better to allow for an additional way in which something can touch upon fullness, namely, by actually being full. This yields an easy sense in which the body can by itself touch upon fullness – by being full. Moreover, the reading makes good sense of the argument: if the body is empty, it cannot touch upon fullness because this would require actually being full. Ogihara rejects this interpretation on the grounds that, at 35a6–7, only touching upon fullness by perception and memory were mentioned.[11] But this claim is made about a person *who is empty* (for the first time) (ὁ τὸ πρῶτον κενούμενος).[12] Hence, it is not surprising that actually being full is not mentioned as a third way of touching upon fullness; for if the person touched upon fullness, he would no longer be empty, contrary to the assumption of the scenario. I do not see any reason, therefore, to take the claim that touching upon fullness can occur by perception or memory to state an exhaustive list of ways in which something can touch upon fullness.

[10] Harte, "Desire", 50; Ogihara, "Independence", 121. Harte (ibid., fn. 25) hedges this claim and says merely that "perceptual awareness" provides the context in which one might attribute touching upon to the body. But Socrates seems to be simply speaking of perception, not of a weaker state such as perceptual awareness that, unlike perception, does not require the soul.

[11] Ogihara, "Independence", 119–120.

[12] Or alternatively, a state that is empty to begin with (Delcomminette, *Agathologie*, 333).

Harte brings up two further objections. First, she says that the interpretation explains only why body cannot touch upon fullness, not why soul *can.*[13] Second, she argues that the reading cannot explain cases of purely psychological desires.[14] Let me begin with the second objection. Building on Delcomminette's case for pains and pleasures involving purely psychological harmonies (see, e.g., 32c3–5.34c6–8),[15] Harte argues that in the later discussion of true pleasures such as the pleasures of learning (51e7–52a2), there are purely psychological *desires*, such as the desire for learning. Such desires cannot be explained by a reading on which the desire argument rests on a claim about the way in which the *body* can touch upon fullness. But it is quite clear that the desire argument concerns bodily desires.[16] Hence, it is not a strike against an interpretation *of the desire argument* that it cannot account for non-bodily desires.

As for the first objection, it is true that, in the cited passage, Socrates does not close with the claim that the body cannot touch upon fullness. Rather, he goes on to conclude that the soul touches upon fullness, and that it does so by means of memory (35b11–c1). But I do not see why we should think that a single argument has to explain both why body cannot touch upon fullness *and* why soul can. Instead, there may be separate arguments for these conclusions. The argument for the second conclusion seems to be simple: if some part of the thirsty person must touch upon fullness, and it cannot be the body (by the earlier argument), then the only part left that could touch upon fullness is the soul. Moreover, Socrates adds an explanation of how the soul can touch upon fullness, namely, by memory.

The argument for the latter claim is again an argument from exclusion: the soul must touch upon fullness by memory, "for by what else could it touch upon it?" (35c1). Surprisingly, no argument for the exclusion of perception is given. But perhaps the thought is that perception is of a *current* state, but the soul has to touch upon a state that is opposed to the current state.[17] For instance, the soul of an empty person may perceive the state of emptiness but not the state of fullness. Hence, the only way of touching upon the opposite of the current state is to remember it from a previous occasion.

This remark on memory leads to the third key juncture in the desire argument, namely, the inference from claims about whether body and soul touch upon fullness to claims about whether thirst (and desire more generally)

---

13 Harte, "Desire", 47.

14 Harte, "Desire", 47–49.

15 See Delcomminette, *Agathologie*, 300.

16 See Evans, "Meaning of Pain", 86; Ogihara, "Independence", 118.

17 One might support this suggestion with 35a8–9 where undergoing fullness "in the present time" seems correlated by parallelism with perception, whereas undergoing it previously is correlated with memory.

is *of* body and soul. Socrates claims that it follows from the desire argument that desire is not of body (35a6–7) and that desire is of soul (35d1–3). On an increasingly popular reading, memory is central for establishing both that desire is not of body and that desire is of soul.[18] For it is only by memory that one can touch upon an affection opposed to the affection that one is currently undergoing, and because only the soul, but not the body, has memory, it turns out that desire is of soul and not of body. In my view, this interpretation unduly inflates the role of memory in the desire argument.

Here is how Socrates concludes that desire is not of body but of soul:

S: Do we understand, then, what results for us from these arguments?
P: Which is what?
S: This argument of ours denies that desire is of the body.
P: How?
S: Because it declares that the impetus (ἐπιχείρησις) of every animal is always opposite to the affections (παθήματα) of that [i.e., the body].[19]
P: Very much so.
S: And indeed, the rush leading to what is opposite to the affections shows presumably that there is memory of the opposites of the affections.
P: Indeed!
S: Thus, the argument, having demonstrated memory leading to the desired states (τὰ ἐπιθυμούμενα), has shown that every rush and desire and principle of every animal is of soul.
P: Most correct.
S: Thus, the argument does not support in any way that our body undergoes thirst or hunger or any such thing.
P: Most true. (35c3–d7)

To begin with, the reason stated why desire is not of body (35c9–10) does not mention memory. Rather, the reason is that "the impetus (ἐπιχείρησις) of every animal is always opposite to the affections (παθήματα) of that [i.e., the body]". This is quite clearly a generalization of the earlier point about thirst. One desires the opposite of the affection that one is currently undergoing. But any desire requires that one touch upon the opposite affection. Since the body can touch upon an affection only by actually undergoing it, it cannot be the body that is the subject of touching upon the opposite affection, and thus it cannot be the body that is the subject of desire. Thus, Socrates can infer from the claim that the body cannot touch upon an opposite affection to the conclusion that

---

[18] See Delcomminette, *Agathologie*, 344; Carpenter, "Plato's and Aristotle's Psychologies", 36; Harte, "Desire", 49–59.

[19] There are two issues of translation here. First, I agree with Frede (*Philebus*, 37; *Philebos*, 45) that the subject of the sentence is ὁ λόγος ("the argument") from 35b6, not, as Justin Cyril Bertrand Gosling, *Plato* Philebus. Oxford 1975, 30 and Harte "Desire", 38 fn. 9) think, "desire". For in this section of text, the subject of verbs of saying, showing, etc. (such as μηνύω in our sentence) is generally ὁ λόγος (see 35c6–7; 35d16–18; 35d5–7). Second, I agree with Ogihara, "Independence", 118 against, e.g., Frede's translation, that ἐκείνου at 35c9 refers to body at 35c6, not to "animal" after the ἐκείνου.

desire is not "of body" at least in this sense: body is not the subject of desire. This argument works with the same resources as, on my interpretation, the argument that the (empty) body cannot touch upon fullness – and it does not include any premises that mention memory.

But does Socrates rely on a premise involving memory to conclude that desire is of soul? He first says that the rush (ὁρμή) to the opposite affections shows that there is memory of the opposite affections (35c12–14). This fits my earlier suggestion that the soul must touch on the opposite affection by memory, rather than perception, because it has to touch on a state that is opposed to the current state. But this is not yet to say that the reason why desire is of the soul is that touching upon the opposite affection must occur by memory. This seems to change with the ensuing claim that "the argument, *having demonstrated (ἀποδείξας) memory leading to the desired states*, has shown that every rush and desire and principle of every animal is of soul" (35d1–3). For here Socrates may appear to say that the conclusion that desire is of soul follows from the claim that memory leads to the desired states.

However, we need not take the passage this way. Socrates' point may simply be that the argument for the claim that the soul touches upon the desired states implies that desire is of the soul. For if the soul is the subject of touching upon the desired states, and being able to touch upon the desired states was the crucial necessary condition on desire that body failed to meet, it is natural to suppose that the soul is also the subject of desire – and that desire is in this sense "of the soul". The weight is on the claim that the soul touches upon the desired states, not that it does so by memory. Of course, memory matters because, as shown by the earlier argument from exclusion (35c1), the soul can touch upon the desired states only by memory. But, as argued above, it is not because the soul must touch upon the desired states by memory that it is the subject of touching upon these states. Rather, once it had been shown that the soul touches upon the desired states, there was the further question of how it does so and the further answer that it must do so by memory. Similarly, the soul is the subject of desire because it touches upon the desired states, not because it does so by memory.

The key ingredients to the interpretation of the desire argument that I have defended are the following. First, Socrates argues that the body cannot touch upon a desired state on the grounds that a desired state is an affection opposed to the current affection of the body and that the body can touch upon an affection only by actually undergoing it. Second, by an argument from exclusion, he argues that the soul can touch on a desired state and he adds, by another argument from exclusion, that it does so by memory. Third, he concludes that the subject of touching upon a desired state is also the subject of desire, and that, therefore, desire is of the soul but not of the body.

If we return to Socrates' initial questions about desire, namely, what it is and where it comes about, we have made progress concerning the second question.

According to the desire argument, desire is of the soul rather than the body in the sense that it is the soul, not the body, which is the subject of desire. This negative conclusion comes out nicely at the very end of the passage cited above: the desire argument rules out "that our body in any way undergoes thirst or hunger or any such thing" (35d5–6). The positive conclusion emerges clearly from a later summary passage where Socrates says that "the soul was what desires the states opposite of the body" (41c5–6). If the soul is the subject of desire, presumably the answer to the second question is that desire comes about in the soul. Carpenter objects to this reading on the grounds that desires are (essentially) psychophysical.[20] It is time, then, to turn to Socrates' answer to the first, definitional question concerning desire. I will argue next that the definition does not refer to body and that therefore desires are not essentially psychophysical.

2. Defining Desire

The main debate about the definition of desire in the *Philebus* concerns the role of the body. Two sorts of views have been adopted. On the one hand, Gosling holds that no (type of) "physical state" is either necessary or sufficient for thirst (or any other desire). For desire is to be understood solely in terms of perception, memory, and a "move towards replenishment", all of which are operations of the soul.[21] Similarly, Delcomminette concludes that desire is "purely psychological" ("purement psychique").[22] On the other hand, Carpenter argues that desire is a "split phenomenon" that involves both body and soul.[23] She emphasizes that desire is for a state which *the body* is not in, which suggests that desire is not a purely psychological phenomenon but rather a psychophysical one. Similarly, Harte argues that "this bodily process is itself a component in his analysis of thirst",[24] which implies not only that (bodily) desire is not purely psychological, but that it is essentially psychophysical: its definition refers to both soul and body.

In this section, I will argue that, as far as the definition of desire is concerned, scholars in the first camp are right. The definition of desire does not contain any reference to the body. But this is not to say that the second camp is simply wrong. On the contrary, I think that Carpenter and Harte are right to insist

[20] Carpenter, "Plato's and Aristotle's Psychologies", 37.

[21] Gosling, *Philebus*, 105.

[22] Delcomminette, *Agathologie*, 344. In his commentary (Sylvain Delcomminette, *Platon* Philèbe, Paris 2022, 372), he says that "desire is exclusively a matter of the soul" ("le désir relève exclusivement de l'âme").

[23] Carpenter, "Plato's and Aristotle's Psychologies", 36–37.

[24] Harte, "Desire", 43.

against their opponents that the body plays a crucial role in Socrates' discussion of desire. However, this role is not a definitional one. Instead, I will argue that the body plays a central role in the explanation of why a desire occurs, namely, as the immediate efficient cause of desire (by providing pleasure or pain). Thus, I advocate a revised version of the first view: desire is not essentially bodily, but the body is still crucial for Socrates' understanding of desire as the cause of occurrences of desires.

Our first task is to reconstruct Socrates' definition of desire. Scholars rarely do so explicitly, with the notable exception of Frede, who offers the following definition:[25]

(Desire$_F$) Desire is a pain (of the soul) with respect to fulfilment ('Schmerz-mit-Bezug-auf-Erfüllung').

Frede explicates this definition further to characterize desire as "a kind of pain of the soul that is at the same time directed towards an object that can compensate the lack and that the soul knows from memory".[26] Her definition relies heavily on the examples of hunger and thirst. For (Desire$_F$) generalizes the characterization of hunger and thirst as directed towards fullness to all desires. Moreover, Frede assumes that desires are pains, based on the previous characterization of hunger and thirst as pains (31d6–e5). Finally, Frede belongs to the first camp above, since (Desire$_F$) does not contain any reference to body.

On the last point, I agree with Frede (see below). But, as formulated, (Desire$_F$) does not correspond to what we find in the desire argument. For, even if desires are pains, they are not called "pains" in the argument. Further, the terms that correspond to "fulfilment" (πλήρωσις, πληροῦσθαι) are used only in the context of the example of thirst and Socrates himself does not generalize them to characterize all desires. Furthermore, (Desire$_F$) does not contain any reference to terms which seem crucial for Socrates' understanding of desire, such as the notion of an "opposite" (τοὐνάντιον) or a "rush" (ὁρμή) (see, e.g., 35c12). It is unlikely, then, that (Desire$_F$) is the definition of desire Socrates has in mind. Let us return to the text of the desire argument with a finer comb.

The most promising passages where we might find Socrates' definition of desire are, first, his general remarks about desire at the end of the desire argument (35c3–d7), and second, his later summary remark about desire (41b11–c8). In the first passage, quoted above, Socrates makes two crucial claims about desire:

(1) "[T]he impetus (ἐπιχείρησις) of every animal is always opposite to the affections (παθήματα) of that [i.e., the body]." (35c9–10)

---

[25] Frede, *Philebos*, 236.

[26] Frede, *Philebos*, 236. In German, Frede calls desire "eine Art von Schmerz der Seele ..., der zugleich auf ein Objekt ausgerichtet ist, das den Mangel zu kompensieren vermag und welches die Seele aus der Erinnerung kennt". See also Frede, *Philebus*, 35 fn. 2.

(2) "[T]he rush (ὁρμή) leading to what is opposite to the affections shows presumably that there is memory of the opposites of the affections." (35c12–14)

In my view, both "impetus" and "rush" refer to desire, and hence desire is characterized in terms of them. For, at 35b3–4, Socrates said that the thirsty person desires what he does not undergo, that is, the opposite of his present state. And in (1) and (2), the impetus and rush are said to lead to opposite affections. Moreover, (1) is meant to argue that desire is not of body (35c6–7), and this argument is effective only if it can show that desire is for an affection opposite to that of the body. Thus, the claim about "impetus" in (2) must be a claim about desire, since the impetus is described as being towards that which is opposite to the body's affection. Finally, at 35d2–3, Socrates concludes that "every rush and desire and the principle of every animal" is of soul, which suggests that desire is understood as a kind of rush. Since I cannot detect any difference between the meanings of ἐπιχείρησις ("impetus") and ὁρμή ("rush"), I suggest that the first ingredient of the definition is simply that desire is a rush.

The second key ingredient is the notion of an opposite affection. For desire is not just any rush but a rush for "the opposite of the affections" (τοὐναντίον ... ἢ τὰ παθήματα) (35c12–13) that the desiring person presently has. In the case of the thirsty person, for example, desire is a rush for fullness with drink. To this we can add that desire is a rush of the soul (35d2). Thus, we get the following definition of desire:

(Desire) Desire is a rush of the soul towards an affection opposite to the present affections of the desiring person.

Unlike (Desire_F), this definition does not refer to pain, nor to fulfilment. Moreover, contrary to Frede's fuller formulation and despite the mention of memory in (2), there is no reference to memory in the definition. As I argued above, Socrates claims that, given that desire is a rush for an affection, the argument has also shown that there is memory of the opposite affections. Memory thus explains how there can be a desire of the soul for the opposite affection, but it is not mentioned in the definition of desire itself.

In (Desire), then, there is clearly a reference to the soul. But what about the body? There are two ways in which one might argue that there should be a reference to body in the definition of desire. The first is to argue that desire is not a rush for an affection other than the current affection of the desiring *person*, as (Desire) has it, but rather for an affection other than the current affection of *the body* of the desiring person. The second way is to argue that, even if (Desire) is accepted as formulated, there is a tacit reference to the body, because the desiring person is not just a soul but also involves a body.

The first objection can take its starting point from (1) where Socrates says that "the impetus of every animal is always opposite to the affections *of that* (ἐκείνου)" (35c9–10), where "that" (ἐκείνου) seems to refer to the body (see also 41c5–6).[27] One may argue, then, that it is part of the definition of desire that it is a rush towards an affection opposite to a current affection of the body – and hence that there is a direct reference to body in the definition. The issue is complicated by the fact that, in the desire argument, Socrates speaks both of the affection of the person and of the affection of the body. For instance, at 35a3–4, he claims that "the empty person" (ὁ κενούμενος) "desires the opposites of what he is undergoing". But at 35b9, he says that the body is empty. In the case of the thirsty person, then, it is true both that the person is empty, and that the person's body is empty. Thus, it is true both that the desire is for a state opposite to the current state of the person and that it is for a state opposite to the current state of the body. Which of these claims should enter the definition of desire?

On balance, I think that it should be the former. For in (1), as well as at 35b9, Socrates is concerned with a sub-argument that concerns specifically the body, namely, that the body cannot touch upon the opposite affection and that, therefore, desire is not of body. In the context of this sub-argument, it is important that the state of the body is discussed; for it is specifically because *the body* is empty that it cannot touch upon fullness, and similarly for other desires. By contrast, outside of this specific argumentative context, Socrates ascribes the affections to the person, as at 35a3–4. Hence, if we look for a definition of desire, we should rely on these more general characterizations of desire where it is a rush towards the affections opposite to the current affections of the person.

At this point, one may be driven to the second objection. If Socrates is happy to speak of both the person and the person's body as empty, perhaps he is not overly worried about this distinction. And perhaps he is not overly worried about the distinction because, in speaking of an affection of the person, there is anyway an implicit reference to the body. Hence, even if there is no explicit reference to the body in (Desire), there is an implicit one, and therefore desire is an essentially psychophysical phenomenon after all.

Implicit reference is not enough, however. For desire to be essentially bodily, its definition must contain an explicit reference to the body. Moreover, it is far from clear that the reference to the thirsty person implies a reference to the body of the person. After all, if the soul is the subject of thirst, in speaking of the thirsty person, Socrates must be, strictly speaking, referring to the thirsty soul. In that case, the empty person is also, strictly speaking, the empty soul, and hence the reference to an affection opposite to the current affection of the person is a reference to an affection opposite to the current affection of the soul.

There is also a more general reason for resisting the inclusion of a reference to body. For Socrates' discussion of desire contrasts strikingly with his preceding treatment of perception. For there, he argued that perception is a

[27] For the reference of the ἐκείνου, see fn. 19 above.

"motion" (κίνησις) that comes about for soul and body "in one affection" (ἐν ἑνὶ πάθει) and "commonly" (κοινῇ) (34a3–5). However exactly we understand this difficult claim, it surely contrasts with the account of desire as of the soul but not of body. In *some* sense, body must be more intimately involved in perception than in desire. But if desire is *essentially* bodily, I cannot see *any* sense in which body could be even more intimately involved in perception than in desire.

My argument may seem to have led me straight back into the first camp of interpreters who regard desire a purely psychological phenomenon. This is true if we have *definitional* purity in mind: there is no reference to body in the definition of desire, and hence desire is not an essentially psychophysical phenomenon. Nonetheless, Carpenter and Harte are clearly right to emphasize against their opponents that the body plays a crucial role for Socrates' discussion of desire. But I think we can take this on board without sacrificing the definitional purity of desire. Here, the second passage mentioned earlier is finally relevant, namely, Socrates' later summary of the conclusion of the desire argument:

S: Yet truly, we said, if we remember, a little while ago that when the so-called desires are in us, then the body is therefore seized by the affections (τοῖς παθήμασι) apart from (δίχα) and without the soul.
P: We remember, and these things have been said before.
S: Hence, the soul was what desires the states (ἑξέων) opposite to the body, and the body was what provides (παρεχόμενον) the pain or, because of an affection (πάθος), some pleasure?[28]
P: It surely was. (41b11–c8)

In this passage, Socrates pulls apart the contributions of body and soul. First, he says that the body "is seized by the affections (τοῖς παθήμασι) apart from (δίχα) and without the soul" (41c2–3). As becomes clear a few lines later, these affections are pleasures or pains, or at least they directly cause pleasures or pains.[29] These affections, and hence the pleasures and pains, are purely bodily, as Socrates emphasizes with both the "apart from" (δίχα) and the "without the soul". In a second step, the body provides the animal with the pain or pleasure, and on the basis of this provision, the desire of the soul arises – namely, a desire for the opposite affection from the one with which the animal has been

[28] Frede (*Philebus*, 46; *Philebos*, 53) takes παρεχόμενον to mean that the body "undergoes" pleasure or pain, not that it provides them. But in the discussion of desire in the *Philebus*, "undergoing" is expressed with πάσχειν and its cognates, including in these very lines (41c2; 41c7).

[29] There is a question of how we take "because of an affection" (διὰ πάθος) at 41c6–7. The expression applies to the provision of pleasure only, but it might suggest a general picture on which the body is affected and only then, on the basis of this affection, provides pleasure or pain. In that case, the affections of the body are distinct from the pleasures or pains that the body provides.

provided by the body.[30] Thus, the body plays an indispensable role in the causal history of a desire. Contra Gosling,[31] then, it is a necessary condition for the occurrence of the desire. Indeed, it is more than a mere necessary condition: the body, with its provision of pleasure or pain, is the immediate efficient cause of the desire.[32] But this is compatible with my claim that the body is not part of the *essence* of desire. For, while caused by the body, desire is defined only with reference to soul.

One might object that this interpretation does not go far enough. For instance, according to Harte,[33] the provision of pain or pleasure by the body is part of the "analysis" of desire. In an innocuous sense of "analysis", this seems certainly right: the provision of pain or pleasure are part of the overall description of (the occurrence of) desire. But if "analysis" is meant to imply that the provision of pleasure and pain by the body is part of the essence of desire, matters look different. For Socrates emphasizes that *the soul* is "what desires" (τὸ ἐπιθυμοῦν) (41c5), not the body, and he ascribes a different role to the body that does not directly concern desire. It seems hardly natural, then, to take Socrates to include the provision of pleasure and pain by the body in the definition of desire.

I have argued that, in the *Philebus*, Socrates defines desire as a rush of the soul towards an affection opposite to the present affection of the desiring person. This definition does not contain any explicit reference to the body. Hence, desire is not an *essentially* psychophysical phenomenon. Rather, desire is essentially only a psychological phenomenon. Still, desire is a purely psychological phenomenon only in this definitional sense. For the provision of pleasure and pain by the body is not only a necessary condition for the occurrence of a desire but its immediate efficient cause. Thus, although desire is not defined with reference to body, the body plays an indispensable role in explaining the occurrence of desire.

---

[30] The mention of the provision of pleasure is odd. After all, the soul presumably desires the opposite of painful states, not of pleasurable ones. Perhaps Socrates wants to allow that there are desires for states opposite of pleasurable states (Reginald Hackforth, *Plato's Examination of Pleasure*. Cambridge 1945, 78), but more likely, 'pain or pleasure' is a generic expression for the sort of entity that the body provides, without implying that both the provision of pains and pleasures may cause desires.

[31] Gosling, *Philebus*, 105.

[32] I am in sympathy, then, with the view that pain is a trigger of desire (Delcomminette, *Agathologie*, 331 fn.54; Ogihara, "Independence", 119). But this need not rule out that desire is also itself a (type of) pain.

[33] Harte, "Desire", 44.

3. The *Philebus* and Aristotle

Socrates' claim that the soul is the subject of desire seems to be precisely the sort of view that Aristotle attacks in the so-called "Rylean passage" in *De anima* I 4. For there, Aristotle argues that the whole human being "with the soul" is the subject of affections, such as anger, not the soul itself (408b11–15). If this claim extends to desire,[34] Aristotle disagrees with the Phileban claim that the soul is the subject of desire. Still, it has been argued by both Carpenter and Harte that the Phileban account of desire is closer to Aristotle's own than it might seem. Their case for this rapprochement rests, first, on the supposed psychophysical nature of desire in the *Philebus*, and second, on the role of soul as a principle (ἀρχή) of the animal. In my view, while a modest case for the second similarity can be made, the first point of comparison does not bring out a similarity with Aristotle but rather a contrast.

Let us begin with the claim that the soul is a principle of the animal. At the end of the desire argument, Socrates says:

> Thus, the argument, having demonstrated memory leading to the desired states, has shown that every rush (ὁρμή) and desire (ἐπιθυμία) and principle (ἀρχή) of every animal is of soul. (35d1–3).

Above, I have made a lot of the connection between rush and desire, but I did not comment on the claim that every "principle (ἀρχή) of every animal is of soul" (35d3). We have not been prepared for this additional move in the desire argument. How are we to understand it?

According to Carpenter and Harte, the conclusion that every principle is of the soul is the culmination of the desire argument.[35] They translate ἀρχή as "rule" or "authority" and take Socrates to argue that, in some sense, the soul rules over desire and the animal. Carpenter holds that the soul has "responsibility" for psychophysical phenomena and "determines the event as the specific event it is".[36] Harte takes this view a step further and argues that the soul has an "authority" over the animal that the body lacks. Indeed, she claims that, for Socrates, "desire is a psychological mechanism responsible for directing and regulating the body in line with the prescriptions of harmonious nature".[37] Moreover, Harte seems to think that this claim marks a similarity with Aristotle.[38]

---

[34] Aristotle does not explicitly mention desire. But he speaks of a large range of affections, e.g., at 408b1–3, of suffering, rejoicing, being brave, fearing, being angry, perceiving, and thinking (διανοεῖσθαι). This suggests that his point is a general one that applies also to desire.

[35] Carpenter, "Plato's and Aristotle's Psychologies", 36–7; Harte, "Desire", 63–70.

[36] Carpenter, "Plato's and Aristotle's Psychologies", 37.

[37] Harte, "Desire", 68.

[38] Harte, "Desire", 34.

But I prefer a less inflationary reading of the ἀρχή-claim that is closer to the text of the desire argument: if a desire is a rush towards some affection, it is also a principle of motion of the animal. This principle of motion belongs to the soul just as the rush, and hence the desire, belong to the soul. Of course, this picture is suggestive of further views of the soul as a principle of the animal or its body. But by itself, the ἀρχή-claim does not imply any such consequences. Rather, Socrates says simply that the soul is the subject of the rush and desire, and thus also of the principle of motion of the animal. Similarly, *pace* Carpenter, although I agree that the soul determines what (an occurrence of) a desire is since desires are essentially psychological, I see little evidence for the view that Socrates says this *in the the ἀρχή-claim*. For the latter is not a claim about the essence of desires but about the subject of rushes and principles of motion. It is not even clear that Socrates makes a general claim about every principle of motion of the animal, the "every" (σύμπασαν, 35d2) notwithstanding. Since Socrates speaks of "every rush and desire and principle", the quantifier is plausibly restricted to the principles at hand, namely, desires. He concludes merely that, in cases of desire, the principle of motion belongs to the soul.

Where does this leave us with respect to the comparison with Aristotle? First, the central disagreement with the Phileban account persists. For the soul, rather than the whole animal, remains the subject of the desire. But second, there is a path forward for Aristotle (see, e.g., *DA* I 4, 408b5–18). He agrees that the principle of motion belongs to the soul (at least in the sense that the motion is "by" (ὑπό) the soul, 408b7) but can divorce this claim from the view that the soul is the subject of affection such as desire. For although the animal is the subject of desire, it is so in virtue of the soul, and hence the principle of motion belongs to the soul, just as Socrates claims in the *Philebus*. But the latter point of agreement is less noteworthy than the point of disagreement. For the focus of the desire argument was on the subject of desire, and here, Aristotle parts ways with the *Philebus*.

What about the first path towards a rapprochement, based on the psychophysical nature of desire? Carpenter draws on Aristotle's discussion of "the affections of the soul" (τὰ πάθη τῆς ψυχῆς, 403a3) in *De anima* I.1, 403a3–b26.[39] Since Aristotle includes "desiring" (ἐπιθυμεῖν) among the affections to be covered (403a7), this passage promises insights into the relation of his account of desire to the Phileban account.[40] Although the details of the passage

[39] Carpenter, "Plato's and Aristotle's Psychologies", 43–44.

[40] However, Aristotle does not define desire in *DA* I.1. He may come closest to a definition in *DA* III.7, 431a8–14, where the capacity for striving or desire (τὸ ὀρεκτικόν) seems characterized in terms of the capacity for avoidance and the capacity for perception (431a14–15) (see Klaus Corcilius, "Aristotle's Definition of Non-Rational Pleasure and Pain and Desire", in: Jon Miller (Hg.), *Aristotle's* Nicomachean Ethics: *A Critical Guide*, Cambridge 2011, 117–143). For our purposes, it is sufficient to note that this characterization

are controversial, it is clear that, for Aristotle, affections of the soul ought to be defined with reference to both body and soul.[41] In this minimal sense, then, desire is essentially psychophysical for Aristotle.[42] But we have seen above that, according to the *Philebus*, desire is not defined with reference to body but only with reference to soul. Hence, unlike for Aristotle, desire is not essentially psychophysical even in the minimal sense. There is, then, no rapprochement here, but only divergence.

One could retort that the *Philebus* does seem to characterize other affections as essentially psychophysical. In particular, as mentioned earlier, perception is said to be common to body and soul (34a3–5), and this claim is at least open to an interpretation that takes perception to be essentially psychophysical. In that case, Aristotle would agree with the Phileban account of perception but disagree with its account of desire. This outcome may appear surprising: should there not be agreement or disagreement across the board? But the fault, if it is a fault, seems to lie with Plato rather than Aristotle. For Aristotle, in *DA* I 1, aims at a general hylomorphic account of the affections of the soul (except for intellect) that applies equally to desire, perception, and "emotions", such as anger (403a5–10.403a16–19). In the *Philebus*, by contrast, it is unclear whether there is a unified account of affections. For desire is not essentially psychophysical, whereas perception may turn out to be. Hence, we have hit on yet another difference between Aristotle and the *Philebus*. Whereas Aristotle clearly strives for a unified account of the affections of the soul, Socrates in the *Philebus* does not, or at any rate it remains far from obvious that he ends up, or wishes to end up, with a unified account.

---

does not undermine the basic point from *DA* I 1 that desiring (ἐπιθυμεῖν) is defined with reference to body and soul.

[41] At 403a25, for instance, Aristotle says that "affections are enmattered forms" (λόγοι ἔνυλοι) or, depending on the manuscript reading, "forms in matter" (λόγοι ἐν ὕλῃ), and he criticizes both definitions that mention only the matter and definitions that mention only the form (403a29–b9). I take these claims to imply that affections are defined with reference to body and soul because, regardless of how we spell out the details, reference to the matter of the affection will involve reference to the body of the affected organism, and reference to the form of the affection will involve reference to the soul of the affected organism.

[42] According to Charles ("Aristotle's Psychological Theory", *Proceedings of the Boston Area Colloquium of Ancient Philosophy* 24 (2008), 1–29; *The Undivided Self: Aristotle and the 'Mind-Body Problem'*, Oxford 2021), affections of the soul are essentially psychophysical in a strong sense since the physical and psychological entities mentioned in the definition of the affection are interdefined. By contrast, Caston ("Commentary on Charles", *Proceedings of the Boston Area Colloquium of Ancient Philosophy* 24 (2008), 30–49) argues for a weaker view according to which the physical and psychological entities mentioned in the definition of the affection are not themselves defined with reference to each other. The weaker view is sufficient for our minimal sense in which desire is essentially psychophysical.

4. Conclusion

I have argued that in the *Philebus*, desire is defined as a rush of the soul towards an affection opposite to the current affection of the desiring person. I have also argued that this definition does not contain any explicit reference to body, and that therefore, unlike for Aristotle, desire is not essentially psychophysical. But this is not to say that the body is not important for the Phileban account of desire. For the body, by providing pleasure or pain, is the efficient cause of the occurrence of desires, even though desire is defined only with reference to the soul.

Bibliography

Carpenter, Amber, "What Is Peculiar to Plato's and Aristotle's Psychologies? What Is Common to Them Both?", in: Verity Harte / Mary Margaret McCabe / Robert William Sharples / Anne Sheppard (eds.), *Aristotle and the Stoics Reading Plato* (*BICS* Supplements, Vol. 107), London 2010, 21–44.

Caston, Victor, "Commentary on Charles", *Proceedings of the Boston Area Colloquium of Ancient Philosophy* 24 (2008), 30–49.

Charles, David, "Aristotle's Psychological Theory", *Proceedings of the Boston Area Colloquium of Ancient Philosophy* 24 (2008), 1–29.

–, *The Undivided Self: Aristotle and the 'Mind-Body Problem'*, Oxford 2021.

Corcilius, Klaus, "Aristotle's Definition of Non-Rational Pleasure and Pain and Desire", in: Jon Miller (ed.), *Aristotle's* Nicomachean Ethics: *A Critical Guide*, Cambridge 2011, 117–143.

Delcomminette, Sylvain, *Le* Philèbe *de Platon : Introduction à l'agathologie platonicienne*, Leiden / Boston 2006.

–, *Platon*, Philèbe, Paris 2022.

Erginel, Mehmet, "Plato on Pleasures Mixed with Pains: An Asymmetrical Account", *Oxford Studies in Ancient Philosophy* 56 (2019), 73–122.

Evans, Matthew, "Plato and the Meaning of Pain", *Apeiron* 40 (2007), 71–93.

Frede, Dorothea, *Plato* Philebus, Indianapolis / Cambridge 1993.

–, *Platon* Philebos, Göttingen 1997.

Gosling, Justin Cyril Bertrand, *Plato* Philebus. Oxford 1975.

Hackforth, Reginald, *Plato's Examination of Pleasure*. Cambridge 1945.

Harte, Verity, "Desire, Memory, and the Authority of Soul: Plato, *Philebus* 35c–d", *Oxford Studies in Ancient Philosophy* 46 (2014), 33–72.

Lee, J. M., "*Philebus*, 35a6–10", *Phronesis* 11 (1966), 31–34.

Migliori, Maurizio, *L'uomo fra piacere, intelligenza e Bene*, Milano 1993.

Ogihara, Satoshi, "The Independence of the Soul from the Body", in: Panos Dimas / Russell Jones / Gabriel Richardson Lear (eds.), *Plato's* Philebus: *A Philosophical Discussion*, Oxford 2019, 106–123.

Phantasia in Plato's *Sophist*: An Un-Aristotelian Precursor to Aristotle[1]

Fiona Leigh

The term, "*phantasia*" is a Platonic neologism, occurring first in the *Republic* at 382e10 to refer to the way the Gods appear (to mortals or one another). It is used twice in the *Theaetetus* (152c1, 161e8). In its first use there it is an explicit gloss of "it appears" (*phainetai*, 152b12), and evidently serves as a substantive equivalent to that term to indicate, in the context of the dialogue, the way something in the world appears to someone (e.g. the wind appears cold). As such, the term refers to things in the world being certain ways, such that each exhibits a variety of appearances, which can and often do vary with the condition under which the thing is experienced.[2] Since these features, appearances, are features belonging to things, they can be contrasted in an ontology with the cognitive states that arise for people who experience them. This contrast can be marked by describing the appearances of things as objective, and the cognitions arising from our experiences of things and their appearances as subjective. The second occurrence of *phantasia* in the *Theaetetus* at 161e8 comes after the elaboration of the Protagorean view that our perception of something correlates with its appearance, and the double assimilation of appearance with reality, and of perception with knowledge. There, Socrates speaks of the futility of investigating and trying to cross examine the appearances (*phantasias*) and beliefs of one another's experience,

---

[1] I am grateful to the audiences of the Platon-Tage conference held in Tübingen (2024), the Yale ancient Philosophy workshop (2024), the ancient philosophy seminar at the National Autonomous University of Mexico (UNAM) (2024), and the Institute of Classical Studies' Ancient Philosophy Seminar (2025) for their comments, critical insights and suggestions. In particular, I would like to thank Joachim Aufderheide, Elena Cagnoli, Klaus Corcilius, Dan Ferguson, Samuel Meister, Melissa Lane, M.M. McCabe, Edgar González Varela, Ricardo Salles, Jan Szaif, and especially Tim Clarke, Verity Harte, and Leonardo Serafini for their written comments on earlier drafts.

[2] The objective appearance of some object, then, does not depend on the object in fact being experienced. For further discussion see McDowell, "Values", 137–139; Harte, "*Republic* X", 82. The *locus classicus* for the view that Plato's Protagoras is suggesting that the properties of things are objectively real (rather than subjective projections or ideas), see Burnyeat, "Idealism", *passim*.

if they are assumed to be correct, as Protagoras maintains. Here, too, Socrates must have in mind his earlier use of the term, viz., to indicate the way things appear to someone – hence Rowe's translation "...examining the things that appear to and are believed by one another, ...". The second occurrence of *phantasia* in the *Theaetetus*, therefore, is objective in the sense outlined above.

Phantasia is most prevalent in the corpus in the *Sophist* – it occurs four times. Strikingly, as we will see, the term is used unambiguously in our dialogue to mark out a specific kind of cognition, a state or activity (or, perhaps, a capacity) of the soul. This subjective use of the term in a semi-technical way to denote a specific kind of thinking is of interest in its own right, psychological taxonomy being rare in Plato's works. But more importantly, I will argue, for Plato's purposes in the dialogue, *phantasia* in both its objective and subjective uses plays a central role in demonstrating the doxastic vulnerability of the inexperienced and ignorant youths receptive of the sophist's art. *Phantasia* (in its subjective use) in the *Sophist* will turn out to be the cognitive capacity not simply of having certain appearances, but rather of having perceptually caused beliefs. The content of this kind of belief is the precise way that what is perceived appears to the subject of this type of cognition, *phantasia*. Images, generated in mimetic production, are epistemically unreliable, since they represent singular appearances of things, and things are not always as they appear. The sophist's spoken images in words are especially epistemically unreliable, and liable to be false, with the exception of the image of himself as prodigiously wise, which is straightforwardly false. In its original use in ancient philosophy of mind, then, *phantasia* in Plato's *Sophist* according to its subjective use (to refer to a perceptually caused belief) turns out to be a remarkably un-Aristotelian precursor to the *phantasia* we find in Aristotle's psychology, particularly *De anima* III 3.

The chapter proceeds as follows: §1 reviews the passages in *Sph.* containing *phantasia*, the central questions arising from them, and suggests problems with previous interpretations. §2 presents the relevant texts in *Sph.* concerning the sophist's art of mimetic production of semblances, rehearses the main issues, and discusses problems with some influential interpretations. A new reading of the sophist's productive art is argued for in §3; before the case for *phantasia* as productive of beliefs that are particularly epistemically unreliable in the case of the sophist's students is sketched in §4. I conclude with some remarks on Aristotle's apparent criticism of Plato on *phantasia* (in its subjective use), in his departure from his teacher on this kind of psychological state or condition.

1. *Phantasia* in the *Sophist*: The Texts

Towards the end of the dialogue, the Stranger introduces the word, "*phantasia*" (260c9). Having shown that *not being* or *what is not* is a genuine component of reality, the Stranger outlines his next task as showing that not being is associated with belief and speech. For if it is not so associated, then everything will be true, and there will be no false speech or belief. Alternatively, if the Stranger can show that falsehood is possible – in believing or saying what is not – then deception will likewise be possible, and everything will be full of images and likenesses, and appearance (*phantasia*).[3] In the immediately following lines, the Stranger elaborates further on his reasoning, and uses the newly introduced term, *phantasia*, a second time (260E). He reminds Theaetetus that the (fictional) sophist earlier denied the possibility of falsehood – false speech and belief – since these are about what is not, which in turn presupposed the impossibility of not being having a share in being. But now, at this stage in the dialogue, they have demonstrated that not being does in fact share in being. Nonetheless, the sophist can still insist that while some kinds or forms do share in not being, others do not, and maintain that speech and belief are among those that do not. And if so, he can also contend, as he did earlier (239C–241D), that the alleged practice of sophistry, image-production, semblance-production, and falsehood are not possible, since belief and speech do not share in not being. The Stranger concludes that they must first investigate exactly what speech and belief and *phantasia* are, so that once they are illuminated, the pair might see their association with not being.

Now, earlier in the dialogue (as we will see in §2 below), images (*eidōla*) are mimetic depictions or representations of things, produced in plastic or visual art or in spoken words, and likenesses (*eikona*) constitute one kind of mimetic representation, i.e. that which preserves in the artefact crucial properties of the subject, the thing it represents, such as proportion or colour. The other kind of mimetic depiction delineated earlier in the dialogue is a semblance (*phantasma*, 236C). This has suggested to some scholars that in its first use at 260c8–9, *phantasia*, as the third item in the list "images, likenesses and *phantasia*", is intended to refer to *phantasmata* ("semblances"), and they have translated accordingly.[4] But this is extremely unlikely, since *phantasia* is

---

[3] (260c1–10) STR: If it [what is not] doesn't mix with them [belief and speech] everything is necessarily true, whereas if it does, then belief (*doxa*) can be false and so can speech (*logos*). For presumably believing and saying things that are not is what falsehood is when it occurs in thought (*dianoiai*) and speech (*logois*). TH: It is. STR: But if there is falsehood, there is deception. TH: Yes. STR: And surely, as soon as there is deception, everything will be full of images (*eidōlōn*) and likenesses (*eikonōn*) and appearance (*phantasias*). TH: Obviously. (Except where noted otherwise, translations of the Greek are my own.)

[4] E.g. Taylor, *The* Sophist, 170; Diès, *Le* Sophiste, 377; and Cordero, *Le* Sophiste, 188, all translate *phantasia* as "illusion", and Rosen as "fantasms" (*Plato's* Sophist, 152) as noted by Notomi (*The Unity of Plato's* Sophist, 252, fn. 90). To this list can be added Duerlinger (*A Translation,* 131), who gives "semblance". Crivelli (*Plato's Account of Falsehood*, 260) argues that the context of the use of *phantasia* at 260c9 indicates that it is intended to suggest a connection with semblance, but translates as "appearance". His treatment of *phantasia* (in

singular, while *eidōla* and *eikona* are plural:[5] if Plato had wanted to use *phantasia* as a synonym for, or to put the reader in mind of, *phantasma*, we would expect the third item in the list to be the plural *phantasiai*, which could then with some plausibility be read as synonymous with, or very similar in meaning to, *phantasmata*.[6] Alternatively, following Cornford's suggestion that *phantasia* should be understood as the substantive equivalent to the verb *phainesthai*, we can understand the first occurrence to claim that "appearances" of things will be everywhere, in the sense that each can appear in a multitude of ways, some of which will be at variance with the way the thing is, thus making falsehood and deception in speech and belief possible. If this is right, *phantasia* at 260C can be taken to refer to the objective appearance that belongs to things, as opposed to a cognitive state.[7] At any rate, it is the association of appearances, as well as belief and speech, with what is not that the Stranger tasks himself and Theaetetus with uncovering.[8]

By contrast, however, a number of readers have understood *phantasia* at 260C to introduce a kind of cognition. The reason for this has been consistency of translation: since one of the later uses, at 264a6, clearly indicates a cognitive state, it has been thought that all occurrences of the word must have this meaning.[9] But this reading should, I think, be resisted, on textual grounds. For, there is no sign at 260C or 260E that the Stranger is referring, by way of

---

all its occurrences in the *Sophist*) is only brief, but his suggestion seems to be that it is the cognitive correlate of semblance, *phantasma* (probably resulting from experiencing the semblance). The interpretation of *phantasia* (from 264Aff.) I will argue for below has some resonances with this suggestion, but is less narrow, in that subjective *phantasia* is the cognitive correlate of perceptual appearances.

[5] 260c8–9: *Stranger*: Καὶ μὴν ἀπάτης οὔσης εἰδώλων τε καὶ εἰκόνων ἤδη καὶ φαντασίας πάντα ἀνάγκη μεστὰ εἶναι.

[6] Notomi also notes the singular *phantasia*, and suggests that therefore the three terms do not constitute a list, but that *kai phantasia* is an explanatory addition, meant to be read in apposition to *eidōlōn* and *eikonōn*. It does not seem obvious to me that kai at c9 is epexegetical, but at any rate for my purposes the important point is that the singular is problematic for reading *phantasia* as synonymous with *phantasma* in these lines. Interestingly, some translators have glossed over the singular in their translations: White (Sophist, 55) and Ambuel (*Image and Paradigm*, 237) give "appearances".

[7] Cornford, *Plato's Theory of Knowledge*, 319, fn. 1. Note however, that Cornford himself does not read *phantasia* at 260C in what I am calling its objective use, but rather as the cognitive state of imagination. In this, Cornford seems influenced by the Protagorean thesis in the *Theaetetus*, in the sense that appearing is assimilated to perception by the senses at *Tht.* 152B–C. As a result Cornford seems to take it that *phantasia* at *Sph.* 260Cff. must also indicate a cognitive state. I take issue with this suggestion below.

[8] Notomi also seems to understand *phantasia* in its use at 260c to refer to objective features of things, as opposed to a kind of cognitive state (Notomi, *The Unity of Plato's* Sophist, 252–253).

[9] E.g. Cornford, *Plato's Theory of Knowledge,* 319–320; Crivelli, *Plato's Account of Falsehood,* 260.

phantasia, to a kind of cognition, or psychological state. Similarly, if a new concept had been introduced to Theaetetus by way of a new use of a word that is itself rare, it seems more likely he would have asked for further details or explanation.[10] But instead, he agrees without hesitation to the suggestion that if there is deception, then everything will be full of images, likenesses and *phantasia*. So to read a subjective use of *phantasia* at 260C or 260E would be both jarring and unmotivated. Moreover, the trio are presented as going together, suggesting – though admittedly not decisively – that they are necessary elements, perhaps jointly necessary, of the sophist's product.[11] And indeed the sophist's product, semblances (*phantasmata*) were earlier described (or defined) as the kind of images that appear (*phainetai*) to be likenesses of the things of which they are images, but are not, in fact (236b4–7). So it is plausibly quite natural to read *phantasia* here as the substantive of *phainesthai*, to remind Theaetetus (or the reader) that things, specifically images, appear certain ways, namely as likenesses, but also, are sometimes mere appearances, images that are other than likenesses.

The third appearance of *phantasia* is at 263D, straight after the Stranger's analysis of false statement (or speech, *logos*) as a statement that says or attributes, to some subject, properties that are in fact other than the subject's properties (and so say, of that subject, what is not). The Stranger then says "What then? Isn't it thereby clear that all these kinds – thought, belief, and *phantasia* – come about in our souls as both false and true?" (263d6-8) Here we have an explicitly subjective use of the term, to indicate a kind of cognition, something in the soul alongside thought and belief. But the grounds for the Stranger's claim, that these can be false, are opaque to Theaetetus, who asks, "how?". To properly grasp how they can be false requires, the Stranger says,

---

[10] Similarly, if Plato had wanted to introduce a term into the dialogue that was new with him and not well attested elsewhere, and then use it in a way that was wholly unfamiliar to his readers, we would expect him to do so more carefully, perhaps by introducing it with some fanfare, but in any case by giving some indication of its intended meaning. For instances of Theaetetus not following and asking for further details, see for instance 233e1-234a2, 237a2, 238d9, 263d9 and compare the use of *phantasia* (which is unambiguously a subjective use) at 263D.

[11] It is suggested at 236Bff. that the sophist's practice is the production of *phantasmata* (confirmed at the end of the dialogue), which are defined as kinds of images that appear (*phainetai*) to be likenesses of the things of which they are images, but are not. Moreover, the thrust of the short stretch of reasoning of 260B–C better fits (what I will call) the objective reading of *phantasia*. The Stranger reasons at 260B–C that if not being doesn't blend with speech and belief everything will be true, while if it does, the sophist will no longer deny the possibility of falsity (saying and believing what is not). But with falsity, the sophist cannot deny the possibility of deception (being brought to believe or speak falsely). And finally, he cannot deny that there are kinds of images that bear likenesses to things but are not those things, as well as images that appear to be likenesses but are not, namely, *phantasmata*.

first grasping what they are and how they differ from one another. In the course of analysing them, the Stranger uses *phantasia* for the fourth time at 264a6. There, having analysed belief as an asserted or denied statement that comes about in silent thought, he proposes that *phantasia* is an affection (of the soul) that arises whenever a belief, an asserted or denied statement, is present for someone not by itself, but through perception. He then sums up at 264a8–b4, saying:

> So since there is true and false statement (or speech, *logos*), of these, thought is the soul's silent dialogue with itself, belief is the completion of thought, 'appearing' (*phainetai*) is that which we say is a mixture of perception and belief, then indeed necessarily, being akin to speech, some of these too are sometimes false.

It is evident that *phainetai* corresponds to, and so is a gloss of, *phantasia* from 264A. Given that the context also makes it plain that, consistent with *phantasia* at 264A, *phainetai* refers to a cognition of some sort, we should understand *phainetai* – literally, "it appears" – as having the sense of the cognitive experience of having something appear to oneself.

Two main questions, then, arise from Plato's deployment of the term, *phantasia*, in the *Sophist*: First, if it is right to read the first two uses of *phantasia* as objective as I have argued, why would Plato use the very same term to indicate a cognitive state, as he evidently does in the second two uses of the term? Why use the same word, one freshly minted with him, as it were, to refer to such radically different things? The second question is how to understand the conception that Plato seems to offer of the cognition of being appeared to, in perception, as a belief – is every case of having an appearance, according to Plato, a belief? If so, isn't he just wrong, since, as Aristotle pointed out in *An.* III 3, seeing is not believing?

A complete response to these questions depends upon the analysis of mimetic image-production and semblance-production provided earlier in the dialogue, as the Stranger's allusion to these crafts at 260C suggests. For, this analysis concerns the objective appearance of things that we experience when we encounter things *via* mimetic images. We will then be in a position to return to 260C, where the Stranger picks up on the earlier analysis of objective appearances *via* mimesis. We will then be in a position to see that he asserts, at 264A–B, a causal connection between these objective appearances and specific cognitive states, which he calls *phantasiai*, by way of a subjective use of that term.

2. Mimetic Production in *Sph.*: Texts and some Influential Interpretations

Mimesis is introduced in the dialogue as a game, liable to trickery and deception (234B), in the context of the seventh attempt to articulate the expertise or craft of sophistry. The imitator produces images of things, through which these things appear a certain way (234C, 235B, cf., 265). The painter, who is able to paint anything, can fool mindless young children that he can make anything at all (234b5–10).[12] The sophist is said by the Stranger to produce word-images (*eidōla legomena*, 234c5–6) that seem true to his hearers. These images, labelled semblances (*phantasmata*), when heard by ignorant and inexperienced youths give rise to beliefs (*doxai*), which, however, they reject in time, once they have gained experience (234c2–e2). For example, the things they previously thought were large (or perhaps important, *mega*), now appear small (or insignificant) (234d6–7). The sophist also produces images for his audience of himself as being prodigiously wise, that is, wise about every topic whatsoever.

As is well known, the Stranger distinguishes two kinds of mimetic production, crafting of a likeness (*eikōn*) and of a semblance (*phantasma*). The expertise of likenesses-production occurs whenever someone contrives to create an artefact that itself replicates and preserves features of the original or model in its material form, such as proportion and colour (235d6–e2). Such an image, produced by focusing on the original or model of which it is an image, faithfully represents its model. Thus, in the case of a beautiful model, the likeness, to which the artist has given the true proportions of the model, appears as it ought, i.e. as an image of the model that correctly presents (or represents) it as beautiful.

The faithfulness of likenesses is brought out by its immediate contrast with the second kind of image, semblances. With the example – familiar to a Greek audience – of a sculptor or painter of monumental artworks, the Stranger points out that if the practitioner of this mimetic expertise were to give the artefact the true proportions of the beautiful things the artefact is to represent, the upper

[12] It is unclear from the text whether the children are deceived into thinking that, because the painter's images are so impressive (at a distance), that a) he is so talented he could accomplish any deed he desired to perform, or b) he is not producing images but the real things themselves, so he is able to manufacture anything he wishes. Although both are conceptually plausible in the case of mindless young children, I prefer a) as capturing a deception that could plausibly be a feature common to all mimetic production, namely, deception about the power (and the knowledge) of the mimetic producer. Against b) it is far less credible to take Plato to think that viewers of statues of gods, for example, are deceived into thinking that the god herself stands before them (a view, however, Crivelli attributes to Plato, as we will see below).

parts of the statue (or painting) would appear (*phainetai*) smaller than they ought and the lower parts would appear larger than they ought. This is because the audience is viewing the former from a distance and the latter up close (235e5–236a2).[13] So if the artist did this with the semblance, i.e. gave it the same proportions as the model, it would not be an image that artistically presents (or represents) its subject, the model, as it ought, because the parts of the statue would appear to be of the wrong size to the audience. Hence, *these* sculptors (and painters) bid goodbye to the truth, producing in their images not the real proportions but those that seem to the audience to be beautiful (236a4–6).

Continuing the contrast, the Stranger says that because the one is like the original, it is correctly called a likeness. The other, however, appears to be like the beautiful original because it is viewed from a non-beautiful or non-ideal position (*ouk ek kalou*), and since it appears like it, though it is not in fact like it, it is correctly called a semblance (*phantasma*). In support of this claim he points out that if, *par impossible*, someone were able sufficiently to view such large things, the semblance would turn out not to be like that which it is said to be like (236b4–7). So, in semblance-production, which the Stranger says constitutes the bulk of mimesis (236c1), the production of the artefact is not constrained by the features of the original. The artefact is, instead, adjusted for the audience where necessary, for the specific conditions under which they experience the artefact, the image.

Commentators have generally taken the kind of image-production the sophist is associated with, semblance-production, to be analysed here by Plato as the generation of an image that, through deception, induces a false belief in the audience. This is, I will maintain, a mistake. To show why, I will first raise some problems for two influential recent interpretations in the literature, those of Paulo Crivelli and Noboru Notomi, before presenting my alternative interpretation in §3 below.

Crivelli reads Plato as understanding mimetic images to deceive by inducing the audience to have the false belief that the imitative image is in fact the very thing it imitates. This element of the deception, common to both likenesses and images, results in a misidentification of the image or artefact with the original or model. Likenesses, according to Crivelli, achieve this deception by creating an image that shares some properties with the model, whereas semblances achieve it by appearing to have, but not in fact having, some of the same properties as the model. So in the case of semblances there is a double

---

[13] The huge gilded ivory statue of Athena in the Parthenon on the Acropolis is an example of such monumental artworks (as was the gigantic statue of Zeus at Olympia). Both would have been very familiar to any Greek. Note the second-person singular *oistha* at 235e7 "you know", and the second-person plural *hēmōn* at 236a2 "our seeing".

deception.[14] Now, one serious problem with Crivelli's reading is that it is not plausible to take Plato to suppose that the viewers of a monumental statue, e.g. Phidias's Athena Parthenos, are deceived into believing that they are in the presence of the goddess herself, or to suppose that viewers of a mural faithfully depicting the proportions and colours of a man's face take themselves to be confronted by the man himself. In a footnote, Crivelli appeals to a monograph by Jan Szaif, who "emphasises that an imitation's cognate deception is at a psychological level whereby it can coexist with the knowledge that the imitation *is not* what it imitates".[15] As well as conceptually implausible, this interpretation faces the further, equally serious textual problem that Plato does not have the Stranger say or suggest that likenesses and semblances, or images in general, deceive the audience into misidentifying the depiction with the thing depicted. At 234b6–10 he says that mindless or foolish young children standing far away are deceived by the painter into thinking he can accomplish anything in his products. Even if we were to read the far-away simple children as deceived into thinking that the painter's product is identical to what it depicts,[16] there is no suggestion that bright children, or foolish children close up – let alone adults – would be so deceived. To be sure, a little later the production of semblances is said to bid goodbye to the truth (236a4–5), which might be taken to suggest some sort of deception. But crucially this is what distinguishes semblances from likenesses, so however it is understood, the remark could not describe deceptiveness in images generally. Indeed, there is no hint in the text that likenesses produce falsehoods or deception in the minds of the audience.

Notomi interprets the text very differently. He reads it as analysing likenesses as being correct representations of the original or model, while semblances are distorted representations of what they depict.[17] Semblances, though not likenesses, are thus false and deceptive. This interpretation, however, cannot be right either. For, insofar as the monumental statue depicts – and in that sense represents – its subject or model, e.g. the goddess Athena, as beautifully proportioned, it represents its subject or model correctly. If instead the sculptor produced his work as the likeness-maker produces his work, the monumental statue of Athena would be a distorted representation of Athena, since it would represent her as having a too-small head and oversized feet, i.e. it would represent her falsely, as having ugly proportions.

A final issue for both Crivelli's and Notomi's interpretations is found in a passage towards the end of the dialogue. As Lesley Brown has pointed out, this

[14] Crivelli, *Plato's Account of Falsehood,* 24–25.

[15] Crivelli, *Plato's Account of Falsehood,* fn. 40, 24; Szaif, *Platons Begriff der Wahrheit,* 401–402.

[16] It is not clear, however, that this is what the Stranger has in mind: see fn. 11 above.

[17] Notomi, *The Unity of Plato's* Sophist, 149–154.

passage speaks strongly against any interpretation either of image production generally, or of semblance production in particular, as defined in terms of the systematic production of falsehoods.[18] In the final division of the dialogue, that of production (which quickly becomes a division of kinds of image-production), some semblances are produced by knowledgeable people (267B–E), such as someone who knows Theaetetus and imitates him by speaking just as he does. Note that, *contra* Crivelli, there is no indication that the imitator deceives people into thinking, falsely, that he is, in fact, Theaetetus. The point seems rather to be that the imitator produces an accurate imitation, in respect of Theaetetus's voice, in sounding recognisably like him. As Brown has argued, it is doubtful that knowledgeable people would produce false representations or depictions (and the Stranger's example does not suggest otherwise). But then, *contra* Notomi, it cannot be the defining characteristic of semblances to produce distorted representations that are false and deceptive. I turn now to my own interpretation of likeness- and semblance-production, and of the sophist's craft.

3. Semblance-Production and Sophistry

The key difference between likenesses and semblances in the *Sophist* lies in the correspondence, in the case of the former, between significant properties of the artefact and the subject or model depicted (e.g. proportion and colour), and the absence of such correspondence in the case of the latter. The key difference, then, does not lie in the accuracy or otherwise of what they represent about the subject, i.e. how they depict it as being. Likenesses, artefacts whose significant properties correspond to that of the subject they depict, almost always represent their subject correctly in respect of these properties. Semblances, by contrast, are artefacts that seem like their subject in respect of the relevant properties, i.e. to correspond to them in this respect, but are not in fact like them in that their relevant properties do not in fact correspond.

Crucial to this interpretation is the distinction between the imitator's immediate product, the artefact, and the way that it appears to the person who experiences it. In the case of human imitative arts, the way that the artefact appears is as an image, that represents or depicts its subject as being some particular way to the audience, as a result of the imitator's efforts.[19] Plato has

---

[18] Brown, "Definition and Division", 161.

[19] In the case of divinely produced semblances (e.g. in reflections in water), the way they appear to the person who experiences them, as a depiction or representation of some subject, seems unlikely to be a matter of divine design or the result of divine effort – and nor does Plato have the Stranger suggest as much at 266B–C. But although, therefore, the mode of semblance production differs in the divine and human cases, that which marks divine

the Stranger make this distinction quite deliberately in the example of the monumental statue. There he carefully distinguishes between the measurable proportions of the parts of the statue and the way it *ought* to appear: he says that if the sculptor were to give the statue's parts or limbs the true proportions, those higher up would appear smaller than they should, or what is necessary (*tou deontos*), and those lower down would appear larger than they should, the former being seen from further away, the latter from close to (235e6–236a2). The normative point being made here, I take it, is that there is a correct way that the artefact ought to appear, namely, beautifully proportioned, in order to succeed in its function of depicting, and in that sense representing, its subject (e.g. the goddess Athena). In adhering to the normative standards of their craft as having a representational function, then, the sculptors produce in their images proportions that are not the real proportions, but those that seem to be beautiful (236a4–6). A few lines later the Stranger further emphasises the distinction between the properties of the thing that appears (the artefact) and how it appears to its audience: he says that which appears (*to phainomenon*) to be like the beautiful thing would be seen as not like it if such large things could be sufficiently viewed. Hence, the properties of that which appears, the artefact, are not like those of the model, even though they appear like them. He goes on to reason that because the artefact appears like the model, but is not, it is a semblance (*phantasma*) (263b7). Now, as the Stranger has already made clear, this appearing but not being is not a failure of the sculptor's expertise, but is on the contrary a condition of the craft's successful operation, in the form of a norm or standard, if it is to perform its core function of depiction or representation.

The example of the monumental statue also makes clear two further features of the representative function of a semblance, *qua* image. First, that there is a very specific, singular way in which the imitator wants the subject depicted to appear to the audience (the achieving of which in the relevant medium will, in turn, standardly require a high level of expertise). In our example, this is that the statue depicts Athena as beautifully proportioned. Call this the "target representation" of the subject (or model or original). Second, the particular condition of the audience must frequently be taken into consideration when fashioning the artefact – in our example, this is that the viewer is human-sized and far from the upper parts of the huge statue, but close to the lower parts (a factor considered in light of the laws of optics). The mode of production, then, that the semblance-producer employs, is entirely different from that of the likeness-producer (who, we have seen, proceeds by looking to, and reproducing in the artefact produced, certain properties of the subject). Semblances, by

semblances as such is the same as with human-produced semblances, i.e. the lack of correspondence between the semblance's properties and those of the model or original. I am grateful to Tim Clarke for making me think harder about this point.

contrast, are made by a kind of reverse-engineering, whereby the imitator decides upon the target representation and, mindful of the relevant conditions of the audience, fashions the artefact accordingly. In their choice of and production of the properties of the artefact, then, the imitator is not constrained, in the way that the likeness-producer is, by the properties of the subject (or model or original). Indeed, we might think, it is generally not the skill or even the business of the imitator to preserve in their artefacts the truth of the model or original, but rather to produce something that depicts or represents the model in some particular way for their audience. It is in this way that the mode of production of semblance-makers bids "goodbye to the truth" (236a4).

As in the example of the statue, the audience conditions for which the features of the artefact are adjusted can be physical. The same will hold, in very similar ways, of the other example in view, monumental paintings. A different kind of audience condition is pointed to in the other example of semblance-production in our passages, that of sophistry. At 234c4–6, the sophist's audience are described as young and at a distance from the truth of things. The condition of their exposure to the sophist's "spoken images" (or "images in words") (*eidōla legomena*, 234c5–6) is thus the general inexperience of youth and overall ignorance about things (*pragmata*, c4). Under these conditions, the sophist is able to bewitch their ears with their spoken-images, in order to make it seem to the audience that the words spoken are true, and the one speaking them, the sophist, is the wisest of all people about all things. The nature of the bewitchment is the adoption of beliefs that the sophist's students overturn when they get older and gain experience of the realities themselves, so that what they previously believed to be large or important through the sophist's images now appear small or insignificant, and what they had believed was easy, now appears difficult. The semblances (*phantasmata*) in words they had earlier embraced are overthrown by their experience (234d2–e2). We are not told how exactly how the sophist fashions his word-images or how they accommodate his hearer's inexperience or ignorance, with the result that he so effectively convinces them that he speaks the truth and is wisest of all. But we can, I think, plausibly conjecture from other dialogues that the sophist will appeal either to beliefs that his hearers already hold or are likely to accept (on authority from the poets, say, or majority opinion),[20] in arguing for his overall claims or conclusions, or else craft an appealing, if fanciful, story that purports to explain (in a literal sense) observable facts or an anthropological or historical development.[21] In very general terms, then, the audience conditions of which

[20] E.g. *Gorgias* 471E–472D. Note, too, that the imaginary sophist in the *Sophist* manages to hide and escape from the enquiry on the strength of the authority of Parmenides, who declares the impossibility of speaking or thinking "what is not" – thereby supporting the sophist's claim that he (the sophist) cannot be a producer of falsehoods (236C–237B).

[21] E.g. Protagoras's long speech in *Prt.* 320Dff.

the sophist is mindful, and in light of which he fashions his spoken-images, can be described as doxastic conditions – epistemic conditions under which they experience his arguments or speeches that contribute to making the word-images seem true, and the sophist himself seem wise. Under such doxastic conditions, moreover, the sophistic semblance-producer is even less constrained by the actual properties of the subjects depicted in his images. For, in an act of reverse-engineering, the sophist will determine what his audience are likely to believe, and will then craft his words accordingly, to pander to their pre-existing beliefs, exploit their antecedent beliefs about who ought to count as authoritative, appeal to their willingness to be entertained by stories, and, of course, take advantage of their inability to reason at a high level.[22]

In the plastic and visual arts, too, the audience's pre-existing epistemic conditions will be relevant to the production of semblances, so that they represent their subjects in ways the audience will find fitting or deem correct. This will be especially true when the audience are in a condition of ignorance or inexperience regarding the subjects depicted. Similarly in poetry, semblance producers will produce images in words that chime with their audience's culturally-determined conceptions of things such as the virtues, statesmanship, and generalship and about which, in Plato's view, they almost universally lack proper knowledge. These cases of semblance-production, then, will be just as unconstrained by the actual, real properties of their subjects as the sophist's production of his images in words.

Note that it does not follow from this interpretation of semblance-production in the *Sophist* that semblances as a kind of image are artefacts that by their nature depict or represent their subjects falsely, or in a systematically deceptive way. Semblances are artefacts that are distinguished, recall, from the other kind of images, likenesses, by their appearing to, but in fact failing to, be like or correspond with the subject (model, original) they depict in respect of the possession of significant properties. Moreover, this distinguishing feature is connected to the depiction or representation they offer their audience, in the deep sense that this feature is what makes the particular representational content possible, regardless of whether the content of the depiction or representation is true or false of the subject depicted.

To see this, consider some examples. In the Stranger's example, the large statue appears to have beautiful proportions (though it does not), but thereby succeeds in depicting or representing Athena. In another example, the couch in a painting, painted as if viewed at an angle, appears just as its physical model would appear to a viewer viewing it from an angle, and thereby appears to have four legs of the same length (though in fact the painted couch does not, as its painted legs, on the artefact's surface, are of uneven length). Nonetheless the painted couch's having legs of uneven length is essential for its depiction or

[22] I am grateful to Melissa Lane and Elena Cagnoli for this last point.

representation of a couch, as if viewed at an angle. Next, consider the actor on stage portraying Hector, who purely by cosmetic means appears to be the very picture of health and physical strength (although the actor does not in fact possess the muscular, gleaming strength Hector was said to possess). Nevertheless, this appearance of the actor's is part of the device by which he depicts and so in that sense represents Hector. Finally, Homer's description of Achilles as fierce and fearless in battle presents him as a paradigm case of bravery (though, by Plato's lights, Homer's character is not in fact courageous in respect of this behaviour). But since the behaviour of Homer's character chimes with his audience's preconceived notions of courage, the description facilitates the character's being a depiction or representation of a case of courage. In the first example, the statue of Athena accurately and so truthfully depicts or represents the goddess in respect of her bodily proportions; in the second example, though the painted couch accurately depicts the perceptible *appearance* of a physical couch, it fails to represent the subject or model, the physical couch, as something with legs of even length, and so does not truly represent the subject or model's actual properties; in the third example, the stage actor accurately or truly depicts or represents the hero Hector in his physical prime; while in the fourth, Homer's character inaccurately or falsely represents an instance of rage as a case of courage.

The mode of semblance production, then, centres on its goal or *telos* of producing some specific depiction or representation, the content of which is understood by the audience as fitting, appropriate, or beautiful in the relevant context. To the extent that the production of the semblance itself, *qua* artefact, is determined by this target representation, in contrast to the way the subject it depicts or represents really is, it is no part of the expertise of semblance production to preserve the truth in the artefact. For this reason, but also since the content of the target representation (the goal of semblance-making) is designed to accommodate the particular audience's viewing conditions, including doxastic conditions, the content of the depiction or representation itself may turn out to be either true or false. Since what a semblance depicts or represents – its representational content – may be true or false, semblances are epistemically unreliable. Moreover, if, as the Stranger suggests at 234C–E, the content of semblances can influence the beliefs of those who are ignorant, then the audience to semblances is doxastically vulnerable to its epistemically unreliable content. Before moving on to the special sub-class of sophistic semblance production, let me pause to note that a merit of my interpretation is that as well as accommodating Plato's examples of semblance-making, monumental sculpture and painting, and the sophist's word-image semblances (as I hope I have shown above), it is able – as rival interpretations are not – to make sense of the Stranger's mention of knowledgeable semblance-makers towards the end of the dialogue (267B). For, on my interpretation, the gap between the features of the artefact and the way it appears to its audience (and therefore the gap between the features of the artefact and the content of what it depicts) makes it possible for a knowledgeable semblance-maker to adjust the features of the artefact so as to deliberately depict its subject truthfully, as being exactly as it is. Indeed, as indicated above, I take it that the monumental statue furnishes the reader with a clear example.[23] In such cases of semblance-production, the artefact appearing like, but not being like, the subject (or model or original) it depicts, is no barrier to the artefact's representational content being true.

I have argued that according to Plato in the *Sophist*, semblances are not, by their nature, false and deceptive, but merely epistemically unreliable. Because of the sophist's particular employment of the mode of semblance production, however, his semblances (images in words) are not merely epistemically unreliable, but especially likely to be false. As is frequently the case with the "artistic" semblance-maker (at least in Plato's view), the sophist's audience is frequently ignorant about the subjects depicted by the semblances that are crafted. So, like the artist, the sophist will frequently aim at a target representation that chimes with, reflects, and builds upon his ignorant audience's pre-existing views – a potent factor in making them epistemically unreliable. But unlike the artistic semblance-maker who, as we have seen, may possess knowledge of the subjects depicted, Plato presents the sophist as lacking knowledge of the subjects about which he speaks. First, the Stranger describes the sophist as willing to controvert on any subject whatsoever, before eliciting agreement from Theaetetus that it is impossible to have knowledge about everything (232B–233C). Second, and more decisively, the Stranger and Theaetetus agree that the sophist is unable correctly to controvert or contradict someone who has knowledge about the subject the sophist speaks of (232E–233A), even though he appears correctly to contradict others, and his arguments appear to give him a claim to wisdom (233B). This entitles the Stranger to conclude that the sophist is not knowledgeable about those subjects his word-images depict, but only has a kind of "reputed knowledge" about everything (*doxastikē epistēmē*, 233c10), and not the truth.[24] Therefore the sophist cannot knowingly produce a word-image that depicts or represents his subjects truthfully, but could only do so by pure luck – and this would, presumably, be rare.

There is a further reason, however, that the sophist's products constitute a special subclass of semblance. His products appear to have a very particular property, in virtue of which they appear like the subjects they depict, namely, the property of being true (234C). So the sophist's semblances appear true, and

[23] Athena is beautifully proportioned, and knowing this, the expert sculptor depicts her as such for a human-sized audience by crafting a sculpture not beautifully proportioned.

[24] I here follow (at least partially) Cornford's translation of *doxastikē epistēmē* as "reputed and apparent knowledge" (Cornford, *Plato's Theory of Knowledge*, 193).

thus like the real or true things they depict or represent, but are not in fact like them in respect of being true. It is precisely because they appear true, though without being so, that they succeed in depicting, for their particular audience, the reality of anything and everything.[25] As a result, unlike the artist's semblances, the sophist's artefact appearing like, but not being like, the subject (or model or original) it depicts in the relevant respect (i.e. it appears true but is not), is indeed a barrier to the artefact's representational content being true.

Let me clarify that I do not mean to attribute to Plato the highly implausible thought that in practicing his craft, the sophist cannot utter a statement to his audience or students that is true. For it seems likely that by "spoken-images" (*eidōla legomena*, 234c5–6), the Stranger has in mind the entire "argument" or line of contention articulated by the sophist, to which he aims to have his hearers acquiesce. That is, the sophist presents the individual statements (or rhetorical questions) as both acceptable because they seem true to his audience, and as acceptably linked to the other statements he makes, so that the central claim or conclusion asserted appears to them correct, and as something they should accept. By taking into account the audience's ignorance and inexperience, and presuming a background of popular beliefs and attitudes, the sophist is able to fashion his contention and its support so as to seem maximally acceptable. Like the artistic producer of mimetic semblances, the sophist aims to craft a product that appears a certain way (in the sophist's case, it appears true) and which represents things as appearing a particular way (e.g. the virtues appear easy to understand and acquire). And like the artistic semblance-maker's product, the sophist's product is not designed to be engaged with, beyond the passive reception and acceptance of the representation it is designed to project, for a particular audience, experiencing it under particular conditions. The sophist's various statements and the way they are presented as hanging together are not to be reflected upon, questioned, or critically examined, but are rather to be adopted, as both plausible and persuasive to the particular audience to whom they have been presented. So understood, the sophist's products – "images in words" – are the sorts of linguistic entities that are able to be wielded by the sophist to contradict or "countersay" (*antilogein*, 232B; 233B–C) his interlocutor convincingly enough to his audience (233B). If this is right, then, given the ignorance of both the sophist's students and the sophist himself regarding the subjects of which he speaks, as well as his student's

[25] They do not, of course, in fact depict the reality of each and every thing that is, as it really is *tout court*, but only as such *to their particular audience*. In suggesting this interpretation, I am not supposing, as many interpreters have done, that a true declarative statement is a word-image that counts as likeness, and one that is false counts as a semblance. I am instead proposing that semblance-making is a kind of production that only succeeds when the artefact appears like, but is not like, what it depicts (while a likeness is an artefact that appears like and is like what it depicts).

inexperience and understanding of proper (i.e. logically valid) argumentation, the chances of the sophist's *eidōla legomena* being, as well as appearing, true, are vanishingly small.[26] Moreover, the self-image the sophist creates, by way of the practice of his craft, as prodigiously wise because supremely knowledgeable, will be false.

With this interpretation of semblance-making, and of sophistry as a specific sub-class of this expertise, in hand, we are in a position to return to the Stranger's puzzling use of *phantasia* in the closing stages of the dialogue.

4. *Phantasiai* and Doxastic Vulnerability to Sophistry

I argued in §1 above that the Stranger's first two uses of *phantasia* (260C–261A) in the *Sophist* were, consistent with the small number of other uses of this Platonic neologism in previous dialogues, "objective" in the sense that it refers to some feature or other of something in the world independent of any experience of it. I further argued, in light of a suggestion by Cornford (and followed by others, e.g. Notomi) that in such uses we can regard the term, *phantasia*, as a substantive equivalent to *phainesthai*, to refer to an appearance that belongs to something, irrespective of whether there is anyone to whom it appears. I also argued that the second two uses of *phantasia* (263D–264B) were radically different, in being "subjective" uses, in the sense that they referred to a kind of cognition (or thought, or cognitive state). The puzzle was to see why Plato would use his own relatively recently invented term in such radically distinct ways, and relatedly, how precisely to understand the kind of cognition he calls "*phantasia*". I will now argue that the puzzling switch in uses turns on a familiar conception of appearance, according to which an objective appearance of something gives rise to a cognition of its being a certain way to

[26] It remains, of course, logically possible, even if highly unlikely given the sophist's lack of knowledge of his subjects, for the sophist to produce several true statements connected by logically valid inferences, in the service of whatever claim the sophist is contending against his interlocutor. In such a case, in light of the definition of semblance as appearing but not being a certain way (236b4–7), and the characterisation of the sophist's semblances as appearing but not being true (233c6–9), the sophist's word-image (or some part of his word-image) will be a likeness, not a semblance. Significantly, however, the word-image that is in fact like, as opposed to merely appearing like, its subject, will have been produced by way of the method of semblance-making, i.e. it will have been reverse engineered in light of a target representation or depiction, and not by the method of likeness-making, i.e. produced by looking to the properties of the subject or original and deliberately reproducing them in the artefact (in this case, the word-image). The sophist's product will, therefore, be a merely accidental likeness, and so remains, from the ignorant student's perspective, as epistemically unreliable and as likely to be false as any semblance produced by the sophist, even though it happens, in fact, to be true.

someone who experiences it under the right conditions. We will see that this cognition is, according to Plato, a perceptually caused belief (*doxa*). I will then suggest that, in light of the particular kind of semblance the sophist produces, this effect of appearances reveals the extent to which the sophist's audience are doxastically vulnerable to his practice.

In this later section of the dialogue, just prior to the introduction of *phantasia*, the Stranger has given an analysis of the basic form of statement or speech (*logos*) as a naming term (*onoma*) together with a predicate term or verb (*rhēma*) (262A–E), along with either assertion or denial (263E). This follows his lengthy discussion of Forms or kinds, in which he has argued that there is a Form of Not Being, closely associated with Difference, which legitimates his earlier assertion, against the sophist, that it is possible to think and speak of what is not, or not being. He then proceeds to analyse both true and false statement. The details of this somewhat controversial analysis need not detain us – for our purposes, the important point is that, since not being and the possibility of falsehood have been established, the possibility of deception has likewise been established, along with the possibility of images, likenesses, and appearances being deployed for that purpose.

The Stranger then turns from the means of deception to its psychology. He sets out to distinguish what each of thought (*dianoia*), belief (*doxa*), and appearance (*phantasia*) are, in order to demonstrate that they can be either true or false (263D–E). Thought is said to be the same thing as speech (*logos*), excepting that it is a silent discourse (*dialogos*) of the soul with itself, and he clarifies that speech or statement always includes assertion or denial. He then defines belief as speech, or a statement (asserted or denied) that comes about silently in the soul in accordance with thought (264a1–2), before introducing a second kind of belief in the next lines. At 264a3–4 he says that whenever belief should come to be present in someone not on its own (*mē kath' hautēn*),[27] i.e. in the way just described,[28] by the operation of silent thought alone, but instead through perception, this sort of state is called appearance (*phantasia*).

---

[27] Reading the mss's *kath' hautēn* at 264a4 instead of Stobaeus's suggested *kath' hauto*.

[28] I read the reflexive *kath' hautēn* at 264a4 as referring to *doxa* (264a2), so that the Stranger is saying that whenever a belief should come to be present to someone not by itself but through perception it is *phantasia*. Another alternative, adopted by Grönroos, is that *kath' hautēn* refers to *psuchē* (264a1), so that the Stranger is saying, somewhat elliptically, "when affirmation or denial occurs to someone not by the soul on its own…but through sense perception…" it should be called *phantasia* (Grönroos, "Two Kinds of Belief", 5). Although this interpretation gives an overall sense very like my own, I don't think it is very likely to be what Plato intended. For, most naturally read, the subject of the reflexive *kath' hautēn* is the same as the subject of the sentence: the phrase *mē kath' hautēn alla di' aisthēseōs* is most easily read as describing the cause or manner of the action denoted by the verb, *parēi* ("should become present in"), in which case they share the same subject. But the subject of the sentence cannot be *psuchē* since a soul does not come to be present in someone through

I interpret the two kinds of belief described here as follows. The first is the product of active intellectual effort, an internal dialogue within the soul, so that the "intellectual belief" (or "belief" as I shall call it from here on) is the soul's discursive conclusion that things are a certain way, through inference or recognition, or a similar effortful cognitive process. This is why the Stranger a few lines later describes belief as "the conclusion of thought (*dianoia*)" (264b1). The second kind of belief, called appearance (*phantasia*), is not a belief present in a person by itself, arising from silent thought in the way just described, but is caused by perception, and so brought about passively. Through perceptual experience of the world, an activity involving the sense organs, a statement (or speech) coupled with affirmation or denial arises in the soul. In the case of appearance (*phantasia*), the affirmed or denied statement is not the result of the intellectual efforts of the soul, such as inference or recognition.[29] Rather the soul is passive in this process, the content of the statement (or speech) being determined by how things are experienced in perception, that is, by how things appear by way of our perceptual experience. This difference in the causal process results in a different kind of belief, described by the Stranger as "this sort of state" (*to toiouton pathos*, 264a5), which he gives the name "appearance" (*phantasia*).

Behind this first subjective use of *phantasia*, I suggest, is a certain conception of appearance, that licences the assumption that if something, *a*, is such as to appear F to a person, then if someone does in fact experience *a*, the cognitive state they enjoy is an appearance that has the content, F*a* (note that this content is not, usually, "it appears F*a*"). So understood, the type of cognition here labelled *phantasia*, is the contentful cognition, an appearance, that arises for us when encountering the perceptual appearance of things. If this is right, Plato's use of *phantasia* in the objective and subjective sense mirrors the use of "appearance" in English whereby it describes both the way something is, objectively, such as to appear a certain way (under certain

perception. And if we accept the manuscripts' reading, *kath' hautēn*, over the interpolated *kath' hauto* (as I take it we ought to do if possible), it would be impossible to take *kath' hautēn* to pick up on *touto* at 264A, and so impossible to take the subject of *kath' hautēn* to be "assertion or denial" (263e12).

[29] See also M.L. Gill, who understands the distinction between the two kinds of judgement or belief at 264A–B, *doxa* and *phantasia*, in a similar but slightly more narrow way than that proposed here, in terms of inferential and non-inferential truth-assessable states of judgement respectively (*Philosophos*, 169–170). For an alternative reading, which takes it that any kind of belief must be the result of a cognitive process (in contrast to a perceptual one), see Notomi, *The Unity of Plato's* Sophist, 259. Notomi evidently takes *kata dianoian* at 264a1 to be a defining feature of any kind of *doxa*, while I have suggested an alternative reading whereby one kind of *doxa* (the "by itself" or pure kind) is the product of an effortful intellectual process, which the Stranger goes on to contrast with another kind (the "through perception" kind), which is the product of a passive perceptual process.

conditions), and the corresponding cognition that results for someone who experiences it (under those conditions).[30] On the reading I am suggesting, then, appearance *(phainetai*, a clear gloss on *phantasia)* is a "combination of perception and belief" (264b1–2) just insofar as it is a perceptually caused belief.

Just like their artistic counterparts, the products of sophistry – semblances that are word-images – are experienced perceptibly, and, as we have seen, also possess a representational content, expressible as a statement. In the earlier section on mimetic production, the Stranger emphasises that the sophist's products are audible: it is his students' ears that are bewitched with words (234c5), the sophist is described as the "one speaking" (*ton legonta*), who appears most wise, and his product is described as "spoken images" (*eidōla legomena*) and semblances in words (*ta en tois logois phantasmata* 234e1) which seem to be spoken (*legesthai*) truly (234c5–7). So too in the final division at the end of the dialogue, sophistry is described as performed by the kind of semblance producing expert who gives short speeches in private and forces his interlocutor into contradiction (268B–C).[31]

The sophist's spoken images express a content concerning the various subjects he presents claims or lines of contention about, with which content he contradicts his interlocutors (e.g. subjects are said to be large or significant, or difficult), and his images also appear true. At 234C–E, the Stranger emphasises the perceptual nature of the ways in which sophistry is experienced by an audience, or the sophist's students: they are bewitched with words through their ears, so that the display of images in words to them is an audible display (c5–6). The audience are also pointedly described as "listeners" or "hearers" (*akouontōn*, d2–3) of the sophist. Therefore, the semblances (*phantasmata,* e1) that they experienced in words, which are refuted by the time they are older and have experienced things for themselves (*tōn ontōn*, d6, cf. *tōn pragmatōn*, c4), are clearly semblances perceived audibly. I submit that through perceiving – hearing – the sophist's images, his students enjoy a cognition, an appearance, of the same content as those spoken images (one example could be that having power to do what you want is an important and valuable thing).[32] This thought or cognition has the hallmarks of belief, as the Stranger has described it: it is in the form of a statement (subject conjoined with predicate). What is more, as the Stranger's description of the cognitive transformation of the sophist's

[30] Compare: "The tree appears to have a rosy hue in the evening light", "In the evening light, I had an appearance of the tree as rosy hued".

[31] Note that the plastic and visual arts in the Stranger's examples are experienced through the sense modality of vision (and perhaps touch, in the case of the former). Similarly, someone who imitates Theaetetus's comportment and voice (267A) produces an imitation that can be experienced auditorily and visually.

[32] *Gorgias*, 466E.

students over time makes plain, the earlier cognitive state of the students, while under the spell of the sophist, does indeed contain assertion (or denial): they are described as changing their beliefs (*doxas*, d6), so that what they previously thought was important, now appears insignificant (d6–7).

Let me pause briefly to clarify that although I am attributing to Plato in the *Sophist* the claim that a great many beliefs (perceptually caused beliefs, *phantasiai*) will arise through the experience of verbal statements, I am not claiming that, on the interpretation proposed, all verbal statements cause the corresponding belief to arise in the mind of the hearer. I am claiming that, for Plato in the *Sophist*, all simple declarative statements, which are not asserted within the context of critical reflection or intellectual examination, and so are asserted in a manner that seeks and urges straightforward passive acceptance on the part of the hearer, result in a perceptually caused belief, *phantasia*, arising for the hearer. On the view proposed, statements framed as questions (other than rhetorical questions), which do require intellectual effort on the part of the hearer for the statement to be accepted or rejected, do not issue in *phantasiai*. Moreover, statements embedded in a propositional attitude, such as desiring, wishing, hoping, dreaming, fearing, expecting, and intending, do not result in a *phantasia* (perceptually caused belief) arising for the hearer, the content of which corresponds to the embedded statement. Rather, they result in a *phantasia* arising for the hearer that interprets such statements as reportage (at least where the speaker appears sincere). For example, if Jones declares she expects a promotion at Christmas, her hearer forms the perceptually caused belief that "Jones expects she will be promoted at the end of the year". The contrast between *phantasia* and *doxa* at the end of the *Sophist*, then, is that between a belief that arises passively for the subject, through perception, and one that is the result of an active, intellectual process. I expand slightly on the reading proposed in the next section, and offer a brief defence of it.

If the foregoing is right, in the *Sophist* Plato analyses the sophist's products as semblances that have the power to inculcate beliefs in their hearers, beliefs passively absorbed through perception, which reflect the representational content of the spoken word-images he produces. In the next section I will expand slightly on, and briefly defend, the interpretation of subjective *phantasia* proposed. For now, however, it is important to note that the power of the sophist's products is further amplified by their persuasiveness and verisimilitude, their appearing true. As we have seen, the products of sophistry are especially problematic: the products of sophistry, like all semblances that are reverse engineered with a view to some target appearance, are epistemically unreliable. But in addition, unlike other mimetic crafts, sophistry's particular use of semblance-production (whereby producer and consumer are equally ignorant, yet his products appear true) ensures that his spoken word-images are especially likely to be false. This makes the sophist's power to inculcate beliefs in his hearers especially dangerous.

5. An Un-Aristotelian Precursor to Aristotle on *phantasia*

On the view presented, the capacity for having appearances in the sense described by the Stranger, that is, the capacity for having a belief as a result of perception, is a feature of our psychology that makes us vulnerable to sophistry, and to mimetic production in general, the majority of which is concerned with semblance production. One of the guiding thoughts behind such a view, I take it, is that the perceiver will take on, or absorb, the content of the target representation, in the form of an asserted or denied statement, i.e. a belief, as her own. The assent or denial coupled with the subject and predicate in this way becomes the perceiver's assent or denial. And this guiding thought, we might think, is surely specious. After all, seeing is not believing. So cognising things, in the form of having an appearance of things, as being some way or other, as a result of perceiving those things through sight, is not believing. For example, as Aristotle argues in *de Anima* III 3, through sight the sun appears to us to be a foot across, but we don't believe it. Therefore, he argues, *phantasia* must be distinguished from belief, not identified with it, let alone understood as a species of it (428a19–428b9). Aristotle goes on to mount the objection, apparently with the *Sophist* in view,[33] that if appearances were beliefs, the soul would therefore suffer contradictory beliefs, contrary to the facts. Isn't it obvious, we might think, that Aristotle is right, and Plato is just wrong about the having of appearances?

Not necessarily, is the answer I want to give here. First, it is not immediately clear how to understand "*doxa*" as Plato uses the term. *Republic* X, for instance, gives us reason to think that Plato uses "*doxa*" in a sense that would equate to a fairly broad use or even a loose way of using our contemporary conception of belief (which can in a minimal sense be understood as "taking it that thus and such is the case, or is true"). In *Rep.* X Socrates argues that when we perceive a stick in water as bent, two opposing beliefs (*doxai*) arise in the soul, from distinct soul-parts: the belief of the non-rational element that it is bent, which arises directly from the perception of it as such, and the belief of the rational element that it is not bent, which arises from calculation and measurement, if not of the perceived stick directly, of other relevantly similar cases. The familiar nature of the example strongly suggests that the non-rational belief is (or is very much like) the cognition one has when some object or state of affairs clearly and distinctly strikes one as being a certain way, even in cases where we know that it is not so. Another way to describe such a cognition (at least in English) would be as a strong or striking impression.[34]

---

[33] See, for instance, Lycos, "Aristotle and Plato on 'Appearing'", *passim*.

[34] For a similar view of the sense of *doxa* in use in *R.* X, see Lorenz, *The Brute Within,* 66–67.209. For further discussion of this example of opposing beliefs and its connection to *mimēsis*, see Leigh, "Mimesis", 312–315.

Moreover, in Socrates' example, there is no suggestion that the perceiver adopts the *doxa* that the stick is bent in any permanent way. Rather, the example strongly suggests that the rational belief is, in such quotidian cases, regular cause for the rejection of the non-rational belief.[35] On this view of *doxa*, then, it is plausible to think that in the absence of a rationally produced belief to the contrary, in such clear and distinct perceptual cases, an appearance is a strong impression that is, in our contemporary sense, a weakly held kind of belief: If you didn't know better, you'd believe the stick was bent.

A second counter-objection that Plato, at any rate, would seem likely to make against Aristotle is that people simultaneously hold contradictory beliefs very often, as Socrates shows in numerous early dialogues.[36] In the *Sophist*, too, Plato affirms his commitment to the frequent presence of opposing beliefs in the soul: at 230B the Stranger describes a method of cleansing the soul of false belief, in which the questioner "collect(s) those beliefs together and puts them side by side, thereby revealing them as contradicting one another not just on the same subjects but in relation to the same things and in the same respects" (tr. Rowe). As I hope to have shown in this chapter, by way of the type of cognition Plato calls *phantasia* in the *Sophist*, one of the central means of acquiring false beliefs is passive, largely naïve, and thereby nefarious – *via* perception, when someone without knowledge of the subject of discussion is exposed through sensation to highly persuasive imitative semblances in spoken images, expertly crafted for him by a sophist who is similarly ignorant of the subject about which he speaks.

---

[35] To be sure, in *R.* X Socrates says that the non-rational *doxa* remains for the agent. But we need *not* take this to suggest that in cases where it is obviously in error (such as the bent stick), such perceptually caused beliefs are not overridden and rejected by the agent. For Socrates can be taken to suggest that for as long as the agent gazes at the stick in water, it will strike her as bent (and so she will have the perceptually caused belief for as long as she looks at it), but nonetheless a moment's reflection will see her reject that belief, which is why she does not act on it. In giving such a familiar, everyday example, then, Plato shows himself to be aware that such perceptually caused cognitions, in which things powerfully strike us as thus-and-so – and so which he labels "belief" or *doxa* – nonetheless regularly do not form the basis for action.

[36] In these dialogues, Socrates reveals to his interlocutors that they all along held, antecedent to speaking with him, beliefs that contradict other avowed beliefs, despite disavowing those beliefs. As Socrates says to Polus "...I do believe that you and I consider doing what's unjust worse than suffering it, ..." (before going on to secure agreement from Polus that this is indeed what he thinks, *Grg.* 474B). For further discussion, see Leigh, "Self-knowledge", 257–258, and for the opposing view, see Raphael Woolf, "Socratic Authority", *passim*.

Bibliography

Ambuel, David, *Image and Paradigm in Plato's* Sophist, Las Vegas 2007.

Brown, Lesley, "Definition and Division in Plato's *Sophist*", in: David Charles (ed.), *Definition in Greek Philosophy*, Oxford 2010, 151–171.

Burnyeat, Myles, "Idealism and Greek Philosophy: What Descartes Saw and Berkeley Missed", *Philosophical Review* (1982), 3–40.

Cordero, Nestor-Luis, *Le* Sophiste *de Platon: traduction inédite, introduction et notes*, Paris 1993.

Cornford, Francis M., *Plato's Theory of Knowledge: The* Theaetetus *and the* Sophist, Abingdon / New York 1935.

Crivelli, Paolo, *Plato's Account of Falsehood: A Study of the* Sophist, Cambridge 2012.

Diès, Auguste, (ed., tr.) *Platon Le* Sophiste, Paris 1969.

Duerlinger, James, *A Translation of Plato's* Sophist *with an Introductory Commentary*, New York 2005.

Gill, Mary Louise, Philosophos*: Plato's Missing Dialogue*, Oxford 2012.

Grönroos, Gösta, "Two Kinds of Belief in Plato", *Journal of the History of Philosophy* 51 (2013), 1–19.

Harte, Verity, "*Republic* X and the Role of the Audience in Art", *Oxford Studies in Ancient Philosophy* 38 (2010), 69–96.

Leigh, Fiona, "Mimesis, Art, and the Metaphysics of Appearances", in: Mary Margaret McCabe / Simon Trépanier (eds.), *Rereading Plato's* Republic. Edinburgh 2025, 291–324.

–, "Self-knowledge, Elenchus and Authority in Early Plato", *Phronesis* 65 (2020), 247–280.

Lorenz, Hendrick, *The Brute Within: Appetitive Desire in Plato and Aristotle*, New York 2006.

Lycos, Kimon, "Aristotle and Plato on 'Appearing'", *MIND* 73 (1964), 496–514.

McDowell, John, "Values and Secondary Properties", in: Russ Shafer-Landau / Terence Cuneo (eds.), *Foundations of Ethics: An Anthology*, Malden, MA 2007, 137–44.

Notomi, Noboru, *The Unity of Plato's* Sophist: *Between the Sophist and the Philosopher*, Cambridge 1999.

Rosen, Stanley, *Plato's* Sophist: *The Drama of Image and Original*, South Bend, Ind. 1983.

Rowe, Christopher (tr.), *Plato:* Theaetetus *and* Sophist, New York 2015.

Szaif, Jan, *Platons Begriff der Wahrheit,* Freiburg 1998.

Taylor, Alfred Edward (tr.), *The* Sophist *and the* Statesman, London 1961.

White, Nicholas P. (tr.), Sophist, Indianapolis / Cambridge 1993.

Woolf, Raphael, "Socratic Authority", *Archiv für Geschichte der Philosophie* 90 (2008), 1–38.

Soul, Life, and Living Beings in Plato's *Timaeus*

Andrea Falcon

1. Introduction

My contribution to this volume, which is devoted to Plato and the soul, is rooted in my critical engagement with Aristotle. I would like to shed some light on how Plato thinks about soul, life, and living beings starting from the vantage point offered by Aristotle's *De anima.* This goal can be approached in more than one way. One can concentrate, for example, on the points of contact between Aristotle and Plato and use them as a useful platform for an in-depth study of how Plato thinks about the soul. This exegetical strategy has been adopted by several scholars. Here I single out the book on Plato's *Timaeus* by Thomas K. Johansen.[1] Johansen outlines his exegetical strategy in the introduction to his book, where he finds it instructive to place the *Timaeus-Critias* within the context of Aristotle's philosophy.[2] By his lights, both Aristotle and Plato adopted the same style of natural philosophy to the extent that they both considered teleology indispensable for a successful study of the natural world. As a result, the book is introduced as a study of the teleological outlook shared by both philosophers:

> [T]he teleological outlook that drives both philosophers often makes them confront the same kinds of questions and objections. I hope therefore to convey a sense of the ways in which Plato anticipates the concerns of Aristotle's natural philosophy, even where their specific answers differ.[3]

One of the goals of this valuable book is to reduce the conceptual distance separating Plato from Aristotle when it comes to the question of how we should study the natural world.[4] In the pages to follow, I employ a diametrically

---

[1] Johansen, *Plato's Natural Philosophy*.

[2] Johansen, *Plato's Natural Philosophy*, 5.

[3] Johansen, *Plato's Natural Philosophy*, 5–6.

[4] This exegetical approach has prompted several reactions. Here I would like to single out the late Rob Bolton, who insisted on Aristotle's strictures when it comes to teleological explanations. As a result of these strictures, according to Bolton, the teleology adopted by Plato in the *Timaeus* is not to be counted as an instance of *natural* teleology (Bolton, "The Origins of Aristotle's Natural Teleology", 121–143). Johansen, for his part, has continued to think and write about teleology in Plato and Aristotle. In a recent attempt to return to this

opposed strategy; I instead try to learn something about Plato and his theoretical commitments via a *contrast* with Aristotle. Rather than engaging in an exercise of assimilation, I explore the conceptual differences between the two philosophers. I use those differences as a springboard to cast light on what is distinctive about their respective contributions on the topic of soul, life, and living beings.

To be as clear as possible, I do not dispute that Aristotle and Plato have a great deal in common when it comes to the topic of the soul. Both Aristotle and Plato share the same starting point to the extent that they conceive of the soul as the principle of living beings. For both, the soul is the provider of life – namely, that which makes a living being alive. As a result, both Plato and Aristotle think of the living being as an ensouled thing.[5] And yet, there are also salient differences. Let me recall the most obvious one: in the *Timaeus,* Plato is critically engaged with the *peri phuseôs* tradition. He does so by adopting the distinctive cosmogonic framework employed by his predecessors.[6] This framework is quite flexible and can be used to reach different results. By his own admission, Plato concentrates his attention on the coming to be of the present world order (*kosmos*) from the beginning all the way down to the coming to be of the human being. We infer this research focus from the following two programmatic passages which outline the scope and boundaries of the cosmogonic account advanced in Plato's *Timaeus:*

> *Critias:* All right, Socrates, what do you think of the plan we have arranged for our guest gift to you? We thought that because Timaeus is our expert in astronomy and has made it his main business to know the nature of the universe, he should speak first, *beginning with the origin of the world and concluding with the nature of human beings.* Then, I will go next, once I am in possession of Timaeus' account of the origin of human beings and your account of how some of them came to have a superior education. (Plato, *Ti.* 27A, trans. Zeyl, emphasis mine)

---

topic (Johansen, "From Craft to Nature", 103–120), he has sketched out his own account of the emergence of natural teleology. While he argues (unsurprisingly) that Aristotle is responsible for the shift from unnatural to natural teleology, he thinks that artificial teleology (*alias* unnatural) remains a case of proper teleology for Aristotle (Johansen, "From Craft to Nature", 102). In due course I will argue that there is no room for artificial teleology in Aristotle's natural philosophy.

[5] The expression "ensouled being" (*to empsuchon*) is itself a piece of philosophical jargon. We can safely say that this phrase is native to the ancient Greek philosophical reflection on and around the soul as a principle of life. It is the most abstract way of thinking about a living being. For both Plato and Aristotle, this is the most general way to refer to a compound of soul and body. While they have different (indeed competing) ways to conceive of this compound, they both adopt this phrase to convey the point that the living being has a soul.

[6] By "cosmogonic framework" I mean the narrative framework which consists in telling the story of the emergence of the world order from the beginning (*ab initio*).

> *Timaeus:* And now indeed, it seems, *we have all but completed our initial assignment, that of tracing the history of the universe down to the emergence of humankind*. We should go on to mention briefly how the other living things come to be – a topic that won't require many words. (Plato, *Ti.* 90E, trans. Zeyl, emphasis mine)

These two passages mark, respectively, the beginning and the end of the account offered by Timaeus; jointly taken, they make it abundantly clear that Plato's main goal is to give an overall picture of the world order and the place that human beings occupy in it. There are serious limitations as to what he can achieve by narrowing the scope to humans. For sure, a systematic study of perishable living beings is beyond Plato's ambition and stated goal in the *Timaeus*. But we cannot rule out that results achieved in this way might be applied beyond the case of the human being. Based on what we read in the stretch of text that is presented as a coda to the main cosmogonic account, we can even say that Plato is ready to explain not only the emergence of sexual difference but also the emergence of non-human animals by way of a derivation story. But what Plato says in this context is too sketchy to even try to supply a derivation story on his behalf. In the end, it remains unclear just how far beyond the case of the human being Plato is willing, or even able, to apply the results achieved in the main part of his *Timaeus.*

Unsurprisingly, this is also one of Aristotle's major sources of dissatisfaction with Plato's *Timaeus.* I will have more to say on this topic in due course. For the time being, I am content to recall that in his own review of what his predecessors say on the topic of breathing, Aristotle complains that the narrow approach adopted by Plato in the *Timaeus* makes it difficult to see how this account can be applied to non-human animals. One concrete example will clarify why Aristotle is dissatisfied with Plato's account: Do fish breathe? Based on what we read in the *Timaeus* we simply do not know how Plato would have answered this question. Moreover, we do not know whether he was ready to extend his complicated explanation of how human beings control their bodily temperature to fish. And yet, whether fish breathe was an important scientific question at the time, which was recognized as such and intensely discussed before Plato. We do know (mostly thanks to Aristotle) that not only Anaxagoras but also Democritus argued that fish breathe.[7] Aristotle does not follow his predecessors on this point. By his lights, fish do not breathe because

[7] The relevant information can be found in Aristotle's critical review of what was achieved by his predecessors. The relevant stretch of text is *Juv.* 2–4 (*Respir.* 8–10). For the reader who is not familiar with this double numeration should keep in mind that the short essay *On Respiration* (= *Respir.*) is embedded in a larger discussion traditionally transmitted with the conventional title *On Youth, Old Age, Life and Death, and Respiration* (= *Juv.*). The unwelcome decision to separate the second part of the treatise and treat it as an independent essay on respiration is a modern convention that is not reflected in the manuscript tradition and is not supported by the extant evidence. More to the point: it is neither suggested nor encouraged by Aristotle, so it must be resisted.

they control their bodily temperature by using water instead of air. How does Plato fit into this scientific debate? The best answer is that we simply do not know, since we are not given clear instructions on how to extend what we are told about breathing in the case of the human animal to the case of the non-human animals.

To reiterate a point that I have already made, the narrow scope adopted in the *Timaeus* is not dictated by the cosmogonic style of investigation; rather, it is a self-imposed limitation on the part of Plato. As such, it tells us more about Plato and his research focus than about the cosmogonic framework itself.

2. The Nutritive Soul as Primary Cause in Aristotle's *De anima*

Arguably, the major contribution, indeed innovation, in Aristotle's *De anima* is the nutritive soul (also known as vegetative soul, even though Aristotle does not use this phrase as a technical expression).[8] With the nutritive soul, Aristotle expands the domain of the soul beyond the limits of what was known at the time, and its introduction entails a criticism of all his predecessors, no one excluded. Among other things, this expansion also suggests that "psychology" is a misnomer when it is applied to Aristotle's theory of the soul. According to Aristotle, the soul is the ultimate principle controlling several life activities that we do not want to associate with what we today call psychology.

To fully understand the Aristotelian innovation, we must return to the obvious, but too often neglected, fact that in his *De anima* Aristotle is concerned with providing a theoretical foundation for a systematic study of all perishable living beings. To be sure, nutrition, growth, and reproduction are the most conspicuous life activities associated with perishable living beings. It is by means of these activities that perishable living beings not only maintain themselves in existence but also succeed in replicating and perpetuating their distinctive form of organization. For Aristotle, any scientifically adequate explanation of self-nutrition, growth, and reproduction must involve a causal reference to the soul. At least for him, the soul is the primary cause of all these activities.

Both "primary" and "cause" call for a few words of elaboration. To begin with, "cause" must be understood in a distinctively Aristotelian manner. As Aristotle himself tells us in *An.* II 4, the soul is the formal, final, and moving

[8] Johansen, *The Powers of Aristotle's Soul,* 116: "In Aristotle's survey of earlier thinkers, there is not a single one who appears to have accounted for the nutritive soul. The impression is created that Aristotle is innovating the study of the nutritive soul in a way which makes up for a major shortcoming in the predecessors' approach to psychology." Of course, this is not just an impression artfully created by Aristotle, but it is a hard fact about the ancient debate on and around the soul. More on this in due course.

cause of self-nutrition, growth, and reproduction in all the ensouled perishable living beings. Let us read the relevant text:

> The soul is a cause and principle of the living body. And these things are said in more than one way. At any rate, the soul is cause in three of the ways determined. For the soul is cause as (a) the whence motion comes, (b) that for the sake of which, and (c) the essence of ensouled bodies.
>
> Now, that the soul is cause as essence is clear, for the essence is the cause of being for all things, and being alive is the being of living beings, and the soul is their cause and principle. Moreover, the actuality is the account of what is in potentiality, and it is clear that the soul is the cause for the sake of which. *For just like* nous *creates for the sake of something, so too soul does in the same way, and this is its end. But the soul is this sort of things in living beings and in accordance with nature.* The reason is that all natural bodies are tools for the soul. And just as the bodies of animals, so too those of plants, are for the sake of the soul. For the sake of is twofold: of which and for which. But the soul is also the whence locomotion comes in the first place. Such a power is not present in all living beings. But both alteration and growth are in accordance with soul. For perception seems to be a kind of alteration, and nothing perceives which does not have a soul. Things hold in the same way with respect to growth and decay: nothing naturally decays or grows unless it is nourished, and nothing is nourished which does not participate in being alive. (*An.* II 4, 415b8–28; emphasis and translation are mine)

The soul works as the formal cause for the ensouled perishable living beings in the sense that it is the cause of their specific mode of existence, which is being alive as the kind of perishable living beings they are. Put differently, perishable living beings are alive as humans, cats, elephants, or plants because they are ensouled, and they are ensouled because they possess a specific kind of soul. What keeps them alive in their distinctive way is their own soul, which takes care of their nourishing, growth, and decline. The soul does so without being itself moved. According to Aristotle, the soul nourishes the living body as an unmoved mover. We can restate this point by saying that the nutritive soul controls the relevant activities involved in self-nutrition, growth, decline, and reproduction taking place in the living body without undergoing any change itself. A further key point for Aristotle is that the goal of these activities is the soul itself. It is also a point that is often missed in the secondary literature: the living body is at most a beneficiary of these activities, but it should not be mistaken with the goal (*to hou heneka*). For Aristotle, the goal is the soul, not the living body, and *the soul acts from within the living body as an immanent goal.*

The words highlighted in italics at the end of the previous paragraph are important for my argument. *Nous* too acts for the sake of a goal. In the above passage, however, Aristotle makes it very clear that the soul does *not* act in the way *nous* does. *Nous* acts as an external agent. Unlike *nous*, the soul does not act as something separate. This explains how the soul, unlike *nous,* enters as the key ingredient in natural teleology. For Aristotle, all goals in nature are intrinsic and there is simply no place in his scientific treatment of nature for the implementation of goals by means of an external agent. Articulating Aristotle's position with greater precision and greater detail is not called for here.[9] What matters for my present purposes is that the causal involvement of the soul in the explanation of self-nutrition, growth, and reproduction must meet all the strictures of Aristotle' theory of causality as outlined in *Physics* II.

The causal involvement of the soul in self-nutrition is a case of *direct* involvement of the soul. As Aristotle himself says, it is the soul that does the nourishing (with the soul being *to trephon*, and the living body *to threphomenon*):

> Since there are three things – (a) that which is nourished, (b) that by which it is nourished, (3) and that which does the nourishing – *that which does the nourishing is the primary soul* [*sc.* the nutritive soul], that which is nourished is the body that possesses this soul, and that by which it is nourished is the nourishment. [...] *And that by which it is nourished is twofold, just as in the case of the pilot the hand and the rudder, the former being the moved mover and the latter being the moved thing.* All nourishment must be capable of being concocted, and the heat produced concoction. *That is why every ensouled being has heat.* (*An.* II 4, 416b18–29: emphasis and translation are mine)

It is important to see that for Aristotle the soul is the primary but not exclusive cause of self-nutrition. On his account, some internal fire understood as natural heat is also necessary – but only as a contributory cause (*sunaition*).[10] In his *De anima*, as well as elsewhere, Aristotle goes out of his way to argue that biological growth cannot be explained as the result of the action of fire alone.[11] At the same time, he is adamant that the presence of internal natural heat alongside the soul is necessary. The action of this heat is controlled and shaped by the nutritive power of the soul. Aristotle illustrates this point with the help of the example of the hand and the rudder. Both the hand of the pilot and the rudder are required for navigation to take place. One cannot steer a ship, and so one cannot have an instance of navigation, without a rudder and the hand of a pilot. If I understand the analogy correctly, the hand is the equivalent of the vital heat with which the soul nourishes the living body; just as the pilot uses the hand as a tool to steer the ship, so the soul uses the vital heat as its tool. The rudder is then, on this reading, the equivalent of nourishment employed for the nourishing.

---

[9] For more on this point, I refer the reader to Menn, "Aristotle's Definition of the Soul", 117–128; Johansen, *The Powers of Aristotle's Soul,* 116–127, and Corcilius, "Soul", 13–34. They all endorse a version of the traditional reading I sketch out in the main text. I remain skeptical of the alternative solution recently offered by Jessica Gelber (in Gelber, "Aristotle on Seed", 104–121).

[10] The word is borrowed from Plato (*Plt.* 281D and 289D, and *Ti.* 46D).

[11] For another key passage where Aristotle insists on the need for nature (soul) understood as a final cause *in addition to fire* in any scientifically adequate explanation of natural (biological) processes, I refer the reader to the very end of *Generation of Animals* (*GA* V 8, 780b3–15). Aristotle singles out Democritus as his critical target in this passage.

There is, for our purposes, at least one other important aspect in the pilot-hand-rudder causal chain. I will come back to it momentarily. For the time being, let me insist on the *non-expendable* nature of the hand. Change cannot be transmitted from the pilot to the rudder without using a hand. In this sense, the causal chain envisioned by Aristotle is not like the one we find in the case of the hand-stick-stone. The hand can move the stone without employing a stick, so the stick is an *expendable* moved mover.[12] By contrast, the hand of the pilot is an *indispensable* moved mover. When we transfer this result to self-nutrition and growth, we can conclude that both the nutritive soul and some internal, natural heat must always be present at the same time. Let us refer to this fact as the necessary co-presence of the nutritive soul and some internal, natural heat.

Here is how Aristotle envisions this integration of fire and soul at the most general (and most abstract) level:

> (a) The nature of fire seems to some people to be the cause of nutrition and growth. For it alone of bodies and elements appears to nourish and increase itself. And for this reason, one might think this to be at work in both plants and animals. (b) *But while this is in a way a co-cause, it is not simply a cause, but rather the soul is [a cause].* (c) For the growth of fire proceeds indefinitely, as long as there is something burnable, but for everything composed by nature there is a limit and a proportion (*logos*) in size and growth. These are features of soul rather than fire, and of an essence (*logos*) rather than matter. (*An.* II 4, 416a18–29; emphasis mine)

So much for Aristotle and his own account of self-nutrition, growth, and reproduction, which crucially involves the soul as the proper cause of these life activities. It is time to turn to Plato's *Timaeus*, where we will see how Plato relates self-nutrition to respiration.

3. Nutrition and Respiration in Plato's *Timaeus*

Let us begin with what is more obvious before turning to what is less obvious and is also more controversial: *there is nothing equivalent to the nutritive soul in Plato's Timaeus*. And this is so for at least two reasons. To begin with, Plato, unlike Aristotle, sees no connections between nutrition, growth, and decline on the one hand, and reproduction on the other. Quite tellingly, his account of self-nutrition and his account of reproduction are offered in different parts of his likely story. His account of reproduction is given in a coda at the very end of the *Timaeus* where an account of the generation of the sexual parts is also given. By contrast, the phenomenon of self-nutrition is approached by dealing with the human body and the way in which this body sustains itself. But we are in a

---

[12] Unless the stone is outside of our reach, or we use the stick as a lever to move a heavy stone, we normally do not need to posit any intermediate between the hand and the stone.

completely different conceptual scenario from the Aristotelean one outlined above for another, more important, reason. In the *Timaeus,* the explanation of self-nutrition, understood as the complex process by which the human being takes in food and transforms it into blood, makes no reference to the soul. For Plato, the soul is not involved in the explanation of how a human being (and more generally any perishable living being) assimilates the relevant nourishment.

It is worth recalling, briefly, how the assimilation of nourishment and its distribution in the living body is explained in the *Timaeus*. Plato invokes *the image of an irrigation system* that pumps the digested nourishment in the form of blood to all the corners of the human body by means of the blood vessels. It is worth pausing to reflect on the choice of this image. An irrigation system is something that is set up by *nous*, not by soul. Unlike (an Aristotelian) soul, *nous* is separate from the living being. Whatever is done by *nous* (whether it is a divine *nous* like Plato's demiurge or a human *nous* makes no difference here) is *not an instance of natural teleology*. Think of a gardener who has connected all the relevant pipes to a source (e.g., a cistern) so as to supply all the plants in the garden with enough water to sustain them through the dry season. Once the irrigation system is set up, the gardener need not be present. In fact, the gardener can attend to other more urgent business, or can even go on vacation, because the irrigation system works on its own. In other words, the irrigation system does not require the presence of the gardener. In fact, the whole point of installing an irrigation system is to free oneself from having to water the plants in our garden. Contrast the idea of the irrigation system with the Aristotelian image of the hand of the pilot steering the rudder. The hand always has control of the rudder, and the pilot must be present on board the ship. As Aristotle himself tells us in *Physics* II, not only is the presence of the pilot the cause that explains why the ship has made it safely to harbor, but also the absence of the pilot is the cause that explains why the ship sank (*Phys*. II 3, 195a11–14).[13] Also in light of this, we can safely conclude that the image of the irrigation system and the one of the hand steering the rudder entail different, indeed competing, conceptions of causation.[14]

Let us look more in detail at how the analogy of the irrigation system works in the case of the living body. Water is pumped to all the plants in the garden so as to help them live through the dry season. In an analogous way, blood is pumped to all the corners of the human body for as long as the latter is alive. But how does Plato envision the irrigation system at work? In this context, Plato famously invokes another image: the fish trap. The internal structure of the fish trap envisioned by Plato as working in the human body is made of air

[13] Repeated *verbatim* in *Metaph.* V 2, 1013b12–16.

[14] At some point the analogy breaks down: the pilot is a self-mover whereas the soul is an unmoved mover.

and fire. This fire plays a key causal role in breaking down the food that descends into the stomach of the human being. Inhalation and exhalation (breathing in and out) also play a crucial role; they are jointly responsible for the oscillation of the fish trap in the human body, which is required for the fire to be in constant motion so as to be able to cut the food inside the stomach and to constantly pump food-turned-into-blood into the blood vessels and move the blood away from the stomach to the rest of the body. In dealing with this stretch of text, interpreters routinely speak of self-nutrition and respiration as distinct physiological processes. I do not think that this manner of speaking quite captures the strong integration that Plato envisions between self-nutrition and respiration.[15] Hard as it may be for us to place ourselves in Plato's shoes, we need to try our best: there is a single system, analogous to a hydraulic system, working on its own to sustain the human body for as long as the latter is alive. This system does not need the causal intervention of the soul. Quite the opposite. Let us read the relevant passages:

> *The gods proceeded to fashion the irrigation system as follows.* We will come to see it more easily if we can first agree on this point. Whatever is made up of smaller parts holds in larger parts, while whatever consists of larger parts is incapable of holding in smaller parts. Of all the elemental kinds, fire is made up of the smallest parts, and that is the reason why it can pass through water, earth, and air and any of their compounds. Nothing can hold it in. Now we must apply this point to our stomach. When food and drink descend into it, the stomach holds them in, but it cannot hold in air and fire, consisting as they do of a smaller part than it does. *And so, the god availed himself of air and fire to conduct moisture from the stomach to the blood vessels.* He wove together an interlaced structure of air and fire, something like a fish trap. At its entrance it had a pair of funnels, one of which in turn he subdivided into two. And from the funnels he stretched reeds, as it were, all around throughout the structure, right to its extremities. All the interior parts of this network he made of fire, the funnels and the shell he made of air. (*Ti.* 77E–78c3, trans. Zeyl, emphasis mine)[16]
>
> He took this structure and set it around the living thing that he had fashioned in the following way. The funnel part got inserted into the mouth, and, consisting as it did of two funnels, he let one of them descend into the lungs down the windpipe, and the other alongside the windpipe into the stomach. He made a split in the first one and assigned each of its parts a common outlet by way of the nostrils, so that when the one part fails to provide passage by way of the mouth, all of its currents also might be replenished from that one. The shell, the other part of the trap, he made to grow around the hollow part of the body, and he made this whole thing flow together onto the funnel – gently because they are made of air – and now, when the funnels flow back, he made the interlaced structure sink into and through the

---

[15] Shroeder, "Replenishment and Maintenance", 317–346, is a refreshing exception to the rule.

[16] Note how Plato switches from the plural (gods) to the singular (god) in the passages I italicized for the sake of emphasis. This is no slip of the pen but an intentional choice on the part of Plato the writer. The lesser gods imitate the divine demiurge, so they apply the same (perfect) rules of rationality in the production of the irrigation system. Switching from plural to singular is perfectly alright in this context: the demiurge and the lesser god are instantiation of the same productive rationality.

body, a relatively porous thing, and pass outside again. The interior rays of fire bound from side to side, he made to follow the air as it passed in both directions. *This process was to go on nonstop for as long as the mortal living being holds together, and this is the phenomenon to which the name-giver* (so we claim) *assigned the names of 'inhalation' and 'exhalation'. This whole pattern of action and reaction irrigating and cooling our bodies, supports their nutrition and life.* (*Ti.* 78c3–78e5, trans. Zeyl, emphasis mine)

The fire cuts up the nourishment [in the stomach] and as it follows the breath it oscillates inside us. As the oscillation goes on, the fire pumps the cut-up bits of nourishment from the stomach and packs them into the blood vessels. This is the mechanism by which the stream of nourishment continues to follow throughout the bodies of all living beings. The bits of nourishment, freshly cut up and derived from things like themselves – from fruits or from vegetables which the god had caused to grow for this very purpose, to serve as nourishment – come to have a variety of colors as a result of being mixed together but a reddish color pervading them predominates, a character that is the product of the cutting and staining action of fire upon mixture. This is why the color of the liquid that follows in our bodies looks like the way we have described, this liquid we call blood, which nourishes our flesh and our whole bodies. From this source the various parts of our bodies are watered and so replenish the supports of the depleted areas. *Both processes, the replenishment and the depletion, follow the manner of the movement of anything within the universe: everything moves toward that which is of its own kind.* (*Ti.* 80d3–81a2, trans. Zeyl, emphasis mine)

The details of the explanation offered in the above passages are notoriously difficult.[17] What matters to us is only this: replenishment is needed because the air and the fire surrounding the living body are responsible for its depletion.[18] As a result, the lesser gods contrive a replenishing system that is based on the fish trap. What is especially interesting about this replenishing system is that it is envisioned as a closed system that works for as long as the perishable living body breathes in and out. While *Aristotle sees a close connection between self-nutrition and reproduction*, to the point that he is willing to trace both life activities back to one and the same soul, namely the nutritive soul, *Plato sees an important connection between self-nutrition and respiration.* Aristotle has a great deal to say on Plato's account of respiration in the so-called dialectical section of his own treatment of respiration. There is much that he does not like about what Plato says on the topic. Here are his most important complaints:

The circular thrust (periôsis) described in the Timaeus *has made no determinations at all as to the way in which the preservation of the heat occurs in the other* [sc. *nonhuman*] *animals*, whether it is the same process or it is due to some other cause. (*Juv.* 11 [= *Respir.* 4], 472b6–9, emphasis and translation are mine)

Furthermore, *the mode of causation is a fabrication*. (*Juv.* 11 [= *Respir.* 4], 472b12, emphasis and translation are mine)

Furthermore, with respect to that for the sake of which this whole process is present in animals (I mean inhaling and exhaling), *those who speak in this way have said nothing at all but deal with it as if they were dealing with a mere concomitant fact (sumptôma).* And yet,

[17] On how to think about the fish trap see, most recently, Pelavski, "Physiology in Plato's *Timaeus*", 61–74 and Schroeder, "Replenishment and Maintenance", 317–346.

[18] *Ti.* 77a1–3.

we see that these processes have control over life and death: when animals that breathe can no longer do so, then their destruction ensues. (*Juv.* 11 [= *Respir.* 4], 472b24–27, emphasis and translation are mine)

Aristotle levels three main criticisms against Plato. To begin with, because of its programmatic restriction to the human body, it is unclear how Plato's account applies to non-human animals. As soon as we move away from the human being, and move down the *scala naturae*, it becomes increasingly more difficult to see how this account is supposed to work. We can elaborate further on this first point by noting that in the passages from the *Timaeus* I quoted above, Plato speaks of the mortal living being, not of the human being. A perceptive reader may legitimately wonder what sort of changes (if any) we must make if we want to extend Plato's account beyond the central case of the human being, or the case of the land animals equipped with lungs. It remains unclear how Plato would like to answer this question. Furthermore, at least for Aristotle, the mode of causation envisioned by Plato is a fabrication. The air that is inside the body goes out, the outside air goes inside, and the two pockets of air exchange their places due to the fact that there cannot be any void in the natural world. Note that, in his account of how this happens, Plato takes the whole process to begin with exhalation. By his lights, the hot air inside the human body goes out first in virtue of the principle that like is attracted by like. It is only at this point that the air which surrounds the body moves in. Aristotle objects to this reconstruction by arguing that it is an implausible piece of fiction. Among other things, it reverses the correct order in which the process we call respiration unfolds: first inhalation, then exhalation. Finally (and this is the most important criticism) respiration so understood is a merely coincidental result or a concomitant fact – a *sumptôma*. By "*sumptôma*" Aristotle means something that happens at the same time as something else, but it is not related to it in any causally meaningful way. At most, we can say that the process as envisioned by Plato is coopted so as to obtain a new result. This new result is the moving up and down of the fish trap, the breaking down of ingested nourishment, and the nutrition of the living body. And yet, there is no causal relation (or, at the very least, no casual relation of the relevant kind) between being alive and respiration in Plato's account. *Respiration happens at the same time as we are alive, and for as long as we are alive, but we cannot trace it back, either directly or indirectly, to the soul understood as our own principle of life.*

With this we have reached an important conclusion: self-nutrition and respiration are closely connected in Plato's mind. However, the explanation of how they jointly work so as to keep the human body alive does not involve any reference to the soul. As a result, we can say that self-nutrition combined with respiration (to be understood as a single process of replenishment) are necessary for life in the sense that we cannot live if we do not nourish ourselves and do not breathe, and we live for as long as we are capable of doing so. But this does not amount to a life activity (again one activity rather than two) if by "life activity" we mean an activity that can be traced back to the soul as the principle of life. Quite the opposite: at least for Plato, this activity of constant replenishment does not require a direct causal involvement of the soul. As a result, it is not properly or strictly speaking a life activity even if life is contingent upon the perishable living body performing this activity.

4. Plato on Living Beings and Life

As we reflect on the different ways in which Aristotle and Plato approach the topic of self-nutrition, growth, and reproduction, it becomes clear that *Aristotle and Plato are not only operating with different conceptions of causation, but they are also working with different conceptions of the soul.* Aristotle is enlarging the domain of the soul in an unprecedented way. By contrast, Plato is on this front much closer to his predecessors than we may initially think. In fact, he agrees with them on this very point.[19] We come to a similar conclusion when we turn to Plato's notion of the living being (*zôion*).

We have seen that the human being has a body that is constantly depleted by the surrounding air and fire.[20] As a result, the human being requires nourishment to keep its body constantly replenished. To this end, in addition to designing the irrigation system as well as the fish trap, the lesser gods – understood as the relevant manifestation of practical rationality (*nous*) at this stage of the cosmogonic account – need to provide for suitable nourishment. They solve this problem by creating *another living being* (ἕτερον ζῷον):

> the cultivated trees, and more generally the plants, with the fruits and seeds they produce. (*Ti.* 77a6, trans. Zeyl)

All this is well known and relatively uncontroversial. Let me make just two points in connection with this aspect of the likely story offered in Plato's *Timaeus*. At this stage of the story, there are no perishable living beings next to the human being. There is only the human being, to which the lesser gods now add another living being. The outcome of this observation is that we must place a great deal of emphasis on ἕτερον. Plants cannot be just another living being next to the human being. Plants must be another *kind* of living beings. In other words, they must be sufficiently different from the human beings to serve as their food. The story told by Plato works only if the two kinds of living beings are separated by a real (that is, categorical) difference. This leads me to my

---

[19] This is true regardless of our ability to shed light on any intellectual debt Plato may have incurred on this front. Our ability to trace Plato's claims back to particular medical sources is notoriously limited.

[20] *Ti.* 77a1–3.

second point: it would have been very easy for Plato to demote plants to the status of nonliving things. And yet, he chose not to do so. The ancient (pre-Aristotelian) debate on and around plants is quite complex, and I do not need to recall it.[21] In fact, it does not take a great deal of imagination to envision a scenario in which the lesser gods create plants as non-living beings – regardless of what Plato's predecessors and contemporaries may have thought on the topic of plants. But this is emphatically not how Plato proceeds: he does not demote plants to the status of nonliving things; rather, he takes the opposite route adding, quite emphatically, that

> everything that partakes of being alive (ζῆν) may *justly and with perfect truth* be called a living being (ζῷον). (Ti. 77b1–3, trans. Zeyl, emphasis mine)

In this passage, Plato establishes an etymological connection between being alive (ζῆν) and living being (ζῷον). I will come back to this connection momentarily. For the time being, however, let me focus on another aspect of his likely story. Since Plato endorses the view that plants are perishable living beings, one may legitimately wonder what exactly he has in mind when he calls them ζῷα. Any attempt to answer this question entails a reference to "the third kind of soul".[22] This is the soul that Plato locates between the midriff and the navel, and the powers that he associates with this soul are *aesthesis,* understood as the capacity to feel pleasant and painful sensations, and the power to have appetitive desires. What Plato tells us in the *Timaeus* may not be sufficient to settle the question of how Plato envisions these powers to be working in plants.[23] In fact, I suspect that Plato has little interest in pursuing this topic. What matters to me in this context is this: Plato seems to be willing to ascribe a rudimentary form of cognition in the form of pleasant and painful sensations to plants. This also seems to be the reason why he insists, quite emphatically, that plants are rightly and justly called a different (kind of) living being (ζῷον).

This last observation brings me to the larger question of how Plato uses the word "living being" in the *Timaeus.* When we look at the actual use that Plato makes of ζῷον in the *Timaeus*, we discover that he uses this term to refer to things as different as:

1. the *cosmos*, which is described as an intelligent, ensouled ζῷον (*Ti.* 30b1), and a visible ζῷον containing all the ζῷα that there might be (*Ti.* 30d3–31a1).
2. the *fixed stars* and the *planets*, which are described as ζῷα (*Ti.* 92b5).

---

[21] Diogenes of Apollonia may have argued that plants are non-living beings. For one thing, he makes respiration *the* sign of life, and he reportedly denied that plants breathe. For another, he sharply distinguished the mode of reproduction of plants (*phuesthai*) from the mode of reproduction of animals (*gignestai*).

[22] This is a clear reference to the doctrine of the tripartition of the soul as presented in *R.* IV.

[23] For an attempt to answer this question see Carpenter, "Embodied Intelligent (?) Souls", 281–303 [2021: 35–53]. Cf. Wilberding, "The Secret Sentient Vegetative Life", 249–268.

3. *animals*, which are called ζῷα (*Ti.* 92c2).

4. *plants*, which are collectively referred to as another (kind of) ζῷον (*Ti.* 77a5, and *Ti.* 77c3).

5. the *sexual parts* of the male and the female human being. Plato describes the male genitalia as "a self-willed and unruly ζῷον" which can be "driven crazy by desire" (*Ti.* 91a2).[24] With less drama, Plato speaks of the woman's uterus as a ζῷον with a desire for childbearing (*Ti.* 91c2).

At least at first sight, this looks like a quite confused (and confusing) shopping list. We can provide some order and structure to the items on the list with the help of the following remarks. By Plato's lights, there exist both perishable and imperishable living beings. Among the imperishable living beings, we can count the cosmos, the fixed stars and the planets. The earth is described as the first and most senior amongst the gods in *Ti.* 40c2–3. As a result, the earth too must be regarded as an ensouled ζῷον. Among the perishable living beings we can count plants, animals, and human beings. But note that, by Plato's lights, even the sexual parts of men and women are described as living beings. Toward the end of the *Timaeus* they are regarded as an inchoate form of life.

It is not immediately obvious what (if anything) these different kinds of things have in common so as to deserve to be called "living beings". One may be tempted to say that *self-motion* and *cognition* are what jointly hold all of them together. This would be in line with what Aristotle says about his predecessors when he tells us that they all identified in motion and cognition the basic signs of life. For one thing, this would confirm that Plato, like all his predecessors, sees the soul as being causally involved only in the explanation of motion and cognition. For another, this would underscore the narrow connection between soul and life that we have already seen at work in the explanation of nutrition and respiration. And yet, this interpretation does not solve all problems, especially if we keep in mind that cognition takes radically different forms for Plato. More directly, it is far from obvious that reason and "unreasoning *aisthesis*" have much in common.[25] There is a large and very deep gulf separating reason and unreasoning *aisthesis* and everything suggests that Plato does not want to bridge this gulf. Quite the opposite. It is not trivial that the divide between perishable and imperishable soul, as well as the distinction between the different kinds of perishable living beings, is cashed out in terms of presence or absence of reason and understanding. While plants have a share in pleasant and painful sensations plus appetites, they have no access to the

---

[24] I note, in passing, that Aristotle adopts a similar language in *Mot. An.* 11, 703b20–22. He speaks of each of these parts as a *separate* living being (ὥσπερ ζῷον κεχωρισμένον).

[25] It is an educated guess that Plato speaks of "unreasoning *aisthesis*" to underscore that there is a categorical difference between reason and *aisthesis*. This leads to the further question of what, if anything, holds them together *qua* forms of cognition.

higher forms of cognition which are based on *aisthesis.* And *a fortiori* they have no access to reason and understanding.

In sum, it is unclear how strong a unity Plato is presupposing behind his use of the word "living being" in the *Timaeus*. One thing is clear, however: *Plato's use of ζῷα in the sense of living beings is a theoretical achievement*. The emphasis that Plato places when he employs the word "living beings" (ζῷα) to plants suggests that this extension is not obvious. Quite the opposite: it is an extension that calls for defence and elaboration. This elaboration, I am afraid, is not given in the *Timaeus,* which is programmatically restricted to the account of the generation of the cosmos all the way to the generation of the human being. There is a great deal that is simply outside this scope. Plato is not obligated to give us this elaboration in *the Timaeus*. My guess is that he is not even interested in giving it – either in the *Timaeus* or elsewhere. But put yourself in the place of a thinker who, unlike Plato, is greatly concerned with these distinctions. This thinker may also be a person who, unlike Plato, has the ambition to provide an as complete as possible conceptual map of perishable life. This person will be deeply dissatisfied with the situation left by Plato. Aristotle is such a person. Part of the task that he sets upon himself in his study of the soul consists in trying to tackle the difficult questions left unanswered by Plato. I mean questions such as the scope of the domain of the soul, how exactly we should think about the connection between soul and life, and the connection between different forms or levels of life and different kinds of living beings.

It is emphatically *not* a coincidence that Aristotle's *De anima* begins with the statement that the soul is a sort of principle of living beings (οἷον ἀρχὴ τῶν ζῴων).[26] This is a statement which is, to say the least, vague. Part of what follows in Aristotle's *De anima* is a long and complex attempt to articulate this claim. Elsewhere I argued that this claim is to be taken as equivalent to an indistinct whole.[27] It is the sort of thing one starts with at the outset of a scientific investigation. While it is a true claim, it is also a claim which requires a great deal of conceptual work to be turned into a scientific truth. This is not the place to look at this conceptual work in any detail. Let me only say that this conceptual work results in a complete reconfiguration of the domain of perishable living beings. The most important outcome is this: ζῷα will no longer be equivalent to living beings as suggested in Plato's *Timaeus*. More directly, the etymological connection that Plato establishes between living being and being alive is broken in Aristotle's *De anima.* Except for the opening statement (and another passage in *An.* I 1) the term ζῷον is used to refer to a specific kind of perishable living beings: animals (including the human

[26] *An.* I 1, 402a6–7.

[27] Falcon, "*The Architecture of the Science of Living Beings*", 29 fn. 50.

beings), to the exclusion of plants.[28] For sure, the great divide that separates animals from plants is confirmed by Aristotle. But Aristotle, unlike Plato, is now able to speak of plants as a distinct kind of living beings. Plants are engaged in self-nutrition, growth, and reproduction, but all these life activities can be fully explained with reference to the nutritive soul without making any reference to cognition. There is a clear link that connects Aristotle's expansion of the soul beyond the case of cognition and motion to his ability to identify a specific non-cognitive kind of life, namely plant life.

The task Aristotle sets for himself in his *De anima* is to provide a theoretical foundation for his own science of perishable living beings. It is far from shocking to discover that this theoretical foundation entails a drastic revision of some of the most significant results reached by Plato. But this observation only confirms that when it comes to the topic of the soul as the source of life there was a serious disagreement separating the two philosophers. Tracking their disagreement can help us better appreciate the reasons Plato and Aristotle had to approach the topic of life in their own distinctive way.

Bibliography

Bolton, Robert, "The Origins of Aristotle's Natural Teleology in *Physics* II", in: Mariska Leunissen (ed.), *Aristotle's Physics: A Critical Guide*, Cambridge 2015, 121–142.

Carpenter, Amber, "Embodied Intelligent (?) Souls: Plants in Plato's *Timaeus*", *Phronesis* 55 (2010), 281–303. [Reprinted, with minor changes, in Fabrizio Baldassarri / Andreas Blank (eds.), *Vegetative Powers: The Roots of Life in Ancient, Medieval, Early Modern Natural Philosophy*, Cham (Switzerland) 2021, 35–53.]

Corcilius, Klaus, "Towards a Science of Life: The Cosmological Method, Teleology, and Living Things", in: Liba Taub (ed.), *The Cambridge Companion to Ancient Greek and Roman Science*, Cambridge 2020, 58–78.

–, "Soul, Parts of the Soul, and the Definition of the Vegetative Soul", in: Fabrizio Baldassarri/Andreas Blank (eds.), *Vegetative Soul: The Roots of Life in Ancient, Medieval, and Modern Natural Philosophy*, Cham (Switzerland) 2021, 13–34.

Falcon, Andrea, *The Architecture of the Science of Living Beings. Aristotle and Theophrastus on Animals and Plants*, Cambridge 2024.

Gelber, Jessica, "Aristotle on Seed", in: Caleb M. Cohoe (ed.), *Aristotle's* On the Soul*: A Critical Guide*, Cambridge 2022, 104–121.

Johansen, Thomas Kjeller, *Plato's Natural Philosophy: A Study of the Timaeus-Critias*, Cambridge 2004.

–, *The Powers of Aristotle' Soul*, Oxford 2012.

[28] For example, Aristotle can say that being alive (ζῆν) belongs to all living beings (ζῶσι), but animals (ζῷα) alone have a share in sense-perception because there is more to animals than merely being alive (ζῆν). See *An.* II 2, 413a22. (Cf. *Juv.* 1, 467b18–25 and *passim.*) More on this front in Falcon, "*The Architecture of the Science of Living Beings*", Chapter 1.

–, "From Craft to Nature: The Emergence of Natural Teleology", in: Liba Taub (ed.), *The Cambridge Companion to Ancient Greek and Roman Science*, Cambridge 2020, 102–120.

Menn, Stephen, "Aristotle's Definition of the Soul and the Programme of the *De anima*", *Oxford Studies in Ancient Philosophy* 22 (2002), 83–139.

Pelavski, Andrés, "Physiology in Plato's *Timaeus*: Irrigation, Digestion, and Respiration", *The Cambridge Classical Journal* 60 (2014), 61–74.

Schroeder, Lea Aurelia, "Replenishment and Maintenance of the Humam Body (*Timaeus* 77 A-81 E)", *Apeiron* 54 (2021), 317–346.

Wilberding, James, "The Secret Sentient Vegetative Life of Plants", in: Peter Adamson / Rotraud Hansberger / James Wilberding (eds.), *Philosophical Themes in Galen*, London 2014, 249–268.

Zeyl, Donald J. (trans.), *Plato's* Timaeus, Indianapolis, Ind. 2000.

Soul and Essence in the *Phaedo:* Socrates' Final Proof and Aristotle's *Categories*

Riccardo Chiaradonna

1. Plato's Eponymy: Forms, Characters, Particulars

Socrates' final proof in the *Phaedo* shows that the soul cannot perish because life belongs essentially to it (this is a tentative paraphrase: as we shall see below, the term 'essentially' does not appear in the *Phaedo*). The demonstration involves several steps, and I will focus on *Phd.* 102, where Socrates begins the argument that will lead to the conclusion that the soul is (essentially) alive and brings life to whatever it occupies, just as fire is (essentially) hot and brings heat to whatever it occupies, snow is (essentially) cold and brings coldness to whatever it occupies, three is (essentially) odd and brings oddness.

The passage begins with Phaedo speaking in his own voice as narrator and recapitulating the agreed conclusion from the first part of the demonstration. There, separate Forms are presented as genuine causes: this is the "straightforward, amateurish and perhaps simple-minded [i.e. uninformative]" (*Phd.* 100d3–4) view that certain characters are based on the participation of the respective object in Ideas bearing the same name: "nothing makes it beautiful other than that Beautiful's presence, or association, or whatever its mode and means of accruing may be" (100d4–6).[1] So, as Phaedo says:

> When these points of his [Socrates] were accepted and it was agreed that each of the forms exists and that other things receive a share of and are named after the forms themselves […] (102a10–b3).[2]

The existence of Forms is therefore agreed upon, and the same holds for eponymy, i.e. the relation in virtue of which participants are named after the Forms themselves. The example illustrating this view is Simmias' participation in largeness and smallness, which explains Simmias' being larger than Socrates and smaller than Phaedo:

---

[1] For the translation of Plato's *Phaedo*, see Sedley and Long, *Plato:* Meno *and* Phaedo. The text in 100d6 is dubious, but this is irrelevant to the present discussion.

[2] Ὡς μὲν ἐγὼ οἶμαι, ἐπεὶ αὐτῷ ταῦτα συνεχωρήθη, καὶ ὡμολογεῖτο εἶναί τι ἕκαστον τῶν εἰδῶν καὶ τούτων τἆλλα μεταλαμβάνοντα αὐτῶν τούτων τὴν ἐπωνυμίαν ἴσχειν […].

> [...] [I]t isn't in Simmias' nature to exceed because of being Simmias, but rather because of the largeness that he happens to have. And do you agree that, again, he does not exceed Socrates because Socrates is Socrates, but because Socrates has smallness relative to his largeness? [...] and again that he is not exceeded by Phaedo because Phaedo is Phaedo, but because Phaedo has largeness relative to Simmias' smallness (102c1–9)?[3]

Scholars have convincingly emphasized that Plato introduces three items here:

1: Forms (i.e. the Form of largeness)

2: Characters in particular participants (i.e. largeness in Simmias)

3: Particular participants (Simmias who happens to have largeness).[4]

As David Ebrey remarks, "Socrates thinks that a commitment to the forms themselves and to things having a share in these forms automatically brings with it a commitment to immanent forms," since "[...] when something has a share of largeness, there is something about it – something 'in it' – that it makes it appropriate to call it 'large' in certain situations."[5] This cannot be the Form, because separate Forms are unchangeable and cannot be destroyed, whereas the immanent forms either retreat or perish when their opposite approaches. Socrates argues that neither Forms nor characters admit contraries; therefore, neither Largeness itself nor largeness in Simmias can ever admit smallness, i.e. neither Largeness itself nor largeness in Simmias can ever be small. Participants can instead admit opposites with due qualification: for example, Simmias is larger than Socrates, but smaller than Phaedo (102B–D). In explaining this section, David Sedley has insightfully suggested that Plato's discussion of largeness in the *Parmenides* sheds light on this argument: largeness is identical with the capacity to exceed, while smallness is identical with the capacity to be exceeded (*Prm.* 150c6–e1). Accordingly, largeness in Simmias is to be identified with his power to exceed, and Simmias exercises this power only when he exceeds someone:

> When he stands next to Socrates, who is smaller than him, his largeness advances; when he stands next to Phaedo, who is larger than him, it retreats again. Largeness is for Plato definable as the capacity to exceed, so Simmias' own largeness will be his own particular capacity to exceed others, which is determined by his particular height, say six feet.[6]

---

[3] οὐ γάρ που πεφυκέναι Σιμμίαν ὑπερέχειν τούτῳ, τῷ Σιμμίαν εἶναι, ἀλλὰ τῷ μεγέθει ὃ τυγχάνει ἔχων· οὐδ' αὖ Σωκράτους ὑπερέχειν ὅτι Σωκράτης ὁ Σωκράτης ἐστίν, ἀλλ' ὅτι σμικρότητα ἔχει ὁ Σωκράτης πρὸς τὸ ἐκείνου μέγεθος; [...] Οὐδέ γε αὖ ὑπὸ Φαίδωνος ὑπερέχεσθαι τῷ ὅτι Φαίδων ὁ Φαίδων ἐστίν, ἀλλ' ὅτι μέγεθος ἔχει ὁ Φαίδων πρὸς τὴν Σιμμίου σμικρότητα;

[4] I would mention Turnbull in particular, "Aristotle's Debt", 132: "[...] it is surely no distortion of the Phaedo to claim that its ontology includes individuals, characters, and forms." The present article is indebted to Turnbull's seminal work, both for the account of Plato's eponymy and for the parallel between Plato's account of eponymy in the *Phaedo* and Aristotle's views on names and predication in the *Categories*.

[5] Ebrey, *Plato's* Phaedo, 257.

[6] Sedley, "The *Phaedo*'s Final Proof", 215.

What matters for the present account is that Simmias can continue to exist and remain himself, while contrary characters come to be in him and cease to exist: this view is conveyed by the contrast between Simmias, who possesses his own identity, and the largeness that Simmias happens to have (*Phd.* 102c1–3, see below). Socrates makes this distinction clear when he answers Cebes' objection that this view goes against the first proof, which is based on the idea that things come from their opposites:

> […] [W]e were talking about the things that have the opposites, naming them after those opposites, whereas now we're talking about those opposites themselves, from whose presence inside them the things that are named get their labels. We are saying that the opposites themselves would never be willing to admit coming to be one another (*Phd.* 103b6–c2).[7]

Here we find the distinction between opposites themselves and things that have opposites and are named after the opposites present in them. It is a matter of debate whether Plato admits the existence of Ideas of objects or natural substances such as human being or fire.[8] But it can hardly be denied that Plato's examples of Forms in this section include not Forms of objects, but Forms of opposite attributes, such as large/small, hot/cold, alive/dead, odd/even. When Plato says that particular participants are named after the Forms, he is not suggesting that Simmias is named 'human' after the Form Human, or that particular instances of fire are named 'fire' after the Form Fire. There is no indication that when Socrates says "it isn't in Simmias' nature to exceed because of being Simmias" (*Phd.* 102c1–3), he is suggesting that Simmias partakes in the Form Human Being and happens to be large in addition to this fact. Eponymy involves not Forms of objects, but Forms of attributes. Socrates' point is that particular participants (e.g. Simmias, the large individual) are named after the attributes ascribed to them ('large', 'small', 'hot', 'cold', etc.), and these attributes are grounded in inherent characters that are in turn grounded in separate Forms. Note that particulars have a crucial position in the later part of Plato's final proof, since, as Sedley puts it, "it is vital to insist that the essential bearers (e.g. soul and fire), are particulars" because they are "a distinct range of *immanent* entities capable of occupying or withdrawing from individual

---

[7] […] περὶ τῶν ἐχόντων τὰ ἐναντία ἐλέγομεν, ἐπονομάζοντες αὐτὰ τῇ ἐκείνων ἐπωνυμίᾳ, νῦν δὲ περὶ ἐκείνων αὐτῶν ὧν ἐνόντων ἔχει τὴν ἐπωνυμίαν τὰ ὀνομαζόμενα· αὐτὰ δ' ἐκεῖνα οὐκ ἄν ποτέ φαμεν ἐθελῆσαι γένεσιν ἀλλήλων δέξασθαι. Here I cannot focus on the analogies and differences between this passage and Plato's statements on qualities and qualified objects in the *Theaeteus* (*Tht.* 182a3–b7).

[8] See Sedley, "Plato and the One-over-Many Principle" who suggests that in dialogues such as the *Phaedo* and the *Republic* Plato admits Forms of opposites and Forms of (human) artefacts, but not Forms of natural kinds or their parts. The situation changes in the *Timaeus*: there Plato abandons his doubts about man, fire and water, and he does so – as Sedley suggests – on the ground that man, fire and water, like the table and couch in *R.* X, are artefacts, albeit divine artefacts.

things."[9] Essential bearers have the alternative options of retreating and perishing, whereas Forms cannot perish in any way. If this is the case, we may wonder whether the lines quoted above (*Phd.* 102c1–9) convey any specific view of the status of particular participants.

2. Essences and Necessary Attributes

This question intersects with a much-debated issue, i.e. whether Plato regards participants as particular objects or rather as mixtures or bundles of characters or Form-instances. Scholars are sometimes inclined to find in the *Phaedo* an anti-essentialist account of particulars as bundles or mixtures of characters, which would be consistent with what Plato says elsewhere, more precisely in the *Timaeus*.[10] Wolfgang-Rainer Mann provides a particularly clear example of this approach, as he compares the status of participants in the *Phaedo* to quasi-Anaxagorean mixtures, where Plato's formal characters play a role similar to Anaxagoras' elemental stuffs. Note that, according to this reading, there are, strictly speaking, no sensible 'objects' constituted from the elements, since objects are nothing else than "mixtures of bits or portions of stuffs".[11] Mann finds evidence for his interpretation in Plato's distinction between unchangeable/uniform vs changeable/multiform items (*Phd.* 78D, 80B).[12] Sensible particulars are multiform because they 'are' (though only derivatively) a variety of different things. Accordingly, as Mann argues:

> [...] There really are no genuine things, because there is nothing to being such a particular 'thing' besides being a certain mixture. So any time the mixture is changed, we have a new 'thing' (because the proportions of the elemental stuffs in the mixture are different). But each mixture can be thus changed in every way. Hence there is no genuine alteration (as opposed to substantial change); rather, all cases of what we ordinarily take to be change are really instances of the generation or perishing of mixtures, in other words, instances of rearranging the eternal, elemental stuffs. And hence there also is nothing the 'thing' actually is. Whatever it 'is', it merely becomes.[13]

However, the evidence in support of Mann's interpretation is meager, and the section of Plato's *Phaedo* investigated in this article goes against his reading (see below).[14] Francesco Ademollo has argued instead that in the *Phaedo* and elsewhere sensible particulars are conceived as unstable and ever-changing in

---

[9] Sedley, "The *Phaedo*'s Final Proof", 213.

[10] For a recent discussion, see Meister, "The Ontology of Images in Plato's *Timaeus*".

[11] Mann, *The Discovery of Things*, 112.

[12] Mann, *The Discovery of Things*, 119.

[13] Mann, *The Discovery of Things*, 124.

[14] Against Mann, see the critical remarks in Ademollo, "On Plato's Conception of Change", 70 fn. 59; Betegh, "The 'In' Relation". On these issues, see also the discussion in Turnbull, "Aristotle's Debt", 137–140.

the specific sense that, where there seems to be one and the same object persisting through time, there is in fact a succession of impermanent objects numerically distinct from each other but similar to one another (*entia successiva*).[15] I will not enter into this debate here, except to note that if we apply Mann's account to the example of Simmias, we should regard largeness as a part or component of that particular mixture that we call 'Simmias', but which in fact has no permanent identity. As Mann himself admits, however, this reading is implausible.[16] Plato regards Simmias as possessing his own identity and largeness as a characters inhering in him or, rather, as something which Simmias happens to 'have': "For presumably it isn't in Simmias' nature to exceed because of being Simmias, but rather because of the largeness that he happens to have" (*Phd.* 102c1–3). The same vocabulary occurs with regard to Socrates and smallness in Socrates, and with regard to Phaedo and largeness in Phaedo: "And do you agree that, again, he does not exceed Socrates because Socrates is Socrates, but because Socrates has smallness relative to his largeness? [...] and again that he is not exceeded by Phaedo because Phaedo is Phaedo, but because Phaedo has largeness relative to Simmias' smallness?". In other words, Simmias, Socrates and Phaedo are not conceived of as mixtures or bundles of characters; rather, they are 'what they are', and they are named after the characters of smallness and largeness which they happen to possess.

If anything in Plato resembles Aristotle's distinction between essential predication and inherence in the *Categories*, it is certainly what we find in this passage, as Alan Code has remarked:

> Aristotle would, I think, find in the *Phaedo* the doctrine that a word may be applicable to an object either in virtue of what that object Has or in virtue of what that object Is. The word 'large' is applicable to Simmias not in virtue of what he Is, but rather in virtue of the largeness that he Has.[17]

What requires further scrutiny, however, is not the idea that we apply the word 'large' to Simmias in virtue of what Simmias has (i.e. largeness), but that we apply other words in virtue of what he is. What words are these? It is tempting to infer that Plato is alluding here to predicates like 'human being' or 'animal', and that we find in this passage from the *Phaedo* the same notions at work in Aristotle's *Categories*. Simmias is a human being in virtue of what he is (the species human being is a secondary substance, and it is essentially predicated of Simmias), while Simmias is large in virtue of what he has (largeness). Nevertheless, I am inclined to disagree, and I think we should give full weight to Plato's choice to not use the species term 'human' but instead proper names such as 'Simmias', 'Phaedo' and 'Socrates': the emphasis is on the individual

---

15 See Ademollo, "On Plato's Conception of Change".

16 See Mann, *The Discovery of Things*, 132–133.

17 Code, "Aristotle: Essence and Accident", 427.

as such, not on the individual insofar as he is ranked under a species.[18] It is worth recalling that Socrates mentions Simmias and 'largeness in Simmias' as a preliminary step in his argument and as an example to introduce the three items necessary for his final proof, i.e. opposite Forms, opposite characters and particular participants named after the opposites. After focusing on Simmias, largeness and smallness, he then uses the three items to convey the status of a special set of participants, such as fire, snow, soul and triplets, which are not only named after the opposites in them (hot, cold, alive and odd), but "always possess the opposites, and they too seem not to admit whatever form is opposed to the form inside them; instead, when it attacks, evidently they either perish or retreat" (*Phd.* 104b8–c1). In addition, such participants bring their permanent character to whatever they occupy. As noted earlier, eponymy deriving from Forms involves opposite attributes such as 'large' and 'small', and does not involve species-membership. In other words, Simmias does not appear in this argument insofar as a being endowed with some nature that depends on a Form (such as the Form Human Being) and is reflected in essential predication. Plato does not oppose 'being human' and 'being large', but he carefully states that it is not in Simmias' nature to exceed because of being Simmias; he then repeats the same point about being Socrates and being Phaedo.

Two kinds of items are implied in Plato's argument: Simmias (who happens to be large) and 'what Simmias is'. Socrates clearly explains that individuals such as Simmias, Phaedo and Socrates are 'what they are' in virtue of their individual souls, as he says in a famous exchange with Crito:

> Gentlemen, I'm not convincing Crito that I am Socrates here, the one who is now holding a conversation – setting out remarks one by one. Instead he supposes that I'm that corpse which he'll shortly be seeing, and he actually asks how he should bury me. As for the argument I have spent a long time propounding, that when I drink the poison I won't stay behind in your company any longer, but will depart and be gone to some happy state fit for the blessed, I seem to be wasting my breath on him, while reassuring both you and myself (*Phd.* 115c6–d6).

Stephen Menn has persuasively emphasized the importance of this passage in Plato's argument, showing that only the soul guarantees the individual's identity through time.[19] Menn's conclusions, it seems to me, can be applied to Plato's reference to what Simmias is in 102C. In other words, I would suggest that in opposing what Simmias is and what Simmias has (e.g. largeness), Socrates is not opposing species-membership based on participation in Forms (Simmias is what he is insofar as he partakes in the Form Human Being) and the inherence of non-essential properties. Rather, he is focusing on the fact that

[18] See also *Phd.* 102e3–5: "I myself, for example, do admit and withstand smallness and, while still being this same who I am [ἔτι ὢν ὅσπερ εἰμί], am small."

[19] See Menn, "On Socrates' First Objections to the Physicists", 60–61.

an individual such as Simmias, whose identity is grounded in his individual soul, is called 'large' because of the largeness inhering in him.

The individual Simmias, who happens to be large, is in fact composed of Simmias' body and Simmias' soul, since, as Socrates says, "[...] aren't we ourselves part soul, part body?" (*Phd.* 79b1–2)[20] and the body is the visible part of the human being (τὸ ... ὁρατὸν αὐτοῦ) (80c2–3). A few remarks are in order here. The soul-body composition in the *Phaedo* is, so to speak, the composition of two entities that remain discrete: the soul – which is incorporeal and the bearer of Simmias' or Socrates' identity (Simmias' soul is what Simmias is, Socrates' soul is the one who is holding the conversation with Crito) – and the body. Socrates characterizes the body, or rather 'what is corporeal' (σωματοειδές), as 'heavy, weighty, earthy and visible' (*Phd.* 81c8–9), opposing it to the invisible and incorporeal Forms, and he also emphasizes that bodies are multiform and impermanent (*Phd.* 80C).[21] I cannot dwell on the details here, but I would just note that Plato's composition differs from Aristotle's hylomorphism: within the framework of Plato's *Phaedo*, the bodies of living beings are not potentially alive. The body is only derivatively alive (it is alive only insofar as the soul, which is an incorporeal and self-subsistent entity, happens to be present in it), so that there is no difference between the body of Socrates talking to Crito and the corpse of Socrates (note the difference with Aristotle's so-called 'homonymy principle'). There are therefore three senses of 'Simmias': (a) his soul (what Simmias is), (b) his visible and tangible body (which is something like a corpse that happens to be vivified by the soul in it), and (c) the composite of Simmias' soul and Simmias' body, where the two items, while being related, remain ontologically discrete. 'Largeness' belongs to the composite Simmias insofar as the body is part of it (accordingly, largeness does not belong to 'what Simmias is', i.e. to his soul). The soul is certainly not one of the characters that make up Simmias' body, and the soul is neither an essential nor an accidental character, but a permanent self-subsisting incorporeal entity that gives life to the body.

One might ask how this account can be applied to the 'bringers' mentioned in the later part of the argument, and more precisely to entities such as fire or snow, which can hardly be associated with an individual soul grounding their identity through time. It seems to me that explaining the status of the 'bringers' in terms of the Aristotelian notion of 'essential predication' can be misleading (I agree with Ebrey, who suggests avoiding the term 'essential').[22] O'Brien, for

[20] [...] ἄλλο τι ἡμῶν αὐτῶν τὸ μὲν σῶμά ἐστι, τὸ δὲ ψυχή;

[21] See the remarks in Betegh, "The 'In' Relation": here Plato "starts to apply the apparently newly coined word, *sōmatoeidēs*, body-like, or bodily, corporeal, to designate collectively the otherwise disparate members of the visible kind [...]." The term covers not only the organic bodies of animals and other ensouled beings, but all physical entities.

[22] See Ebrey, *Plato's* Phaedo, 262–263.

example, remarks that Aristotle's distinction between essential and accidental is already at work in the *Phaedo*, although Plato does not have Aristotle's technical vocabulary to express it:

> Plato has no technical vocabulary for 'accidental' and 'essential' in this sense. In the present argument his simplest way of describing what we may call essential predication is by the use of 'always' and 'never'. Throughout the argument Socrates is made to repeat that fire is always hot and never cold, that snow is always cold and never hot, that three is always odd and never even, that two is always even and never odd. So ultimately Socrates will claim that the soul is always alive and never dead.[23]

I find these remarks unpersuasive. The distinction between 'essential' and 'accidental' predication is not part of Aristotle's vocabulary in the *Categories* (although it is part of the vocabulary of the ancient and modern commentators on the *Categories*). There Aristotle conveys the distinction between essential predication and inherence using a vocabulary that is very similar to (and probably inspired by) that in the *Phaedo*. Therefore, he distinguishes "what a substance is" (a particular horse is horse and animal: horse and animal are secondary substances, i.e. the species and genera under which particulars are ranked) from what inheres in the substance. This is reminiscent of Plato's distinction between 'being Simmias' and what Simmias has or what is 'in Simmias'. Plato's point in 102E that individuals can admit (δέχεσθαι) contraries while still being the same individuals is similar to Aristotle's point that an (individual) substance can receive contraries while remaining one in number and the same (Arist. *Cat.* 5, 4a10–11).[24] An important difference between Plato's and Aristotle's vocabulary, however, lies in the use of proper names, which is crucial in Plato (Simmias, Phaedo and Socrates *are* Simmias, Phaedo and Socrates, whereas they happen to *have* smallness and largeness) and conspicuously absent in Aristotle, who refers to particular substances through expressions like "a particular human being" or "a particular horse" (*Cat.* 5, 2a13–14; I will return to this issue later). What I want to suggest is that (*pace* O'Brien) Plato obviously had all the resources to say, for example, that fire is essentially hot or that hotness is part of the essence of fire or of 'what fire is'. However, Plato does not adopt this vocabulary and prefers a more cautious approach. He therefore prefers to speak of "things that are not opposites of one another, but always possess the opposites, and they too seem not to admit whatever form is opposed to the form inside them" (*Phd.* 104b8–10).[25] Plato's vocabulary in this section is perhaps not as clear as we might hope, but it is significant that he conveys the relationship between the opposites and their bringers using the same verbs,

[23] O'Brien, "The Last Argument of Plato's *Phaedo*. I", 200.

[24] Μάλιστα δὲ ἴδιον τῆς οὐσίας δοκεῖ εἶναι τὸ ταὐτὸν καὶ ἓν ἀριθμῷ ὂν τῶν ἐναντίων εἶναι δεκτικόν. On this, see Beere and Betegh, 'Body and Substance in Aristotle's *Categories*'.

[25] ὅσα οὐκ ὄντ' ἀλλήλοις ἐναντία ἔχει ἀεὶ τἀναντία, οὐδὲ ταῦτα ἔοικε δεχομένοις ἐκείνην τὴν ἰδέαν ἣ ἂν τῇ ἐν αὐτοῖς οὔσῃ ἐναντία ᾖ.

ἔχει and δέχεσθαι, that he applies to the relationship between Simmias and the largeness which Simmias 'has'. In other words, Plato does not say that hotness is or shows 'what fire is' or 'the essence of fire'. The contrast he draws separates what something 'happens to possess' (Simmias happens to possess largeness [... τῷ μεγέθει ὃ τυγχάνει ἔχων], 102c2–3) and what something 'always possesses' (fire always possesses hotness: ἔχει ἀεὶ τἀναντία, 104b8–9): this contrast is different from that between what something is and what something has. If we really want to translate Plato's argument in Aristotelian terms, we could say that the opposites stand in relation to their bringer in the same ways as items such as inseparable or *per se* accidents stand to their subjects: they are not part of their essence, while at the same time being, so to speak, grounded in the essence and necessarily associated with it (note that odd and even are Aristotle's examples of non-essential *per se* attributes in *Anal. Post.* I 4 and that Plato's claim that the threeness is such that it is never deprived of the odd [104A] is comparable to that view).

I suggested above that when Plato mentions 'being Simmias', 'being Socrates' and 'being Phaedo', he is not actually referring to some essential feature, but to the (individual) souls of Simmias, Socrates and Phaedo. Souls guarantee the identity of particulars through time, whereas bodies have no genuine diachronic identity. What about fire, for example? I think that Plato is deliberately silent about the essence of fire or 'what fire is'. Answering this question would perhaps have required a digression on the essential and geometrical principles of the elements, rather than a digression on the 'Idea of Fire'.[26] However, it is perfectly understandable that Plato does not go into such detail in the *Phaedo*, where his focus is on the soul and its immortality. Whatever Plato's view of the 'Idea of Fire' may have been, I would emphasize again that his account of eponymy does not involve any reference to the essence of physical objects or elements. Eponymy is the relation according to which participants are named after the Forms of opposites, and this relation entails that participants have characters based on the Forms and inhering in them; in addition, some participants *always* possess the opposites, and they do not possess whatever character is opposed to those within them. But this does not mean that the opposites are 'the essence' of the participants. Note that my point is not that the opposites are not the essence of the participants, while other characters are; rather, my

[26] A different reading can be found in Trabattoni, *From Death to Life*, 165–166, who regards the reference to the Idea of Fire as a necessary element in Plato's argument. Sedley, "The *Phaedo*'s Final Proof", 213 persuasively argues that ἰδέα in *Phd.* 104D does not involve any reference to separate Forms: "The natural solution [...] is to take ἰδέα as meaning, not a transcendent Form, but a 'character' in a metaphysically less restricted sense. This suggestion is borne out by the fact that ἰδέα has nowhere hitherto in the *Phaedo* or in any dialogue likely to predate it been used as a term for a transcendent Form. Its use in that sense is in fact unexpectedly rare in Plato." See also the insightful discussion in Centrone, *Platone:* Fedone, 230 fn. 166.

point is that the essence of the participants is not classified among their properties or characters. Thus, the soul is necessarily alive, but this does not imply that life is part of the soul's essence. Instead, according to my account, life is a necessary feature of the soul that is grounded in the soul's essence.

3. The Background of Aristotle's *Categories*

I have emphasized that Plato's distinction in this section can be viewed in parallel with Aristotle's ontology in the *Categories*. There Aristotle distinguishes particular substances, general substances, particular properties and general properties (the 'ontological square') (*Cat.* 2, 1a20–b9). Properties are 'in' substances, whereas general substances are said of (i.e. essentially predicated of) particular substances. As noted earlier, Aristotle's distinctions are interestingly similar to those we find in the *Phaedo*. Furthermore, Aristotle opens the treatise by listing three types of items: homonymous, synonymous and paronymous items (*Cat.* 1, 1a1–15). Their definitions are famous: homonymous items are designated by the same name, but the definitions associated with that name are different (e.g. 'leg' applies to legs of animals and to legs of furniture, according to different definitions); synonymous items are designated by the same name, and the definitions associated with that name are the same (e.g. 'mammal' applies to horses and dogs, according to the same definition); paronymous items are called after the name *of something else* with a different ending. For example, the brave is so called after the name of bravery; the courageous is so called after the name of courage, etc.[27] This classification provides a framework for Aristotle's classification of genera and species in the *Categories*. Items in different genera are homonymous, and the same name is applied to them according to different definitions (e.g. 'mouse' is applied to animals and to computer equipment); items in the same genus are synonymous, and the same name (i.e. the name of the genus) is applied to them according to the same definition (i.e. 'mammal' is applied to horses and to dogs); paronymous items are those designated by terms deriving from the names of properties inhering in them: for example, 'the brave' is a human being who has bravery.

Let us now consider the distinction between 'IS predication', i.e. essential predication, predication expressing what something is, and 'HAS predication', i.e. the so-called 'accidental predication' expressing what something has i.e. its properties. In the first case, subject and predicate are synonymous: when I predicate 'animal' of 'horse', 'animal' is the name of a genus, and this name is

[27] *Cat.* 1.1a12–13: παρώνυμα δὲ λέγεται ὅσα ἀπό τινος διαφέροντα τῇ πτώσει τὴν κατὰ τοὔνομα προσηγορίαν ἔχει (see *Cat.* 8, 8b25–26; 10a27–28; 10a30–32; 10b9–10). This sketchy account of paronymy is indebted to Fait, "La predicazione linguistica", 33.

applied to the horse according to the definition of 'animal': as Aristotle explains in the *Categories*,

> [...] the primary substances admit the definition of the species and of the genera, and the species admits that of the genus; for everything said of what is predicated will be said of the subject also (*Cat.* 5, 3b2–5).[28]

In other words, synonymous predication expresses essential species and genus membership. In 'HAS predication', the predicate is instead a paronymous term deriving from the name of a property and expressing the inherence of that property in a subject: so when I predicate 'loyal' of 'dog', I mean that a property whose name is 'loyalty', and not 'loyal', inheres in dogs.[29] In the *Metaphysics*, Aristotle applies these distinctions critically to Plato's theory of Ideas. Consider the Idea 'Human' and its participants. Either (a) 'human' is applied to the Idea and to participants according to the same definition (synonymous predication), but this jeopardizes the very distinction between Ideas and participants, since they are of the same nature or essence, or (b) 'human' is applied to them according to a different definition (homonymous predication), but this jeopardizes any causal connection between Ideas and participants, since they are disparate items. Note that Aristotle's criticism is aimed precisely at Ideas of natural substances like 'Human':

> And if the Ideas and the particulars that share them have the same Form, there will be something common to these [...]. But if they have not the same Form, they must have only the name in common, and it is as if one were to call both Callias and a wooden image a man, without observing any community between them (Arist. *Metaph.* I 9, 991a2–8).[30]

Let us now return to the *Phaedo*. 'Homonymous' is part of Plato's standard vocabulary: the term means that the same name is applied to Ideas (as a proper name) and to participants. For example, 'beautiful' is applied both to beautiful things and to the Form Beautiful. Accordingly, Socrates asks in the *Phaedo*:

> What about the many beautiful things, such as people or horses or cloaks or any other things whatsoever that have that particular property [ἄλλων ὡντινωνοῦν τοιούτων]? Or again, things that are equal, and so on for all the things that share the names of those entities we mentioned [πάντων τῶν ἐκείνοις ὁμωνύμων]? Do they stay in the same state, or, in quite the opposite way to those entities, are they virtually never in the same state at all, either as themselves or as one another (*Phd.* 78d10–e4)?

Once again, it is worth noting that 'homonymous' does not refer to the names of objects. It is not sensible horses that are homonymous with the Form Horse;

---

[28] Trans. Ackrill, *Aristotle's* Categories *and* De Interpretatione.

[29] A borderline situation occurs when the same term can be taken as the name of a property and as a term deriving from that name: e.g. 'white' is both the name of the property whiteness and a term deriving from that property, meaning that whiteness inheres in a subject: 'the white (horse)' (see *Cat.* 5, 2a29–34).

[30] Trans. Ross, in: Barnes (ed.), *The Complete Works of Aristotle*, Vol. 2.

rather, horses, cloaks and people, which have the property of being beautiful, are homonymous with the Form Beautiful. This is the same situation that Socrates describes in *Phd.* 102, where he elucidates this fact by stating that participants receive a share of the Forms themselves and are named after them. In other words, eponymy means that participants are homonymous *vis-à-vis* the Forms.[31] As Socrates explains, "[...] now we're talking about those opposites themselves, from whose presence inside them the things that are named get their labels [περὶ ἐκείνων αὐτῶν ὧν ἐνόντων ἔχει τὴν ἐπωνυμίαν τὰ ὀνομαζόμενα]" (*Phd.* 103b7–c1).

It is at least possible that in the *Categories* Aristotle sets out from Plato's vocabulary while making some crucial corrections to it.[32] First of all, Aristotle's homonymous items are definable objects designated by sortal terms (names) such as 'animal', so that homonymy does not (or at least does not primarily) concern paronymous predicates such as 'beautiful' or 'equal'. As Aristotle says: "Thus, for example, both a man and a picture are animals" (*Cat.* 1, 1a2–3). Eponymy disappears from Aristotle's picture and is replaced by paronymy (large vs largeness), which designates the inherence of non-substantial properties in substantial subjects. This seems somewhat ironic: whereas Plato's eponymy points to the metaphysically fundamental fact that participants are named after Forms (i.e. beings in the full and proper sense, *ousiai*), Aristotle's paronymy and the inherence expressed through paronymy involve non-substantial properties that are inherent in substances. The underlying idea is that *ousiai* are not, as in Plato, Forms of which sensible items receive a share, but subjects to which everything else belongs. Substancehood is now identified with subjecthood (primary substances are primary subjects), and this is Aristotle's characteristically anti-Platonic move in the *Categories* (see *Cat.* 5, 2a34–b6c). Finally, Aristotle adds synonymy to the picture, and synonymy again points to his break with Plato's ontology: sensible particulars are endowed with essences as such (and not insofar as an incorporeal soul occupies them), so that the names designating species and genera are synonymously predicated of them.

It is perhaps no coincidence that proper names such as 'Simmias' and 'Socrates' vanish from Aristotle's *Categories*. In fact, primary substances are best understood as countable items (a particular man, a particular horse), which are the bearers or non-substantial items (properties) and essentially fall under sortals or kinds. Gareth B. Matthews calls this view 'Aristotle's principle': "Everything that exists is a something or other." Accordingly,

---

[31] See the remarks and list of references in Granieri, "The Referents of 'Being'", 349 fn. 3.

[32] My discussion is indebted to two classic papers: Turnbull, "Aristotle's Debt" and Striker, "A Note on the Ontology". The present outline obviously does not rule out that other dialogues are also in the background, in particular the *Timaeus*: see on this Beere and Betegh, "Body and Substance in Aristotle's *Categories*".

[t]here is no Socrates apart from there being a certain man, who is, at the same time, a certain animal and a certain living thing. [...] the relationship between Socrates and man (that is, 'human-ness') is not correctly thought of as a relationship between two quite separate things; rather, Socrates, in being the individual he is, is (already) an individual man.[33]

Christof Rapp conveys a similar view through the expression 'sortal determinacy': "It is by being a member of a species *F* that a primary substance is what it is, has its determinacy, identity and unity."[34] Aristotle's examples of primary substances ('a particular man', 'a particular horse') support conclusions like these: what Aristotle has in mind are not concrete particulars referred to by their proper names ('Socrates', 'Bucephalus'), but countable particulars referred to by sortal terms, i.e. countable particular instances of kinds. In a recent article on Aristotle's account of primary substances in the *Categories*, Francesco Ademollo has argued that Aristotle's primary substances are not ordinary particulars with all their properties, but particulars insofar as they are endowed with essential attributes:

[...] [A] primary substance is [...] an object which *does not encompass all of its attributes*, but only a relevant subset of them. More precisely, this subset consists of the substance's essential attributes and leaves out the accidental ones. Take an instance of "the concrete particulars of common experience", e.g. Socrates with all of his attributes; then strip it of its accidental attributes – his wisdom, his tallness, his being the son of Sophroniscus, etc. – by abstracting them away from it. What is left after this process is the primary substance.[35]

As I see it, Aristotle's reworking of the notions set out in Plato's *Phaedo* also includes his decision to designate essential synonymous predication with the verb *metechein* "to participate".[36] In this way, Aristotle achieves a subversion of Plato's conceptual apparatus. Whereas Plato mentions both eponymy and participation in describing the relationship between separate Forms and participants, Aristotle transforms eponymy into paronymy, which applies to the inherence of properties in substantial subjects, and employs the verb *metechein* in relation to synonymous essential predication, which indicates the species and genus membership of substantial subjects endowed with essences. Plato's account of predication and participation in the *Phaedo* thus provides a framework for elucidating the genesis of Aristotle's account of essence, inherence and predication in the *Categories*. This should not, however, be taken to mean that Plato anticipates Aristotle's basic views. Rather, Aristotle responds critically to Plato and modifies his master's picture. The changes introduced by

33 Matthews, "Aristotelian Categories", 149.

34 Rapp, "Essentialism in Aristotle's *Categories*", 42.

35 Ademollo, "The Anatomy", 151.

36 Aristotle defines μετέχειν as "admitting the definition of the thing in which something participates": ὅρος δὲ τοῦ μετέχειν τὸ ἐπιδέχεσθαι τὸν τοῦ μετεχομένου λόγον (*Top.* IV 1, 121a11–12; cf. IV 5, 126a17–25; V 4, 132b35–133a11). On the issues tackled in this paragraph, see the insightful remarks in Striker, "A Note on the Ontology", esp. 106.

Aristotle point to his break with Plato, since Aristotle replaces participation with the view that sensible particulars are primary substances, i.e. ultimate subjects endowed with essences that are subjects both for their kinds and for the properties inhering in them, so that "if the primary substances did not exist it would be impossible for any of the other things to exist" (*Cat.* 5, 2b5–6).[37]

Bibliography

Ackrill, John L. (trans. and comm.), *Aristotle's* Categories *and* De Interpretatione, Oxford 1963.

Ademollo, Francesco, "On Plato's Conception of Change", *Oxford Studies in Ancient Philosophy* 55 (2018), 35–83.

–, "The Anatomy of Primary Substances in Aristotle's *Categories*", *Oxford Studies in Ancient Philosophy* 60 (2022), 145–202.

Beere, Jonathan/Betegh, Gábor, "Body and Substance in Aristotle's *Categories*", forthcoming.

Betegh, Gábor, "The 'In' Relation and the Functions of the Receptacle in the *Timaeus*", forthcoming.

Centrone, Bruno (comm.), *Platone:* Fedone, traduzione e note di Manara Valgimigli, introduzione e note aggiunte di Bruno Centrone, Roma/Bari 2000.

Code, Alan, "Aristotle: Essence and Accident", in: Richard E. Grandy/Richard Warner (eds.), *Philosophical Grounds of Rationality: Intentions, Categories, Ends*, Oxford 1986, 411–439.

Ebrey, David, *Plato's* Phaedo: *Forms, Death, and the Philosophical Life*, Cambridge 2023.

Fait, Paolo, "La predicazione linguistica nelle *Categorie* di Aristotele", *Rivista di estetica* 26 (2004), 23–36.

Granieri, Roberto, "The Referents of 'Being' in Plato's *Sophist*", in: Luc Brisson/Edward Halper/Richard Perry (eds.), *Plato's* Sophist*: Selected Papers of the Thirteenth Symposium Platonicum*, Baden-Baden 2024, 349–356.

Mann, Wolfgang R., *The Discovery of Things*: *Aristotle's Categories and Their Context*, Princeton 2000.

Matthews, Gareth B., "Aristotelian Categories", in: Georgios Anagnostopoulos (ed.), *A Companion to Aristotle*, Oxford 2009, 144–161.

Meister, Samuel, "The Ontology of Images in Plato's *Timaeus*", *British Journal for the History of Philosophy* 30 (2022), 909–930.

Menn, Stephen, "On Socrates' First Objections to the Physicists (*Phaedo* 95e8–b8)", *Oxford Studies in Ancient Philosophy* 38 (2010), 37–68.

O'Brien, Denis, "The Last Argument of Plato's *Phaedo*. I", *Classical Quarterly* 17 (1967) 198–231.

[37] I have presented drafts of this contribution as papers at the Tübingen Conference and at the 2024 Southern Association for Ancient Philosophy meeting (Cambridge, Sept. 16–17, 2024). I would like to thank the audiences and the organizers for their insightful comments and remarks. I am also grateful to Roberto Granieri for valuable suggestions.

Rapp, Christof, "Essentialism in Aristotle's Categories: Some Queries and Suggestions", 2019, https://www.academia.edu/40326251/Essentialism_in_Aristotles_Categories_ Some_Queries_and_Suggestions.

Ross, W. D. (trans.), *Aristotle:* Metaphysics, in: Jonathan Barnes (ed.), *The Complete Works of Aristotle*, Vol. 2, Princeton NJ 1985.

Sedley, David, "Plato and the One-over-Many Principle", in Riccardo Chiaradonna/Gabriele Galluzzo (eds.), *Universals in Ancient Philosophy*, Pisa 2013, 113–137.

–, "The *Phaedo*'s Final Proof of Immortality", in: Gabriele Cornelli/Thomas M. Robinson/Francisco Bravo (eds.), *Plato's* Phaedo: *Selected Papers from the Eleventh Symposium Platonicum*, Baden Baden 2018, 210–220.

Sedley, David (ed.) and Alex Long (trans.), *Plato:* Meno *and* Phaedo, Cambridge 2010.

Striker, Gisela, "A Note on the Ontology of Aristotle's *Categories*, Chapter 2", in ead., *From Aristotle to Cicero: Essays in Ancient Philosophy*, Oxford 2022, 102–111.

Trabattoni, Franco, *From Death to Life: Key Themes in Plato's* Phaedo, Leiden/Boston 2023.

Turnbull, Robert G., "Aristotle's Debt to the 'Natural Philosophy' of the *Phaedo*", *Philosophical Quarterly* 8 (1958), 131–143.

On the Meaning of αἰτία and Bringing

Participation, Mereological Predication and Property Transmission in Plato's *Phaedo* 96A–105D

Peter Oxenknecht

1. Introduction

'So answer,' said Socrates. 'What is it such that, when it arises in any body, the body is alive?' 'It is soul,' he said. 'Now is this always the case?' 'Yes, of course,' he said. 'In that case, whenever soul occupies anything, does soul always come to it bringing life?' 'Yes, it does.' (105C–D).[1]

Ἀποκρίνου δή, ἦ δ' ὅς· ᾧ ἂν τί ἐγγένηται σώματι ζῶν ἔσται; Ὧι ἂν ψυχή, ἔφη. Οὐκοῦν ἀεί τοῦτο οὕτως ἔχει; Πῶς γὰρ οὐχί; ἦ δ' ὅς. Ψυχὴ ἄρα, ὅτι ἂν αὐτὴ κατάσχῃ, ἀεὶ ἥκει ἐπ' ἐκεῖνο φέρουσα ζωήν; Ἥκει μέντοι, ἔφη.

This line of questioning launches the *Phaedo*'s last argument for the immortality of the soul, in which Socrates infers the soul's indestructibility from the fact that *it always brings life* (105C–107A). The central notion of 'bringing' is developed in the prior section, 103B–105C, as part of the discussion of the "cause (αἰτία) of coming-to-be and ceasing-to-be" (95E). Socrates proposes this discussion to address the problems his interlocutor, Cebes, raised about the soul's supposed immortality (87A–88B). To understand Socrates' claim that the soul always brings life, we need to be clear about what αἰτία and 'bringing' in the relevant passage mean, and whether bringing can be classified as an αἰτία. In this contribution, I will argue that Socrates first establishes three conditions that an αἰτία has to meet to be successful: it must be responsible (in a necessary, sufficient and invariant way) for a thing having the property F. Next, he introduces his well-known participation scheme as meeting those conditions: participation in the form of F-ness determines things to have F (in a necessary, sufficient, and invariant way). Bringing, while not fulfilling those conditions, will emerge as an *intermediary* explanation: it exemplifies ways in which participation can come about. From the relevant passage, one can extract three different ways in which participation can come about: (i) participation plus entailment, (ii)

[1] Unless otherwise noted the translations are by Sedley and Alex Long. However, I modified this first quote in a crucial way, which will be justified in the last section of this contribution.

mereological predication, and (iii) property transmission between particulars. It turns out that, in the *Phaedo*, bringing does not refer to all cases in which an item forces another item to take on a property. The notion of bringing, rather, is tailored to grasp how the soul brings life to the living human being. It does so in two ways that correspond to (ii) and (iii): on the one hand, the soul itself is alive and imports its features to living human beings (soul-body composites) by being a part of them; on the other hand, it transmits the property of life to the body by coming into contact with it. As the relevant passage (95E–105C) is quite long and the positions in the secondary literature are numerous, I will first provide an overview of the text, then set the scene by sketching the pertinent secondary literature, and finally present my own position.

2. Setting the Scene

The relevant section can be divided into five parts:

(1) 95E: Socrates states the goal of studying "the cause (αἰτία) of coming-to-be and ceasing-to-be" (95E) as preparation for the last argument for (or last proof of) the immortality of the soul, which answers to the problems Cebes raised before (in Cebes' own words: 87A–88B; in Socrates' recapitulating words: 91D).

(2) 96B: Socrates discusses the αἰτίαι proposed by the natural philosophers and shows how their proposals generate puzzles.

(3) 97C–99D: Anaxagoras introduces teleological αἰτίαι but fails to use them (according to Socrates).

(4) 99E–101B: The hypothesis method is established as a "second voyage" to find the αἰτίαι. Forms are hypothesised, and Socrates presents the well-known participatory scheme: the presence of the form of F-ness makes things have F. Unlike the αἰτίαι of the natural philosophers, the presence of forms turns out to be an admissible candidate for an αἰτία.

(5) 102B–105C: Socrates develops the notion of bringing and characterises the soul as 'the bringer'[2] of life.

According to a prevalent opinion in the secondary literature, the passages (4) – (5) develop one overarching concept of αἰτία that also covers the notion of bringing. I will refer to such a reading that subsumes bringing under αἰτία as the 'one notion view'. The exact understanding (and translation) of αἰτία, however, is a matter of controversy; the two main contenders for translations of αἰτία are 'reason' and 'cause'. A proponent for the first option can be found in Gregory Vlastos. In his seminal paper "Reasons and Causes in the *Phaedo*",

[2] Plato doesn't use the noun 'bringer' himself, but employs the verb 'to bring' to characterize the doings of certain things. David Ebrey proposes to name them "bringers" (Ebrey, *Plato's Phaedo*, 249) which I will adopt in this contribution.

he defends the view that αἰτία in the *Phaedo* should not be translated as 'cause'. Rather, so he argues, the term refers to the answer to questions of the type 'Why is a thing F?', and gives us the reason, for example, why something is warm.[3] According to Vlastos, Socrates claims that the reason why a thing is warm consists in its participating in the form of warmth. Admissible answers to 'Why is x F?' questions are given by way of the participatory scheme: participating in the form of F-ness makes things F.

Furthermore, Vlastos proposes that the notion of bringing merely consists in amending the participatory scheme and can be put like this: F brings G iff the presence of F-ness makes a thing have F, and the form of F-ness entails the form of G-ness. That means, if a thing participates in F-ness and therefore has F, then it also participates in G-ness and therefore has G. For example, if the form of fire entails the form of warmth, then the particular fire always has to be warm.[4] Vlastos thus reduces bringing to (a) the well-known participatory scheme and (b) an added entailment relation between forms. As participating in the form of F-ness constitutes the αἰτία for a thing having F and bringing can be reduced to participation, Vlastos consequently dubs the 'bringers' "the 'clever' aitai".[5]

Not every commentator agrees with Vlastos's take on αἰτίαι and bringing, but many still subscribe to the 'one notion view'. David Sedley, for example, rejects Vlastos' reduction of both αἰτίαι and bringing to the participatory scheme.[6] According to him, the passages (4) – (5) instead establish three laws of causation that carve out those *items* that constitute the true causes.[7] If a thing conforms to those laws, it can rightly be called an αἴτιον.[8] Furthermore, according to Sedley, αἰτίαι should be understood as causes, rather than explanations, albeit Plato's concept of cause differs from our contemporary

[3] See Vlastos, "Reasons and Causes in the *Phaedo*", 292–296.

[4] See Vlastos, "Reasons and Causes in the *Phaedo*", 317.

[5] Vlastos, "Reasons and Causes in the *Phaedo*", 317. The name 'clever' comes from Socrates' talk of a more clever (κομψοτέραν, 105C) answer that refers to the bringers.

[6] Sedley, "Platonic Causes", 115–116. There, in footnote 2, he claims that he finds no "common ground" with Vlastos' paper as the latter stresses that only forms can be causes (in the *Phaedo*) whereas Sedley emphasizes that the metaphysical status of an object is irrelevant for it being a cause.

[7] "If x causes anything to be F (whose opposite is un-F) (1) x must not be un-F (2) x's opposite must not cause anything to be F (3) x must never cause anything to be un-F" (Sedley, "Platonic Causes", 121).

[8] For an enumeration of interpreters who advance those three laws, see Kanayama, "The Methodology of the Second Voyage and the Proof of the Soul's Indestructibility in Plato's *Phaedo*", 54. Those three laws also come up in Kelsey, "Causation in the *Phaedo*", 28–30. Sean Kelsey argues that Plato uses a teleological model of causation according to which causes follow a "rationally intelligible plan" (23) to bring about F as the purpose of that cause.

usage of that term.[9] Despite his differences with Vlastos, Sedley, too, holds that Plato works out a "unitary notion of" αἰτίαι with bringers falling under that concept.[10]

There have been detractors of the 'one notion view': Nicholas Denyer points out that Socrates never calls the bringers αἰτίαι nor uses the causal vocabulary that he employed along with the term αἰτίαι.[11] Dominic Bailey also alludes to the linguistic evidence and denies that bringing falls under causing.[12] I will refer to such a reading that differentiates between αἰτίαι and bringing as the 'two notions view'.

In this contribution, I will defend the 'two notions view' by showing that bringing does not satisfy the conditions that Socrates establishes for something to count as αἰτία: the αἰτία for something (x) to exhibit the property F has to be invariant, necessary, and sufficient. The 'participatory scheme' fulfils those conditions: participation in the form of F-ness is an invariant, necessary, and sufficient condition for a thing to exhibit F. The notion of bringing, however, will turn out to be only sufficient for a thing having F. Furthermore, regarding the items involved, it will emerge as a wider notion than participation in a form. Whereas participation refers to a relation between a form of F-ness and a particular F-thing, bringing encompasses relations between forms and particulars as well as between two particulars: the particular bonfire, for example, brings warmth to a particular pair of cold hands, just as the particular soul brings life to the body.

The claim that bringing comprises relations between particulars, however, is contested in the secondary literature.[13] The reason is a tricky, dilemma-generating passage in which Socrates maintains that the bringer x of the property G also awards its own defining feature F to the entity that receives G (104D–105A). In the case of the participation relation, this description can be explained easily: The form of fire (F-ness) entails the form of warmth (G-ness). By participating in the form of fire, a particular thing, say, a candle flame, exhibits the feature of fire (F) and also the entailed feature warmth (G). The

---

[9] For the point that αἰτία should be understood as 'cause', see Sedley, "Platonic Causes", 122, and Bailey, "Platonic Causes Revisited", 21. For a discussion of the contemporary usage of 'cause' and the supposedly Platonic one, see Sedley, "Platonic Causes", 124–125.

[10] Sedley, "Platonic Causes", 115. See for other commentators that endorse the 'one notion view': Kanayama, "The Methodology of the Second Voyage and the Proof of the Soul's Indestructibility in Plato's *Phaedo*", 73; Kelsey, "Causation in the *Phaedo*", 22; Stough, "Forms and Explanations in the 'Phaedo'", 24.

[11] Denyer, "The *Phaedo*'s Final Argument", 93.

[12] Bailey, "Platonic Causes Revisited", 25. For another critique of the 'one notion view', see: Ebrey, *Plato's Phaedo*, 265.

[13] Some authors assume Socrates only allows for forms to be bringers. See Vlastos, "Reasons and Causes in the *Phaedo*", 318; and O'Brien, "The Last Argument of Plato's *Phaedo*. I", 225–228.

particular bonfire, on the other hand, does not turn cold hands into fire themselves; it, therefore, does not award the cold hands with its own defining feature. Does that mean that only forms, but no particulars, can be bringers?

There are two strategies to face this problem: (1) As said before, some authors interpret Socrates as indeed allowing only forms to be bringers. As a consequence, those interpreters are confronted with the difficulty that, according to their reading, the text passage on bringing does not cover the *particular* soul as bringer. Insofar as a later passage frames the particular soul as bringer (the last argument for the soul's immortality, 105C–D), this reconstruction produces a tension between the two passages. I will later refer to this problem as the 'context-objection'. (2) The second strategy designed to resolve this tension, suggests that Socrates does not postulate the bringers of G to import their own defining feature F.[14] The particular fire that warms cold hands can be considered a bringer, even though it does not turn those hands into fire. By letting the passage on bringing cover the particular soul, this second strategy dissipates the tension but generates a new problem: it has to explain why Socrates first alludes to the bringers of G as importing their own defining feature F, but then supposedly drops that claim in order to encompass particulars like the aforementioned bonfire. The first strategy excludes particulars, the second one excludes a claim made by Socrates. As a result, both strategies produce tensions in the text.

I propose a third reconstruction that avoids the pitfalls of both strategies. To do this, I have to show how particulars that bring G can award the receiving entity with the bringer's defining feature F. The solution to this problem can be extracted from the explanandum of the passage (which is that of the whole *Phaedo*): the living human being, which can be analysed into a body-soul composite. The soul brings life in two different ways: (i) it transmits the property of life to the body, and (ii) insofar as the soul is alive itself, it brings life to the complex entity 'human being' by being a part of it. The second way of bringing life consists in mereological predication.[15] Through mereological predication, the soul not only brings its entailed feature of being alive (G) to the soul-body composite, but it also imports its own defining feature of being soul (F). *Insofar as the soul is part of the human being, the soul's defining feature can be predicated of the living human being.*

Mereological predication refers to a dyadic relation between two particulars whereby one particular awards (inter alia) its own defining feature F to another (more complex) particular. The working out of this solution allows particular beings to play the role of bringers and sheds light on the three ways of bringing:

---

[14] Theodor Ebert even argues that some bringers of G neither import their defining feature F nor exhibit G themselves (*Platon Werke: Band I, 4 Phaidon*, 383–389).

[15] F is mereologically predicated of a whole entity z iff (i) a part x of the whole z is said to have F, and (ii) the whole z only has F qua being partly composed of x.

(i) participation plus entailment, (ii) mereological predication, and (iii) property transmission. The first one holds between forms and particulars, the second one between particulars that stand in a part-whole relation to each other, and the third one between particulars that are both parts of a complex whole. After discussing what αἰτία and bringing mean, I will conclude by showing that none of the three ways of bringing classifies as an αἰτία.

I will start by arguing that the passage on the αἰτίαι of the natural philosophers (96B) implicitly puts forward three conditions that every αἰτία has to fulfil.

3. The Conditions for αἰτίαι

Socrates presents the section in which he discusses the notions αἰτία and bringing (99E–105C) as a response to issues that he encountered in his youth. As a young man, he tried to learn the αἰτίαι of "coming-to-be and ceasing-to-be" (95E) from the natural philosophers but was entrapped by puzzles and blinded (96C–97B) when he used their methods to explain growth (change in the state of maturity), height difference (change in the relations of being taller or smaller), and one becoming two (change in quantity). In this contribution, I will use the Greek term αἰτία without translating it into 'reason' or 'cause' in order not to introduce a potentially misleading concept into the reconstruction.[16] The term αἰτία designates the A in a wide range of relations shaped like 'A is responsible for B'.[17]

In the secondary literature, there is a dispute about what exactly is puzzling for Socrates in the proposed αἰτίαι of the natural philosophers.[18] As a

[16] Charlotte Stough proposes 'explanation' as a neutral term ("Forms and Explanations in the 'Phaedo'", 1). At the end of the contribution, I will concur that 'explanation' is a fitting translation for αἰτία. However, it is not neutral and excludes, for example, Sedley's reconstruction. He argues that the job of αἰτίαι is to "identify the thing responsible", see Sedley, "Platonic Causes", 122. An item alone, unlike a state of affairs involving an item, does not constitute an explanation: The heater in my room does not explain why my room is flooded with water. The fact that the pipes of my heater burst, on the other hand, does explain it. In order not to exclude a possible reconstruction, I will not translate αἰτία. Furthermore, instead of asking 'what explains B?' I will use the question 'what is responsible for B?'. The latter covers items as well as states of affairs that involve items. For example, if I ask: 'What is responsible for the flooding of my room?', one could answer by referring to the item, 'the heater', or the state of affairs, 'the bursting of the pipes of the heater'.

[17] At this point, I do not want to specify whether A and B refer to (particular or general) things, properties, processes, or states of affairs, which is why I use 'A' and 'B' and not the standard symbols.

[18] In the modern reader, this might provoke "meta-puzzles: what perplexes him is what there is in any of them [the puzzles] that Plato could have thought perplexing". (Vlastos, "Reasons and Causes in the *Phaedo*", 310).

consequence, there are also different reconstructions of how Socrates' own account solves those puzzles.[19] In the following, I will show how the accounts of the natural philosophers left Socrates "utterly blinded" (96C) and that he implicitly puts forward conditions that every account of αἰτίαι has to fulfil to avoid such blindness. Only after introducing those criteria, Socrates presents his own account of αἰτίαι. In light of the overall aim of my contribution, those αἰτίαι conditions play an important role: after reconstructing them and the notion of bringing, I will use the conditions to check whether bringing is a possible candidate for being an αἰτία.

As an example of how the αἰτίαι of natural philosophers lead to blindness, Socrates advances the process of 'one becoming two'. Natural philosophy would proffer as an αἰτία (i) the process of one instance of the number one getting closer to another instance of the number one, or (ii) one instance of the number one being divided. Why do those αἰτίαι lead to blindness on Socrates' part? He voices two misgivings:

> That I'm no doubt a long way indeed from thinking that I know the cause of any of these. I don't allow myself to say even that, when somebody adds one to one, either the one it was added to has become two or the one that was added and the one it was added to became two, on account of the addition of the first to the second. For then there comes to be a cause of coming to be two that is the opposite of the earlier cause. Back then, you see, it was because they were brought together into proximity with each other, and one was added to the other, but now it is because they are brought apart, and one is separated from the other. (96E–97C)

The (contemporary) reader might regard it as a category mistake to even attempt to explain "coming to be two" by the physical processes of "bringing in proximity" and "bringing apart" applied to numbers. According to Vlastos, the moral of Socrates' story about his youthful attempts is exactly that: a warning that one should not mix up arithmetical operations with physical processes.[20] However, that is not what bothers Socrates in the quote above. He does not just dismiss the αἰτίαι of the natural philosophers on the grounds that the mathematical and the physical belong to different realms. Rather – and this constitutes the first misgiving he has –, Socrates complains that if one asks 'What is the αἰτία of becoming two?' the answer 'one getting closer to another one' allows for two different cases: (i) the first one becomes two or (ii) the second one becomes two.

Hence, the answer is unsatisfactory because it allows for different concretisations. What seems to be one answer at first glance turns out to be two

---

[19] In Stough's view, for example, the failure of the natural philosophers (according to Socrates) lies in not discerning bearer from property and using a predicative statement as a "'partial' identity statement" (Stough, "Forms and Explanations in the 'Phaedo'", 6). In her reconstruction, Socrates' solution consequently consists of pointing out the difference between bearer and property.

[20] Vlastos, "Reasons and Causes in the *Phaedo*", 311–314.

answers and, therefore, does not pick out the A that is responsible for the B. In other words, the answer varies in itself. Spoken metaphorically, it leads to 'blindness' for Socrates because it does not single out one invariant A, which is why he cannot 'see' what constitutes A. Conversely, the first condition for αἰτίαι that pick out the responsible item and that avert blindness can be put like this:

(C1) Αἰτίαι have to be invariant.

By being invariant, an admissible αἰτία constitutes a stable point of reference, which cannot be said of the proposed material αἰτία for "coming to be two". Additionally, Socrates posits another qualm – the second misgiving – in the quote above: the same result ("coming to be two") is accounted for by two opposing αἰτίαι ("bringing in proximity" and "bringing apart"). Again, the material αἰτία turns out to be unsatisfactory: not only does it allow for *one* answer that varies in itself but also explicitly states two opposing answers. Why do αἰτίαι in such cases result in blindness? One cannot infer the thing responsible (A) from the result (B). This means that just looking at B and having the two possible αἰτίαι in mind, one cannot 'see' which one constitutes A. To show what constitutes A, αἰτίαι have to reduce the logical realm of possible A to one. Conversely, the second condition for successful αἰτίαι can be phrased in the following way:

(C2) Αἰτίαι have to be necessary for the 'B' they are responsible for.

If one proceeds like the natural philosophers, then there are also cases in which one and the same αἰτία results in two opposing states: a person can be taller than another person by a head, and the same person can be smaller than a third person also by a head (101A). This means that just by looking at A (the head) and having the two possible effects in mind, one cannot 'see' which one constitutes B. This time the material αἰτία (the head) is unsatisfactory because one cannot infer the result from the αἰτία. Conversely, this can be articulated as another condition:

(C3) Αἰτίαι have to be sufficient for the 'B' they are responsible for.[21]

In this vein, one can extract conditions for viable candidates for αἰτίαι from Socrates' presentation of the puzzles. Combining those conditions, one obtains the following 'αἰτίαι conditions':

(AC) Αἰτίαι have to be invariant, necessary, and sufficient for the 'B' they are responsible for.

To adopt a bird's eye perspective, it is not the case that Plato simply dismisses the αἰτίαι of the natural philosophers as categorical mistakes based on his (or our) ontological commitments, as Vlastos would have it. *We* might think that

[21] Bailey reconstruction of the text concurs with C2 and C3. According to him, Plato "adopts some strong form of the Principle of Sufficient Reason" (Bailey, "Platonic Causes Revisited", 16) which states that "causes must be not merely sufficient for their effects but also necessary" (ibid.).

one should not explain arithmetical operations through physical processes, but that alone would not move someone with different ontological commitments to adopt our distinction. Plato instead introduces ontologically neutral criteria that he extracts from our aim to single out the responsible αἰτία.[22] It is this aim that excludes the possibility of opposing answers. AC is not a substantial theory of αἰτίαι but puts forward minimal conditions for one.[23]

Until now, I have only used the symbol 'A' or the word αἰτίαι without clarifying whether they refer to items, processes, or states of affairs. Peculiarly, the αἰτίαι of the natural philosophers, according to Socrates, sometimes consist of physical things (a head, blood, fire, brain, bones, sinews) and sometimes of processes (eating and drinking, decomposing, bringing in proximity, bringing apart) that themselves involve different kinds of things (food and water, the hot and the cold, two instances of 1). At this point of the dialogue, Socrates constrains αἰτίαι neither to items nor to processes or states of affairs. However, if one reconstructs αἰτίαι as necessary and sufficient for B (as I did above), then A cannot consist of items. The physical things, bones and sinews, are not necessary conditions for Socrates to sit in prison, but the fact that he has a body is. The stone is not a sufficient condition for the window to break, but throwing the stone against the window is. If the αἰτίαι conditions are phrased as I have proposed, one would from the outset constrict viable candidates to processes or states of affairs (that involve items) and would exclude the possibility that αἰτίαι in the *Phaedo* only consist of items. So my phrasing of the constraints falls prey to Sedley's critique that

> [...] talk of necessary or sufficient conditions becomes unsatisfactory, since no causal theory could coherently describe such a thing, as distinct from some fact about the thing like its presence on the scene, as constituting any kind of 'condition'.[24]

According to Sedley, one should, therefore, refrain from framing αἰτίαι "in terms of necessary or sufficient conditions".[25] In the next chapter, I will argue for the claim that αἰτίαι refer to states of affairs, thereby neutralising Sedley's objection.

---

[22] Sedley instead aligns himself with the tradition that extracts three laws of causation (Sedley, "Platonic Causes", 121).

[23] Those conditions are standards of reason. Kanayama conjectures that the 'blindness' of the natural philosophers lies in the fact that they relied on their senses and did not employ those standards to work through the perceptual material. For the connection between blindness and this reliance, see Kanayama, "The Methodology of the Second Voyage and the Proof of the Soul's Indestructibility in Plato's *Phaedo*", 45. There he stresses that Socrates does not dismiss the use of senses entirely but only their unreflective usage.

[24] Sedley, "Platonic Causes", 121.

[25] Sedley, "Platonic Causes", 121.

4. Admissible Candidates for αἰτίαι

After indirectly putting forward the αἰτίαι conditions (AC), Socrates introduces two admissible types of αἰτίαι. The first being explanations that refer to an intelligence which orders everything to be in the best state. Such teleological explanations are the result of optimality reasoning. Lacking a teacher who could enlighten him on optimality reasoning and the nature of the good, Socrates turned to a "second voyage" (99D),[26] which consists of two parts (99E–100A): (1) refuge to λόγοι, and (2) the hypothesis-method. According to the latter, one hypothesises as a starting point the λόγος that one thinks to be the strongest (or the most robust). I cannot explain the problems surrounding that passage here. It suffices to say that Socrates continues investigating the αἰτίαι by assuming the following hypothesis:[27]

> 'Well then,' he said, 'I no longer understand those otherwise causes, and I can't recognise them either. Suppose someone tells me why something or other is beautiful, and says that it is because it has a vivid colour or shape, or some other such thing. I ignore those other explanations, because I am confused when they are all around me, and I keep the following at my side, in my straightforward, amateurish and perhaps simple-minded way: nothing makes it beautiful other than that Beautiful's presence, or association, or whatever its mode and means of accruing may be. For I don't go so far as to insist on this, but only that it is because of the Beautiful that all beautiful things are beautiful. (100D–E)

Starting from the hypothesis that there are forms, Socrates proposes to Cebes that the A that is responsible for B (the fact that a thing has the property F) is the presence of the form of F-ness. Socrates does not spell out how exactly the relation between F-things and the form of F-ness should be conceptualised, explicitly leaving it open. However, it is clearly a one-sided, asymmetric relation, in which the form F-ness determines a thing to have the character F.

---

[26] There is a lot of discussion on the topic of how one should understand the term 'second voyage'. See Yahei Kanayama for the view that Socrates just refers to the second voyage as second *in a temporal sense*, an attempt which takes part after the first one and for which one is better prepared by opting for a more secure kind of travelling (Kanayama, "The Methodology of the Second Voyage and the Proof of the Soul's Indestructibility in Plato's *Phaedo*", 95). See Ebrey for the contrasting claim that the second voyage is second in an axiological sense by being second best. According to that reading, the second voyage advances without knowledge (Ebrey, *Plato's Phaedo*, 228).

[27] The questions one would have to address are for example: Does λόγος refer to proposition, argument, theory, definition? And why does one have to take refuge in a λόγος if not does not want to be blinded? (See for a discussion: Kanayama, "The Methodology of the Second Voyage and the Proof of the Soul's Indestructibility in Plato's *Phaedo*", 46–51) Does the hypothesis include one or more λόγοι? How does the method ensure safety? And what does it mean to set down the thing as true which is in accordance with the hypothesis (100A) (See for a discussion of the latter question: Kanayama, "The Methodology of the Second Voyage and the Proof of the Soul's Indestructibility in Plato's *Phaedo*", 62 – 64; Ebert, *Platon Werke: Band I, 4 Phaidon,* 351–354; Ebrey, *Plato's Phaedo*, 237–243).

In the following, I will use two different ways to phrase that relation: 'presence of the form of F-ness makes things have F' and 'participating in the form of F-ness makes things have F'.[28] Both formulations refer to the same relation. This explanatory scheme complies with the conditions αἰτίαι have to fulfil (AC). For example, let B be the fact that a thing is tall. The A would then be the presence of the form of tallness. Although the latter can be phrased in more than one way – the presence of tallness/participation in tallness makes things tall – it refers invariantly to one and the same state of affairs and, therefore, satisfies C1. It does not matter, then, what concrete tall thing is referred to by B. In each case of a thing being tall, its tallness is necessarily generated by the presence of the form of tallness. If a thing is tall (B), one can infer from its being tall that it takes part in the form of tallness (A). The fact that B implies A imbues the answer 'it participates in the form of tallness' with the property of being necessary and secures its compliance with C2. Lastly, if 'presence of the form of tallness' takes the place of A, one can infer B, namely, a thing being tall. As a result, the participation-relation is sufficient for B. Hence, Socrates' hypothesised αἰτίαι fulfil C3.

Concerning Sedley's worry that αἰτίαι refer to items and for that reason should not be framed as conditions, we can respond that the quote above does not only mention items (the forms) but also states of affairs involving those items: According to Socrates, 'the presence of F-ness' or 'participating in F-ness' is responsible for things exhibiting F. It is, therefore, permissible to frame AC in terms of conditions. Furthermore, it is also admissible to render αἰτίαι as 'explanation' since it does not pick out items in isolation.[29]

The scheme 'participation in F-ness makes things exhibit F' allows for easy answers that satisfy AC. Demonstrating this simple path, Socrates replaces step by step some of the αἰτίαι from the puzzles of the natural philosophers with forms (101A–C). The result of that discussion establishes an answer that involves a certain type of thing, namely, forms. However, this scheme does not suffice to elucidate the relation between the soul, the body, and the body's property of being alive. Let us assume we want to single out the αἰτία of the fact that a body has the property of being alive. If one were to plug in the soul and the body into the established scheme, and treat the soul as the form, then

[28] The second version can be found in the *Phaedo* in formulations such as: 'F-things take a "share" (101C) in the form of F-ness'.

[29] Until now, I refrained from translating αἰτία with 'explanation' because in doing so, I would have excluded items as possible candidates for αἰτίαι since items alone do not constitute conditions (see fn. 15). Theodor Ebert argues that Plato was aware that only propositions and not things can constitute explanations and translates αἰτία, therefore, with the German 'Grund'. He also refers to Michael Frede who pointed out that in the *Phaedo*, Plato uses αἴτιον to indicate things involved in causal relations and αἰτία to indicate propositions involving those things (Ebert, *Platon Werke: Band I, 4 Phaidon,* 365–370). I am sympathetic to Ebert's translation but not convinced by Michael Frede's proposal.

the body's participation in that form would turn the body into a soul, the same way participation in the form of fire would turn a particular thing into fire. The participation scheme does not generate the desired effect of the body having life.

Socrates, indeed, does not just plug in the soul and the body in the established scheme, but introduces a further notion: bringing. The soul *brings* life to the body. According to Vlastos, bringing merely extends the established scheme and can be posited in the following way: if the form of F-ness entails the form of G-ness, and if a thing participates in F-ness and, therefore, has F, then it also participates in G-ness and, therefore, has G.[30] If the form of the soul entails the form of life, and the body participates in the form of soul, then it also participates in the form of life and, therefore, has the character of being alive.

I do not share the view that all cases of bringing are just an extended version of the participation-relation. Reconstructions that presuppose bringers to be forms all face the same problem that I dub the '*context-objection*'. It runs as follows:

If Plato were to conceptualise bringing in Vlastos' way, then the entity that 'brings' a property would be a form. Insofar as the soul is supposed to bring life, it has to be a form, too. Yet, forms are eternal (78B), which means that the soul is eternal qua being a form, and its immortality would not need to be proven. However, the soul as bringer constitutes the starting point of the last argument for the immortality of the soul (105C–D). In the argument's proceeding, Socrates also refers to the particular snow (and not the form of snow) as the bringer of coldness. This is made clear by his question whether snow in the co-presence of something hot would stay intact and unmelted if one assumes that the snow's entailed property coldness (G) would imply the property of 'being imperishable' (106A). Since it does not make sense to ask whether the form of snow would melt in the co-presence of something hot, Socrates alludes to the particular snow as the bringer of coldness.[31] As a consequence, bringing should not be reconstructed in such a way that it presupposes the entity that brings to be a form.

This objection hinges on the immediate goal of the passage on bringing. Furthermore, there is also an earlier passage that casts doubt on the soul being a form: Socrates suggests the soul is more akin to forms than to the body in certain respects (79E). If he were to assume the soul to be a form, he would not need to show its mere similarity with forms in certain respects.[32]

---

[30] See Vlastos, "Reasons and Causes in the *Phaedo*", 317.

[31] See Frede, "The Final Proof of the Immortality of the Soul in Plato's 'Phaedo' 102a–107a", 34.

[32] For this point, see Frede, "The Final Proof of the Immortality of the Soul in Plato's 'Phaedo' 102a–107a", 36.

In order to clarify what bringing means, I will reconstruct Socrates' step-wise procedure of carving out the bringers. During that process, I will show how the secondary literature creates a dilemma and present my solution on how to avoid it.

5. Carving out the Bringers

The first step consists of Socrates discerning a character F from its bearer (103B). Some bearers can exhibit opposing characters. Simmias, for example, is taller than Socrates but smaller than Phaedo (102C), whereas neither the character 'tall' nor the form 'tallness' can become their opposite (102D–E). Characters make changes intelligible, and forms are responsible for a thing exhibiting some character, but neither form nor character can undergo changes.

In the second step, Socrates introduces a class of bearers that exhibit a certain character G as long as they have their defining feature F:

> 'Don't you think that threeness should always be called both by its own name and by the name of the odd? The odd is not just what threeness is, but nevertheless threeness, fiveness, and an entire half of the number series are somehow naturally such that each of them is always odd, despite not being just what the odd is. Again, the two, the four and in its turn the entire other column of the number series are each always even, despite not being just what the even is. Do you accept that or not?' 'Of course I do,' he said. (104A–104B)

The examples range from mathematical ones like three being odd to physical objects like snow being always cold and fire being always hot (103D). Socrates carves out a set of entities whose being as the things they are is linked to a specific property G. In the secondary literature, Socrates' predication of such a property is sometimes called 'essential predication'.[33] That is a misnomer if essential predication refers to a predication that sets forth the essence of a thing. The character 'being cold' does not unpack the essence of snow. The polar region, liquid nitrogen, food in the freezer, and outer space are different things that are also cold. Unlike snow, food, of course, does not have to be cold to be food. Therefore, a more adequate term to describe Socrates' examples of properties that are linked to a thing being the thing it is might be 'necessary predication'. He focuses on such properties G that necessarily follow from a thing's defining feature F:[34]

---

[33] See, for example, Frede "The Final Proof of the Immortality of the Soul in Plato's 'Phaedo' 102a–107a", 29.

[34] *Pace* Denis O'Brien, who claims that Plato "has no technical vocabulary for 'accidental' and 'essential' in this sense. In the present argument his simplest way of describing what we may call essential predication is by the use of 'always' and 'never'." (O'Brien, "The Last Argument of Plato's *Phaedo*. I", 200).

(Necessary predication = NP) A thing x with the defining feature F necessarily exhibits G iff G is not the defining feature F of x, but has to be predicated of x in virtue of F.
Part of NP is an entailment relation: F implies G.[35]

After discerning bearers from properties and introducing NP, Socrates, in a third step, aims to show that some things (the bringers) are incompatible with certain predicates, even though they do not stand directly in opposition to them. Snow, for example, does not oppose the property warmth, but coldness does. Insofar as coldness is necessarily predicated of snow, and coldness opposes warmth, then snow cannot exhibit the property of being warm. The last argument for the immortality of the soul hinges on this notion of 'incompatibility without direct opposition'. As central as it is and as easy as it looks at first glance, there is a tricky problem in the passage in which Socrates develops the notion: there are seemingly *two* ways in which he carves out the 'class of things that are incompatible with certain predicates without directly opposing them'. I will refer to the part of the passage that carves out the set in one way as 'T1', and to the part which carves it out in another way as 'T2'. After presenting the text, I will point out how the discussion in the secondary literature creates a dilemma: On the one hand, one can align T1 and T2 and, in doing so, create a lacuna between them and a later text passage (namely, the last argument for the immortality of the soul). On the other hand, one can align T2 with the later text passage, thereby creating a non sequitur between T1 and T2. In my solution, I will align all three text passages by deleting a widespread assumption about T1.

Let us start with the text passages in question:

[T1] 'Now, Cebes,' he said, 'would they be the following: those that, whatever they occupy, compel it not only to have their own form in each case but also, invariably, the form of some opposite of something as well?' 'What do you mean?' 'Just what we were saying a moment ago. For presumably you know that whatever the form of the three occupies, must not only be three but also be odd.' (104D)

The form of threeness (F) implies oddness (G), so that, if it determines something to be three, this thing also has to be odd. Socrates here outlines a relation between something 'occupying' (κατέχειν) and 'compelling' (ἀναγκάζειν) another thing:

(Occupying and Compelling, version A = OCA) Let x have the defining feature F, F imply G, and x occupy y. Then, x awards its defining feature F to y, thereby making y exhibit G.

---

[35] Vlastos proposed for that relation to be called 'entailment' (Vlastos, "Reasons and Causes in the *Phaedo*", 317).

After setting forth the example with the form of three, Socrates continues to specify what he has in mind:

[T2] 'So as regards what I was saying we should determine, namely the sort of things that are not the opposites of something but still do not admit that opposite – such as our present example, threeness, which is not the opposite of the even but all the same does not admit the even, because it always imports the opposite of the even, as twoness imports the opposite of the odd and the fire that of the cold, and as a great many other things do – anyway, see if you make the determination as follows. Not only does the opposite not admit its opposite, but there is also the thing that imports some opposite to whatever it itself attacks, and this further thing, the one that imports it, never admits the opposite of what is imported.' (104D–105A)

The form of threeness (F) here still implies oddness (G), but now Socrates adds that oddness opposes evenness (H). By always determining something to be odd (G), the form of three cannot admit evenness (H):

(Occupying and Compelling, version B = OCB) Let x have the defining feature F, F imply G, G oppose H, and x occupy y. Then, x makes y exhibit G, and it is impossible for x to exhibit H.

There is an important difference between those two versions: In the first case (T1), x awards *its own defining* feature F to y, and since F implies G, the fact that x awards y with F makes y take on the entailed feature G. The second passage (T2) does not mention that clause but adds another one: because x always brings G to y, and G opposes H, it can never be the case that x exhibits H. T2 leaves it open whether x awards G to y by forcing x's own defining feature F onto y.

6. The Dilemma

Next, I will present the aforementioned dilemma. It is set in motion by a common answer to the following question: In T1, what does it mean that x occupies y and compels it to exhibit the defining feature of x? It is assumed to be another way of phrasing the participation scheme: 'x compels y to exhibit F' means that the presence of the form of F-ness (x) makes things (y) have F.[36] Socrates' use of the form of three as an example in T1 suggests such a reading. If this reconstruction holds, OCA, then, would only allow forms to constitute x: the form of fire, snow or three awards its own defining feature to particular things by making them exhibit the character of fire, snow or three. And by

[36] Like Vlastos ("Reasons and Causes in the *Phaedo*", 317), O'Brien argues that Socrates alludes to exactly that participatory relation in the cases of fire, snow and three ("The Last Argument of Plato's *Phaedo*. I", 225–228).

awarding them with F, they (y) will also exhibit G. Bringing, then, is reduced to the participation relation between F-things and F-ness:

('Bringing as participation') F-Ness brings G-ness iff F-ness entails G-ness and F-ness does not only make things have F, but also determines F-things to have G.

Particular things, then, could not be bringers: The form of snow makes something exhibit the features of being snow and therefore to exhibit coldness, but the particular snow, while cooling down wine, for example, does not turn the wine into snow.[37] If 'bringing G' can be reduced to participation and entailment, then particulars cannot bring G (at least not in the technical sense of bringing introduced in T1).

Let us proceed to T2 and demonstrate how one horn of the dilemma is generated. The quoted passage does not mention that x brings its own defining feature F to y. In the proceedings of the dialogue, however, T2 comes right behind T1. The most desirable way to reconstruct that passage would be to frame T2 as amending T1. It could be a tacit assumption that T2 adopts all determinations brought forth in T1 while introducing new ones. If so, then T2 would also exclude particular things from the class of bringers. This led interpreters to assume that Socrates refers to the *forms* of fire, snow, and the soul in T2.[38] The reading's drawback lies in the fact that it creates a lacuna between the passage on the notion of bringing (the text of both T1 and T2) and the last argument for the immortality of the soul. Following the context-objection, the last argument for the soul's immortality treats the *particular* soul (and not the form of soul) as the bringer of life.[39] In short: If we reconstruct bringing by reducing it to the participation scheme with the added entailment relation, and if we assume T2 to retain all determinations of T1, then there is a tension between the passage that introduces the notion of bringing and the later passage that uses that notion to frame the particular soul as the bringer of life (105D). The notion of bringing would be established with the target object of the particular soul in mind, but would exclude the particular soul as a possible candidate for a bringer. That is one horn of the dilemma.

---

[37] Concerning the example of snow cooling down another particular thing, Denyer points out that it was used in ancient Greece to cool down wine ("Platonic Causes Revisited", 94). The cooling effect was brought about in combination with two vessels: a ψυκτήρ and a κρατήρ. The wine was placed into one of those vessels, the snow in the other one.

[38] Vlastos assumes that Socrates refers to the forms of three, fire, snow, and soul in that section (Vlastos, "Reasons and Causes in the *Phaedo*", 318).

[39] O'Brien concurs with Vlastos that threeness, fire, and snow all signify forms here. He avoids the lacuna between the passage on bringing and the last argument for the soul's immortality by granting the soul to refer to the form of soul as well as to the particular soul. ("The Last Argument of Plato's *Phaedo*. I", 225–228). But, he adds, the "ideal nature of fire and soul is suggested only by context" (ad loc.).

To avoid that problem (and, in doing so, to generate the other horn of the dilemma), we can argue that T2 retains the determination 'x awards y with G' from T1 but drops the clause 'x awards y with x's defining feature F'.[40] By renouncing the latter determination, T2 would allow x to refer to particulars, too: the snow brings its entailed feature coldness to wine without turning wine into snow. If we take that route, two problems arise: First, we have to explain why Socrates starts by focusing on the form of three and the determination 'x awards its own feature F to y' only to drop it in the next step without telling the reader so. One might propose a pedagogical reading: T1 is not yet meant to define the bringers, but figures as a starting point. Socrates wants his interlocutors not to focus on the fact that the form of three makes something partake in three. He, rather, aims to direct their attention to the fact that *by always compelling* other things to exhibit G, the bringers can never exhibit the opposite of G. This pedagogical reading just accepts that there is a tension in the passage in question.

In short: If we reconstruct bringing in T1 by reducing it to the participation scheme with the added entailment relation, and if we assume T2 *not* to take over all determinations of T1, then there is a tension between two consecutive passages that are supposed to characterise the same notion. That is the other horn of the dilemma. As a result, both strategies accept that there is a non sequitur in the dialogue; the first one creates the lacuna between the passage on bringing and the last argument for the soul's immortality, the second one instils it directly into the passage on bringing.

7. Avoiding the Dilemma: Mereological Predication

There is a way to avoid this dilemma. I suggest deleting the common assumption that in T1, the determination 'x compels y to have x's own form' is just another way of phrasing the participation relation. Using "the form of the three" (104D; ἡ τῶν τριῶν ἰδέα) as an example suggests that reading. However, Plato does not use the vocabulary that comes with the participation scheme. 'Occupying' and 'compelling' might refer to *all* relations in which a thing x awards its own defining feature to another thing y.[41] Participation in a

---

[40] Theodor Ebert argues that T1 and T2 contain two different definitions. Numbers are covered by T1, things like the particular fire and snow by T2 (*Platon Werke: Band I, 4 Phaidon,* 383–386).

[41] Frede calls them "military metaphors" that allow Plato to leave open the question of how exactly 'bringing G' works in each case (Frede, "The Final Proof of the Immortality of the Soul in Plato's 'Phaedo' 102a–107a", 34f).

form might be just one of many such relations.[42] What other possible relations are there that fit that description? I suggest using the explanandum of the whole text passage, and of the entire dialogue, as an example from which to extract such a relation: the soul-body composite that is separated by death (64C), in other words, the living human being. In what way does the soul occupy the body and compel it to have the soul's own form?

In the challenge that started the whole discussion on αἰτίαι and bringers, Cebes compares the relation between the soul and the body with the one between the weaver and his cloak (87B). Amending that example, we might say that the weaver (x), while wearing that cloak (y), produces a new complex entity z made of the weaver and the cloak. The weaver has as his defining feature 'being human' (F) and some entailed features (G) like his upper body's circumference and his arms. After putting on the cloak, the garment does not magically become human. It does not exhibit the defining feature of its wearer (F). Instead, it only exhibits features like the circumference of the wearer and having arms (G). In this respect, the weaver and the cloak resemble the example of the snow and the wine: the snow does not turn the wine into snow but awards its entailed feature, coldness, to the wine. The soul also does not turn the body into soul but awards it with the soul's entailed feature, being alive.

However, there is a way in which the weaver, snow, and the soul award things their own form: The complex entity z that is composed of the weaver and the cloak does exhibit the feature of 'being human' insofar as it is partly composed of a human. The same holds for the complex entity composed of snow, wine, and the vessels they are placed into: on the one hand, snow awards its entailed feature, coldness, to the wine by cooling it down; on the other hand, snow awards its own form to the composed entity by being a part of it.[43] While it might be awkward (but not impossible) to say that the weaver and his cloak or the conjunction of snow, wine, and the two vessels compose a complex whole, it is natural to refer to the living human being, the soul-body composite, as a unity. Therefore, I do not insinuate that Socrates projects an inappropriate framework onto his target object, the soul-body composite.

What is the textual basis for my reconstruction? In the presently discussed section, Plato only states the scheme of bringing and does not spell out its mechanism. He also does not work out a theory of mereological predication,

---

[42] Frede suggests such a reading, too, and does not choose one of the two horns of the dilemma: she neither restricts the bringers to forms nor drops the claim that bringers of G import their defining feature F. However, she does not spell out how particulars import their defining feature F. She leaves it, rather, to the reader's feeling for language ("bleibt aber dem Sprachgefühl überlassen"), whether it is permissible to say that a particular fire compels an oven not only to be hot but also to be 'fiery' ("Das Argument aus den essentiellen Eigenschaften (102a–107d)", 149). In the following text, I aim to deliver an explanation of how particulars can be said to import their defining feature.

[43] For the practice of cooling down wine with snow, see fn. 37.

but he implies it from the start: In the beginning of the *Phaedo*, Socrates investigates which human being is best in gaining knowledge of forms (65E). He maintains that it is a human being which "uses thought alone by itself and unalloyed" (66A). The method of focusing on the intellect is achieved by separating the soul from the body's disturbing influences. That means that, for Socrates, the soul serves as the source of knowledge. Socrates, thus, views human beings as composed of the soul and the body; furthermore, he discerns what activities and goals can be traced back to the soul and which ones to the body (66A–67B). Insofar as living humans are partly composed of the soul, they can be said to exhibit the soul's defining features (intellectual thinking and striving for knowledge, 66A–B). The *Phaedo* concerns itself, from its start until the last argument for the soul's immortality, with thinking about parts and wholes, composition and separation, and the predicates that come along with the soul and the body as parts of a complex entity.

By being a part of the soul-body composite, the soul's defining feature F (and its entailed feature G) can be predicated of the living human being. A way for particulars to 'occupy and compel', that is, for them to award something with their own defining features, lies in:

(Mereological Predication) While x and y compose the complex entity z, x imports its defining feature F to the whole entity z by being a part of z, and hereby determines z to exhibit F and G.

I do not claim that Socrates restricts 'x awards something with its own form' in T1 to mereological predication. Rather, I propose that 'occupying' and 'compelling' refer to all relations in which a thing x awards its own defining feature to another thing y. In the case of participation, the form of F-ness compels a particular to exhibit F. In the case of merelogical predication, a thing F compels a complex entity made out of different things to exhibit F by being part of that complex whole. If my proposal holds, then T1, although claiming 'x awards something with its own feature', still allows x to refer to particulars. Since it was the refusal to allow particulars to constitute x that generated the non sequitur between T1 and T2, as well as the lacuna between them and the text passage they prepare for (the last argument for the immortality of the soul), the dilemma has been dissolved.

After eluding the dilemma, we can state how Socrates carves out the set of entities that bring G:

(Bringer): a kind of thing x that (i) has some defining feature F, (ii) necessarily exhibits some other property G qua having F, and (iii) never admits of the opposite of G because it always brings G.

In the discussion above, I have unearthed two ways for x to compel another thing to exhibit its defining feature: participation and mereological predication. In both cases, x compels something to have its defining feature (F) and, in doing so, brings its entailed features (G). In the case of participation, x refers to forms; in the case of mereological predication, it signifies particular things. In the next step, Socrates maintains that particular things can bring their entailed features not only to complex entities through mereological predication, but also to other particulars through property transmission.

8. Property Transmission

After carving out the bringers, Socrates discerns two kinds of safe answers:

'Then tell me again from the start,' he said. 'And don't give as your answer whatever I say in my question, but follow my example. I say this because, besides that safe answer I gave at first, I see another kind of safety, thanks to what we are saying now. For if you were to ask me what it is that, when it comes to be present in anything's body, makes the thing hot, I will not give that safe, ignorant answer – namely that it is hotness – but, thanks to what we now say, a more ingenious one: that it is fire.' (105B–C)

If a thing x with such a defining feature F that entails another feature G comes in contact with a thing y that does not yet exhibit G, but is capable of exhibiting G, then y takes on G. This third way of bringing is called:

(Property Transmission between Particulars) During the co-presence of x and y, x alters y by importing its entailed feature G to y.

Particular things, by always bringing *with them* some entailed feature G, also bring that feature *to* other things they come into contact with. There are two schematic differences between mereological predication and property transmission: (i) The first difference concerns the question of which properties are imported by the bringer. In the case of mereological predication, the bringer x is the subject of the predicates F and G, and, through mereological composition, the complex entity z is also the subject of F *as well as* G. The complex entity composed of wine, snow, and cups, for example, exhibits, at least in part, all the snow's features. In the case of property transmission, the receiving entity y only exhibits G and not the bringer's defining feature F. The wine is cooled down by snow, but it does not turn into snow. (ii) The second difference concerns the ontological relation between the bringer and the receiving entity. By transmitting a property, the bringer forces a thing separate from itself into assuming the character G. In mereological predication, the receiving entity is not a thing separate from x but partly consists of x.

In the *Phaedo*, Plato only establishes the basic scheme of property transmission; he does not spell out how it works in concrete cases.[44] I restrict the name 'property transmission' to a relation that holds between particulars.

[44] See for an affirmative discussion Sedley, "Platonic Causes", 123.

Here, transmission can take place through a physical process: the particular snow gives some of its coldness to the wine to cool it down. Property transmission, in my usage, does not refer to the relation between the form of F-ness (that brings G-ness) and F-things (that exhibit G).[45] In the case of the soul transmitting life to a body, one could flesh it out by resorting to Plato's *Timaeus,* in which he explains the interaction between soul and body by ascribing spatial properties and movements to both.[46]

In the case of property transmission between particulars, the receiving entity y does not take on the bringer's defining feature F. Does not Socrates, then, generate a tension between T1, in which the bringer of G is said to import its own defining feature F, and the presently discussed section? Indeed, property transmission does not take place *by way of* awarding the receiving entity y with F and thereby forcing y to also take on F's entailed feature G. But this does not imply that property transmission blocks mereological predication from taking place. If snow and wine are placed into a ψυκτήρ and a κρατήρ, then there are two things happening at the same time: during the co-presence of snow and wine, (i) the complex entity which is composed of snow, wine, and the two vessels takes on the snow's defining and entailed features and (ii) the wine takes on the property of being cold.

9. Two-Part Explanatory Account: Bringing and αἰτία

The quote above (105B–C) not only establishes property transmission but also integrates the bringers into an explanatory framework. The safe but ignorant answer responds to the question 'What is the αἰτία for a thing exhibiting F?' by stating 'Participating in the form of F-ness makes a thing have F' whereby the presence of the form of F-ness constitutes the αἰτία. The new safe answer refers to the question 'whose presence makes a thing G' and reacts to it by stating 'the bringer of G makes a thing G'. Take the example of the cold hands held above a fire. According to the first answer, participating in the form of

[45] My reconstruction, therefore, does not fall prey to Kelsey's objection to the transmission theory. He dismisses that model because it does not hold "for the great majority of effects Socrates is interested in (namely, those for which there are forms)" (Kelsey, "Causation in the *Phaedo*", 24). He even calls it "a silly way to think about the production of equality, beauty, and justice" (Kelsey, "Causation in the Phaedo", 24). I argue that Plato, in the case of the *Phaedo*, uses the transmission theory not for explaining the participatory relation between forms and particulars, but for fleshing out another way of bringing G. In doing so, he aims to elucidate how the particular soul brings life to a particular body.

[46] Thomas Johansen argues that Plato already champions a weak substance dualism in the *Phaedo* (Johansen, "The Separation of Soul from Body in Plato's *Phaedo*", 17). According to this position, the soul and the body "can share some accidental or non-defining properties" (ibid.) which allows for interaction.

warmth makes the hands warm. According to the second answer, fire (as a bringer of warmth) compels the hands to become warm. Thanks to this parallelism, Vlastos called the bringers "the 'clever' αἰτίαι".[47] This made history and led to bringers being widely understood as αἰτίαι.[48]

Do bringers satisfy the 'αἰτίαι-conditions' (AC) worked out above? According to these conditions, the A that is responsible for B has to be invariant, necessary, and sufficient. None of the three ways of bringing holds up to the conditions of invariance and necessity: (i) Regarding 'participation plus entailment', the property of oddness (G) can be brought by the form of threeness as well as every other form that entails oddness. The participation in the form of oddness, on the other hand, is necessary for something to be odd; the form of oddness, however, does not count as a bringer of oddness. (ii) Regarding property transmission, bonfires, as well as heated stones or any particular warm thing, by being warm, can warm up cold hands. (iii) Lastly, every particular thing that partly composes a complex thing and that has the entailed property G qua its defining feature F, brings G by way of mereological predication. A house that is partly composed of a straw roof can be said to have a roof and be combustible. The reason is that the house is partly made out of a straw roof and, therefore, exhibits the defining features F of a straw roof as well as the straw roof's entailed feature G of being flammable. The same can be said about a house that is partly composed of wooden walls: it is combustible because it is made of walls that are combustible. In summation, 'bringing' fulfils the sufficiency-criterion but lacks necessity and invariance, and, therefore, fails to be an αἰτία.[49] The second safe answer, thus, is not a reaction to the question 'What is the αἰτία for a thing exhibiting F?'. It rather reacts to the question 'What has to occupy a thing so that it participates in the form of G-ness?'. This result backs the 'two notions view' according to which bringers cannot be subsumed as αἰτίαι.[50]

---

[47] Vlastos, "Reasons and Causes in the *Phaedo*", 317.

[48] See for example Kanayama, "The Methodology of the Second Voyage and the Proof of the Soul's Indestructibility in Plato's *Phaedo*", 73; Kelsey, "Causation in the *Phaedo*", 22; Sedley, "Platonic Causes", 115; Stough, "Forms and Explanations in the 'Phaedo'", 24.

[49] Gail Fine suggests that "'bringing-on' just is the generic relation of sufficiency" (Fine, "Forms as Causes: Plato and Aristotle", 386).

[50] Bailey, too, argues that there are two different questions (Bailey, "Platonic Causes Revisited", 25). So do Ebrey (*Plato's Phaedo*, 264f.) and Denyer ("The Phaedo's Final Argument", 93). As justification, they point to the fact that Socrates uses different vocabularies when referring to αἰτία and to the bringers. While focusing on αἰτία, Socrates employs the following three locutions: (1) αἰτία, (2) διά + accusative or causal dative, (3) ποιεῖν = to make (Sedley, "Platonic Causes", 115). When Socrates refers to the bringers, he is not using those locutions anymore. Bailey calls to attention, that "often expressions that refer to forms are put in the (causal) dative" ("Platonic Causes Revisited", 25), whereas the bringers "are connected to those things to which they inevitably bring various properties only by dative relative pronouns" (ibid.). Moreover, the verb ποιεῖν is not to be found in the Greek text that fleshes

The two notions, despite being different, can be integrated in a two-part explanatory account for a thing coming to have G:

(1) Participation in the form of G-ness explains (in a necessary, sufficient, and invariant way) why things exhibit G. It, therefore, counts as αἰτία.

(2) Being occupied by a bringer of G is sufficient for a thing to participate in the form of G-ness.

The bringer of G compels another thing to participate in the form of G-ness. It therefore constitutes an intermediary explanation. The examples that Socrates uses to flesh out 'bringing' establish three different ways it can be realised. The first one holds between forms and particulars. The second one, mereological predication, and the third one, property transmission, take place between particulars. One such occurrence of bringing between particulars is the case of the soul bringing life to the body.

10. Conclusion

During our earthly existence, soul and body compose an entity (64D) in which the soul plays the role of the bringer of life in two ways.[51] The first manner of bringing consists in mereological predication: By being a part of the animated animal, the soul awards its defining feature to the complex entity and, in doing so, its entailed features as well. At the beginning of the *Phaedo*, Socrates discerns the soul from the (living) body by identifying its own activity and its own goal. Hence, the soul is defined by intellectual thinking and desiring the truth (66A–B). Since thinking and desiring are phenomena of life, the soul's defining features entail the property of 'being alive'. Insofar as the living

---

out the second safe answers containing the bringers; still, many translators used 'make' to describe the doings of the bringers. Sedley, for example, translates "For if you were to ask me what it is that, when it comes to be present in anything's body, makes the thing hot" (105B). The difference in the Greek original is glossed over in many English translations (for an enumeration of the translations using 'make', see Denyer, "The Phaedo's Final Argument", 93f).To convey the linguistic difference and to refrain from employing 'make', Ebrey proposes: "For if you should ask me, what is such that, whatever it arises in, [...] this thing will be hot" (*Plato's Phaedo*, 264). I used his proposal as a model for the quote at the beginning of this contribution. In her German translation, Frede also provides us with a text without 'make' ('machen'): "Wenn du mich nämlich fragen würdest: 'Was tritt in einem Körper auf, so daß er warm sein wird?'" (*Platons Phaidon*, 61).

[51] That the soul takes the role of the bringer of life in animated animals is not proven in Socrates' answer to Cebes' challenge. Both rather start from the assumption that the soul is the determining agent insofar as it 'weaves' its body (87E). The argument for the soul's independence from the body and its commanding power over the body comes earlier in the dialogue, namely, in Socrates' answer to Simmias' challenge (93A).

human being is partly composed of the soul, it can be said to have a soul and, therefore, be alive.

However, not all life phenomena can be explained by composition. Socrates characterises the body through its activities and goals. He ascribes to the body sense-perception (65B) and the desire for food, drink, sex, and goods like clothing, ornament (64D), and possessions in general (66C). Although Socrates refers to the subject of those features as "the body" (65B), he cannot mean the body by itself but only the living, that is, the ensouled body, because the dead body neither perceives nor strives. Those attributes, therefore, are a common achievement of soul and body. Since they are not the defining or entailed features of the soul by itself, they do not arise by mereological predication. Rather, they result from the soul transmitting life to the body.[52]

Bibliography

Bailey, Dominic, "Platonic Causes Revisited", *Journal of the History of Philosophy* 52 (2004), 15–32.

Denyer, Nicholas, "The *Phaedo*'s Final Argument", in: Dominic Scott (ed.), *Maieusis. Essays on Ancient Philosophy in Honour of Myles Burnyeat*, Oxford 2007, 87–96.

Ebert, Theodor (2014), *Platon Phaidon.* Übersetzung und Kommentar, Göttingen / Bristol 2014.

Ebrey, David, *Plato's Phaedo. Forms, Death, and the Philosophical Life*, Cambridge 2023.

Fine, Gail, "Forms as Causes. Plato and Aristotle", in: Gail Fine (ed.), *Plato on Knowledge and Forms*, Oxford 2004, 350–396.

Frede, Dorothea, "Das Argument aus den essentiellen Eigenschaften 102a–107d", in: Jörn Müller (ed.), *Platon: Phaidon*, Berlin 2011, 143–157.

–, *Platons Phaidon: Der Traum von der Unsterblichkeit der Seele*, Darmstadt 2011.

–, "The Final Proof of the Immortality of the Soul in Plato's 'Phaedo' 102a–107a", *Phronesis* 23 (1978), 27–41.

Johansen, Thomas Kjeller, "The Separation of Soul from Body in Plato's *Phaedo*", *Philosophical Inquiry* 41 (2017), 17–28.

Kanayama, Yahei, "The Methodology of the Second Voyage and the Proof of the Soul's Indestructibility in Plato's *Phaedo*", in: David Sedley (ed.), *Oxford Studies in Ancient Philosophy* 18 (2000), 41–100.

Kelsey, Sean, "Causation in the *Phaedo*", *Pacific Philosophical Quarterly* 85 (2004), 21–43.

O'Brien, Denis, "The last Argument of Plato's *Phaedo*. I", *The Classical Quarterly* 17 (1967), 198–231.

Sedley, David, "Platonic Causes", *Phronesis* 43 (1998), 114–132.

Sedley, David/Long, Alex, *Plato: Meno and Phaedo*, Cambridge 2011.

Stough, Charlotte, "Forms and Explanation in the 'Phaedo'", *Phronesis* 21 (1979), 1–30.

[52] This contribution is based on a talk I gave at the Platon-Tage 2024 in Tübingen. I would like to thank its organizers, Klaus Corcilius, Irmgard Männlein, and Samuel Meister for this opportunity and the audience for their helpful comments.

Vlastos, Gregory, "Reasons and Causes in the *Phaedo*", *The Philosophical Review* 78 (1969), 291–325.

The *Philebus* on the Source of Good Governance in the Soul

Jan Szaif

From Plato's mature dialogues, we can extract an idea of how certain metaphysical features of the world provide a basis for what should be our basic ethical orientation. This can be summarized as follows:

- The existence of goodness and beauty in the phenomenal world is owed to ordered structures thanks to which fluctuating multitudes can gain stability and unity.
- Such structures involve certain proportions among their components.
- Creating or maintaining such proportions is a task that requires understanding or wisdom.
- The execution of this task points, hence, to the workings of an intelligent agent-cause.
- The wisdom that guides this agent-cause is based on the comprehension of self-subsisting paradigmatic ideas or "forms" that constitute eternal truths. First and foremost, such wisdom requires an understanding of what it means for something to be in a good state.
- While such wisdom firmly rules the visible cosmos, its realization in individual human souls is a difficult endeavor and the chief task for human souls. It requires the help of philosophy.

My essay aims to show that a puzzling remark by Socrates in *Philebus* 64B, at a significant juncture of the dialogue, is linked to this philosophical vision. Socrates compares the argumentation he has just completed to an *incorporeal order (kosmos) apt to rule over a soul-body compound.* The argumentation in question was about the ingredients of the good life, and thanks to its completion, the interlocutors now find themselves in front of the entrance to the "dwelling-place of the good". I am going to argue that the comparison in 64B is meant to suggest an affinity between their argumentative discourse and the intelligent agent-cause that ought to be the governing principle within the soul.

Extant translations have often obscured the precise meaning of this comparison. My interpretation seeks to stay close to the literal meaning and grammar of the sentence and to situate it within its context. However, in order to appreciate the significance that the context lends to this passage, we first need to discuss the basic structure of this dialogue as a whole (section 1). Moreover, for a correct understanding of the concepts evoked in this passage, we also need to recall the core ideas of the ontological and cosmological segment 23C–31B, with a focus on the notion of an intelligent agent-cause that is introduced there (section 2). I shall also point to certain kindred ideas in the *Timaeus*. After these preparations, the main part of this essay will offer a close reading of the passage in question (section 3). As a result, we will be able to understand the comparison in 64B as an expression of Plato's view that their discourse about the good prefigures the soul's ideal rational condition, apt to function as a source of structure, beauty, and stability.

1. The Four Tasks that Structure the Argument of the *Philebus*

The *Philebus* aims to demarcate some middle-ground between hedonism and radical anti-hedonism (or strict intellectualism), presumably in response to debates within the Academy and, previously, among Socratic circles.[1] While Plato's own standpoint is closer to the intellectualists, he does here also offer a partial justification of the value of pleasure. Protrachus' role in the dialogue is to defend the hedonist position (on behalf of Philebus), whereas the lead-speaker Socrates introduces himself as defending the claim that the human good resides in the cognitive condition of insight or understanding (φρονεῖν, 11d9) and that cognitive states, in general, have greater value than pleasure (11b6–c2). In this context, and throughout the dialogue, the notion "good" relates to what renders a life eudaimonic (11d6).[2]

Since the conversation has the form of a Socratic refutation of a proposal defended by a respondent, it is Socrates' role to develop a certain course of argumentation that leads to the refutation of the respondent's proposal and, in

[1] We know about Eudoxus and Speusippus as proponents of hedonism and anti-hedonism in the Academy; among the earlier Socratics, Aristippus the Elder and Antisthenes represent hedonism and anti-hedonism respectively.

[2] In the *Philebus*, ἀγαθόν (in the neuter) is mainly used in two ways: 1) to designate what is the (ultimate) final goal for humans (or highest practical human good), either by identifying τὸ ἀγαθόν with a certain kind of phenomenon, e.g., pleasure or mixture (13b7, 14b4, 20b8, 21a2, 22c2, *et passim*) or by predicating ἀγαθόν (without the article) of the entire class in question (e.g., all pleasures) with the implication that nothing else qualifies as good *in its own right* (cf. 11b4, 13a8, 13e6, 20e6, 27e8, 32d5f, 44b2, 54c7, 55a10, 64a2); and 2) as the designation of an intrinsic good that can render other things desirable by being present in them or being related to them (20d10, 22b4, 28a3, 32d6, 60b2–4, 65a1–5). While *the good* completes human *eudaimonia* (cf. 11d4–6, 22d6f.) and serves as the requisite target (σκοπός, 60a7), comparative evaluative terms such as "better" (ἄμεινον, βέλτιον, e.g., 11b9, 66e8) or "better good" (19d4) are used to assert the higher value of cognition in relation to pleasure. Such *relative* goods may also be called "assets" (κτήματα, 19c6, 66a5).

doing so, to obtain an agreement to each argumentative step from his respondent. Protarchus can resist or counter any argumentative move that he finds implausible, provided his answers are honest and he does not object just for the sake of winning the debate. This is how their exchange maintains the character of a collaborative investigation.

At first blush, the ensuing dialogue might seem poorly organized. Yet a clear framework emerges if we pay attention to the questions or tasks that Socrates introduces and then works to resolve in his exchange with Protarchus. I count four such guiding tasks.[3] The first section of the dialogue (11A–12B) identifies the overarching purpose of their conversation by introducing the following two interconnected tasks (11DE, cf. 66DE):

Task 1: Clarify whether the human good is pleasure (*hedonism*), or a cognitive state (Socratic *intellectualism*), or some third item.

Task 2: If the human good should turn out to be some third item, clarify which of the first two – pleasure or cognition/wisdom – has the higher value on account of its greater kinship with the third.

Socrates gets Protarchus to admit that there are great dissimilarities between different kinds of pleasure, just as there are between different kinds of cognition. Different and opposing kinds might also differ, and be opposed, with respect to value. Instead of making a generic claim about the value of pleasure and the value of cognition, the investigation ought to start with a distinction of kinds and evaluate these kinds individually (12B–14B). This means that they are facing a third task:

Task 3: Distinguish the *kinds* of pleasure and *kinds* of cognitive states, and then relate the value question to each kind individually.

The scientific method for a division of kinds, described in the excursus 14C–18D, turns out to be too difficult for Socrates' interlocutor Protarchus. Socrates therefore resolves Task (1) through a simpler argument (19A–23A) that is based on three plausible criteria for the highest good: The good has to be a thing that is complete and sufficient and that anyone who recognizes it couldn't fail to desire. The interlocutors agree that neither a life defined by wisdom and understanding but devoid of all pleasure nor a life of pleasant sensation but without cognitive awareness could realize such complete fulfillment. They conclude that the human good must be a mixture that includes cognitive states and pleasures. This outcome activates the second task, which is also described as a contest for the "second prize".

Socrates' next move is to introduce a cosmological theory (22C–31A) that is based on a distinction of four foundational genera in nature: limit; the unlimited; things arising from the combination of limit with the unlimited; and,

[3] These "tasks" provide a different (and perhaps more fine-grained) structuring principle for the dialogue than the one employed by Dorothea Frede (*Plato: Philebus* and *Platon: Philebos*), who divides the dialogue into a "dialectical", a "critical", and a "synthetic" part.

finally, the agent-cause responsible for introducing limit into the unlimited. At first, this section purports to provide an answer to Task 2 (22C–23B, cf. 27C), gesturing toward a proof of the greater value of cognition based on how wisdom and understanding function as the agent-cause that introduces limit into the unlimited, whereas pleasure lacks measure and determination and thus falls into the class of the unlimited. However, this proof is not carried through to the end, presumably because it would ignore the necessary differentiations between kinds of pleasure and kinds of cognition. Accordingly, Socrates returns to Task (3), which he pursues in the long central part of the dialogue. In 31B–55C, he provides detailed accounts of the causes of somatic and psychic pleasures, and of their alethic qualities and ethical character. He demonstrates the existence both of false pleasures (which are, at least in part, associated with bad conditions in the body or the soul)[4] and of pure and genuine pleasures. In 55C–59D, he explains how pure and genuine forms of *cognition* differ from impure and less genuine ones. After the conclusion of these investigations, he observes that the investigation of the kinds of pleasure and cognition has provided them with the materials from which they now can try to produce an optimal mixture. The conclusion of Task 3 thus gives rise to yet another task (59DE, cf. 61BC):

Task 4: On the basis of the distinction between kinds of pleasure and cognition according to their alethic qualities and purity or impurity, clarify which kinds of cognition and which kinds of pleasure are required as components of a mixture that optimally realizes the human good (i.e., a eudaimonic life).

After a brief recapitulation of how they have resolved tasks (1) and (2), Socrates starts to tackle task (4). He begins his argumentation with the following observation:

> [T-1a:] S. The good, then, needs to be grasped either clearly or, at least, in some rough outline (τύπος τις), namely, as mentioned, for the sake of knowing to whom we should give the second prize. / P. Quite right. / S. Haven't we now found a certain path toward the good? / P. Which path? / S. It is like this: If one is looking for a certain person, it would certainly very much facilitate the discovery of the sought-after person if one first obtained correct information about the home (οἴκησις) where this person dwells. / P. It would. / S. Just so, a certain argumentation has now revealed to us (as it did in the beginning [of our conversation]) that we should not look for the good in the unmixed but in the mixed life. (61a4–b6)

According to this quotation, their conversation has to identify a path that will take them, as it were, to the place where they can find the (optimal) good, which is the thing relative to which everything else has to be ranked in value. They now know the path since they have realized that the good is to be found in the "mixed life", i.e., in a life whose goodness is defined by a certain mixture of

---

[4] Cf. Szaif, "The Place of Flawed Pleasures in a Good Life", for further analysis of the place of certain false or flawed pleasures in a good life.

goods rather than by just one kind of good. Further scrutiny of what constitutes this mixture should get them to a position from where they can grasp the good.

When Socrates reaches the conclusion of his argumentation about the ingredients of the good human life (Task 4), he suggests that this kind of investigation is also apt to reveal the nature of the good for the entire (physical) universe, which is likewise an intelligent and corporeal living being. He then compares their just completed argumentation to an incorporeal *kosmos* apt to rule well over a soul-body compound (64B). In his immediately following remark, he returns to the image of the house of the good:

[T-1b] S. Thus, if we said that we are now already standing in the area in front of the entrance to the Good (ἐπὶ … τοῖς τοῦ ἀγαθοῦ … προθύροις) and to the dwelling-place of such a thing (τῆς οἰκήσεως … τῆς τοῦ τοιούτου), wouldn't we be speaking correctly somehow? / P. I think so. (64c1–4)

Since his reference is to the entrance area (τὰ πρόθυρα) in front of the house in which the good dwells, he doesn't claim that they have entered this house. In other words, they don't yet see the good directly, but they have come very close. T–1b has a well-known textual and interpretative problem: Why does he speak of the entrance not only to the "Good" but to the Good "and" the dwelling-place of "such a thing"? What does "such a thing" refer to – still the good, or something that is merely like the good, or closely related to it, and what could this be? Or is the text perhaps corrupt, and the correct wording would mention only the entrance to the dwelling-place of the good?[5] For our purposes, it suffices to focus on the good. But more questions arise. Does "the good" here signify the universal idea of the good or merely the shared feature of good human and good cosmic life? If the latter, this might be a more specific form or ἰδέα (64a2, 65a1) than the universal good about which the *Republic* says that it is the root of all being (*R.* 509B). Moreover, are we meant to understand that they are going to enter the dwelling place and become directly acquainted with the good? This question is connected with the previous one since the good in its most universal manifestation would seem to lie beyond the scope of a dialogue that talks about the good in the domain of temporal reality.

Returning now to Task (2) – the question of the "second prize" – Socrates first introduces three formal characteristics of good mixture: *first*, measure (μέτρον) and proportion (συμμετρία), *second*, beauty, and *third*, truth. Measure and proportion are constitutive of a mixture that is free of conflict, and the

---

[5] Burnet athetized καὶ τῆς and τοῦ τοιούτου (following Badham), but the text can be understood as is. If τοῦ τοιούτου refers to the form of the Good, the καὶ would be epexegetic and serve to recall the talk of the dwelling (οἴκησις) of the good in 61AB. Alternatively, the τοῦ τοιούτου might refer to forms that are closely related to the Good (e.g., the Beautiful, the Measured, the True; cf. 64D–E). Whatever it is that τοῦ τοιούτου refers to, it is placed inside the house or temple of the Good.

element *beauty* piggybacks on this first characteristic since in Plato's (and Greek) aesthetic understanding beauty results from balanced proportions in a visible or audible object. He justifies the addition of truth by referring to a previous argument about truth as a necessary precondition for the coming-to-be of any good mixture. (I'll come back to this argument later.) The outcome is then summarized in the following statement:

[T-2] S. Hence, if we can't hunt down the good with the help of one single form (μιᾷ ἰδέᾳ), let's capture it with the help of three together – beauty, harmonious proportion (συμμετρία), and truth – and, treating them as one thing, let's claim that this is what we might entirely correctly hold responsible for what is included in the mixture (ὀρθότατ' ἂν αἰτιασαίμεθ' ἂν τῶν ἐν τῇ συμμείξει) and that, because it is good, the mixture too has become so {*i.e.*, has become good} (65a1–5).

Socrates here acknowledges that they are unable to capture goodness as a single form (ἰδέα). This confirms that the dialogue does not claim to provide a unitary account of the universal Good. As a substitute, it proposes a combination of three attributes that jointly characterize the formal cause of the goodness of mixtures in the temporal domain (ἰδεῖν τὴν αἰτίαν, δι' ἣν … παντὸς ἀξία γίγνεται 64d4, cf. 65a3). This kind of answer is probably what Socrates called a rough outline (τύπος τις) in T–1a.

With this list of formal aspects of the human good at his disposal, Protarchus is now himself able to allocate the second prize (65B–66A). He asserts that wisdom and understanding satisfy these formal criteria and are thus akin to the highest good, whereas pleasure lacks this kinship. Socrates supplements the relative ranking of cognition and pleasure with an absolute ranking of six classes of constituents of the human good (66A–D)[6] and then concludes the dialogue with a brief recapitulation of the arguments pertaining to Tasks (1) and (2).

This overview allows us to understand the position of the remark in 64B within the framework of the dialogue as a whole. It occurs at the exact moment when the account of the ingredients of the good mixture (Task 4) has been completed and Socrates is about to introduce a list of formal characterization of the good in order to resolve Task 2. At this juncture, he also claims that they are now positioned at the entrance to the house of the Good. This elevates the passage to being a sort of culmination point. Our expectations are raised to the highest, as we look forward to getting a glimpse at the most precious object of all, the good itself. Even though the dialogue then refrains from giving a direct answer about the essence of goodness, the imagery of this passage reveals the ultimate direction for this kind of discourse.

---

[6] Cf. Szaif, "The Place of Flawed Pleasures in a Good Life", 144, 156 on the intended number of classes of goods (and cf. West, *The Orphic Poems*, 116–193).

2. The Notion of an Intelligent Agent-Cause According to the Cosmological Segment 23C-31B

Since the comparison in 64B, according to the reading I am going to present, harks back to the notion of an intelligent agent-cause in the cosmological section of the dialogue (23C–31A), I'll preface my analysis with a brief review of the theory of the four components of nature developed in this earlier section. The first two components, *the unlimited* and *limit*, were already mentioned in Socrates' discussion of the method of collection and division (16C–E). The leading idea there was that, for each *technê*, there is always an ordered system of numbered kinds or forms, unified under a shared genus and supervening on the indeterminate plurality of particulars. The cosmological segment, by contrast, tackles the role of limit and the unlimited entirely within the domain of temporal particulars in the physical cosmos. Socrates describes its scope as "the things that now are in the universe" (τὰ νῦν ὄντα ἐν τῷ παντὶ 23c4). The exact meaning of this phase is not easy to establish. It suggests temporality; but more specifically, it might serve to contrast the cosmos in its current ordered state against a previous unordered state,[7] which would amount to an implicit reference to the *Timaeus*.

The genus *unlimited* is characterized by the fact that its members allow for increase or decrease on a scale of *more or less*, with no intrinsic limit or stopping point in either direction. Such a scale is typically defined by a pair of opposites. For instance, the concepts *hotter* and *colder* together describe a scale extending in two directions with no defined endpoints. Plato combines this conceptual analysis with an ontological claim: Entities that are solely defined by such scales, lacking any determinate quantity (ποσόν), ceaselessly fluctuate along these scales (24A–D).

The genus *limit* comprises measurable proportions such as *equal*, *double*, and the like (25AB). It is only thanks to the introduction of such limit and, hence, of measuredness (τὸ μέτριον) that the opposites that define an open scale are now bound together, and their fluctuating antagonism comes to rest (25DE).[8]

The third genus, referred to as *mixture*, comprises all items that have attained harmonious proportions (σύμμετρα καὶ σύμφωνα, 25e1) thanks to the application of limit to the unlimited. Examples are health, harmonious musical tuning, mild weather seasons (as opposed to excessive climate phenomena), and virtuous dispositions of the soul supported by "law and order, which have/carry limit" (νόμον καὶ τάξιν πέρας ἔχοντ[ε],[9] 26b10). Since harmonious mixtures

[7] Cf. Delcomminette, *Le* Philèbe *de Platon,* 213, citing Kühn, "Quatre catégories cosmologiques employées en éthique".

[8] On 25DE, cf. Frede, *Platon: Philebos,* 194–199.

[9] I am reading the elided ἔχοντ' (supported by T and W) as a dual form.

presuppose a *process* of mixing, it is always the case that they have *come to be* (γένεσις εἰς οὐσίαν 26d8, cf. γεγενημένη οὐσία 27b8). Such being-that-has-come-to-be stands in contrast not only to the previous indeterminate flux but also to the genuinely stable being of the Forms: Measured proportions that have come together at a certain time are liable to come apart at a later time.

The coming-to be of a measured and temporarily stable state in the unlimited (26D) is a process that requires some goal-directed organizing cause or causes. Under the label of *cause* (αἰτία), such intelligent agency is listed as the fourth constitutive factor of temporal reality. It is also called the "making" or "crafting" factor: τὸ ποιοῦν 26e6, τὸ δημιουργοῦν 27b1), using terms in the neuter that recall their personifying counterparts ποιητής and δημιουργός in the *Timaeus* (*Tim.* 28a6, c3). Correspondingly, the things that come to be (τὸ γιγνόμενον) are also referenced as the things that are "made" (τὸ ποιούμενον 27a1). Whereas this kind of cause "leads", the other contributing factors – viz., *limit* and *the unlimited* – are in a subservient role (τὸ <u>δουλεῦον</u> εἰς γένεσιν αἰτίᾳ 27a9). They are not to be called "cause" because they are mere tools of the cause.[10] Compare the following quotation:

[T-3] S. Doesn't that which makes (τὸ ποιοῦν) always naturally take the lead (ἡγεῖται), and that which is being made follows it (ἐπακολουθεῖ) while it is in the process of becoming? / P. Yes, indeed. / S. Hence, the cause and that which is subservient to the cause in the process of becoming (τὸ δουλεῦον εἰς γένεσιν αἰτίᾳ) are different and not the same. / P. Of course. / S. And didn't the three genera provide the things that come to be and also those out of which they all come to be? / P. They did so, yes. / S. Accordingly, we refer to that which arranges all this in a craftsmanlike way (πάντα ταῦτα δημιουργοῦν) as the fourth item, namely, the cause (αἰτία); for it has become suffciently clear that it is different from those [three]. / P. It surely is different. / S. […] / P. [...] / S. So, in *first* place, I list the unlimited, *second* limit, then, out of these, *third*, being that is mixed and has come to be (μεικτὴν καὶ γεγενημένην οὐσίαν). If I then listed the cause of mixture and coming-to-be in *fourth* place, I would not be out of tune, right? / P. How would you? (27a5–c2)

Up to this point, the "cause" has not yet been expressly identified with reason or intelligence. This step is taken in 28C–30D. Socrates begins by highlighting the function of the intellect as the directing cause of the visible universe as a whole (28C–29A), using again the language of rational leadership or governance. He appeals to the alleged view of "the sages" that "*nous* is the king of heaven and earth" (28c7f.). The universe is not administered (ἐπιτροπεύειν d6) by chance or some random irrational force; rather, some amazing intelligence and understanding (νοῦν καὶ φρόνησίν τινα θαυμαστήν) steers and organizes it (τὸ … ὅλον … συντάττουσαν διακυβερνᾶν d8; cf. διακοσμεῖν e3). In this connection, we have to ask ourselves about the meaning of the term *nous*

[10] In other contexts, Plato has referred to such contributing factors employed by a rational leading cause as συναίτια (cf. *Ti.* 46C–E, 76D; *Plt.* 281C–E, 287B–D) or as ἄνευ οὗ οὐ (cf. *Phd.* 99B).

frequently used in the *Philebus*. In the first quote (about *nous* as the "king of heaven and earth", 28c7f.), we could understand it to mean "intellect", either as a self-subsisting entity or as a faculty of the world-soul. Subsequently, however, this word is clearly used as the name for a certain condition or virtue of the intellectual faculty, often in juxtaposition with the terms *epistêmê* or *phronêsis*.[11]

While the assertions just cited are about *nous* as the governing principle in the cosmos or visible universe, the subsequent segment 29A–30D expands the scope so as to include also the *nous* that operates in the human soul as a cause that administers the human soul-body compound. Socrates argues that the human microcosm must be composed of the same basic constituents as the macrocosm, if through weaker or less perfect manifestations. His argumentation then reverses its course so as to argue from the governing role of *nous* in the human soul-body compound to its analogous role in the cosmic soul-body compound, reconfirming the cosmological thesis:

[T-4] (1) S. Regarding these three, *limit*, the *limitless*, and *what they [both] share in* (κοινὸν), and regarding the genus *cause* (τὸ τῆς αἰτίας γένος), present in all of them as the fourth,[12] – [if we consider] that, among the things that belong to us (ἐν μὲν τοῖς παρ' ἡμῖν), it [i.e., the *cause*] bears the names of all the manifold kinds of wisdom (σοφία) since it renders the soul *** and introduces physical exercise or, when the body is failing, the medical art and also provides other kinds of conjoining and healing in other things,[13] and [if we then also consider] that those same things {*i.e.*, soul and the corporeal elements} are present in large quantities in the universe (οὐρανός) as a whole and, moreover, in a beautiful and pure condition – then, Protarchus, we surely won't believe that it {i.e., the *cause*} has not crafted in them the nature of things most worthy and beautiful (μεμηχανῆσθαι τὴν τῶν καλλίστων καὶ τιμιωτάτων φύσιν). / P. Such a belief wouldn't make sense at all. /

(2) S. If it doesn't make sense, we'd better follow this other argument and affirm that there is (as we have often said) a lot of what is unlimited in the universe, and a sufficient amount of limit, and that there is also a certain cause operating on them (τις ἐπ' αὐτοῖς αἰτία), which is by no means insignificant (οὐ φαύλη) since it arranges (κοσμοῦσα) and jointly puts in order (συντάττουσα) the years and seasons and lunar cycles, which is why it is very appropriately called wisdom (σοφία) and understanding (νοῦς). / P. Very appropriately indeed.

---

[11] Cf. Menn, *Plato on God as Nous,* 15–18.

[12] Based on the following text for a9–b1, with Bury's emendation (1897, *ad loc.*): Οὐ γάρ που δοκοῦμέν γε, ὦ Πρώταρχε, τά <τε τρία> [τέτταρα] ἐκεῖνα, πέρας καὶ ἄπειρον καὶ κοινὸν, καὶ τὸ τῆς αἰτίας γένος ἐν ἅπασι τέταρτον ἐνόν, …

[13] The received text of b1–4 reads: …, τοῦτο ἐν μὲν τοῖς παρ' ἡμῖν ψυχήν τε παρέχον καὶ σωμασκίαν ἐμποιοῦν καὶ πταίσαντος σώματος ἰατρικὴν καὶ ἐν ἄλλοις ἄλλα συντιθὲν καὶ ἀκούμενον πᾶσαν καὶ παντοίαν σοφίαν ἐπικαλεῖσθαι, […]. The παρέχον is puzzling since Plato certainly can't maintain that a person's wisdom provides them with a soul. (Cf. 30c9f. [T-4 (2)] on how wisdom and *nous* presuppose the existence of a soul.) Either an adjective is missing (e.g., καλὴν παρέχον), or the participle παρέχον is a corruption for some other participle that would convey the idea of tending, managing, organizing, or the like. Cf. Frede, *Platon: Philebos*, *ad loc.*

/ S. Surely, wisdom and understanding could never come to be without a soul. / P. They coudn't. / S. [...] / P. [...] /

(3) S. You don't believe, do you, that we have argued this in vain, Protarchus? Rather, you believe that our argument (λόγος) supports (σύμμαχος) those erstwhile revelations, which say that *nous* is what always rules over the universe (ὡς ἀεὶ τοῦ παντὸς νοῦς ἄρχει). (30a9–d8)

The intelligent cause operating in the world soul and the human soul is here referred to as wisdom (σοφία) and understanding (νοῦς). About this agent-cause it is again said that it designs or crafts (μεμηχανῆσθαι) the universe, assembling it so as give it order and structure – a *kosmos* in the proper sense of the word (κοσμοῦσά τε καὶ συντάττουσα). In the case of a human being, this agent-cause is this person's own wisdom, which takes care not only of the human soul in its entirety but also of the body. At the end of this segment, the idea of the governance of *nous* is expressed by the term "ruling" (ἄρχειν), which we will encounter again in 64B.

This ontological segment in the *Philebus* shows a number of significant agreements with the ontology and cosmology of the *Timaeus*. The following are obvious shared features: Both dialogues promote the idea of an intelligent agent-cause, described as a demiurgic force responsible for the cosmic order and especially for the system of heavenly rotations. However, unlike the "verisimilar tale" of the *Timaeus*, the account in the *Philebus* does not personify this demiurgic factor. Both dialogues emphasize the role that measure and proportion play for the coming-to-be of an ordered cosmos, while also evoking the idea of an inherently fluctuating substrate that can attain temporary stability only through the introduction of measure and proportion. In the *Philebus*, the various manifestations of the unlimited take on the role that the *Timaeus* has assigned to receptacle and "wetnurse of being". Finally, in both cases, the understanding of human and cosmic nature is informed by the macrocosm-microcosm analogy.

We should note that the four constitutive *genera* distinguished in the *Philebus* don't have to be mutually exclusive. Thus the intelligent cause might itself turn out to be constituted by a combination of a certain kind of limit and a certain kind of the unlimited. This would, at any rate, be supported by how the *Timaeus* describes the ordered rational soul not only as an intelligent cause but also as a mobile structure created from "soul-stuff". While it is uncertain to what extent this kind of talk is merely a symbolic representation of more abstract facts, Plato seems to be committed to the idea that a soul can become enlightened only thanks to the restoration of some internal structure.[14]

[14] Cf. Szaif, "Truth, Music, and the 'Measured' Mind," 284-290.

3. The Interpretation of *Philebus* 64B

After these preparations, we are now ready to tackle the puzzling comparison in 64B, which concludes the section dedicated to Task (4) (59D–64C). Socrates has addressed this task through a kind of thought experiment in which he "mixes" a good life from scratch, selecting the right ingredients from among cognitive states and pleasures[15] – a process that he even compares to the making of a mixed drink (61c4–8). He maintains that pure and fully genuine ingredients should take precedence over impure or less genuine specimens, but also that impure specimens may have to be added to the mixture if this should be required for an optimal result (61e6–9). The interlocutors quickly reach the conclusion that, in addition to the pure forms of science and understanding (viz., dialectic and pure mathematics), the inferior practical forms of knowledge or expertise also have to be included as they also make a positive contribution to human life. As for the question of the hedonic ingredients of the good mixture, Socrates resorts to the literary device of an imaginary conversation with both the personified pleasures and the personified higher forms of understanding, φρόνησις and νοῦς (63c5). The pleasures reaffirm that they prefer to be joined with the ability to recognize and understand (γιγνώσκειν). Personified reason and understanding, in turn, will admit only those pleasures that do not antagonize them. They consent to cohabitation with pure forms of pleasure linked to cognitive states. They then also welcome all those pleasures that are corollaries of healthy or virtuous activities.[16] Yet they sharply dismiss any pleasure associated with illness of the body or a defective condition of the soul (vice, foolishness). It is from here on that I am quoting the passage that leads up to the claim in 64B:

[T-5] S. […] {*φρόνησις and νοῦς speaking:*} "[…]; (1) yet to mix with reason/understanding (νοῦς) pleasures that follow a foolish/immoderate attitude (ἀφροσύνη) or any other kind of badness (κακία), this would be quite an absurd thing to do (2) for whoever attempts to learn from the sight of a most beautiful and most unconflicted mixture and blend (ὅτι καλλίστην ἰδόντα καὶ ἀστασιαστοτάτην μεῖξιν καὶ κρᾶσιν) which thing is (by nature) good (τί ποτε … πέφυκεν ἀγαθὸν) both in a human being and in the universe, and how one should conjecture (μαντευτέον) about what kind/form (τίνα ἰδέαν) it (αὐτὴν; *i.e., the mixture*)[17] is." […]

[15] The focus on cognitive and hedonic components is the result of the fact that the dialogue as a whole aims to adjudicate the competing claims of hedonists and intellectualists so as to establish some common ground.

[16] Cf. Szaif, "The Place of Flawed Pleasures in a Good Life," for further discussion.

[17] There is a grammatical issue here: The passage claims that the sight of a most beautiful and harmonious mixture, as constructed in their conversation, will provide the inquirer with answers regarding the following two questions: *First*, what thing is (by nature) good (τί ποτε πέφυκεν ἀγαθὸν) in a human being and in the universe? *Second*, how should one conjecture about what ἰδέα "it" (αὐτὴν) is? In most translations or comments, the thing that is the ἀγαθόν is understood to be the antecedent for the "it", but the feminine gender suggests that it refers

(3) S. Yet this too is needed, for not a single thing could come to be in a different way. / P. What is this? / S. Nothing could ever truly *become* [a certain kind of thing] (ἀληθῶς γίγνοιτο) or, having become it, *be* it (γενόμενον εἴη), unless we add truth to the mixture. / P. How could it?

(4) S. It certainly could not; but tell me, you and Philebus, whether this blend (σύγκρασις) is still in need of something. *For to me it seems that our present account/discourse/reasoning (λόγος) has been composed/completed (ἀπειργάσθαι) just like {or: as if it were} (καθαπερεί) some incorporeal structure (κόσμος τις ἀσώματος) that is going to rule well (ἄρξων καλῶς) over an animate body (ἔμψυχον σῶμα).*[18] / P. Socrates, please call this a view that I too have consented to. (63e7–64b9)

The statement contained in (1) concludes the discussion of which kinds of pleasure are fit to be included among the components that jointly optimize human life. In (2), we are told that this kind of investigation has a broader scope than merely to give an account of the good human life. Its ulterior aim is to find out what defines the goodness of embodied intelligent life in general, be it human life or the life of the cosmos. We are thus reminded of the *microcosm-macrocosm* analogy introduced in the cosmological segment (22C–31A).

In segment (3), Socrates claims that the good mixture also requires the addition of truth as a further ingredient. In his justification, he points out that nothing at all can "truly" (ἀληθῶς) *become* or, *having become*, *be* something of a certain kind unless "truth" (ἀλήθεια) is "mixed" into it. The expression γενόμενον εἴη recalls the notion of a γεγενημένη οὐσία in the cosmological segment (27b7–8, cf. 26d8). It indicates that the "true being" talked about here is still merely a temporary kind of being that may last only for a certain time. Given that the *Philebus* makes use of the terminology of truth and falsehood in so many different ways, the claim that the good mixture has to include truth could have a variety of meanings.[19] Yet the argument Socrates employs relies on a specific sense or mode of *ontological truth*. Calling some putative instance of F-ness "a thing that is a true/genuine F" is making the claim either that it is

---

back to καλλίστην … μεῖξιν καὶ κρᾶσιν (the optimal mixture and blend), just as the ἐν ταύτῃ shortly before does. This might be an instance of assimilation or of a construction *ad sensum* (because the common feature of goodness is an ἰδέα). However, the choice of the term ἰδέα harks back to the preceding ἰδόντα, which has μεῖξιν καὶ κρᾶσιν as its object. Since the modeled optimal mixture is, hence, the likely referent of αὐτὴν, Socrates seems to be talking about this mixture as instantiating a specific kind or form.

[18] In Greek, the sentence reads: ἐμοὶ μὲν γὰρ καθαπερεὶ κόσμος τις ἀσώματος ἄρξων καλῶς ἐμψύχου σώματος ὁ νῦν λόγος ἀπειργάσθαι φαίνεται. The words ἄρξων καλῶς ἐμψύχου σώματος after ἀσώματος in 64b7 are missing in T but are present in the other primary text witnesses B/D and W. For the text of the *Philebus*, T and W together belong to one main branch of the tradition as they frequently agree with each other against B (and the related D). The missing words in T are, hence, certainly due to an individual scribal error caused by the homoioteleuton ἀσώματος and σώματος.

[19] Cf. Wolfsdorf, *Pleasure in Ancient Greek Philosophy,* 63–102, Szaif, "The Place of Flawed Pleasures in a Good Life", 135–138.

really (and not just apparently) F or that it is F in an exemplary (and not merely deficient) manner. In the case of this *Philebus* passage, we seem to be dealing with the latter, emphatic notion of ontological truth, which has the effect of raising the applicability bar of the predicate in question.[20] It supplements the normative notion of mixture which is laid out a little further on, as part of Socrates' explanation of what constitutes goodness in mixtures:

[T-6] S. There isn't a single human being who wouldn't know this. / P. What? / S. That every kind and manner of mixture (σύγκρασις) that fails to gain a share in measure and in the nature of measured proportion (μέτρου καὶ τῆς συμμέτρου φύσεως) will necessarily destroy both its ingredients and, first of all, itself. For, every time this happens, this sort of outcome would not be mixture (κρᾶσις) but truly (ἀληθῶς) some unmixed/uncontrolled (ἄκρατος) lumped-together (συμπεφορημένη) real mishap (ὄντως ... συμφορά) to those who have acquired it. (64d7–e3)

According to this quotation, a mixture that doesn't have a share in measure and proportion would be self-destructive and also harmful to its ingredients. As Socrates puts it in a barely translatable sentence that plays with the ambiguities of the words ἄκρατος and συμφορά,[21] such a product "truly" becomes (ἀληθῶς) some unfortunate jumble (συμπεφορημένη ... συμφορά) and thus is "really" (ὄντως) a mishap (συμφορά) to its possessor, falling short of being a mixture and/or of being self-controlled (ἄκρατος). In order to *truly* become a mixture and attain temporary stability free of internal strife (ἀστασιαστοτάτη),[22] it needs to attain a condition of internal harmony and cohesion.[23]

Turning now to segment (4) of T-5, it should be highlighted, first, how little the comparison of their completed argument with an "incorporeal structure that is going to rule well over an animate body" contributes to the further progression of the argumentation. This reinforces the impression that this puzzling formulation was added as an aside that hints at an important idea. Let's then discuss how we are to understand this hint.

---

[20] Cf. Szaif, *Platons Begriff der Wahrheit*, 49–56, on the attributive usage of ἀληθής.

[21] Cf. Friedländer, *Platon, Band III,* 493, fn. 73.

[22] Cf. Frede, *Platon: Philebos,* 194–202, 355f. (also Harte, *Plato on Parts and Wholes,* 189–191) on the ontological basis for this normative notion of mixture. – Note that Socrates carefully avoids attributing "true being" to mixtures, as this is a hallmark of the transcendent Forms. He speaks instead of "truly coming to be" or "truly being *as the result of having become*" (οὐκ ἄν ... ἀληθῶς γίγνοιτο οὐδ' ἂν γενόμενον εἴη; cf. γεγενημένη οὐσία in 27b7–8, γένεσις εἰς οὐσίαν 26d8). Mixtures, even if stabilized thanks to internal structure and proportion, are still temporary and intrinsically perishable entities.

[23] It is still odd that T–5 lists this formal and normative feature of mixture alongside the material ingredients of a good life, knowledge and pleasure. Take Plato's own example of a mixed drink: A Manhattan Cocktail, for instance, is a true specimen of its kind only if the right ingredients have been mixed in the right proportion that guarantees the characteristic tasting experience. Yet the factor "truth" (in the ontological sense of genuineness) cannot be added like a material ingredient alongside the Vermouth etc.

Since this remark follows immediately after Socrates has asked whether or not the mixture they have produced in words still lacks something, it is tempting to translate as if the ἀπειργάσθαι were predicated of the object of the *logos,* i.e., the mixture. This is what we find in several well-known translations,[24] and it also seems to be the dominant view among commentators,[25] if they comment on this phrase at all. Yet the grammatical subject of ἀπειργάσθαι φαίνεται clearly is "the current *logos* (ὁ νῦν λόγος)". The choice of the verb ἀπειργάσθαι conveys the idea that their *logos* is now complete like the finished product of an artisan. The νῦν indicates that this phrase refers not to some abstract content or proportion but to their present verbalized discourse and argumentation. To be sure, by completing a *logos* about how to produce the best mixture, they have also produced a verbal or conceptual representation of such a mixture. But it is still their current *logos*, not this ideal mixture, that is compared to an "incorporeal *kosmos*". The course our interpretation will take depends on this interpretative decision.

Another key decision relates to the question of how we are to understand the καθαπερεί. Does it really serve to introduce a comparison, or does it merely soften the assertion – as if Socrates were saying about the completed *logos* that it is "in a way", *but not strictly speaking*, some kind of (τις) incorporeal *kosmos*? Some of the most widely used translations read it in the latter way.[26] Yet a look at the other occurrences of the word καθαπερεί in Plato's dialogues – three more in the *Philebus*, and single occurrences in the *Timaeus*, *Statesman*, and *Laws* – confirms that Plato always uses it to introduce a genuine comparison, typically so as to create a figurative analogy.[27] Let us briefly review the other three instances of this construction in the *Philebus*. In 22e5, Protarchus remarks that pleasure has succumbed as if it had been "knocked out" (καθαπερεὶ πληγεῖσα) by Socrates' arguments. No literal beatings have occurred, but the comparison vividly illustrates how Protarchus assesses the

[24] Cf. Apelt, *Platon: Phaidon*, Diès, *Platon: Philèbe,* Hackforth, *Plato's Examination of Pleasure,* Frede, *Plato: Philebus,* and *Platon: Philebos*, Delcomminette, *Platon: Philèbe,* also Friedländer's paraphrase (*Platon, Band III,* 325). A noteworthy exception is Schleiermacher's German translation, which follows the text very closely ("…, denn mir scheint, wie eine unkörperliche Ordnung, die schön über einen belebten Körper herrschen soll, die gegenwärtige Rede vollendet zu sein"), as do the early humanist translations by Ficino (1484), Cornarius (1561), and Serranus (1578); e.g., Ficino: *Mihi enim tamquam mundus quidam incorporeus animato corpori pulchre dominaturus sermo hic peractus fuisse videtur.*

[25] Cf. Frede, *Platon: Philebos,* 355, Delcomminette, *Platon : Philèbe*, 559, and (apparently) Hackforth, *Plato's Examination of Pleasure*, *ad loc.*

[26] Cf. Hackforth, *Plato's Examination of Pleasure,* and Frede, *Plato: Philebus* ("of what might be called"). Diès, *Platon: Philèbe* ("une sorte de") and Gosling, *Plato: Philebus* ("a sort of") translate the τις after κόσμος but, like Frede, *Platon: Philebos,* leave out the comparative conjunction καθαπερεί.

[27] Cf. *Phlb.* 22e5, 59e1, 61a9, *Ti.* 86c4, *Plt.* 267a1, *Lg.* 712a4; see also καθάπερ ἂν εἰ in *Lg.* 684c3, 872c4.

outcome. In 59e1, Socrates compares himself and his interlocutor to craftsmen (καθαπερεὶ δημιουργοῖς ἡμῖν) who have gathered all the necessary materials needed to make their product. Yet they are not literally craftsmen since theirs is only a philosophical conversation that tries to construct the human good in theory. In 61a9, he compares (καθάπερ εἴ τις ...) their progress in the search for the *good* to the situation of someone who is trying to find a certain person and has now made an important first step forward since he has learnt where this person lives. Here again, the comparison serves to introduce a figurative analogy that illustrates what they have achieved in their conversation.

It is important to note that in each of these cases, the literal meaning of the figurative analogue is easy to understand. It is clear what it means to knock someone out, or to find someone's address. After all, such comparisons are meant to illustrate a point the speaker is trying to convey, and to this end it would be counterproductive to introduce something more obscure than its *comparandum*. However, the comparison in 64B, while also tied to a comment about the progress they have made, uses a phrase that is much obscurer than the *comparandum*. This gives us reason to suspect that this is a case in which the comparison does not serve to illustrate or clarify a claim but to hint at some analogy that Plato finds important in its own right.

The comparison refers to an incorporeal structure that has a certain *purpose* or *aptitude*, expressed by a participle in the future: viz., to rule well (ἄρξων καλῶς) over a soul-body compound (ἔμψυχον σῶμα). The fact that this "body" is called ἔμψυχον, i.e., endowed with a soul, points to a living and sentient being over which the incorporeal order or structure is said to rule. The notion of an ἔμψυχον σῶμα already came up in the cosmological segment. Socrates resorted there to the *microcosm-macrocosm* analogy in order to argue that the body of the cosmos as a whole must be ἔμψυχον no less than the human body.[28] Accordingly, when Socrates in T–5 talks about an ἔμψυχον σῶμα, he may be hinting at the human or the cosmic soul-body compound, or at both. Yet what is it about the *logos* just completed that makes it comparable to an incorporeal structure apt to rule over an animate body? This *logos* is an argument about how to realize the best kind of human life through the right kind of mixture of the relevant ingredients. From the point of view of a eudaimonist approach, it represents, hence, the kind of reasoning that should *guide* a person in their life, which could then also be described as "ruling" over a human soul-body compound. Moreover, as a complex argument, it also has a certain structure, and while this *logos* is not strictly an incorporeal entity since it is a voiced

[28] 30a3–7: "Won't we say about the body that belongs with us that it has a soul? / P. Of course. / S. But from where, my dear Protarchus, could it have obtained a soul, if the body of the universe (τό γε τοῦ παντὸς σῶμα) didn't happen to be endowed with soul (ἔμψυχον), although it has the same [elemental] parts as this one [*i.e.*, the human body] and even has them in an altogether more beautiful condition?"

conversation between two people, its logical structure can be viewed as something incorporeal.

But why, then, is this *logos* not directly characterized as an incorporeal *kosmos* but only compared to one? Or should we, after all, agree with the translators who read the construction with καθαπερεί as a turn of phrase that merely weakens the force of the assertion? (Socrates might want to weaken it because a voiced discourse cannot be incorporeal strictly speaking.) The combined force of the following considerations weighs against such a minimalist reading: *First*, the other passages that use the καθαπερεί locution do, as we have seen, involve genuine comparisons and don't serve to merely soften the force of an assertion. *Second*, the formulation introduced with καθαπερεί is rhetorically highlighted and memorable on account of how the two phrases κόσμος τις ἀσώματος and ἐμψύχου σώματος closely mirror each other with their equivalent rhythm [29] and their antithetical but similar-sounding endings (ἀσώματος / σώματος). Such rhetorical highlighting has an effect opposite to that of softening an assertion. The fact, moreover, that this sentence belongs to a juncture at which the dialogue reaches a climax also makes us expect that the reference to an incorporeal ruling *kosmos* points to something very significant and worth exploring in its own right.

The key for understanding the reference to an incorporeal *kosmos* apt to rule well lies in the notion of "ruling well" (ἄρχειν καλῶς τινος). It is, to be sure, conceivable that Plato would, somewhat metaphorically, characterize a form or structure inherent in a mixture as that which "rules" over the mixture structured by it. We have also seen that the next segment does, in fact, talk about the formal cause of good mixture (cf. T-2). However, the cosmological section of the *Philebus* has assigned the task of *ruling* over an ensouled human body to the genus *intelligent cause*, identified as *nous* and *sophia* (cf. T-4 [2]). The reference to the microcosm-macrocosm analogy in segment (2) of T-5 already forces attentive readers to think back to this previous discourse. They will thus also link the notion of "ruling *well*" (ἄρξων καλῶς) in T-5 to how this discourse described the intelligent cause as that which rules (ἄρχειν), steers (διακυβερνᾶν), crafts (δημιουργεῖν, μηχανᾶσθαι), manages (ἐπιτροπεύειν), or organizes (κοσμεῖν, διακοσμεῖν, συντάττειν) both the universal cosmos and its microcosm counterpart, the human person.

But why is this intelligent agent-cause described as an "ἀσώματος κόσμος"? The cosmological section identifies this cause with *nous* and *sophia*, which Plato certainly views as incorporeal qualities or powers of the incorporeal soul. Yet it also ascribes to *nous* the function of producing order and harmony in a disorganized substrate. Its task is to produce *kosmos* (τὸ διακοσμεῖν). Doesn't this mean that it would be wrong to describe the agent-cause itself, and not only its product, as a *kosmos*?

---

[29] The patterns – – ◡◡ – ◡◡ and – – – – ◡◡ are metrically equivalent.

We have already noticed several significant points of agreement between the cosmological account of the *Philebus* and the cosmological tale of the *Timaeus*. The *Timaeus* also provides an important clue with regard to the current question: It uses the ordered celestial motions of the physical cosmos as the model for describing the workings of both the human and the cosmic intellect (*Ti.* 36CD, 37A–C, 43A–44C). This tells us that Plato conceives of the condition of the rational part of the human soul, in its enlightened state, as a balanced dynamic structure – in other words, as itself a *kosmos*. As long as the rational core of the human soul is still reduced to a condition of foolishness, it is like a dynamic compound deprived of its natural proportions, and its parts cannot perform according to their nature; it still fails to be a *kosmos*. In order to become a *kosmos*, it needs to restore its proper dynamic state, emulating the world-soul, whose balanced motions consistently produce true discourse about ideal and physical realities (37A–C). Only thus restored will the human mind have the wisdom and understanding needed to rule well over its entire soul-body compound.

Basically the same idea seems to underlie a remark in the *Sophist* about the causes of error.[30] The lead speaker claims that ignorance resulting in false judgment is a sort of ugliness (αἶσχος) caused by some disproportion (ἀμετρία). While the lack of *symmetria* among the parts of a body causes the body to look ugly, the lack of *symmetria* within our cognitive apparatus results in ignorance and error (227D–228E). This is further illustrated by a comparison of the act of judging with an act of archery (228CD): Just as an archer misses the target if his posture is out of balance, the act of judging also misses its target – the truth – due to an internal ἀμετρία. In other words, only a cognitive apparatus that has restored its proper internal proportions, its natural *symmetria*, will be able to produce correct judgment and understanding.

We can now see what Plato has in mind when he evokes the idea of an incorporeal *kosmos* as the governing agent-cause in animate bodies. *Measure* and *proportion* are constitutive not just of the good life as a whole but also of the enlightened state of wisdom. Only by restoring its internal proportions – and, hence, as a kind of *kosmos* – can the mind function as the agent-cause that conveys balance and right proportion to the person's entire soul and body, and also to other things within the person's scope of action (cf. section [2] of T-4).

Why does Socrates draw a comparison between this kind of agent-cause and his current conversation with Protarchus about the human good? Their current discourse exemplifies and anticipates the kind of reasoning that should guide us in our lives. It is, however, merely an episode of conversational reasoning, limited to a certain time and situation and expressed phonetically. As such, it is merely an *image* and *prefiguration* of the perfected internal reasoning that

---

30 Cf. Szaif, "Truth, Music, and the 'Measured' Mind", 289f.

should become the ruling principle within us. For this reason, it is comparable to, but not identical with, this enlightened state of mind.[31]

In this connection, it is also instructive to recall how the *Phaedrus* has developed the notion of a "living *logos*" internal to the soul as the key to wisdom and happiness (276E–77A). This dialogue compares the reception of an argumentative account (*logos*) to the planting of a "seed" in the soul. A fully developed *logos*-seed will be "written into the learner's soul conjoined with *understanding* (ἐπιστήμη)" (276a5–6, cf. e6–7). It is called a "living *logos*" (276a8) since it is a dynamic and creative rational condition, able to grow and sustain itself, formulate responses to objections, and communicate itself to other souls by planting "new seeds" through the medium of philosophical conversation.[32] The key take-away is that the agent-cause that rightly governs a human soul-body compound can be conceived as a dynamic condition of the mind linked to its internal reasoning activity. This lends additional context to our conclusion that Socrates' and Protarchus' argumentative exchange about the good is an image or prefiguration of the kind of internal state of mind that would amount to wisdom. We can also tell why Socrates gestures at this connection at the precise moment when their conversation has taken them to the entrance of the "house of the good": The ultimate purpose of engaging in such conversations is the discovery and full understanding of the good, as this would fully restore the enlightened agent-cause within the soul.

[31] Some read the comparison as introducing an analogy involving four elements (Bury, *The Philebus of Plato,* Rudebusch, *Plato's Philebus*): As the incorporeal *kosmos* is to the animate body, so the present *logos* is to a certain x (left unnamed). The question then is: "What is this x?" Since the *tertium comparationis* would here be the relation of ruling well, this question then becomes: "What is the x that the present *logos* rules well?" However, the text, as it is, does not describe two analogous relations of ruling. In my reading, the present *logos* is compared to a certain incorporeal *kosmos* (*nous*, wisdom) that rules well over a soul-body compound because it foreshadows the internal condition of *nous* or wisdom, which Plato views as an incorporeal *kosmos* and ruling principle realized in the soul. The only object in play here that needs to be ruled well is this soul-body compound (i.e., the whole human person). The current *logos* takes us in this direction.

[32] In the *Phaedrus*, this kind of internal *logos* is set in opposition to written texts that stay fixed and cannot react to new questions and objections or clear up misunderstandings. An argument developed orally and in conversation with an attentive interlocutor shares many of the virtues of this internal "living" *logos*, yet it is still limited in certain ways; namely, by being confined to a certain time and constrained by how far the interlocutor is willing or able to follow the course of the investigation.

4. Conclusions

To conclude, let's recapitulate the main results of our interpretation of the comparison in 64B:

1) The subject of the assertion (the *comparandum*) is the *logos*, not the mixture; and this *logos* is their just completed argumentation about how to produce the best mixture of goods that together would constitute a good human life.

2) This verbalized argumentative discourse is not directly characterized as an incorporeal structure (*kosmos*) apt to rule well, but likened to such a *kosmos*.

3) The reference in the comparison to a structure that is apt to rule well *over a soul-body compound* (which could be an individual human being or the physical cosmos as a whole) harks back to the notion of an intelligent agent-cause introduced in the cosmological segment of the dialogue (23C–31B).

4) As in this previous segment, the intelligent agent-cause is to be understood as *nous* or *phronesis* (also *sophia*), which is an intellectual virtue realized in the rational core of a soul and tasked with ruling over the whole soul-body compound.

5) This enlightened condition of the soul is called a *kosmos* since Plato conceives of the rational soul in such a state as a harmoniously structured dynamic system (as set out in the *Timaeus*).

6) As such a structured system, the enlightened rational soul is characterized by the formal criteria of goodness: measure and proportion, beauty, and truth. It also aims to implement these qualities in the soul-body compound as a whole and in whatever else it rules over. But before it can function as a source of goodness in other things (*qua* agent-cause), the rational soul itself first has to be shaped by the good (as the formal cause of its goodness).

7) Socrates' conversational argument and discourse (*logos*) about the good is likened to the *kosmos* that shapes the dynamic state of an enlightened soul since such discourse is a sort of image and prefiguration of the internal reasoning of a fully restored rational soul.

To be sure, the complex theory that, according to my reading, provides the background to the remark in 64B has to be reconstructed with the help of other passages in the *Philebus* and in other late dialogues such as the *Timaeus*, *Sophist*, and *Phaedrus*. My aim here has been to show that, and how, the suggestive but obscure comparison in 64B hints at this complex of ideas and why it has been placed at this specific juncture of the dialogue.

Bibliography

Apelt, Otto, *Platon: Phaidon*, Leipzig [3]1923.
Burnet, Ioannes, *Platonis Opera, tomus II*, Oxford 1901.
Bury, Robert G., *The Philebus of Plato, with introduction, notes and appendices*, Cambridge 1897.
Delcomminette, Sylvain, *Le* Philèbe *de Platon. Introduction à l'agathologie Platonicienne*, Leiden 2006.
–, *Platon: Philèbe. Introduction, traduction et commentaire*, Paris 2022.
Diès, Auguste, *Platon: Philèbe* (= *Œuvres complètes IX.2*), Paris 1941.
Frede, Dorothea, *Plato: Philebus. Translated with introduction and notes*, Indianapolis, Ind. 1993.
–, *Platon: Philebos. Übersetzung und Kommentar*, Göttingen 1997.
Friedländer, Paul, *Platon, Band III*, Berlin [3]1975.
Gosling, Justin C.B., *Plato: Philebus. Translated with notes and commentary*, Oxford 1975.
Hackforth, Reginald, *Plato's Examination of Pleasure (The* Philebus*)*, Cambridge 1945.
Harte, Verity, *Plato on Parts and Wholes*, Oxford 2002.
Kühn, Wilfried, "Quatre catégories cosmologiques employées en éthique (23b-26d)", in: Monique Dixsaut (ed.), *La fêlure du plaisir. Études sur le Philèbe de Platon. 1: Commentaires*, Paris 1999, 89–154.
Menn, Stephen, *Plato on God as* Nous, Carbondale, Ill. 1995.
Rudebusch, George H., *Plato's Philebus: A Commentary*, Norman, Okla. 2023.
Schleiermacher, Friedrich, *Platons Werke, II.3*, Berlin 1809.
Szaif, Jan, *Platons Begriff der Wahrheit*, Freiburg / München 1996.
–, "The Place of Flawed Pleasures in a Good Life. A Discussion of Plato's *Philebus*", *Plato Journal: The Journal of the International Plato Society* 22 (2021), 133–157. https://impactum-journals.uc.pt/platojournal/article/view/10336
–, "Truth, Music, and the 'Measured' Mind", in: Peter D. Larsen / Vasilis Politis (eds.), *The Platonic Mind*, London 2025, 279–293.
West, Martin L., *The Orphic Poems,* Oxford 1983.
Wolfsdorf, David, *Pleasure in Ancient Greek Philosophy,* Cambridge 2013.

Compensating for Fragmentation

Philosophical Methods in Plato's Later Dialogues in Light of the *Timaeus*

Klaus Corcilius

1. The Human Condition in the *Timaeus*

In his *Timaeus*, Plato depicts the rational part of the human soul as similar to the world soul. He then describes the essential characteristics of the *conditio humana* as the result of the fact that the rational human soul, which is immortal, is put into a mortal body. The outcome of this is the human situation. We may describe that situation as a peculiar kind of *inversion* of the situation the world soul finds itself in. To understand how this is the case, it will be helpful to first consider the characteristics that both the world soul and the human rational soul have in common. Firstly, and most importantly, both are immortal. They *must* be immortal, given that they are the immediate products of the demiurge's work, and the demiurge is incapable of producing anything mortal (41c2–3). The lesser parts of the human soul and the human body are mortal, however, which is also why the demiurge delegates their creation to the lesser deities of traditional religion (41A–D). Secondly, the human rational soul and the world soul consist of the same ingredients or parts, namely divisible and indivisible being alongside identity and difference, which are mixed and arranged in the exact same ways, which is to say according to the structure exhibited by the different macroscopic parts of the universe – the circle of the same and the circle of the different, including its internal differentiations; thirdly, they are moved in the same ways, namely according to the system of the circular movements that the macroscopic parts of the world soul exhibit, even if, as Plato puts it, the mixture and the ingredients of the human rational soul enjoy a lesser degree of purity (*deutera kai trita*, 41D; and the same, I take it, should also hold for their movements). I shall refer to this remarkable commonality between the ingredients, the structure, and the movements of the world soul and the rational core of the human soul as their 'identity in kind'. Identity in kind is clearly significant. It forms the basis for the understanding of the human condition in the *Timaeus* as a kind of inversion of the world soul's condition. Identity in kind implies not only the immortality of the human rational soul but also the latter's capacity to engage in the same kind of activity as the world soul, namely true rational thinking about both intelligible and perceptible things. Timaeus (the character) even says that we humans, when engaged in successful intellectual activity, can actually *keep up with* and *understand* the movements of the world soul (*Ti.* 90d1, '*sunhepesthai*' has both of these meanings). This is certainly good news for us human beings and, from an epistemological point of view, also a strong commitment to a fundamentally optimistic attitude in regard to the possibility of epistemic success for human beings on Plato's part. The identity in kind between human and cosmic rationality has many further consequences that I cannot go into here. What is important for now is that the rational part of the human soul is the core and essence of the human soul and the same in kind as the world soul.[1]

Let us now turn to the dissimilarities. The human rational soul is, as Plato puts it, bound to a body, or, to be more precise, "implanted" or, perhaps better even, "engrafted" in a body (*emphyteutheis*, 42a3). And the body, as we will see in more detail below, is the main reason why it is prevented from exercising its own original nature, which is to engage in the same kind of activity as the world soul (*archaia physis*, 90d5). It is important in this regard that, very much unlike the world soul, which encloses and pervades the entire body of the cosmos (34b3–4; 36D–E, thus making it a divine and self-sufficient causally closed system, 34b4–9), the human rational soul has no such extension. On the contrary, each human soul is but a tiny fragment of the leftover materials from the production of the world soul that the demiurge cut into many pieces, namely exactly as many as there are stars in the sky (41d8–e1). And each of these fragments is bound to, or engrafted in, a body "into and out of which things flow" (43a5–6). In other words, the human rational soul *is enclosed* in a body, while the world soul *encloses* the body of the universe. The consequences of this confinement are drastic from both an epistemological and a moral point of view (which, for Plato, of course are closely linked).

It is no overstatement to say that the predicament of human existence – the *conditio humana* according to the *Timaeus* – results from this confinement of the human rational soul. The hostile environment the embodied rational soul encounters in the cosmos contrasts with the situation of the world soul, which is a self-sufficient and self-regulating spherical body that moves in perfectly regular circular motions (33b7–34b9). Plato thinks of the world soul as having full control over its body, which is the body of the world (34c5). It thus can perform its cognitive activities without any interference from its body. The world soul's movements and its corresponding thinking remain entirely undisturbed by its body, while it cognizes everything in the cosmos it has contact with (*ephaptestai*, 37a6). And since it pervades the entire body of the universe,

---

[1] Sameness in kind excludes parthood. Human rational souls, even if coming from the same mixing bowl as the soul of the world, are not parts of the world soul. See Petrucci, *Platone. Timeo*, 303.

it has contact with everything in it, which makes it that it also *cognizes* everything in the universe. Plato credits the world soul with an "unceasing life of rationality" (*apaustos kai emphronos bios*, 36e4), calling it the single most excellent thing that has come to be (*aristê genomenê tôn gennêthentôn*, 37a1–2, the formulation here, I take it, carries overtones of moral excellence), precisely because it permanently and eternally engages in its cognitive activity. The human soul, by contrast, since it is of lesser purity, fragmented, and enclosed by a body, is shut off from immediate access to the outer world. Its embodied state precludes it from having immediate contact with things in the world. The human soul's way of cognitively accessing the outside world therefore is indirect. It takes place by way of an affection, namely perception (*aisthêsis*). Perception, however, does not reveal the true being of things. It does not show how things actually are; it only reveals the *power of the source* of the perceptual affection to affect the perceiver thus and so:

> When even a minor disturbance affects that which is easily moved by nature, the disturbance is passed on in a chain reaction with some parts affecting others in the same way as they were affected (i.e. the media), *until it reaches the phronimon and reports the power of that which produced* (i.e. the affection; *exangeilêi tou poiêsantos tên dunamin*). (64B)

What this means is that the cognition of the human soul has to operate with a set of data that is inferior to the data with which the world soul operates. While the latter – we do not know how – has direct contact with things themselves,[2] the human soul must work on the basis of how things affect it. What is revealed to it by perception is not the true being of things but only the "power of that which produced the affection." This is an interesting expression. It says that the information the human rational soul (the *phronimon*) gets from perception is not the nature of things themselves but the way in which perceptible things affect it through the body, perhaps, as I tend to think, including the information *that* there is some outside object that is the cause of the affection.[3] The thinking soul will then, on the basis of the data given to it by perception, have to *figure out* what the true nature of things is. And in addition to this indirect and

---

[2] See the discussion of the notion of "contact" in the *Timaeus* in Corcilius, "Ideal Intellectual Cognition", 84–94.

[3] This is a matter of whether we interpret the genitive in the expression "the power *of* that which produced the affection" as part of the *content* of the report delivered by perception or not. In the latter case, the human rational soul would merely receive reports about the powers (presumably perceptual qualities corresponding to the affections like "hot" or "cold", "red" or "white" etc. This seems to be the way Johansen, *Plato's Natural Philosophy*, 170–171, reads the passage), whereas in the former case (which I favor), it would receive reports about there being an external producer of its affection, namely that it has the power to affect it thus and so ("hot thing out there" or "cold thing out there" or "white thing out there" etc.). In this former case, Plato's characterization of perceptual affection would capture the intentionality of perception. On perception through the whole body in the *Timaeus* see Johansen, "Plato on Perceiving".

informationally inferior access to data about external things, the human soul must also deal with the constant bombardment of incoming and outgoing movements that affect its body, as well as the various natural processes to which its body is subject (growth, nutrition, perception and the resulting emotional reactions). All these movements prevent the human soul from cognizing things adequately. Plato says that they distort and stupefy her internal movements rendering the human being "mindless" and "silly" (43D–44B, *anoêtoi*, *anous*). And as if this wasn't enough, the human soul is also subjected to the disturbances that result from the five non-circular (and hence non rational) kinds of inner cosmic movements.

They [i.e. the disturbances] mutilated and disfigured the circles [of the human rational soul] in every possible way so that the circles barely held together and though they remained in motion, they moved without rhyme or reason (*alogôs*), sometimes in the opposite direction, sometimes sideways and sometimes upside down – like a man upside down, head propped against the ground and holding his feet up against something. In that position its right side will present itself both to him and to those looking at him as left, and his left side as right. It is this very thing – and others like it – that had such a dramatic effect upon the revolutions of the soul. (43E)

Ontogenetically, at first at least, the result of all this is utter and unthinking confusion. With the passage of time, however, humans can gain control over these disturbances (44B–C). When they succeed in this, they can hope to *restore the original constitution of the motions of the rational soul* before incarnation – i.e. the state these motions were in before they were distorted by embodiment. The way this works in a nutshell is by aligning the motions of their rational souls with the circular motions of the world soul. The magic word is 'control,' which here means 'self-control' in the sense that the rational core of the human soul gains control over the body and the non-rational parts of the soul. The way Plato puts it, the removal of the hindrances for human rational thinking as they result from embodiment, alongside the restoration of the original course of the rational soul's movements, is the *goal* of human education and indeed the goal of human existence on earth. Plato says that we *ought* to strive to join the motions of the world soul (*skeuasteon*, 90c7–d7), and that it is the job of our moral upbringing and education (*paidagôgia*, 89d7) to bring about the removal of the (bodily) hindrances that prevent us from engaging in undisturbed rational thinking. This is what we are here for according to Plato, namely to restore our original rational nature by mastering our bodily predicament with *logos* (*logôi kratêsas eis to tês prôtês aphikoito eidos hexeôs*, 42d1–2) and to thus become as happy as human beings can be:[4]

We should redirect the revolutions in our heads that were thrown off course around the time of our birth, by coming to learn the harmonies and revolutions of the universe, and so bring

[4] On the cosmological ethics in the *Timaeus* see Sedley, "The Idea of Godlikeness" and Betegh, "Cosmological Ethics".

into conformity with its objects our faculty of understanding, as it was its original condition (*archaia physis*). And when this conformity is complete, we shall have achieved our goal: that best life offered to humankind by the gods, both now and forevermore. (90d1–7)

The path towards gaining control over our bodies with *logos*, very roughly, starts with gaining control over the movements of the body. And this is achieved through gymnastic 'counter-movements' to the environmental movements to which our bodies are naturally exposed. These gymnastic movements are *harmonious* because they imitate the order of the universe (88D–89A). It turns out, then, that for Plato movements are both, one of the main causes of the predicament of the embodied soul but also the main part of the solution to the problem, provided the movements we engage in are tamed and ordered in the right way. But gymnastics is only the first step towards full self-control through education. The end result of the process, if all goes well, is the alignment of the movements of the rational soul with its original nature and thus also the alignment of its cognition with the cognition of the world soul. (88b5–90d7).

These are the outlines of the human condition and the path towards redemption in the *Timaeus*. As said above, the human condition presents us with an *inverted image* of the situation of the world soul: while the world soul encloses and pervades the body of the universe so that the body is in it, the human rational soul is trapped in a body that prevents it from doing what it is designed to do by its nature. Embodied human rational souls are thus very much unlike the world soul, even if their true nature is identical with it in kind. But they are unlike the world soul in a way that is explicable in terms of their fragmentation and embodiment. I will only mention some of the epistemic inversions. As it encloses the body of the universe, the world soul has direct contact with all beings in the world (37A–C). Human rational souls, by contrast, are fragmented. This means that they only have access to a very limited number of beings in the cosmos. Human rational souls furthermore are enclosed in bodies, which cut them off from having direct contact with things in the world and distort the internal motions of the rational soul with a constant avalanche of incoming and outgoing movements. The result is stupidity and confusion. In sum, we may say that embodiment has an effect on human rational souls which can be compared to a particularly severe version of solitary confinement. The only contact human souls have with the outside world is through the window of perception (*aisthêsis*, 64B). But even this window does not show us the outside world as it is but only as it affects our bodies.[5]

In the remainder of this chapter, I wish to explore the idea that the description of the human condition in the *Timaeus* offers an interesting and unifying perspective on many of Plato's remarks on human cognition and philosophical

[5] Of course, all of this is compatible with the fact that the human body also has an enabling function for cognition. On this see below and Campbell, "Biology in the *Timaeus*".

method in his later dialogues. More specifically, I wish to explore the idea that they can be usefully interpreted as offering *strategies of coping with the negative epistemic consequences of human embodiment* as it is described in the *Timaeus*. My contention will be that we understand them as offering strategies of *compensating* for the fragmentation and 'imprisonment' of our rational souls, and that looking at these passages in this way provides us with a philosophically fruitful perspective on important aspects of Plato's discussions of human knowledge. I will begin with a brief description of the details of the cognitive workings of the world soul as they are described in the *Timaeus*. I will use it, as I think Plato does, as a precise model for successful intellectual cognition generally. I will then, without pretension to exhaustiveness, look for remarks on human cognition and philosophical method in Plato's later dialogues that can be interpreted as offering strategies to compensate the embodied human rational soul for the loss of its original cognitive powers.

2. The Model. Ideal Intellectual Cognition

Plato's account of the thinking of the world soul in *Timaeus* 37A–E offers a general philosophical account of intellectual cognition by offering a picture of what the best-case scenario of worldly thinking looks like.[6] If this is correct, that account should offer a fairly precise standard by which to identify and measure less perfect forms of worldly thinking such as the thinking of human beings. According to Plato's account in the *Timaeus*, the world soul's cognition exhibits the following relevant features:[7]

(i) The world soul cognizes everything it has contact with.

---

[6] Or so I have argued in a 2018 paper. See Corcilius, "Ideal Intellectual Cognition".

[7] Here is the relevant piece of text. "Since it [i.e. the world soul] has been mixed out of these three parts – the nature of the Same and the Different, and of Being – and [since] it has been divided and bound together in proportionate ways, and circles round upon itself, [it follows that] whenever it touches something that has divisible being or [something that has] indivisible [being], it, being moved throughout its whole self, declares whatever something is the same as and whatever it is different from, especially in relation to what each thing is [the same as or different from] as well as where and in which way, and when each thing happens to be or to undergo [something] regarding the things that come to be and the things that are always in the same state. But given that the declaration turns out to be equally true whether it is concerned with the Different or the Same, and given that it is borne along in that which is moved by itself without sound or echo, [it follows that] whenever it is concerned with what is perceptible, and the circle of the Different, moving straight, proclaims it to the whole of its soul, firm and true opinions and convictions come about; whenever, on the other hand, it is concerned with what is intelligible, and the circle of the Same, moving smoothly, reveals it, intellect and knowledge necessarily result." (*Ti.* 37a2–c3)

(ii) The world soul, while rotating, at every moment of time has contact with every single thing inside the cosmos that *has* being, both divisible, perceptible being and indivisible, intelligible being.

(iii) The world soul cognizes each of the things it has contact with in the cosmos (i.e. all things in the cosmos), by subjecting them to an exhaustive comparison (the 'GREAT COMPARISON'). During the GREAT COMPARISON each item the world soul has contact with is compared to each other item it has contact with, which is to say to all other things in the cosmos. This comparison takes place in four different respects, namely in relation to what (*pros hoti*), location (*hopêi*), manner (*hopôs*), and time (*hopote*). It is unclear whether Plato intends these four respects to exhaust all respects in which the world soul compares things in the cosmos or not. But for our present purpose we can ignore this difficult question.[8]

(iv) Given the above, the world soul's thinking amounts to a full and exhaustive census of all the identities and differences that every single thing in the cosmos exhibits with relation to every other single thing in the cosmos at every moment of time in these four respects.

(v) The world soul's cognition consists in pronouncements or, as we would say, comparative judgments that express all the identities and differences that things in the cosmos have with relation to each other in the above four respects. They take the following form.

X is the same as *Y* in respect *R*
and respectively
X is different from *Y* in respect *R*
where *R* stands for the following four respects
(a) what *X* and what *Y* are,
(b) where *X* and *Y* are,
(c) the manner in which *X* and *Y* are, and
(d) at which time *X* and *Y* are.

(vi) The outcome of the GREAT COMPARISON is true propositions (*logoi*) about every single thing in the cosmos. When they regard intelligible things, the resulting propositions form knowledge (*epistêmê*), and when they regard perceptible things, the resulting propositions form true opinion (*doxa alêthês*).

In Plato's description, the world soul does not cognize things by intuiting them either by perception or intellectual intuition, but only by subjecting them to the GREAT COMPARISON. The world soul will know exhaustively how each single thing in the cosmos either is identical with, or different from, every other thing in it. But it will not have any immediate and intuitive knowledge of things, either perceptual or intellectual. The words 'idea', 'form' or 'kind' do not occur in the description of its knowledge. The world soul possesses only

---

[8] See the brief discussion in Plutarch, *De animae procreatione* 1023E.

relative knowledge of all things in the cosmos by cognizing not things themselves but their interrelatedness and order consisting in a full list of all the systemic properties that things have with relation to each other. I feel entitled to say "*all* systemic properties", because identity and difference are the most fine-grained relative properties in Plato's conceptual repertoire. It is plausible, therefore, that Plato's description of the world soul is meant to render it *omniscient* of everything that happens or is the case in the cosmos, albeit in this non-intuitive and comparative 'negative copy'-way of cognizing things. I shall call this the world soul's 'worldly omniscience' in what follows, as Plato does not mention anything about extra-cosmic items being part of the world soul's knowledge. It is plausible that this cognition of all identities and differences of things which are the case will result in further cognition of everything that might *follow* from, or supervene on, that exhaustive cognition of the actual, even if Plato does not mention this explicitly. But nothing in the account would prevent the world soul from having knowledge of the patterns and further relations that in one way or the other supervene on, or can be inferred from, its cognition. This may include knowledge of forms or even of the world soul itself. But however that may be, given that the *Timaeus* conceives of the world soul as an ideal worldly cognitive agent, it is highly likely that the objects of the world soul's cognition should include *everything that can be truly cognized by human beings*. This, I think, follows anyway from Plato's description of our task in the world as becoming as much as possible like the world soul by aligning our cognitive movements to the world soul's movements and to think like it as much as we can (90B–D). The world soul's worldly omniscience should therefore comprise *everything* that can possibly be cognized by any human being in the world.[9] What that means is that *further facts* about the order of things that are less fine-grained than the complete list of identities and differences between individual things, and generic facts in particular, should be implied or, as it were, come for free to anyone who possesses the knowledge that results from the GREAT COMPARISON. It is of course conceivable that someone who

[9] In this respect the world soul's knowledge, which at any moment comprises the entirety of all the facts about the world, and therewith everything that can possibly be known by anybody, is – to some extent – similar to Immanuel Kant's *Ideal of Pure Reason*, which is the transcendental principle of the possibility of all things (KdrV. 601–606 B). Kant describes it as follows. "Thus if the thoroughgoing determination in our reason is grounded on a transcendental substratum, which contains as it were *the entire storehouse of material from which all possible predicates of things can be taken*, then this substratum is nothing other than the idea of an All of reality (*omnitudo realitatis*). All true negations are then nothing but limits, which they could not be called unless they were grounded in the unlimited (the All)." (KdrV. 603–604 B, emphasis mine). It should however be added that, for Kant, Plato would be guilty of an unlicensed hypostatisation of that principle, due to what he takes to be a dialectical transformation of the distributive unity of our use of experience into the collective unity of the whole of experience.

knows the differences between every single x-thing and every single y-thing in the world happens not to know that *x*-things thereby form a general kind which is different from the kind y-things. But there is no good reason I can think of why Plato would have conceived of the world soul as devoid of the ability of forming thoughts of general facts, including thoughts of the interrelatedness of the generic facts themselves. It seems to me that his account of the thinking of the world soul as an ideal worldly cognitive agent should imply this. If this is on the right track, the GREAT COMPARISON presents us with only the first and most basic step of the world soul's cognitive activity, namely the full census of all the identities and differences that all things have in relation to each other. Since Plato thinks of the world soul as an ideal cognitive agent that leads the best and happiest intellectual life among all generated things, it is likely that he endows it with the best possible cognition of *everything* that there is to be known about the cosmos on the basis of the GREAT COMPARISON, including generic facts and everything that follows from them, even if he does not explicitly say so. This, at any rate, is the hypothesis based on which I shall work in the remainder of the chapter.[10]

---

[10] In support of my thesis of the worldly omniscience of the world soul, let me point out that the different respects in which the world soul compares things in the cosmos with each other are sufficiently vague, but also sufficiently weighty, to cover all sorts of differences and identities, not only of the individual objects in the cosmos that the world soul has contact with (perceptible and intelligible), but also to cover them under various different descriptions. For example, the *manner* (*hopôs*) in which things are identical or different from each other may include their being active and passive or their being causes or effects of one another. It may well also cover different kinds of priority and other logical, modal, and ontological relations in which things in the cosmos stand towards each other. Since it is *possible* to interpret, for instance, the fact that the world soul's exhaustive list of identities and differences of all things with relation to each other should dispense her from having to engage in inductive *inference towards universal knowledge* without depriving her of the corresponding *universal knowledge*, we should, I think, go with that possibility. A cognitive agent who understands of each individual cow that it is ruminant will thereby understand that all cows are ruminants. Note also that the identities and differences that generic entities exhibit with relation to each other are identities and differences as well, and they are identities and differences that are different from the identities and differences that individual entities exhibit with relation to each other. Again, there is no reason to suppose why Plato should have prevented the world soul from having cognition of these identities and differences too (the discussion of *Tht.* 186b2–9 below will support this idea of a recursive character of the world soul's cognition). It is not likely that Plato wanted to exclude the world soul from the cognition of such differences. Plato conceives of the world soul as an ideal cognitive agent that serves as a model for human thinking. I therefore think it best to credit her with worldly omniscience. And this omniscience should include not only the knowledge of facts but also knowledge of facts about these facts. This may very well also include the knowledge of forms. Knowledge of forms is certainly *compatible* with the kind of knowledge Plato attributes to the world soul; it is not an alternative to it. See below.

3. Human Intellectual Cognition

How can the human rational soul compensate for the predicament resulting from its imprisonment in a body 'into and out of which things flow' and restore, as Plato thinks is possible, its original nature (*archaia physis*, 90d5)? While on earth, it will not be possible for the rational soul to restore the full extent of bodiless happiness it enjoyed before it was brought into this world. This follows from embodiment and, as we will see now, also from the cognitive costs that come with the accretion of the two non-rational parts of the soul. These non-rational parts of the soul, in spite of the necessity with which they are said to come about once a human rational soul is implanted into a body (42a3–b1), are each in their own ways *enabling conditions* for the rational soul to dwell in the cosmos, both biologically (*epithumia*, "appetite") and socially (*thumos*). The lesser gods designed the two non-rational parts of the soul to mediate between the rational soul and the body to ensure the survival of the mortal body in a hostile environment (69c5–70e5, *eiper ti melloi pote thnêton esesthai genos*). Notwithstanding their hypothetically necessary enabling role, appetite and *thumos* on their part themselves present major obstacles for the rational soul's well-functioning. They bring irrational drives with them that present additional hindrance to the rational soul's pursuit of its own rational goals (see especially 69c8–d6).[11] However, Plato does not demand their complete suppression but instead suggests overcoming them in such a way so as to make these drives subservient to the rational part of the soul. They must be "mastered" and be subjected to self-control. As we have seen, the way to do this is by the creation of *harmony* among the parts of the soul, which Plato understands as a reciprocal, but hierarchically organized, collaboration among the soul-parts (89e3–90a2, *summetrous kinêseis*). Harmony among the parts of the soul, in his understanding, amounts to the teleological subordination and subserviency of the non-rational parts under the rational part, which in return thinks on their behalf and takes care of them. Harmony among the parts of the soul, then, does not require the *absence* of bodily movement or the inactivity of *epithumia* and *thumos* but only a harmonious way of exercising them (89e5–90a2). Hence, our best state in this world will have to include the exercise of the non-rational parts of our souls and of our bodies. But this, as I've suggested above, comes not without significant cognitive costs. To start with, our intellectual activity will not be continuous. It will be interrupted by sleep and our other basic needs, desires, emotions etc. insofar as they present a hindrance to the exercise of our intellect. Plato also emphasizes that the symmetry of the motions of our soul-parts requires constant physical exercise, so as to keep the

[11] This is so despite the intelligent design of the human body which posits the non-rational parts of the soul in separate places of the body to facilitate their subservience to the rational part (69d6–70a7). It still is a major effort to bring this subserviency about.

ensouled body in the *right* kind of movement that, by keeping it busy in the right way, prevents it from disturbing the activity of the rational soul. There is of course much more to be said about all this. But leaving he details aside for the moment, we can say that not only the body but also the two non-rational parts of the soul present the rational soul with considerable obstacles. To master them in the right way is the goal of primary education. Once these bodily obstacles are removed, we next must ask how Plato thinks we human beings can restore the original movements of our rational souls. The *Timaeus* is relatively brief on this. Plato says that we should provide our souls with the appropriate motions and nourishment. We should straighten out the distorted revolutions in the rational part of our soul by learning the harmonies and revolutions of the universe and thus "bring into conformity with its object our faculty of understanding, as it was our original condition" (90d3–5). This emphasizes, as is typical for the *Timaeus*, the physical aspects of intellectual education. I will now ask what contribution Plato's statements on human knowledge and philosophical method outside the *Timaeus* can make to our question of how we can regain our original rational nature.

At first, the answer seems obvious. To restore our original state, we must practice dialectic. In the *Sophist,* Plato says that dialectic is the art or science of finding out what kinds are the same and what kinds are different from each other (*Sph.* 253d1–3), or in short, it is the art of making distinctions in the right kind of way.[12] This sounds like what we have been looking for. For it does seem that this is exactly what the world soul's GREAT COMPARISON is doing when it detects the identities and differences among things in the cosmos that result in her knowledge and true opinion. So, even though the word 'dialectic' does not occur in the *Timaeus*, there is no good reason to doubt that the thinking of the world soul as described in the *Timaeus* provides a framework that helps us understand why the art of dialectic makes sense in the first place: to join the cognitive movements of the world soul is to engage in her thinking of the identities and differences among things, even if only partly. And this is what dialectic according to the above description from the *Sophist* promises to deliver. It seems, then, Plato thinks that dialectic is the *technê* that can help us in restoring our original rational nature.

Visitor: So, Theaetetus, what shall we label this knowledge? Or for heaven's sake, without noticing have we stumbled on the knowledge that free people have? Maybe we've found the philosopher even though we were looking for the sophist?

---

[12] I take this description to be compatible with the description of the dialectical person in *Cratylos* 390c10–11 "And what would you call someone who knows how to ask and answer questions? Wouldn't you call him a dialectician?" (trans. C.D.C. Reeve). It seems to me that this is just a matter of perspective. The best person to ask and answer questions is the person in command of the structure of reality as it is reflected in the web of identities and differences between things.

Theaetetus: What do you mean?
Visitor: Aren't we going to say that it takes expertise in dialectic to divide things by genera and not to think that the same kind is a different one or that a different kind is the same?
Theaetetus: Yes.
Visitor: So if a person can do that, he'll be capable of adequately distinguishing a single kind spread out all through a lot of other things, each of which stands separate from the others (i). In addition he can distinguish kinds that are different from each other but are included within a single kind that's outside them (ii), or a single kind that's connected as a unit throughout many wholes (iii), or many kinds that are completely separate from others (iv). That's what it is to know how to distinguish by genus how things can associate and how they can't.
Theaetetus: Absolutely.
Visitor: And you'll assign this dialectical activity only to someone who has a pure and just love of wisdom. (*Soph.* 253c6–e6, transl. White, modified)[13]

Dialectic is the art of making distinctions about kinds and sub-kinds in philosophical discourse and of making them in the right kind of way, namely by identifying correctly the relations of compatibility and incompatibility in which they stand towards each other according to (i)-(iv), namely inclusion within a larger kind, exclusion within a larger kind, connectedness (or continuity) of one kind over different kinds, and complete separation of kinds. Doing this in the right way will, I take it, eventually yield taxonomical systems that correspond to bodies of knowledge (cp. *Phdr.* 265d3–e3). Elsewhere, Plato says that if we apply this method to the beautiful, the just, and the good, it will make the person who internalizes the resulting *logoi*, provided she is suitably receptive of them, as happy as this is possible for us (*Phdr.* 276E–277A, cp. *Ti.* 90d1–7, quoted above). Here, then, is the argument for why dialectic is the method of our choice for restoring our original nature. The world soul's thinking of the identities and differences among things in the cosmos yields *logoi* that correspond to knowledge and true opinion. The art of dialectic is concerned with identities and differences among kinds. Dialectic is all about *logoi*.[14] When used correctly, it provides us with the identities and differences of kinds, thus promising us knowledge and true opinion, as far as we are able to possess them. In this way, the art of dialectic compensates for the loss of our original nature.

Unfortunately, even though much in the above argument is right, things are not that simple. Remember that the human rational soul works on the basis of data that is inferior to the data with which the world soul works. Unlike the world soul, we have no direct contact with things themselves, let alone with intelligible things. What we have access to is perceptible things, which are only images of intelligible things. This is the reason why we have to work hard to extract intelligible information about things *from the data that perception provides us with*, especially since, as we have seen, our access to perceptible things is only through perception, i.e. through the *affections* that perceptible things

[13] On this passage see Gill, *Philosophos*, 211–214.
[14] *Plt.* 285d8–286b2; *R.* VII 533b1–535a1, especially 534b3-4.

bring about in us. This regards our information about intelligible objects but it also regards the concepts we employ in our investigations, including the very concepts we employ in grasping perceptible things. We cannot access the being of kinds just like that. Human thinking requires concepts, and Plato is clear that we must *extract* our concepts from our perceptual affections. Dialectic is about distinguishing kinds, but we depend on our concepts to be able to think kinds. Our concepts are not given to us by nature and without further ado; we must extract them, or work them out, from what perception provides us with.[15]

In the above passage from the *Sophist,* the Eleatic Stranger describes dialectic as expertise (*epistêmê*) in dividing *genera* (*genê*) without thinking that the same kind (*eidos*) is a different one or that a different kind is the same. This kind of distinguishing kinds clearly does *not* work on the basis of the same set of data that the world soul works with. To start with, there is no misrepresentation of being in the world soul whose thinking is necessarily true. Also, there was no mention of *genê* and *eidê* in the description of the world soul's thinking. It is true that I argued above that her worldly omniscience would give her the information about kinds "for free". The world soul would gain that knowledge of *genê* and *eidê* and so on on the basis of her exhaustive census of identities and differences of all individual things in the cosmos as a kind of surplus. But as far as the text allows us to tell, the world soul does not generate its knowledge on the basis of a comparison of *genê* and *eidê* but solely on the basis of a comparison of individual things in the cosmos. Hence, even if it is good news for us that there is an expertise that allows us to do something that looks like what the world soul does (even if not exhaustively), things are far more difficult for us than they are for the world soul. We humans have to work with far inferior data. We cannot work with things themselves but must content ourselves with how things affect us through perception. It is from what perception provides us with that we must *form* the concepts we use in dialectic.[16]

Concept Formation Step 1

How do we acquire our concepts? How does the extraction of concepts from perceptual experience work for Plato? It seems to work in a way not altogether different from the way in which the world soul gains knowledge in the *Timaeus*, namely by comparison, only that human beings operate on an inferior set of data. We can only compare the data that perception provides us with. This is clear from the *Theaetetus* where Plato offers an account of the formation of simple perceptual concepts such as 'hardness'. The dialogue makes it very

---

[15] On concepts in Plato and in the classical period see now Caston, "Concepts in Classical Greece". On concepts in ancient philosophy generally see Betegh/Tsouna, *Conceptualising Concepts*.

[16] In that picture, in order to ensure the possibility of human cognitive success, there must be a sufficiently high degree of rational order in the perceptual data.

clear that the acquisition even of such basic empirical concepts is a matter neither of sensory affection nor of immediate and intuitive intellectual cognition but the outcome of a process of juxtaposition and comparison of a plurality of perceived items.

Not so fast now. Wouldn't you say that it is through touch that the soul perceives the hardness of what is hard, and similarly the softness of what is soft. "Yes." But as regards their being – the fact that they both are and also their opposition to one another, and the being, again, of this opposition, the soul itself attempts to discriminate for us by going over them [viz. the hard and soft perceptual objects etc.], and comparing them in relation to one another. (*Tht.* 186b2–9, transl. by Levett, rev. Burnyeat, modified)

This passage tells us that mastering concepts,[17] even such basic empirical ones as hardness and softness, requires some kind of holistic and *systematic framework*, however minimal this framework might be. For an epistemic agent to come to possess a concept of hardness, for instance, he must compare the hard objects he perceives with other perceived objects that relate to the hard objects in systematic ways, for example by being contrary or otherwise opposed to them. If one engages in this comparison, one will come to be aware of a candidate for the *being* of hardness (*ousia*). This is how the soul "attempts" (*peiratai*, 186b9) to discriminate such beings. According to the above passage, our rational souls (the soul "by itself", 185e6) *generate* their empirical concepts by juxtaposing and comparing perceptual objects with each other in their minds in this way, i.e. by "going over them" and discriminating them in relation to each other. This, I take it, is to detect identities and differences of perceptual things by comparing them to each other. Our acquisition of the corresponding concepts is the result of that discriminatory process. It is, in other words, the identities and differences of perceptual things *as we detect them*.[18] This means

[17] In our example this is not the soft or hard thing (*F*-thing) but the concepts of softness and hardness (*F*-ness) taken in themselves. D. Frede, "The Soul's Silent Dialogue", "The Philosophical Economy", and recently Brown, "Do Forms Play the Role", argue for a reading of the *koina* passage in the *Tht.* as being about concepts. See main text below.

[18] ἐπανιοῦσα καὶ συμβάλλουσα πρὸς ἄλληλα κρίνειν, *Tht.* 186b6–9. Note that *krinein* here need not mean "to judge" or "to decide" (McDowell and similarly Lovett/Burnyeat, Rowe, also Gill and Lienemann in this volume). I think it is much better rendered as "to discriminate", "to discern" or "to distinguish" (on this point see A. Schmitt, *Denken ist Unterscheiden* and earlier publications). In my view Plato tells us here how he thinks the soul *acquires* its concepts of the being (*ousia*) of *F* as for instance of hardness, namely by juxtaposing perceptual data and detecting their identities and differences as they result from that juxtaposition ("going over them"). "Decision" or "judgement" do not in my view capture the *generative character* of that process as Plato seems to emphasize it here. Let me add that I do not see that the *Theatetus*-passage under discussion offers an account of perception inconsistent with the role of perception in *Republic* VII in the acquisition of concepts (*mutatis mutandis*, of course). The fact that perception is said to "announce" (*parangellein*) in *R.* VII 524a2–3 need, and I think should, not be taken in a way that attributes beliefs to it (on Plato's usage of *diangellein* and *mênuein* see Corcilius, "Ideal Intellectual Cognition", 80–81, on

that when we have arrived at a concept as for instance the concept of hardness as a result of having successfully distinguished hard from soft and other related objects in some such way, we are in possession not only of an isolated concept of hardness but of the concept of hardness as part of a whole *network* of related concepts such as softness and other ones. Plato says here that we possess the being of hardness only once we are aware of how hardness relates to other concepts that systematically relate to it. In the text, the example for such a network of systematic relations is the relation of opposition (*enantiotês*), but the context suggests that something like that holds good for all sorts of systematic relations.[19] The main point is that we *generate* our concepts of perceptible things *by way of comparing them with each other* and that the result of this comparison is not isolated concepts but entire networks of concepts that most basically consist in the differences and identities of things that perception provide us with. Hardness and softness and the entire network of related concepts *emerge* from the souls' comparisons of perceptual objects with each other. Plato does not countenance the possibility of acquiring isolated concepts. He thinks of concepts holistically, as he also thinks holistically about the comparative thinking of the world soul. But for us humans to acquire them requires hard work involving a great deal of "trouble and education".[20]

One may object here that I render as "concepts" what in the above text Plato refers to as "being (*ousia*)". However, my understanding of "concept" here corresponds only to whatever arises in the soul as the outcome of the act of comparing and discriminating described above. In our case this outcome is the *mental presence of the being of hardness and softness*, which I take to be the *concepts* of hardness and softness. Now, certainly Plato does not want to say that the *being* of hardness and softness (*F*-ness) results from our acts of comparison and discrimination. Also, the above text explicitly says that the outcome of our comparisons etc. is our souls' *attempts* to discriminate the being of things (*tên ousian .... krinein peiratai*, 186b6-9). Plato talks here about our concepts of beings.[21] And it is extremely unlikely that every concept we generate in this

the "summoners of understanding" passage in the *Republic* see, most recently, Warren, "Early Learning").

[19] Lorenz, *The Brute Within*, 87 and 91, seems to agree when he speaks of "structural features".

[20] "And thus there are some things which all creatures, humans and animals alike, are naturally able to perceive as soon as they are born; I mean, the affections which reach the soul through the body. But comparisons (*analogismata*) regarding their being and their advantageousness come, when they do, only as the result of a long and arduous development, involving a good deal of trouble and education." (*Tht.* 186b11–c5, transl. by Levett, rev. Burnyeat, modified). On the holistic theory proposed in this passage and its similarity to the thinking of the world soul, see Corcilius, "Ideal Intellectual Cognition", section 3.

[21] What he in *Parm.* 132b3–c8 calls a *noêma*. On the distinction between forms and our concepts of them in Plato and his use of the term '*noêma*' see Caston "Concepts in Classical Greece", 18-20.

way will be adequate and match an existing being or kind. Much can go wrong, in spite of the latent knowledge Plato attributes to our souls (*Men.* 81A–86B; *Phd.* 72E–76E; *Phdr.* 249B–C).[22]

Concept Formation Step 2

But the above text goes beyond a description of the formation of basic empirical concepts such as hardness and softness. It also tells us how we generate our concepts of the *relations* in which perceptual data and our concepts of them stand to each other. We do this in the same way that we generate our concepts of perceptible things themselves, namely by 'going over' them again, only this time we do not compare our perceptual data with each other, but, as I understand it, our acquired *concepts*:

> But as regards their being – the fact that they both are and also their opposition to one another, *and the being, again, of this opposition*, the soul itself attempts to discriminate for us by going over them etc. (*Tht.* 186b6–9)[23]

Plato here says that we apply the same comparative process by which we generate our empirical concepts to its own output. Our souls can in this way go 'meta' and form concepts of our concepts, namely by juxtaposing and comparing them to each other in the same way in which we compare our perceptual data. In the text the example is the relation of opposition. The relation of opposition was already 'at work' in the formation of the perceptual concepts of hardness and softness but it was not itself an object of cognition. What Plato here describes is how we arrive at our conception of these very concepts. First, we come to be aware that hardness and softness are opposed to each other. Then we compare ("go over") the relation of opposition with some other relation (Plato does not tell us which), with the result that we acquire a concept of the relation of opposition, or, as he puts it, "the being, again, of this opposition". The process of concept formation as described by Plato is productive and, to some extent at least, *recursive*. Presumably, the iterability of the application of the comparative process of concept-formation to its own output will at some

---

22 The fact that perceptual experience is a necessary condition for us coming to develop our conceptual repertoire and abilities is fully compatible with Plato's realism in regard of the existence of separate forms, which is a fundamentally anti-empiricist tenet. It is also compatible with Plato's idea in the *Timaeus* that our rational souls, which consist of the circle of the same and the circles of the different, *are* themselves in some sense "made of" conceptual components, namely being and the reflexive concepts of identity and difference (*Ti.* 35a1–36d7). The point is only that neither our empirical concepts nor the concepts which constitute our rational souls are naturally *given* to us as objects of cognition – we have to work hard to extract them from the data our perceptual experience provides us with.

23 Τὴν δέ γε οὐσίαν καὶ ὅτι ἐστὸν καὶ τὴν ἐναντιότητα πρὸς ἀλλήλω καὶ τὴν οὐσίαν αὖ τῆς ἐναντιότητος αὐτὴ ἡ ψυχὴ ἐπανιοῦσα καὶ συμβάλλουσα πρὸς ἄλληλα κρίνειν πειρᾶται ἡμῖν.

point come to an end. Presumably, this will be the case when we reach the highest universal concepts such as being, identity, and difference. As we have seen above, Plato thinks of identity and difference not as empirical concepts but as constitutive parts of the rational soul. In the process of concept formation, we *employ* identity and difference when we compare things with each other and go "over them", so as to generate the corresponding concepts.[24] If this is right, the human rational soul, by employing identity and difference (its constituent parts) by comparing perceptual data and concepts with each other, can eventually come to have a conception of its own constitutive parts.

Concept Formation and the World Soul

All of this suggests that for Plato our concepts are structures that we do not intuit but *generate* by locating them in systematic frameworks of features that emerge from our comparisons both of perceptual things and of our concepts of them. Of course, the *Theaetetus* does not tell us how *exactly* the soul's comparison is supposed to generate our grasp of hardness or softness or the relation of opposition. But the parallel to the passage about the thinking activity of the world soul in *Ti.* 37a2–c5 should be clear enough.[25] The *Theaetetus* shows that the comparison of things by way of detecting identities and differences with other things is *only the first step* in the generation of our full repertoire of concepts,[26] as is clear from the fact that the dialogue also offers a brief account of the formation of our concepts *of concepts*, thus pointing out the recursiveness of the process of concept formation. This should at least be a good starting point for a fuller account of concept formation in human beings.

But however that may be, we now see better how Plato thinks human beings acquire the concepts that form the basic material for dialectical practice. Dialectic operates with concepts, and we acquire concepts in the way explicated above. The basic mechanism of human concept formation is the same as the mechanism by which the world soul generates its cognition of things in the cosmos, namely by comparing things with each other in a – more or less –

---

[24] Identity and difference are among the *megista gene*. Mary-Louise Gill refers to them as "structural forms / kinds". See Gill, *Philosophos*, 235–236; and "Method and Metaphysis": "The nature of a structural kind is determined by its functional role in enabling categorial kinds to be what they are and / or to associate with or differ from one another." See also Brown, who suggests that we should think of structural kinds more in terms of their associative / dissociative function in sentences ("Do Forms Play the Role", 106–111).

[25] See Corcilius, "Ideal Intellectual Cognition", 96–99.

[26] There is additional reason, therefore, to think also of *Ti.* 37a2–c5 as giving a perfectly general account of ideal intellectual thinking by giving us only the first step of the process, namely the formation of an exhaustive system of concepts by way of what I have called the GREAT COMPARISON. The Description of the world soul's thinking in the *Timaeus*, if I am right, gives us only the foundational process of intellectual cognition on the basis of which further and also higher forms of cognition can take place.

systematic setting. The difference is that we have to work on the basis of an inferior set of data; our perceptions only give us data about how things affect us. Our concepts are therefore probably of much lower quality than the identities and differences that Plato imagines for the world soul as its thoughts, since these are said to result from direct contact with the things themselves. The world soul has no need of concepts as they result from the comparison of perceptual objects. It doesn't perceive to begin with. And – no less importantly – due to the fragmentation of our rational souls our data set does not cover all the available evidence, but only a tiny fraction thereof. Our comparisons will therefore be far less systematic, if at all, as our data is far from complete. The cognitive costs of embodiment and fragmentation, then, are twofold. Our dependency on perception causes a dramatic loss in the quality of our data, while the lack of exhaustivity of our data is responsible for a no less dramatic lack in their quantity and resulting systematicity. Therefore, even if the underlying mechanism of comparison appears to be the same in both cases, we (not the world soul!) must apply procedures to verify the *adequacy* of our concepts. This is dialectic.

Dialectic

I will skip the process of the formation of judgment in Plato which does not directly contribute to the issue at hand and confine myself to very briefly showing how dialectic can be usefully conceived as an art that compensates for the cognitive losses that go along with the fragmentation and embodiment of our rational souls. As we have seen in *Sph.* 253D–E, dialectic is the art of dividing (*dihaireisthai*) genera in such a way as to detect the identities and differences of kinds (*eidê*) and to ascertain how they can be combined – or not – in accordance with (i)–(iv) above. This includes not only the analytic distinction of kinds by division but also the synoptic identification of kinds by different varieties of collection. Accordingly, the product of that art should be an awareness of these identities and differences. This awareness can be realized to different degrees. The worldly omniscience of the world soul is based on the possession of an exhaustive census of all identities and differences that the things in the cosmos exhibit. This, as we have seen, gives her knowledge of the entire web of identities and differences that make up the order of things in the cosmos. Human dialectic, by contrast, can at best produce fragmentary knowledge of the overall conceptual order. But obtaining exhaustive knowledge of the conceptual order among kinds should certainly be a (perhaps approximative) goal for the art of dialectic.[27] As we have seen, from the standpoint of the *Timaeus*, the

[27] The competence of the *dialektikos* as described in *R.* VII 534b3–c1 consists in the ability to grasp the definition of the being of each thing and to distinguish it from all other things (537C adds the synoptic ability). Being able to grasp the definition of any given kind does not require a full census of the identities and differences of all kinds (as Speusippus

goal of the art of dialectic should be to achieve knowledge and true opinion and to thus join the cognitive movements of the world soul and restore the original condition of the rational part of the soul as much as this is possible for us. In the rest of the chapter, I shall focus only on those features of the art that strike me as the most important to compensate for the cognitive losses that the fragmentation and the embodiment of our rational souls cause in us.

Finding the genus

The most important feature is to find a proper starting point for scientific inquiry, namely finding the subject genus of a given science. To identify a subject genus in the unlimited multitude of phenomena is to discover a domain that a given scientific inquiry will be concerned with. A genus is such precisely because it is a *closed domain* that can be set off from all other things and be made an object of systematic study. This, I take it, is because the correct identification of a scientific genus gives us a *totality*. A genus is a limited camp, field, or domain of reality, the analysis of which can lie in our power precisely because of the limitedness of the domain. To have identified a domain puts us in a situation where we can start to look for a more or less *exhaustive* grasp of its internal order (see e.g. *Phlb.* 16c5-18d2) and to thus compensate for the quantitative shortcomings of the data we have to work with. This is presumably also why the first discoverer (the *prôtos heuretês*) of a science is so important for Plato. To identify a genus requires an exceptional synoptic talent, which is why Socrates in the *Philebus* refers to Theuth, the discoverer of the art of literacy, as a god or a god-inspired man. Indeed, without the identification of a domain, done in the right way by collecting either similar things or things that share a common feature or common core, we would not even be able to know *what* to divide, where to look etc. It therefore makes sense for Plato to speak about the identification of a scientific genus as a heroic act; a genus gives us a closed and manageable domain. That allows us to study a field in a way that mimics in

seems to have thought, cp. Aristotle, *Anal. Post.* II 13, 97a6–22) but having a complete census of all identities and differences is certainly not excluded by the description in the *R.* (Menn, "Collecting the Letters", argues that the characterization in *R.* VII is concerned only with definitions as verbal formulae as opposed to the real elements of things, 301). Lesley Brown discusses the ability to define given target kinds as an *alternative* to the ability of possessing the conceptual order of things ("taxonomic grasp of a fragment of reality" in her words, Brown, "Do Forms Play the Role", 102). But it seems to me that these two aspects of dialectic are inseparable from each other. A given target kind is a possible object of definition only because there is a taxonomical order of kinds, while to define a given target kind just is to uncover parts of the relevant taxonomical order. And the knowledge of the taxonomical order of a given domain in the Platonic sense presupposes the ability to define any kind of that domain.

miniature the exhaustive grasp of the unrestricted domain of all things in the cosmos that the world soul enjoys.[28]

Dividing kinds in the genus

Next comes the art of making the right distinctions within the genus. This is to be done by way of *methodologically ordered divisions*.[29] Everything going well, the process of methodologically ordered divisions will end up with a well-ordered and numbered series of hierarchically arranged conceptual kinds that adequately reflects the order of that area and that constitutes the scientific knowledge of the respective domain. In a nutshell, division divides genera and kinds into sub-kinds, either dichotomously or by a greater number of sub-kinds, the conjunction of which will *exhaust*, and thus be coextensive with, their superordinate genus. Again, everything going well, these sub-kinds should be *immediately subordinated* to their respective superordinate genera, which means that there is no kind in-between a given kind and its sub-kinds. In this way, the dialectician proceeds by further dividing the resulting sub-kinds etc. until *all* the distinctions to be drawn within a given domain are in fact drawn without leaving out any divisional step. According to Plato, this procedure, if properly applied, not only allows one to generate an adequate picture of the interrelatedness of the kinds that constitute a given scientific domain, but it also puts one in a position to identify, and define, each kind within the domain. This is done by recounting the divisional steps in the divisional history (or the divisional "tree") that lead to the target kind. In the example of the domain of articulate sounds from the *Philebus* the division into kinds is described as follows.

(…) *Socrates:* The way some god or god-inspired man discovered that vocal sounds is unlimited, as tradition in Egypt claims for a certain deity called Theuth. He was the first to discover that the vowels in that unlimited variety are not one but several, and again that there are others that are not voiced, but make some kind of noise, and that they, too, have a number. As a third kind of letters he established the ones we now call mute. After this he further subdivided the ones without sound or mutes down to every single unit. In the same fashion he also dealt with the vowels and the intermediates, until he had found out the number for each one of them, and then he gave all of them together the name "letter". (*Phlb.* 18b6–c6, transl. D. Frede)

This gives us the following picture of the outcome and result of a successful case of division of a domain:

[28] Of course, the world soul has an exhaustive grasp of all particular things in the cosmos. Dialectic has to work with kinds. On the passage in the *Philebus* see Striker, *Peras und Apeiron*; Frede, *Philebus*, 130–166; and Menn, "Collecting the Letters".

[29] Doing this, as has been emphasized by Stephen Menn ("Collecting the Letters", 299), will probably require collection as well.

ONE	MANY		UNLIMITED
Spoken sounds	Mutes	B	Spoken Sounds
		T	
		etc.	
	Sonants	L	
		S	
		etc.	
	Vowels	A	
		E	
		etc.	

Fig. 1: Division of the domain of articulate sound

A crucial point here is that this division presents an exhaustive picture of the order of all kinds that make up the domain.[30] Here, again, it is *exhaustivity* that drives the scientific character of the resulting body of knowledge. Plato says so explicitly:

And as he realized that none of us could gain any knowledge even of a single one of them taken by itself without understanding them all, he considered that the one link that somehow makes them all one and called it the art of literacy. (*Phlb.* 18c7–d2, transl. Frede slightly modified)

The knowledge here consists in the conceptual awareness of the order, or *interrelatedness*, of the kinds that constitute the scientific genus. That is why one cannot really know a single letter without knowing all of them. To know a letter is to understand its role in the order of letters. The order of letters is the link (*desmos*) that unifies the letters *qua* being kinds of their genus. To understand the order of the genus in this way can compensate for the inferior quality of our data because the order of letters consisting of the numbered series of hierarchically arranged divisions corresponds to knowledge of a *unity*, namely the internally differentiated order of the genus.[31] Since that order will not be subject to change, our corresponding knowledge will be reliable and stable. The corresponding knowledge should also be *explanatory* because it is knowledge of the *logos* that *makes the genus be one* (see above "the one link that somehow

[30] It is doubtful whether the art of reading and writing (*grammatikê*) is a very good example for a science. I cannot go into this here.

[31] *Phlb.* 16c9 speaks of the objects of dialectic as *tôn aei legomenon einai*, which is ambiguous between "whatever is said to be in each case" and "of the things that are said to be always". In the latter case he would simply affirm that the subject matter of dialectic is immutable, while in the former case he would point out the universal applicability of the divine method. In any case, the proper object of scientific knowledge is the *order* of the scientific domain. This order is not to be identified with ideas, which, if at all, are the items responsible for that order. See the discussion in Frede, *Philebus*, 139–142.

makes them all one"). These features make scientific knowledge better in quality than any less hierarchically organized body of knowledge.[32] The person who has that kind of knowledge has a *logos*, i.e. a definitional account, of the genus, of each kind of the genus down to the *infimae species*, and of the numbered series of divisions that constitute the genus' internal order.

To conclude, what dialectic, thus construed, gives us is a certain compensation for our quantitative and qualitative cognitive shortcomings as they result from the fragmentation and the embodiment of our rational souls in this world. But, of course, this can only work because there is identity in kind between our rational souls and the world soul. Our thinking, just as the thinking of the world soul, is fundamentally *systemic* or *holistic* in character. We, like the world soul, come to know things not by intuiting them but by grasping their interrelatedness. The compensation therefore regards only the (even if dramatically) *lesser degree* of completeness of our data and the resulting lesser degree of systematicity of our intellectual grasp of things. The identification of a scientific domain in human scientific reasoning compensates for the lack of exhaustivity of our conceptual data by giving us certain very limited regions where exhaustive information about kinds can be obtained ("fragments of reality" in Lesley Brown's words), while the knowledge of the order of a scientific kind – the unifying link (*desmos*) of the kinds that constitute the domain – compensates for the inferior quality of our empirical data by way of its reliability and explanatory power. This is why dialectic is a gift of the gods "hurled down from heaven by some Prometheus along with a most dazzling fire."[33] Or it can at least be usefully described as such, when we look at Plato's remarks on philosophical methods in light of the *Timaeus*.[34]

---

[32] Plato seems to think of the *desmos* as *the* order of the genus. It does not occur to him that there could be various equivalent orders of one and the same genus.

[33] Cp. *Phdr*. 266B.

[34] I would like to thank the participants of the Platon-Tage for their questions and remarks. I would also like to thank the participants of the history of philosophy workshop at the university of Stockholm, especially Miira Tuominen and Felix Maier. Thanks also go to Daniel Vorotyntsev for correcting my English and to Laura Bottenberg for her help in preparing the manuscript. Translations from the *Timaeus* are taken from Zeyl (slightly modified).

Bibliography

Betegh, Gabor, "Cosmological Ethics in the *Timaeus* and Early Stoicism", in: David N. Sedley (ed.), *Oxford Studies in Ancient Philosophy* 24, Oxford 2003, 273–302.

Betegh, Gabor/Tsouna, Voula (eds.), *Conceptualising Concepts in Greek Philosophy*, Cambridge 2024.

Brown, Lesley, "Do Forms Play the Role of Concepts in Late Plato", in: Betegh Gábor / Voula Tsouna (eds.), *Conceptualising Concepts in Greek Philosophy*, Cambridge 2024, 96–118.

Campbell, Douglas, "Biology in the *Timaeus*' Account of *Nous* and Cognitive Life", in: Melina G. Mouzala (ed.), *Cognition in Ancient Greek Philosophy and its Reception: Interdisciplinary Approaches*, Baden Baden 2024, 147–174.

Caston, Victor, "Caston "Concepts in Classical Greece," in: *A Philosophical History of the Concept*, Stephan Schmid / Hamid Taieb (eds.), Cambridge 2026, 16–44.

Corcilius, Klaus, "Ideal Intellectual Cognition in *Timaeus* 37 A2–C 5", *Oxford Studies in Ancient Philosophy* 54 (2018), 51–105.

Frede, Dorothea, "The Soul's Silent Dialogue: A Non-Aporetic Reading of the *Theaetetus*", *Proceedings of the Cambridge Philological Society* 215 (1989), 20–49.

–, "The Philosophical Economy of Plato's Psychology: Rationality and Common Concepts in the *Timaeus*", in: Michael Frede / Gisela Striker (eds.), *Rationality in Greek Thought*, Oxford 1996, 29–58.

–, *Philebus*, in: *Platon Werke. Übersetzung und Kommentar*, Göttingen 1997.

Gill, Mary-Louise, *Philosophos. Plato's Lost Dialogue*, Oxford 2012.

–, "Method and Metaphysis in Plato's *Sophist* and *Statesman*", in: *Stanford Encyclopedia of Philosophy*, 26.02.2020, https://plato.stanford.edu/entries/plato-sophstate/.

Johansen, Thomas Kjeller, *Plato's Natural Philosophy*, Cambridge 2004.

–, "Plato on Perceiving Through the Whole Body", *Oxford Studies in Ancient Philosophy* 60 (2022), 95–143.

Lorenz, Hendrik, *The Brute Within. Appetitive Desire in Plato and Aristotle*, Oxford 2006.

Menn, Stephen, "Collecting the Letters", *Phronesis* 43/4 (1998), 291–305.

Petrucci, Federico, *Platone. Timeo. A cura di federico M. Petrucci. Introduzione di Franco Ferrari*, Milan 2022.

Sedley, David, "The Idea of Godlikeness", in: Gail Fine (ed.), *Plato 2: Ethics, Politics, Religion, and the Soul* (*Oxford Readings in Philosophy*), Oxford 1999, 309–328.

Schmitt, Arbogast, Denken ist Unterscheiden. Eine Kritik der Gleichsetzung von Denken und Bewusstsein (Studien zu Literatur und Erkenntnis 18), Heidelberg 2020.

Striker, Gisela, *Peras und Apeiron: das Problem der Formen in Platons* Philebos, Göttingen 1970.

Warren, James, "Early Learning in Plato, Republic 7", in: Betegh Gábor / Voula Tsouna (eds.), *Conceptualising Concepts in Greek Philosophy*, Cambridge 2024, 56–73.

Motion in a Mathematical Cosmos

Plato's *Timaeus* on the Principles of Change

Thomas K. Johansen

Aristotle criticizes Plato for misunderstanding the role that mathematics can play in explaining the natural world. Mathematicians study number and geometrical figures in abstraction from the material bodies to which they belong (*Phys.* II 2). Nature, however, is an inner principle of change and rest. Not only are both form and matter required to account for how natural things change; the form also has to be of a certain sort, one whose presence in matter will cause the thing to change or be at rest. Mathematical forms such as shapes and quantities will not do that. Mathematical forms can be studied and understood without reference to change, in abstraction from sensible objects, even if they ultimately only exist as aspects of such objects (cf. *An.* I 1 403b11–16). There are certainly interesting areas of applied mathematics, optics would be one, but it is not clear that these employ mathematical forms as such. The Platonists, like the Pythagoreans (cf. *Metaph.* I 8, 989b30–32), were then fundamentally misguided in their attempts to explain the natural world through mathematics.

One might think that Aristotle has put his finger on a theoretical blind spot in Plato. Perhaps Plato just rather naively thought that change would sort itself out once one had explained mathematical structure. Perhaps the proposal in *Republic* VII (529c7–530c3) that astronomy can be studied as the motion of purely abstract geometrical solids supports the impression that motion can be understood independently of material bodies.[1] Or perhaps Plato thought that change in material bodies eluded rational explanation. In the *Timaeus* one might perhaps think that change like becoming is simply a brute fact inherited by material bodies from the pre-cosmos. So perhaps change should not be treated as a rational explanandum at all.

[1] Cf. *Metaph.* A.8 (989b33) where Aristotle himself acknowledges that astronomy is an exception to the claim that the mathematical sciences do not study motion. Astronomy is itself part of mathematics (cf. *Anal. Post.* I 14, 79a18–20; *Metaph.* XII 8, 1073b3–8), studying the motions of the heavenly bodies understood as perfect rational spheres.

These thoughts would in large part be wrong, at least as far as the *Timaeus* is concerned. Change is a key feature of the universe,[2] and mathematics has a lot to do with the explanation. This becomes clear both when we look at Timaeus' account of the world soul and when we look at the composition of the world body. The world soul is circular in shape and revolves with the spherically shaped world body (34A–B). The soul has this ability to move by virtue of its composition. The soul is composed of three elements which together lend it spatial location and moveability in accordance with its geometrical structure. I shall suggest that this explanation of the soul's mobility is of the same kind as the explanation of how the geometrical solids that form the four basic bodies move. We shall then find a more general model for how geometrically extended figures move in space, and thereby we shall be able to give an answer to Aristotle's objection.[3]

1. The Soul in Space

Let me begin by taking a closer look at the composition of the world soul. The interpretation I shall develop resembles that of Xenocrates, as reported by Plutarch, and is supported by the evidence of Aristotle, our two best sources for how the *Timaeus* was read in its own age. To many modern readers these reports may seem too far from Plato's text to be recognizable. I hope in this contribution to show their pertinence.

The passage setting out the composition of the world soul, described by A. E. Taylor as "the most perplexing and difficult of the whole dialogue",[4] begins as follows:

[T1] And he [sc. the Demiurge] composed it [sc. the world soul] in the following way and out of the following constituents. From the indivisible, eternally unchanging being and the being that becomes divided around bodies he mixed a third kind of being intermediate between them; again with the same and the different he made, in the same way, compounds intermediate between their indivisible element and the element that is divisible in relation to bodies; and taking these three components he mixed them into single unity, forcing the different, which was by nature difficult to mix, into union with the same, and mixing both with being. Having thus made a single whole of these three, he went on to make appropriate

---

[2] Cf. *Ti.* 28B–C: the cosmos "has come into being; for it is visible, tangible and corporeal, and all such things are perceptible by the senses, and, as we saw, perceptible things are objects of opinion and sense perception and come into being and are generated".

[3] This is of course not to say that it is an answer with which Aristotle or we would be happy.

[4] Taylor, *A Commentary on Plato's Timaeus*, 106.

subdivisions, each containing a mixture of same and different and being.[5] (*Ti.* 35A–B, transl. D. Lee, revised Johansen with further alterations)

The main difficulty of the passage lies in discerning how many elements and mixtures Timaeus has in mind. Cornford's interpretation, which goes back at least to Proclus, has become widely accepted today, and I shall follow it without further argument here. According to this reading, the material of the world is a mixture of three mixtures. Being, sameness and difference each have one sub-kind that is indivisible and another sub-kind that is divisible around bodies. These sub-kinds first get mixed with each other. The results are in turn mixed to form the final soul stuff.

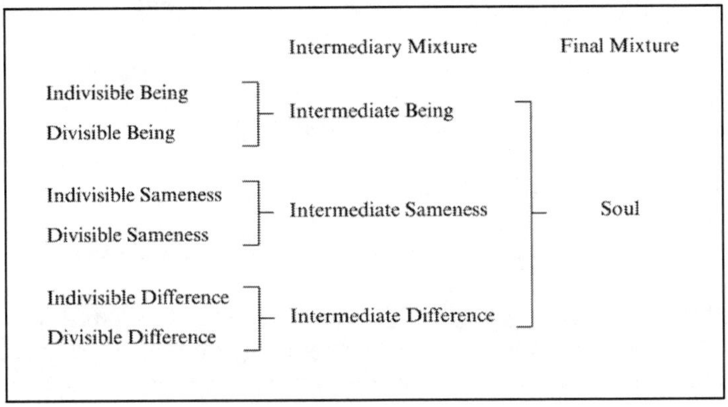

Fig. 1: Proclus' view of the composition of the world soul[6]

[5] συνεστήσατο ἐκ τῶνδέ τε καὶ τοιῷδε τρόπῳ. τῆς ἀμερίστου καὶ ἀεὶ κατὰ ταὐτὰ ἐχούσης οὐσίας καὶ τῆς αὖ περὶ τὰ σώματα γιγνομένης μεριστῆς τρίτον ἐξ ἀμφοῖν ἐν μέσῳ συνεκεράσατο οὐσίας εἶδος, τῆς τε ταὐτοῦ φύσεως αὖ πέρι καὶ τῆς τοῦ ἑτέρου, καὶ κατὰ ταὐτὰ συνέστησεν ἐν μέσῳ τοῦ τε ἀμεροῦς αὐτῶν καὶ τοῦ κατὰ τὰ σώματα μεριστοῦ: καὶ τρία λαβὼν αὐτὰ ὄντα συνεκεράσατο εἰς μίαν πάντα ἰδέαν, τὴν θατέρου φύσιν δύσμεικτον οὖσαν εἰς ταὐτὸν συναρμόττων βίᾳ. μειγνὺς δὲ μετὰ τῆς οὐσίας καὶ ἐκ τριῶν ποιησάμενος ἕν, πάλιν ὅλον τοῦτο μοίρας ὅσας προσῆκεν διένειμεν, ἑκάστην δὲ ἔκ τε ταὐτοῦ καὶ θατέρου καὶ τῆς οὐσίας μεμειγμένην.

[6] As adopted by Cornford: Cornford, *Plato's Cosmology*, 61.

We should note for later reference the alternative reading proposed by Plutarch (followed e.g. by Taylor and John Dillon).[7] Plutarch cuts out the intermediate sameness and intermediate difference from the first mixing. Instead, he uses intermediate being as a sort of glue to bind together sameness and difference, which mix with difficulty.[8]

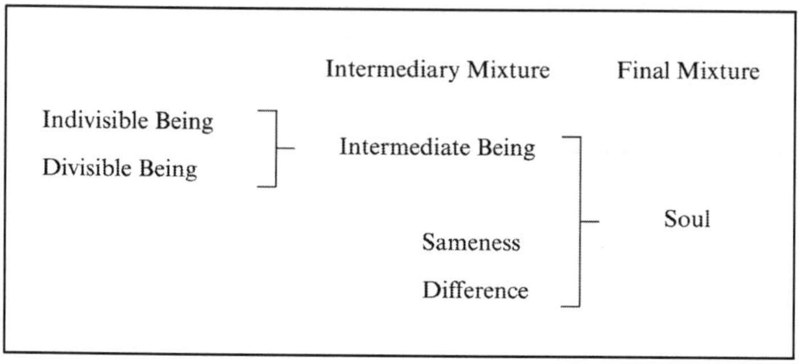

Fig. 2: Plutarch's view on the composition of the world soul

On either reading, the next stage in the construction of the soul is dividing the final mixture into harmonic intervals. Using the geometrical, arithmetical and harmonic means, Timaeus structures the soul into a musical scale, before dividing it up into the eight strips that will constitute the motions of the fixed stars, i.e. the circle of the same, and the seven planets, the circles of the different. These circles then move in different directions according to their different ratios (35B–36D).

What I shall focus on here is not the details of the mathematical structure. Nor do I want to address the question about how the composition of the soul equips it to reason.[9] Rather I want to take up a question which is prior to this, insofar as thinking is a kind of motion: what might there be in the composition of the soul in [T1] that would enable it to move in the first place? There are two related features that need to be explained here: 1) how is the soul extended as a spatial magnitude, and, 2) how is this magnitude such as to move? These are the questions that seem particularly pressing in light of Aristotle's

[7] See Dillon, "The *Timaeus* in the Old Academy", 80–94.

[8] See Plutarch, *De Animae Procreatione in Timaeo*, 2.

[9] The question is well addressed by Dorothea Frede, "The Philosophical Economy of Plato's Psychology: Rationality and Common Concepts in the *Timaeus*"; Klaus Corcilius, "Ideal Intellectual Cognition in *Timaeus* 37 A2–C5", and by Gabor Betegh, "The Ingredients of the Soul in Plato's *Timaeus*".

criticisms of Plato and the Pythagoreans: how can a mathematical account of the soul begin to explain the fundamental features of nature?

There are no explicit answers to these questions in the *Timaeus*, but we do have reports from within the Academy of a range of answers based on [T1]. It is clear from various sources, and confirmed by Plutarch, that the questions were something of a hot potato for the first readers of the *Timaeus*. What I want to do now is to present a story that is a possible reading of the *Timaeus*, which enjoys the support of at least some of the reports of how members of the Old Academy, particularly Aristotle and Xenocrates, understood Plato.

Let me start with the first of the first mixtures, that of indivisible being and "the being divided in relation to bodies". There is broad agreement that the indivisible being that is always the same is the forms. Calling the forms "indivisible" is not unproblematic as there will surely be conceptual distinctions within them. A human being will be, say, a featherless, biped animal. However, whatever conceptual differentiation we may see within a form, it is not going to involve a division that should threaten its essential unity and sameness. In [T1] the contrast is here clearly with the divisibility of the other element "divisible being", the sort of being that becomes divisible *around bodies*. It must be this sort of body-related divisibility which does not affect the form.

The expression "the being that becomes divided around bodies" (*tês au peri ta sômata gignomenês meristês*) has been taken in various ways, as Plutarch's discussions show, to refer to change, body, matter, extension, necessity, or a combination thereof, not to mention Plutarch's own suggestion of an evil world soul.[10] While "becomes" (*gignomenês*) is clearly marked in contrast to the changelessness of the first kind of being, it is still ascribed to an *ousia*, so it could hardly be marking a becoming-being contrast of the sort we get at the beginning of Timaeus' account (27D–28A). I take it (with Cornford) that *gignomenês* works as a copula with "divisible" (*meristês*): the *ousia* is becoming divisible or divided in relation to bodies, suggesting that it might not be divisible or divided before or unless it comes to stand in this relation to bodies. D. Zeyl translates the phrase "the one that is divisible and comes to be in the corporeal realm".[11] However, it is a stretch to say that an *ousia* that comes into being in relation to bodies is available for mixing with the other (indivisible) being before any bodies have come to be. On the alternative construction, the *ousia* is available though it is not yet divisible or divided before it comes into relation to bodies. The phrasing thus suggests that the soul insofar as it contains this element will be essentially related to bodies. The "*peri*", "around", picked up by "*kata*", "in relation to", is vague enough not to require that bodies will divide the soul, or make divisible the soul that has this element, but more weakly mean that the soul will be divided or divisible in the presence of bodies.

---

[10] Plutarch, *De Animae Procreatione in Timaeo*, 21–28.

[11] *Plato. Timaeus*, translated by D. J. Zeyl.

In other words, the element may be such as to make the soul divided or divisible without the bodies being the direct agent or cause in actualizing this feature of the soul. Whether, finally, to translate *meristês* as "divided" or "divisible" is an issue: if "divisible", the soul might as a function of this component become divisible around bodies without necessarily always being divided when embodied. But one would expect that the soul will by virtue of its composition have in its nature a potential for division around bodies, which surely in some circumstances will be realised in the presence of bodies.

What can we say now about the various interpretations canvassed by Plutarch? If Plato by "divisible being" had in mind body or matter in some sense, it would be oddly periphrastic to say that this element becomes divided around or in relation to bodies. Similarly, necessity is not itself divisible in relation to bodies other than in the sense that it may attach to various bodies, as their constitution dictates their behaviour.[12] But I see no point in introducing necessity in the composition of the world soul here.

Extension, in contrast, has a stronger candidature. Of course, "extension" is an Aristotelian term but may capture nonetheless the function of this element. Consider Aristotle's account of place as extension in *Phys.* IV 2:

[T2] But [if one considers it] in the way in which place (*topos*) is thought to be the extension (*diastêma*) of the magnitude, [place is] the matter (*hulê*). For this [extension of the magnitude] is different from the magnitude; this is that which is surrounded and bounded by the form, as by a surface and a limit; and it is this kind of thing that matter and the indefinite are. For when the limit and the properties of the sphere are removed, nothing is left but the matter. That is why Plato, too, says in the *Timaeus* that matter and space (*chôra*) are the same thing (for "the participative" (*metalêptikon*) and space are one and the same thing. Though he gave a different use to "the participative" in what are called his "unwritten doctrines" from that in the *Timaeus*, he still declared that place and space were the same thing. While everyone says that place is something, he alone tried to say what it is.) (*Phys.* 209b6–17, transl. E. Hussey)

The thought here would be that extension is contained and defined by the form of the body that occupies it. Aristotle's example of the sphere is to the point: take away the boundary and nothing remains but an indefinite extension or matter. Whatever else we may think of Aristotle's report on the *chôra* as space or matter, we get an idea here, I suggest, of how extension might match the description of a being that becomes divided in relation to bodies. It is when a body occupies the *chôra* that the *chôra* becomes the extension of some magnitude.[13] The soul would, by having extension or indefinite spatial magnitude in its composition, possess the potential to become divided or divisible in relation

[12] On the relationship between necessity and bodies, see further Johansen, *Plato's Natural Philosophy*, 95–103.

[13] Or if we think of the cases collectively, we might say that it is when the *chôra* becomes occupied by bodies that it generally becomes divis*ible*. We could then accommodate both senses of *meristê*.

to bodies. If this is right, honours go to Posidonius for identifying the divisible *ousia* in [T1] as extension.[14]

If the soul has spatial extension in virtue of the being that becomes divided around bodies, it would explain why the soul can be divided and extended in space, as in the circles of the same and the different. The soul "stuff" is extended in space in a way that makes it determinable as a distinct magnitude. Compare here the way the *chôra* will receive the geometrical figures of the four simple bodies (49B–53C). If we take the geometrical figures to configure the space they occupy,[15] we may say the space becomes divided according to these figures, while previously it was a being divisible around bodies, it now becomes actually divided by them. Similarly, the thought would be that the soul in virtue of this element is spatially determinable. It is because it has an element of *chôra* in its composition that the world soul would be able to receive its characteristic spatial shape.

Let me now consider four objections which may help clarify this suggestion. First, one might object that referring to the *chôra* as an *ousia,* albeit one that is divisible around bodies, is assigning too much substantiality to this elusive, barely intelligible kind. Admittedly the *chôra* is not referred to in the *Timaeus* as an *ousia*, though it is referred to as a *phusis* (50b6, cf. 49a5, 50e2), Timaeus' term for the kinds of the same and the different in [T1]. "*Ousia*" also appears in the gold analogy as the answer to the *ti esti*? question for those appearances that are constantly changing (50B), which are further said to hold on in some way (*amôsgepôs*) to *ousia* (52C) by being in the *chôra*. One might also note that the *chôra* does not fall on the *genesis* side of the *ousia-genesis* contrast since it is not itself subject to *genesis*, but rather a condition of the *genesis* of other things (52D–E). Second, one might object that the reference to the being that becomes divisible *around bodies* is too specific to "bodies" to be consistent with the soul's incorporeality. This is going to some extent to be a difficulty for any interpretation. However, several answers suggest themselves on the current proposal. One is that being "divisible around bodies" may also be the right potential to be divisible in the way the soul stuff is. The point, going back to [T2], is after all about being determinable by a certain shape. Aristotle's example of the sphere is appropriate: it hardly matters to the point whether the geometrical form that determines extension is the sphere, the shape of the circles of the soul or the geometrical shapes that inform the *chôra* to form the simple bodies. At least it hardly matters on the literal interpretation of the soul (to which some of us subscribe) since Plato's soul is not distinguished from

[14] Plutarch, *De animae Procreatione in Timaeo*, 22.

[15] For this kind reading, see Harte, *Plato on Parts and Wholes: The Metaphysics of Structure*, 255–258, and Johansen, "A Cosmos before the Cosmos? Aristotle's Criticism of the pre-Cosmic Traces in the *Timaeus*", 59–74.

body by body's being extended in space.[16] More importantly, soul will be divided in a way that will also determine the motions of the heavenly bodies, and not coincidentally so, since it is in the nature of the world soul to rule the world body (34C, 36E). To refer to the being that is divisible around bodies is then proleptically to refer to a division in the soul that will be fully realized in its embodiment in the heavenly bodies. Ultimately, to be divisible "around" bodies may be to refer to a divisibility of a kind to be realized around bodies, the "around" here being vague enough (as was noted before) not to make the body the agent of the division, since this comes from the role of the world soul in ruling over the world body. A final objection would be that Timaeus can hardly be referring to the *chôra* in [T1] since it is only introduced at 49A. If the *chôra* was required to understand how the world soul is composed, Timaeus would hardly say, as he does at 49a2, that we thought earlier that the other two kinds would suffice. The answer to this objection must lie in an extension of the answer to the previous objection: the reference to the *chôra* is proleptic in that we need to understand the *chôra*'s role in relation to bodies in order to grasp generally what it means to be divisible around bodies. Indeed, one might say that the reference to "bodies" itself will ultimately have to be clarified in relation to the *chôra*, according to what Timaeus says at 49A–B.

2. The Soul in Motion

I have suggested that the world soul is endowed with spatial extension by virtue of its composition, specifically the element of the *ousia* that becomes divisible around bodies, which may be taken as a proleptic reference to the *chôra*. I want now to turn to the soul's moveability. There is no need for something that is spatially extended as such to be subject to motion. We might think of a possible cosmos with a variety of objects all mathematically structured that is entirely static. But this is clearly not our world, which has come into being and keeps moving. *Ignorato motu, ignoratur natura.* So if Timaeus cannot explain change, he has hardly explained our world. I recall in parenthesis that Socrates' original request (19B), which set the whole explanatory enterprise going, was to see his virtuous citizens, which he had presented as if figures in a painting, in movement (*kinoumena*). Accounting for motion has been on the agenda from the beginning.

The answer to the question, which was identified from the early Academy on, was that change was to be explained by sameness and difference. Plutarch reports Xenocrates' view as follows:

---

[16] See Johansen, *Plato's Natural Philosophy*, Ch. 7.

[T3] The former (i.e. Xenocrates et al.) believe that nothing but the generation of number is signified by the mixture of the indivisible and divisible being, the one being indivisible and multiplicity divisible and number being the product of these when the one bounds multiplicity and inserts a limit in infinitude, which they call indefinite dyad too (this Zaratas too, the teacher of Pythagoras, called mother of number; and the one he called father, which is also why he held those numbers to be better that resemble the monad); but they believe that this number is not yet soul, for it lacks motivity and mobility, but that after the commingling of sameness and difference, the latter of which is the principle of motion and change while the former is that of rest, then the product is soul, soul being a faculty of bringing to a stop and being at rest no less than of being in motion and setting in motion.[17] (*de an. proc. Ti.* 2, transl. H. Cherniss)

John Dillon notes rather cautiously that "there is at least nothing in Plato's text that makes Xenocrates' interpretation impossible".[18] I think we can do slightly more on Xenocrates' behalf. Xenocrates' interpretation seems to have a Pythagorean pedigree, probably not Zaratas, but more realistically Archytas. So we have the testimony of Eudemus "that Archytas held that motion was caused by inequality (*anison*) or unevenness (*anômolon*) (A23)".[19] Archytas' view bears a striking resemblance to what Timaeus says at *Ti.* 57E–58A.[20] Here Timaeus operates with the same two terms as Archytas to explain motion: inequality (*isotês*) causes motion by causing disequilibrium:

[T4] We have already said something about them, but must now add that motion can never take place in conditions of uniformity. For it is difficult, or rather impossible, for what is moved to exist without what causes its motion, or what is to cause motion without that which is to be moved; without them there can be no motion and they cannot be in equilibrium. So we must assume that rest and equilibrium are always associated, motion and equilibrium always dissociated; and the cause of disequilibrium is inequality, whose origin we have already described.[21] (*Ti.* 57D–58A, transl. Lee, revised Johansen)

---

[17] οἱ μὲν γὰρ οὐδὲν ἢ γένεσιν ἀριθμοῦ δηλοῦσθαι νομίζουσι τῇ μίξει τῆς ἀμερίστου καὶ μεριστῆς οὐσίας· ἀμέριστον μὲν γὰρ εἶναι τὸ ἓν μεριστὸν δὲ τὸ πλῆθος ἐκ δὲ τούτων γίγνεσθαι τὸν ἀριθμὸν τοῦ ἑνὸς ὁρίζοντος τὸ πλῆθος καὶ τῇ ἀπειρίᾳ πέρας ἐντιθέντος, ἣν καὶ δυάδα καλοῦσιν ἀόριστον (καὶ Ζαράτας ὁ Πυθαγόρου διδάσκαλος ταύτην μὲν ἐκάλει τοῦ ἀριθμοῦ μητέρα τὸ δὲ ἓν πατέρα· διὸ καὶ βελτίονας εἶναι τῶν ἀριθμῶν ὅσοι τῇ μονάδι προσεοίκασι), τοῦτον δὲ μήπω ψυχὴν τὸν ἀριθμὸνεἶναι· τὸ γὰρ κινητικὸν καὶ τὸ κινητὸν ἐνδεῖν αὐτῷ. τοῦ δὲ ταὐτοῦ τοῦ καὶ τοῦ ἑτέρου συμμιγέντων, ὧν τὸ μέν ἐστι κινήσεως ἀρχὴ καὶ μεταβολῆς τὸ δὲ μονῆς, ψυχὴν γεγονέναι, μηδὲν ἧττον τοῦ ἱστάναι καὶ ἵστασθαι δύναμιν ἢ τοῦ κινεῖσθαι καὶ κινεῖν οὖσαν.

[18] Dillon, "The *Timaeus* in the Old Academy", 87.

[19] Supported as genuine by Huffman, *Archytas of Tarentum. Pythagorean, Philosopher and Mathematician King*, 509.

[20] As noted by Huffman, *Archytas of Tarentum. Pythagorean, Philosopher and Mathematician King*, 513–514.

[21] τὰ μὲν οὖν ἤδη περὶ αὐτῶν εἴρηται, πρὸς δ' ἐκείνοις ἔτι τάδε, ἐν μὲν ὁμαλότητι μηδέποτε ἐθέλειν κίνησιν ἐνεῖναι. τὸ γὰρ κινησόμενον ἄνευ τοῦ κινήσοντος ἢ τὸ κινῆσον ἄνευ τοῦ κινησομένου χαλεπόν, μᾶλλον δὲ ἀδύνατον, εἶναι: κίνησις δὲ οὐκ ἔστιν τούτων ἀπόντων, ταῦτα δὲ ὁμαλὰ εἶναί ποτε ἀδύνατον. οὕτω δὴ στάσιν μὲν ἐν ὁμαλότητι, κίνησιν

Huffman suggests that "Plato's presentation of motion in this whole section of the *Timaeus* is confused and contradictory".[22] I would argue, on the contrary, that Timaeus carefully articulates the causal relationship between Archytas' two terms. Inequality is the geometrical term that explains the unevenness in the powers of the bodies in the receptacle, the receptacle moving them in different directions as a response to their different powers. This is what Timaeus means by the "origin we have already described", namely at 52D–E:

[T5] Now as the wet nurse of becoming turns watery and fiery and receives the character of earth and air, and as it acquires all the properties that come with these characters, it takes on a variety of visible aspects, but because it is filled with powers that are neither similar nor evenly balanced, no part of it is in balance. It sways irregularly in every direction as it is shaken by those things, and being set in motion it in turn shakes them. And as they are moved, they drift continually, some in one direction and others in others, separating from one another [...].[23] (transl. D. Zeyl)

The scenario is one where the geometrical differences between bodies result in a disequilibrium and shaking in the *chôra* (*kat' ouden autês isoropein ... seisthai*). Disequilibrium is then the dynamic expression of inequality of qualities in the *chôra*. [T4] is a generalization of this scenario: motion in general presupposes unevenness because it is this that produces disequilibrium.

It would be misleading to think of the affections of the *chôra* as different geometrical figures *entering it* as if from the outside. Of course, these geometrical figures already need to be in the *chôra* to be spatially extended. Nor do they move into the *chôra* as if they already had a motion of their own before coming into the *chôra*. This would just push the question back of what accounts for their motion. Rather the point is that the difference in the geometrical properties as realized in the *chôra* brings about a disequilibrium in the *chôra*. This clearly only happens because the *chôra* already has a dynamic potential, somewhat like Aristotle's matter, only here restricted to spatial motion. *Chôra* is then not simply extension. It is also a receptacle which responds dynamically to the different qualities it receives.[24]

δὲ εἰς ἀνωμαλότητα ἀεὶ τιθῶμεν: αἰτία δὲ ἀνισότης αὖ τῆς ἀνωμάλου φύσεως. ἀνισότητος δὲ γένεσιν μὲν διεληλύθαμεν.

[22] Huffman, *Archytas of Tarentum. Pythagorean, Philosopher and Mathematician King*, 514.

[23] τὴν δὲ δὴ γενέσεως τιθήνην ὑγραινομένην καὶ πυρουμένην καὶ τὰς γῆς τε καὶ ἀέρος μορφὰς δεχομένην, καὶ ὅσα ἄλλα τούτοις πάθη συνέπεται [e] πάσχουσαν, παντοδαπὴν μὲν ἰδεῖν φαίνεσθαι, διὰ δὲ τὸ μήθ' ὁμοίων δυνάμεων μήτε ἰσορρόπων ἐμπίμπλασθαι κατ' οὐδὲν αὐτῆς ἰσορροπεῖν, ἀλλ' ἀνωμάλως πάντῃ ταλαντουμένην σείεσθαι μὲν ὑπ' ἐκείνων αὐτήν, κινουμένην δ' αὖ πάλιν ἐκεῖνα σείειν· τὰ δὲ κινούμενα ἄλλα ἄλλοσε ἀεὶ φέρεσθαι διακρινόμενα ...

[24] One might explore in this context Donald Zeyl's image of the sea in which waves move around. So the *chôra* would be the matter in which geometrical solids are realized and move around, without their material moving with them. The material basis would explain how the

If we now return to [T1], we can see the relevance of sameness and difference to motion. By containing difference as well as sameness in its composition the soul may be characterized by an internal unevenness. This unevenness will result in motion when combined with the *chôra,* which was how we interpreted "the being that becomes divisible around bodies". As one would expect if difference in particular is responsible for change and sameness for rest, greater changeability and variability are associated with the circles of the different than with the circle of the same. [T5] suggests that where there is a great difference between the properties there is a correspondingly greater disequilibrium and shaking of the *chôra*. In the case of the four basic bodies, the unevenness of properties, particularly in the pre-cosmos where there is no regularity in their geometrical characteristics, causes the *chôra* to shake without order (30A, 53A–B, 69B). In contrast, the orderly harmonies of the world soul, whose circles of the different are under the control of the circle of the same (36D), are hardly such as to trigger disorderly motions in the *chôra*. Recall here that the *chôra* is without motions of its own, as it is without its own qualities (51A, 52E), yet it has the ability to respond dynamically to the qualities that enter. Motion is essentially a dynamic response of the *chôra* to geometrical differences. Given our previous analysis of the soul as extended in the *chôra* we can apply this notion also to explain the soul's motion: the soul moves around because the element of *chôra* moves in response to the mathematically ordered combination of sameness and difference which also feature in its constitution. The relevant difference that the soul displays is primarily that of its constituent harmonies according to which it moves (36C–D).[25]

---

geometrical bodies have solidity and how their shapes (like the waves in the sea that crash into each other) alter or break up when they meet. See Zeyl, "Visualizing Platonic Space", 117–130.

[25] At the *Platon-Tage* Klaus Corcilius pointed out that the Demiurge seems to set the world in motion. Perhaps, then, we need not look to the composition of the world-soul itself to find a principle of motion. So at *Ti.* 34a3–5 we read διὸ δὴ κατὰ ταὐτὰ ἐν τῷ αὐτῷ καὶ ἐν ἑαυτῷ περιαγαγὼν αὐτὸ ἐποίησε κύκλῳ κινεῖσθαι στρεφόμενον, τὰς δὲ ἓξ ἁπάσας κινήσεις ἀφεῖλεν καὶ ἀπλανὲς ἀπηργάσατο ἐκείνων or in Zeyl's translation, "And so he set it turning continuously in the same place, spinning around upon itself. All the other six motions he took away, and made its movement free of their wanderings". My own take on this and similar passages (cf. 36C–D) is not that the Demiurge pushes the world soul into motion but that he shapes it in such a way that it will move in a circular way, and not in the other ways. The aim, in other words, is to show how the soul, given its demiurge-given constitution, will move itself. But even if one conceded the claim that the Demiurge gave the world soul the first push, we would need to explain how the world soul is capable of engaging in continuous self-motion. Furthermore, I think that a unified account of motion that explains how motion was present in the universe also before the Demiurge created the cosmos is preferable (cf. 30A, 52D). On the current account, differences in properties in the *chôra* are sufficient to initiate motion without the need of the Demiurge, though the Demiurge is required to order motion.

3. Difference and Motion

Aristotle took issue with the claim that difference or unevenness could explain motion:

[T6] In the first place, one would not be able to put change and alteration into another genus; and, again, it is clear when we consider how some people treat it, asserting that change is difference and inequality and that which is not – it is not necessary for any of these things to change, either different things or unequal things or things which are not; nor, even, does alteration take place into or from these things more than it does [into or] from their opposites. The reason why they assign change to these things is that change is thought to be something indefinite, and the principles in the second column [of correlated opposites] are indefinite because they are privative.[26] (*Phys.* III 2, 201b18–25, transl. E. Hussey)

The nexus of difference and unevenness points, I take it, to the coupling of these terms in Archytas, the *Timaeus* and in Xenocrates. Aristotle's objection is clearly correct if one considers sameness and difference as such, as eternal forms or simple concepts. If sameness and difference were sufficient to cause motion, then all things that are defined by genus and specific difference would *ipso facto* be in motion. Plato, as the *Sophist* (254E) clearly shows, also wants to talk about sameness and difference at the formal level where there is no motion. However, this concession underlines the importance of taking seriously that the composition of the soul in [T1] included, as per Proclus' reading, the kinds of the sameness and difference that become divisible in relation to bodies. If Timaeus had simply mixed the indivisible and eternal kinds of sameness and difference into the composition of the world soul, then there would be little or less hope of avoiding Aristotle's objection. For at the level of indivisible eternal kinds there would be nothing about sameness and difference as such to cause motion.[27] But the kinds of difference and sameness that become

---

[26] οὔτε γὰρ τὴν κίνησιν καὶ τὴν μεταβολὴν ἐν ἄλλῳ γένει θεῖναι δύναιτ᾽ ἄν τις. δῆλον δὲ σκοποῦσιν ὡς τεθέασιν αὐτὴν ἔνιοι, ἑτερότητα καὶ ἀνισότητα καὶ τὸ μὴ ὂν φάσκοντες εἶναι τὴν κίνησιν· ὧν οὐδὲν ἀναγκαῖον κινεῖσθαι – οὔτ᾽ ἂν ἕτερα ᾖ, οὔτ᾽ ἂν ἄνισα, οὔτ᾽ ἂν οὐκ ὄντα – ἀλλ᾽ οὐδ᾽ ἡ μεταβολὴ οὔτ᾽ εἰς ταῦτα οὔτ᾽ ἐκ τούτων μᾶλλόν ἐστιν ἢ ἐκ τῶν ἀντικειμένων. αἴτιον δὲ τοῦ εἰς ταῦτα τιθέναι ὅτι ἀόριστόν τι δοκεῖ εἶναι ἡ κίνησις, τῆs δὲ ἑτέρας συστοιχίας αἱ ἀρχαὶ διὰ τὸ στερητικαὶ εἶναι ἀόριστοι…

[27] Simplicius anticipates this objection to Aristotle, though he does not link it to the interpretation of [T1]: "It is clear to all that Plato made no reference to otherness in this passage (sc. [T4]). But even if Plato or the Pythagoreans say that there are these three, otherness itself regarded as a form, the other through partaking in otherness, and becoming other, when they said that becoming other was change they meant that sort which was alteration and activity. But Aristotle switched to the otherness which is form, by participation in which things became other. Thus he reduced the account to absurdity by saying that 'it is not necessary for any of these to change, whether they be other or unequal or non-existent'. For, if otherness were change, things which participate in otherness would change at once, these being the other." (in *Phys.* 432.34–433.7)

divisible around bodies are exactly of the sort to get realized in the *chôra*, the difference and sameness being thus instantiated in spatially extended entities. And as we know from [T4] and [T5] the *chôra* responds to the differences in the properties that are instantiated in it dynamically, through motion.[28]

We should also address Plutarch's objection that the greatest kinds of the *Sophist* undermine Xenocrates' interpretation:

[T7] It is manifest too that these interpreters have failed to understand the part about sameness and difference, for they say that to the generation of the soul the former contributes the faculty of rest and the latter that of motion, whereas by Plato himself in the *Sophist* existence and sameness and difference and besides these rest and motion are distinguished and set apart from one another as being five things different each from each. (*de an. proc. Ti.* 3, transl. H. Cherniss.)

Plutarch suggests that sameness and difference cannot be responsible for rest and motion in the *Timaeus*, since Plato in the *Sophist* posits motion and rest, next to being, sameness and difference, as the five *megista genê.* Why would motion and rest appear as distinct kinds if they could be explained by sameness and difference? Without going into details about the *Sophist*, we should note, with G. Betegh and D. Sedley,[29] that motion and rest do not mix with each other in the *Sophist*, and so would be ill-suited as elements in the soul's mixture in the *Timaeus*. Indeed, the Demiurge in [T1] has enough of a job on his hands in "forcing the different, which was by nature difficult to mix, into union with the same". Clearly Timaeus wants the world soul both to undergo motion but also to be at rest with respect to other kinds of motion (34A). So to insert elements of motion and rest into the soul that were incompatible would incapacitate the soul. Better to derive the soul's ability to move and be at rest from elements that are combinable and combinable in a way that allows for different kinds of rest and motion in the soul. In any event, there remain doubts about whether motion and rest in the *Sophist* should be treated as greatest kinds of the same standing as sameness, difference and being,[30] in which case an explanatory reduction of the sort the *Timaeus* seems to envisage would not be ruled out.

I have talked somewhat loosely about what the elements of the composition of the soul bring to the nature of the soul. But one should not forget that the

[28] Of course, Plutarch will be unmoved by this point since he rejects the relevance of difference to motion. He prefers to invoke the divisible being to get to motion, which he does in terms of necessity and the pre-cosmic soul.

[29] Cf. Betegh, "The Ingredients of the Soul in Plato's *Timaeus*", 4: "In fact, the *Sophist* offers an immediate answer to the question why Motion and Rest are not part of the Demiurge's mixture. As we learn at 250A, these two kinds are 'completely contrary to each other', and then at 254D–255A the Visitor adds that these two kinds don't blend with each other. If so they cannot be part of the same mixture. I thank David Sedley for this point."

[30] See, e.g. Leigh, "Restless Forms and Changeless Causes", 239–261.

soul is composed by a mixture, not a mere juxtaposition of elements. We should not assume that sameness and difference of the divisible sort provide motion to the soul irrespective of the sort of being with which they are mixed. If it is right, as I have suggested, to take the being that becomes divided round bodies, as a reference to the *chôra*, then it is only when the kinds of divisible sameness and difference are combined with this kind of being, that motion comes into play. The concrete scenario of this mixture, I have suggested, is that of geometrical differences manifesting themselves as a degree of disequilibrium in the *chôra*.

In [T6] Aristotle assimilates Timaeus' position on sameness and difference to the Pythagorean *sustoikheia*. In the more developed account in *Metaph.* I 6 986a22ff., where the two rows are headed by "Limit" and "Unlimited", Aristotle included "moved" (*kinoumenon*) under the unlimited or indefinite (*apeiron*). As far as the *Timaeus* goes, the assimilation is problematic not least because it fails to take into account how, at least on my reading, Timaeus means to see motion as arising through the combination of divisible sameness and divisible difference in the *chôra*. That there would be no change without difference clearly does not mean that difference is sufficient to bring about change. As Aristotle himself would recognize, e.g. in *Gener. Corr.* I 7 and *An.* II 5, change involves an opposition given a basic similarity, something he might put in terms of genus-sameness and species-difference, or sameness in potentiality and difference in actuality, prior to the change. In the *Timaeus*' physics, sameness enters, for example, in the account of the intergeneration of the elements: earth cannot become fire because it is made of different triangles, but fire can become water because both of these are made of the same kinds of triangles, though the particular constellation of triangles differs in the two cases (54C).

Now [T6] follows from Aristotle's own discussion of change in *Phys.* III 1, where he accounted for change as the actuality of the potential qua potential. In [T6], he uses the predecessors' accounts as a foil for this account: by putting the element responsible for change on one side of the *sustoikheia*, particularly the one associated with the indefinite and not-being, they failed properly to combine being and not being in change. Clearly the predecessors could not match the careful combination of actuality and potentiality by which Aristotle explains change. But they could, and I think Timaeus did, offer an account that saw change as arising through a combination of sameness, difference and being. One might put the *Timaeus*' position like this: motion is caused by the presence in the *chôra* of geometrical shapes in their difference. So put, change is not difference nor is it the indefinite It is rather difference *in* the indefinite. But the ordering by *sustoikheia* is ill-suited to expressing this sort of relationship across several elements in one column.

4. Conclusion

The motion of the soul, on the interpretation I have presented, is a special case of a more general conceptual complex: the differences within the soul, expressed by the mathematical ratios, are of a sort to trigger a motive response in the *chôra*. Similarly, the differences between the geometrical figures in the *chôra* provoke motion in the *chôra*. So, the interpretation I have offered shifts a lot of the responsibility for motion in the cosmos onto the *chôra*. The *chôra* is not a mere receptacle, nor mere extension; it also has, as Timeaus says, a distinctive power (*dunamis,* 49a4) as the receptacle. One specific power it has is that of responding to the presence of different geometrical entities by moving. One might compare the *chôra* in this respect to a weighing scale that rises and falls according to weights placed on it, an image that is close to Timaeus' own language in [T5] when the receptacle is said to be imbalanced (*talantoumenên*) by the uneven powers present in it. The receptacle's is a responsive power and one that is only actualized by the unevenness in its affections. Plato and Aristotle clearly disagree about the ability of geometrical form to actualize matter's ability to move and be moved. And so they disagree about the potential of mathematics to explain change. But this has as much to do with their different views about matter, and particularly matter's ability to respond to geometrical form. Timaeus' *chôra* is as extension particularly suited to receiving geometrical form. But it is also as a receptacle such as to respond to geometrical differences dynamically. If, on the other hand, you, like Aristotle, operate with a notion of matter which is constructed from the bottom up in terms of qualities, hot and cold, wet and dry, it will seem less clear why this kind of matter should respond dynamically to the imposition of a geometrical form. And if matter, moreover, is designed to accommodate no less than four categorically different kinds of change, not just spatial change as in the *Timaeus*, then it is clear that matter understood as extension will not do this job. But comparing Timaeus' *chôra* with Aristotle's matter in any more detail would be the subject of another discussion.

Bibliography

Betegh, Gabor, "The Ingredients of the Soul in Plato's *Timaeus*", in Fiona Leigh (ed.), *Themes in Plato, Aristotle, and Hellenistic Philosophy: Keeling Lectures 2011-18, BICS Supplement* 141, London 2021.

Corcilius, Klaus, "Ideal Intellectual Cognition in *Timaeus* 37 A2–C5", *Oxford Studies in Ancient Philosophy* 54 (2018), 51–105.

Cornford, Francis M., *Plato's Cosmology*, London 1937.

Dillon, John, "The *Timaeus* in the Old Academy", in: Gretchen J. Reydams-Schils (ed.), *Plato's Timaeus as Cultural Icon,* Notre Dame, Ind. 2003, 80–94.

Frede, Dorothea, "The Philosophical Economy of Plato's Psychology: Rationality and Common Concepts in the *Timaeus*", in Michael Frede / Gisela Striker (eds.), *Rationality in Greek Thought,* New York 1996, 29–58.

Harte, Verity, *Plato on Parts and Wholes: The Metaphysics of Structure*, Oxford 2002.

Huffman, Carl A., *Archytas of Tarentum. Pythagorean, Philosopher and Mathematician King*, Cambridge 2005.

Johansen, Thomas K., *Plato's Natural Philosophy*, Cambridge 2004.

–, "A Cosmos before the Cosmos? Aristotle's Criticism of the pre-Cosmic Traces in the *Timaeus*", *Chôra* 20 (2022), 59–74.

Leigh, Fiona, "Restless Forms and Changeless Causes", *Proceedings of the Aristotelian Society* 112 (2012), 239–261.

Taylor, Alfred E., *A Commentary on Plato's Timaeus*, Oxford 1928.

Zeyl, Donald J. (transl.), *Plato. Timaeus*, Indianapolis, Ind. 2000.

–, "Visualizing Platonic Space", in Richard D. Mohr / Barbara M. Sattler (eds.), *One Book, the Whole Universe: Plato's Timaeus Today*, Las Vegas 2010, 117–130.

Xenocrates and the Soul as a Self-Moving Number in the Ancient Testimonies

Susanna Kinzig

Xenocrates speaks in the form of a riddle, says Philoponus, when he defines the soul as a number moving itself.[1] A riddle that, in antiquity as well as in the present, remains unsolved. As hints for solving the riddle we only have testimonies which were mostly written several centuries after Xenocrates's death. Nonetheless, they are the only source we have for his definition of the soul as self-moving number. Their quality differs, however: some criticize Xenocrates's definition of the soul, but do not explain it in any plausible way whereas others offer various explanations in different places in their work. In this contribution, I will try to disentangle which testimonies are reliable sources, which contradict each other, and which have something in common, by giving an overview of the testimonies that mention the Xenocratean definition of the soul as self-moving number.[2] After a remark on the editions of the testimonies, I will discuss the testimonies that are relevant in attributing to Xenocrates the definition of the soul as self-moving number. Furthermore, I will give a short overview of the non-constructive testimonies that do not help us to understand what Xenocrates meant with his definition, but refer to it anyway, in particular the Aristotelean testimonies in F 87–89 and F 112. Finally, I will discuss different constructive interpretations of Xenocrates's definition of the soul.

---

[1] αἰνίττομαι in F 101 Isnardi Parente/Dorandi 2012 = Phlp. *In de An.* 32.31–33.2 Hayduck 1897, commentary on Arist. *de An.* I 1, 402a22. Cf. the verb/term also in F 109 (Proclus), analyzed *infra* "Xenocrates and the *Timaeus* (F 108, F 109, F 179)".

[2] An extensive discussion of all testimonies with their contexts is absent both from the edition by Heinze 1892 (but see there the nonetheless valuable discussion in 65–67), and Isnardi Parente/Dorandi 2012, who offers many helpful comments on the testimonies both in the second edition and slightly different, but also very valuable, in the first edition Isnardi Parente 1982. On the soul as self-moving number in general see Krämer, "Die Ältere Akademie", 44–46; Thiel, *Die Philosophie des Xenokrates,* 330–333; Cherniss, *Aristotle's Criticism*, 399f. (especially fn. 325); Palmieri, *La dottrine dell'anima*, especially 221–266. De-Cesaris, "Aristotle's Account", 148–173, and Carter, *Aristotle on Earlier Greek Psychology*, 103–122, pay great attention to Aristotle's critique of Xenocrates. For methodological remarks on the analysis of Xenocratean testimonies see Thiel, *Die Philosophie des Xenokrates*, 226–228.

1. A Short Remark on the Editions of the Testimonies

Unfortunately, no work by Xenocrates has been preserved. We only know about Xenocrates's definition of the soul as self-moving number through testimonies in the texts of other authors. These were collected, first by Heinze 1892, then again by Isnardi Parente 1982, and can now be found in the current standard edition by Isnardi Parente/Dorandi 2012.[3] In her edition, Isnardi Parente followed Heinze in the selection of the testimonies: Heinze collected all mentions of Xenocrates's philosophy in earlier authors, but only included those mentions from "later" authors, that, as he says somewhat vaguely, do not deviate too much from Xenocrates's original thought.[4] For this reason, it should be noted that, unfortunately, their editions cannot serve as a basis for a historical study of the reception of Xenocrates or of the interpretation of his thought in "later" antiquity. For the soul in Xenocratean philosophy, we find 50 testimonies in Isnardi Parente/Dorandi 2012:[5]

– 48 testimonies under the title 'psicologia' (F 85–132);
– two testimonies assigned to Xenocrates's work Περὶ φύσεως (F 179–180).

I will not discuss all of these testimonies in detail: I have excluded F 119–F 128 and F 130–132 from my analysis, since they are not concerned with the definition of the soul as self-moving number, but with the soul's properties; among the others I will discuss in more detail the Aristotelean testimonies (F 85–89, 112), Plutarch's testimonies (F 92, 108) and the engaging interpretations of the definition by Philoponus (F 104, 117), Proclus (F 109), Nemesius

[3] There are significant differences between the first edition Isnardi Parente 1982 and the second edition Isnardi Parente/Dorandi 2012: in the second edition the testimonies are split into the biographical testimonies ("Test.") and the testimonies containing information about Xenocrates's philosophy ("F"). F for 'fragment' is misleading: there are no fragments in any stronger sense of the word containing authentic words of Xenocrates's works, besides maybe certain *termini technici* (cf. Thiel, *Die Philosophie des Xenokrates*, 227). (Cf. on the terms '*testimonium*' and 'fragment' in editions Neuerburg/Tsiampokalos/Wozniczka, "Einleitung", 2–10.) The Greek and Latin texts were taken from the most modern editions, but apparently without updating all translations (see e.g. F 81 Isnardi Parente/Dorandi 2012 in comparison to F 161 Isnardi Parente 1982). Furthermore, the critical apparatus was removed and the commentary revised.

[4] Heinze does not state, what he means by "later" authors precisely. See Heinze 1892, XI, and Isnardi Parente 1982, 44–47.

[5] In this contribution, the numbers of the testimonies are cited according to Isnardi Parente/Dorandi 2012; the texts are cited by the best available editions of the texts, the context (often excluded by Isnardi Parente/Dorandi 2012) is usually included in the citation. The collection of fragments F 85–132 and F 179–180 corresponds, with the exception of F 88 (see the discussion *infra* "Non-Constructive Testimonies"), to the fragments 60–75 in Heinze 1892. See also *infra* "List of Testimonies on the Soul, Arranged by the Author".

of Emesa (F 110) and Pseudo-Simplicius (F 113). Mentions of the other testimonies will mainly be restricted to the footnotes.

2. The Soul as Self-Moving Number: A Definition by Xenocrates

How do we know that the definition of the soul as a self-moving number is by Xenocrates? Whereas Aristotle does not mention Xenocrates's name, later authors attribute the definition to Xenocrates. Our most reliable sources for this are, on the one hand, Plutarch, who has great knowledge of Xenocrates's work,[6] and, on the other hand, Aristotle's commentators.[7] We have no reason to distrust them. Themistius tells us that Xenocrates's theory of the soul as self-moving number is to be found in the fifth book of his Περὶ φύσεως.[8]

Beside these clear attributions of the definition to Xenocrates, we have several testimonies that ascribe the definition to Xenocrates in combination with Pythagoras, some of which rely on doxographical reports:[9] F 90 (Aetius),[10] F 94 (Alexander of Aphrodisias), F 110 (Nemesius of Emesa),[11] F

---

[6] F 108, see the analysis *infra* "Xenocrates and the *Timaeus* (F 108, F 109, F 179)". Plutarch references Xenocrates on many occasions. In the *Indice delle fonti* Isnardi Parente/Dorandi 2012 list more than 40 testimonies (Test. and F) from his works, which is almost 15% of all the testimonies we have of Xenocrates. Dillon (Dillon, "Plutarch's Debt to Xenocrates", 1999, 305 = Dillon, "Plutarch's Debt to Xenocrates", 2012a, XI, 305) attests Plutarch "on certain topics at least […] a notable degree of dependence on […] Xenocrates".

[7] E.g. Alexander of Aphrodisias in F 93–95. Cf. Isnardi Parente 1982, 383f.

[8] F 180. Cf. F 179, where Themistius mentions the work without indicating the fifth book. Both testimonies are analyzed *infra* "Xenocrates and the *Timaeus* (F 108, F 109, F 179)". There are several other works, in which Xenocrates might have talked about the soul, whose titles came down to us through Diogenes Laertios (Test. 2 Isnardi Parente/Dorandi 2012 = D.L. IV 6-15 (*Vita Xenocratis*) Dorandi 2013), e.g. Περὶ ψυχῆς (Krämer, "Die Ältere Akademie", 44, thinks on the basis of Themistius's testimony that the two books Περὶ ψυχῆς were part of Περὶ φύσεως), Περὶ μνήμης, Περὶ φρονήσεως, Περὶ παθῶν, Περὶ θεῶν, Περὶ ἐπιστήμης, Περὶ ἐπιστημοσύνης, Τῶν περὶ τὴν διάνοιαν, Τῶν περὶ τὴν διάνοιαν ἄλλα βιβλία, Περὶ ἀριθμῶν, Ἀριθμῶν θεωρία.

[9] Many of them are listed in the "Proximate tradition" to Aetius's *Placita Philosophorum* in Mansfeld/Runia 2020, 1407–1413.

[10] F 90 Isnardi Parente/Dorandi 2012 = Aetius, *Placita Philosophorum* 4.2.3f. Mansfeld/Runia 2020. Cf. F 91 Isnardi Parente/Dorandi 2012 = Theodoretus, *Graecarum affectionum curatio* V 17 Raeder (in Scholten 2015), which is used as a source for the reconstruction of Aetius's *Placita Philosophorum* by Mansfeld/Runia 2020. See on Aetius and the doxographical tradition Mansfeld/Runia 2020, 1393–1420, especially 1393.1398f.1405–1407.1410f. 1417f.

[11] F 110 Isnardi Parente/Dorandi 2012 = Nemesius of Emesa, *De natura hominis* 2, 102f. (p. 29f. Morani 1987). In *De natura hominis* 2, 68 (p. 17 Morani 1987), Nemesius attributes it to Pythagoras alone.

104 (John Philoponus),[12] F 111 (Meletius),[13] F 98 (Iamblichus),[14] and F 119 and F 120 (Cicero)[15]. The definition of the soul as self-moving number was, according to Burkert, attributed to Pythagoras in retrospective, following the 'Pythagorean' interpretation of the *Timaeus* by Speusippus and Xenocrates.[16]

3. Non-Constructive Testimonies

There are several testimonies among the testimonies on the soul that mention Xenocrates's definition of the soul, but do not help us to understand it. The most important figure in this respect is Aristotle. One could assume that Aristotle is an important source for Xenocrates's theory of the soul, as he knew him personally. In fact, however, the majority of his surviving testimonies (in which Xenocrates's name is never explicitly mentioned) do not help us to get a clearer understanding of the definition, as I will show in this section of the contribution.[17] In general, Aristotle did not agree with Xenocrates's definition of the soul and mentions it on six occasions (F 85–89, 112), four of which I will discuss now (F 87–89, 112).[18]

For Aristotle, a first way of attacking the Xenocratean definition is to ridicule it by showing that soul cannot possibly be a number. He does this at

---

[12] While Philoponus talks of Xenocrates in the Pythagorean tradition in F 104 (see *infra* "Cognition and Movement (F 85)"), he ascribes the definition to Xenocrates in F 103 Isnardi Parente/Dorandi 2012 = Phlp. *In de An.* 71.6–14. Hayduck 1897, commentary on 404a20. (Xenocrates is a correct emendation by Hayduck 1897; the manuscripts say Anaxagoras.)

[13] F 111 Isnardi Parente/Dorandi 2012 = Meletius, Περὶ ψυχῆς 146, 31–33 Cramer 1963. Meletius says that Pythagoras called soul a selfmoving number and Xenocrates a "continuous number and an exhalation of the whole" (ἀριθμὸν συνεχῆ, καὶ ἀναθυμίασιν τοῦ παντός). This is, as Heinze 1892, 66, explained, a conflation of different reports by Nemesius, or, as is said by Isnardi Parente/Dorandi 2012, 303, by Aristotle.

[14] F 98 Isnardi Parente/Dorandi 2012 = Stob. *Eclogae* I 49, 32 = 28, 1–15 Finamore/Dillon 2002. Iamblichus most likely relies on other doxographical reports, cf. Finamore/Dillon 2002, 82f., and Isnardi Parente/Dorandi 2012, 298.

[15] F 119 Isnardi Parente/Dorandi 2012 = Cic. *Tusc.* I 10, 20 Giusta 1984; F 120 Isnardi Parente/Dorandi 2012 = Cic. *Academica primus* 11, 39 Reinhardt 2023.

[16] Burkert, *Lore and Science in Ancient Pythagoreanism*, cf. Mansfeld/Runia 2020, 1399, and more cautious Riedweg, *Pythagoras*, 156: "im Kern zumindest könnte die Lehre ebensogut altpythagoreisch sein"; cf. Thiel, *Die Philosophie des Xenokrates*, 333; Opsomer, "The Platonic Soul", 178. For the interpretation of the *Timaeus* by Xenocrates, see *infra* "Xenocrates and the *Timaeus* (F 108, F 109, F 179)".

[17] In addition, the temporal closeness of Aristotle creates challenges for the reliability of his account. We do not know to what extent Xenocrates's philosophy of the soul had been worked out, when Aristotle criticized him, nor do we know, how much personal and academic antipathies distort Aristotle's account.

[18] For the discussion of F 86 see *infra* "Way of Proof (F 86)". For a discussion of F 85 see *infra* "Cognition and Movement (F 85)".

length in his *De anima*:[19] He calls the definition the "most unintelligible" (ἀλογώτατον) of all mentioned, because both aspects, that it is self-moved and that it is a number, entail contradictions. At the center of his complicated and, in part, unclear criticism stands the question of the ways in which the soul could be defined as a number. Although number is conceived of as "sum-total of units"[20] throughout the argument, this is done in very different ways:

> We must In the ensuing discussion, Aristotle implicitly reviews different ways of conceiving of numbers and their features: as without parts (408b32–409a3); as entities capable of entering into arithmetic relations (409a7–10); as akin to Democritean atoms in their simplicity (409a10–20); and as numbers identifiable or not with points in the body (409a16–30).[21]

In addition, Aristotle shows in his *Topica* that soul cannot be a number, because it can neither be an odd nor an even number.[22]

Aristotle's criticism in F 87 and F 112 unfortunately yields nothing for the explanation of the definition of the soul as self-moving number, since it is unclear which interpretation of Aristotle, if any, represents what Xenocrates had in mind. It is generally assumed that Xenocrates would not have agreed to certain assumptions made by Aristotle in his critique.[23] In particular, it is difficult to determine whether, for Xenocrates, number was conceived as a "sum total of units".[24]

---

[19] F 112 Isnardi Parente/Dorandi 2012 = Arist. *de An.* I 2, 408b32–409a30 Förster (in Corcilius 2017). F 112 is the rejection of F 85, which I will discuss later, see *infra* "Cognition and Movement (F 85)".

[20] Hicks 1965, 279 note on 408b34. For Aristotle a number is a πλῆθος μονάδων as Hicks, 1965, 280 note on 409a1, explains with reference to Arist. *Metaph.* VII 13, 1039a12 and X 1, 1053a30. This also explains, why Aristotle switches from the discussion of ἀριθμός to the discussion of μονάς in 408b32–409a1. It does not necessarily imply that Xenocrates used the word μονάς in relation with his definition, as Ross, 1961, 200, cautiously suggested.

[21] Shields 2016, 147.

[22] F 87 Isnardi Parente/Dorandi 2012 = Arist. *Top.* III 6, 120b3–6 Brunschwig 1967. Cf. F 87 and F 112 to Alexander of Aphrodisias in F 93 Isnardi Parente/Dorandi 2012 = Alex. Aphr. *In Top.* 162.5–163.13 Wallies 1891, commentary on Arist. *Top.* II 4, 111b4, and F 94 Isnardi Parente/Dorandi 2012 = Alex. Aphr. *In Top.* 493.21–494.16 Wallies 1891, commentary on Arist. *Top.* VI 14, 151b3.

[23] Cf. Polansky 2007, 120 fn. 31; Hicks 1965, 285: "But it is highly improbable that either the substitution of points for units or the assumption that the number of the soul must be in space (409a6 sq.) would have passed unchallenged by Xenocrates"; Cherniss, *Aristotle's Criticism*, 399.

[24] Cf. to this John Philoponus's critique of Aristotle's refutation in F 112. He criticizes Aristotle's comparison between Democritus and Xenocrates, pointing out that while Xenocrates posits the soul to be a quantity "simply" (ἁπλῶς), Democritus makes it consist of spherical atoms to explain its movement (F 118 Isnardi Parente/Dorandi 2012 = Phlp. *In de An.* 167.20–168.15 Hayduck 1897, commentary on Arist. *de An.* I 4, 409a10 (part of F 112)).

Another point of attack for Aristotle is to say that the definition does not meet the standards of a definition and that it does not explain what the soul is. In his *Topica*, Aristotle speaks about superfluous elements in definitions (F 89):[25] "Simply put, everything is superfluous if after its removal the rest [of the description/λόγος] makes the defined [object] clear."[26] As an example for a superfluous element in a definition, Aristotle gives the definition of the soul as a self-moving number (ἀριθμὸς αὐτὸς αὑτὸν κινῶν). If you define it as Plato did, Aristotle says, solely as self-moving, this either already is the soul, or it is peculiar to the soul, but does not reveal its essence, so that number would be necessary in order to reveal it.[27] We can imagine that Xenocrates would argue this way, namely that number is necessary in order to reveal the soul's essence.[28]

Lastly, Aristotle discusses to which genus the soul pertains ('movement' or 'rest') (F 88),[29] a problem discussed by several of Aristotle's commentators as well.[30] Unfortunately, from these remarks on the genus of the soul we cannot

[25] F 89 Isnardi Parente/Dorandi 2012 = Arist. *Top.* VI 3, 140a33–b15, Brunschwig 2007. Cf. to this the critique of the definition by Philoponus in F 102 Isnardi Parente/Dorandi 2012 = Phlp. *In de An.* 43.28–44.20 Hayduck 1897, commentary on Arist. *de An.* I 1, 402b26.

[26] ἁπλῶς δ' εἰπεῖν ἅπαν περίεργον οὗ ἀφαιρεθέντος τὸ λοιπὸν δῆλον ποιεῖ τὸ ὁριζόμενον. My own translation.

[27] Cf. De-Cesaris, "Aristotle's Account", 158f. (F 88 (right on p. 158) is accidentally called F 87 on p. 159, and F 89 (right on p. 158) F 88 on p. 159).

[28] This is precisely the main thrust of Alexander's commentary on this passage, see F 95 Isnardi Parente/Dorandi 2012 = Alex. Aphr. *In Top.* 429.4–23 Wallies 1891, commentary on Arist. *Top.* VI 3, 140a33, see F 89.

[29] F 88 Isnardi Parente/Dorandi 2012 = Arist. *Top.* IV 6, 127b13–17 Brunschwig 1967. Since Aristotle does not refer to Xenocrates or the Xenocratean definition of the soul explicitly, Heinze 1892 did not include this testimony in his collection. Isnardi Parente/Dorandi 2012, assume that Aristotle is alluding to Xenocrates, since Xenocrates seemed to see the soul as a source of motion and source of rest, as is said in F 108 (not F 109, as it is printed in Isnardi Parente/Dorandi 2012, 297, but F 108, as it is said in Isnardi Parente 1982, 384). See the discussion of F 108 *infra* "Xenocrates and the *Timaeus* (F 108, F 109, F 179)". They follow Cherniss, *Aristotle's Criticism*, 10f. I do not think that an allusion to Xenocrates's definition of the soul is necessarily what Aristotle had in mind, although it can also be directed against him; cf. De-Cesaris, "Aristotle's Account", 159 fn. 583.

[30] Cf. Arist. *de An.* I 1, 402a22–25. They discuss the categories or genera 'quantity', 'number' or 'movement'. 'Quantity' or 'number': F 101 Isnardi Parente/Dorandi 2012 = Phlp. *In de An.* 32.31–33.2 Hayduck 1897, commentary on Arist. *de An.* I 1, 402a22 (John Philoponus is not confident about this, though, and adds: εἰ δὴ τοῦτο ἔλεγεν ἐκεῖνος, καὶ μὴ ἄλλο τι διὰ τούτου ᾐνίττετο. – "if that is what he means rather than something different to which he refers by these words in the form of a riddle." Translation by van der Eijk 2005. Cf. F 118 Isnardi Parente/Dorandi 2012 = Phlp. *In de An.* 167.20–168.15 Hayduck 1897, commentary on Arist. *de An.* I 4, 409a10 (part of F 112)); F 98 Isnardi Parente/Dorandi 2012 = Stob. *Eclogae* I 49, 32 = 28, 1–15 Finamore/Dillon 2002; F 100 Isnardi Parente/Dorandi 2012 = Ps.-Simp. *In de*

gain anything for the interpretation of Xenocrates's definition of the soul as self-moving number. They are Aristotelean interpretations that either follow Aristotle's line of criticism or try to fit Xenocrates's definition into Aristotle's system of genera or categories.

In summary, then, Aristotle's testimonies in F 87–89 and F 112 do not help us to understand Xenocrates's definition of the soul. One can easily imagine that Xenocrates would not agree with Aristotle's assumptions in his refutation of the soul as number as well as in his critique that the genus of the soul is 'number'.

4. Constructive Testimonies

I will now turn to the discussion of the testimonies that attempt to explain the definition of the soul. In my view, among these testimonies the following are the most compelling for further analysis: 1) Aristotle's testimonies in F 86 and F 85, because, again, due to his temporal closeness, his testimonies deserve special attention. 2) Plutarch's account of Xenocrates's definition of the soul in F 108, because he seems to have known Xenocrates's writings first- or second-hand. 3) Pseudo-Simplicius's interpretation of the definition in F 113, because he explains it in a plausible way.

Way of Proof (F 86)

The most interesting Aristotelean testimony on Xenocrates's definition of the soul is Aristotle's comment on it in his *Analytica Posteriora* (F 86). The interpretation of this passage is challenging and therefore renders the reconstruction of Xenocrates' theory difficult.[31]

In the fourth chapter of the second book, Aristotle asks if there is an argument (συλλογισμός) or proof (ἀπόδειξις) for definitions (τί ἐστι) (91a12–

An. 10.34f. Hayduck 1882, commentary on Arist. *de An.* I 1, 402a22; Michael Psellos, Συλλογαὶ διάφοροι καὶ ποικῖλαι ("Various and diverse collections") 35, 23f. O'Meara 1989; F 107 Isnardi Parente/Dorandi 2012 = *Scholia in Dionysium Thracem* 118, 17–19 Hilgard 1901. 'Movement': F 93 Isnardi Parente/Dorandi 2012 = Alex. Aphr. *In Top.* 162.5–163.13 Wallies 1891, commentary on Arist. *Top.* II 4, 111b4.

[31] In the scope of this contribution I will not be able to discuss the problems and different interpretations of this passage in detail. See on this F 105 Isnardi Parente/Dorandi 2012 = Ps.-Phlp. (see Goldin 2009, 1–4) *In APo.* 348.2–4 Wallies 1909, commentary on Arist. *APo.* II 4, 91a35 (part of F 86) in its context; F 99 Isnardi Parente/Dorandi 2012 = Them. *In APo.* 43.1–3 Wallies 1900, paraphrase of Arist. *APo.* 89b24, in its context; De-Cesaris, "Aristotle's Account", 150–157; Barnes [2]1993, 209f.; Detel 1993, 578–586, with extensive discussion of literature. I follow Detel's interpretation. The Greek text is cited according to Ross 1957.

14). His answer is negative. He first shows that such a syllogism can only have the following form (91a15–26):[32] If we have the valid syllogism

p1: A *a*[33] B
p2: B *a* C
c: A *a* C, where C is defined by A,

C is also defined by the middle term B. Therefore, one of the premises (p2) is already a definition of C, which is a *petitio principii*. Aristotle illustrates this with two examples, the second of which is the following:[34]

Δεῖ δ' ἐν ταῖς δυσὶ προτάσεσι καὶ τοῖς πρώτοις καὶ ἀμέσοις σκοπεῖν· μάλιστα γὰρ φανερὸν τὸ λεγόμενον γίνεται. οἱ μὲν οὖν διὰ τοῦ ἀντιστρέφειν δεικνύντες τί ἐστι ψυχή, ἢ τί ἐστιν ἄνθρωπος ἢ ἄλλο ὁτιοῦν τῶν ὄντων, τὸ ἐξ ἀρχῆς αἰτοῦνται, οἷον εἴ τις ἀξιώσειε ψυχὴν εἶναι τὸ αὐτὸ αὑτῷ αἴτιον τοῦ ζῆν, τοῦτο δ' ἀριθμὸν αὐτὸν αὑτὸν κινοῦντα· ἀνάγκη γὰρ αἰτῆσαι τὴν ψυχὴν ὅπερ ἀριθμὸν εἶναι αὐτὸν αὑτὸν κινοῦντα, οὕτως ὡς τὸ αὐτὸ ὄν. οὐ γὰρ εἰ ἀκολουθεῖ τὸ Α τῷ Β καὶ τοῦτο τῷ Γ, ἔσται τῷ Γ τὸ Α τὸ τί ἦν εἶναι, ἀλλ' ἀληθὲς εἰπεῖν ἔσται μόνον· οὐδ' εἰ ἔστι τὸ Α ὅπερ τι καὶ κατὰ τοῦ Β κατηγορεῖται παντός.

1) We must inquire in the case of two propositions and of primitives and immediates; for then what we are saying becomes especially clear. Those people who try to prove through conversion what soul is (or what man is, or anything else which exists) postulate what was set at the beginning. E.g., if someone were to claim that soul is what is itself explanatory of its own being alive, and that this is a number which moves itself: 2) it is necessary to postulate that soul is just what is a number which moves itself, in the sense of being the same thing as it. 3) For it is not the case that if A follows B and B follows C, then A will be what it is to be C. Rather, it is true to say only that A will hold of C – even if A is just what is some B and is predicated of every B.[35]

The Greek text is ambiguous as to the way in which Aristotle thinks this fits into a syllogism and, in connection to this, what exactly Aristotle tried to illustrate with this example.[36]

1) Detel reconstructs the syllogism in the following way (A=number which moves itself, B=being itself explanatory of its own being alive, C=Soul):[37]

p1: (Number which moves itself) *a* (Being itself explanatory of its own being alive)
p2: (Being itself explanatory of its own being alive) *a* (Soul)

[32] Detel 1993, 583 T2 and 578f. (especially b). Cf. Charles, *Aristotle on Meaning and Essence*, 180f.

[33] With A *a* B meaning: A pertains to all B (= every B is A).

[34] F 86 Isnardi Parente/Dorandi 2012 = Arist. *APo*. II 4, 91a33–b4 Ross 1957.

[35] Translation Barnes ²1993, 52, slightly modified.

[36] This is closely connected to the problem what Aristotle means by saying that they "prove through conversion" (91a35: διὰ τοῦ ἀντιστρέφειν). See on this Detel 1993, 586, and Barnes ²1993, 209f.

[37] See for the following Detel 1993, 585; Barnes ²1993, 209; De-Cesaris, "Aristotle's Account", 152–154; Charles, *Aristotle on Meaning and Essence*, 184f.

c: (Number which moves itself) *a* (Soul)

2) It is necessary, Aristotle says according to Detel, to postulate that the soul is defined as a number which moves itself, if one wants the soul to be defined as a number which moves itself.

3) For, Aristotle says according to Detel, this does not follow from the syllogism. It only follows from p1) and p2) that c) is true, not that c) is the (or a) definition.

What can we gain from F 86 for Xenocrates's definition of the soul? We do not know if Xenocrates tried to prove his definition in this or any syllogistic scheme. If we trust Aristotle's account, we can assume that Xenocrates connected his definition of the soul as a self-moving number with the claim that the soul was explanatory of its own being alive. It is probable that Aristotle means to say that for Xenocrates the soul's being alive amounts to it being self-moved in contrast to living beings that are alive because they have a soul. This raises the question as to how self-movement explains being alive and to what extent the soul being a number plays a role in this. Was the soul defined as a number moving itself, *because* it is explanatory of its own being alive?[38] Or was the soul defined as a number moving itself for different reasons, but still *serves* to explain why the soul is explanatory of its own being alive? Either way, we do not know how the soul as a self-moving number accounts for it being explanatory of its own being alive.[39]

Cognition and Movement (F 85)

The second interesting testimony by Aristotle is to be found in his *De anima* (F 85). At the beginning of the *De anima* Aristotle reports the views of his predecessors on the soul, who according to Aristotle, connected the soul with movement (κίνησις) or perception (αἴσθησις). He says the following about Xenocrates's definition of the soul, without naming him:[40]

[38] De-Cesaris, "Aristotle's Account", 155f.

[39] Cf. Cherniss, *Aristotle's Criticism*, 399f. fn. 325; De-Cesaris, "Aristotle's Account", 155f.; Isnardi Parente/Dorandi 2012, 297, connects this with Plutarch's testimony of Xenocrates's interpretation of the *Timaeus* in F 108, see *infra* "Xenocrates and the *Timaeus* (F 108, F 109, F 179)".

[40] F 85 Isnardi Parente/Dorandi 2012 = Arist. *de An.* I 2, 404b27–30 Förster (in Corcilius 2017). It is unclear, how this testimony connects to the preceding sentences that have been attributed to Plato, Speusippus, or Xenocrates. See on this Isnardi Parente/Dorandi 2012, 296; Thiel, *Die Philosophie des Xenokrates*, 333–339.

ἐπεὶ δὲ καὶ κινητικὸν ἐδόκει ἡ ψυχὴ εἶναι καὶ γνωριστικόν,[41] οὕτως ἔνιοι συνέπλεξαν ἐξ ἀμφοῖν, ἀποφηνάμενοι τὴν ψυχὴν ἀριθμὸν κινοῦνθ' ἑαυτόν.

Since the soul seemed both capable of movement/motion and cognition, some plaited it together in this way from both, saying that the soul is a self-moving number.[42]

As Themistius points out, it is implied that the capacity for motion is reflected in the self-movement of the soul and that the capacity for cognition is in some way tied to it being a number.[43]

It is unclear, however, how the soul is capable of cognition by being a number. The text was subject to varied interpretations in antiquity and the Middle Ages as the following three examples will illustrate.

First, F 85 is interpreted using the *like is known by like* principle.[44] In this way, we can find it for example in Michael Psellos,[45] where he implicitly refers to F 85: Xenocrates, he says, understands forms as numbers; since soul can recognize forms, i.e. numbers, soul itself must be a number.

Secondly, John Philoponus explains F 85 by referencing the Pythagoreans:[46] Xenocrates called it a number, he says, for its capacity for knowledge, "as if he were a Pythagorean,[47]" since number for the Pythagoreans was the principle (ἀρχή) of all things. He called it self-moving (αὐτοκίνητον) because of its

[41] The punctuation is disputed: Torstrik 1862, 117, (followed by Rodier 1900, Ross 1961, Hicks 1965, Siwek 1965) puts the comma after οὕτως and reads it, relating it to the previous text, "οὕτως = τῷ ἐκ τῶν στοιχείων εἶναι, so that it limits the sense of γνωριστικόν" (in the words of Hicks 1965, 225). The manuscripts punctuate before the οὕτως, most likely announcing the ἀποφηνάμενοι, cf. the similar use in Bonitz *Index Aristotelicus*, s.v. οὗτος 546b13f. I thank Justin Winzenrieth for his helpful remarks on this.

[42] This is my own translation.

[43] Them. *In de An.* 12.28–33 Heinze 1899, commentary on F 85.

[44] This is the position taken by many modern scholars, see Cherniss, *Aristotle's Criticism*, 400; Hicks 1965, 15; Krämer, "Die Ältere Akademie", 46; Thiel, *Die Philosophie des Xenokrates*, 331f.; Polansky, 2007, 76f.; Isnardi Parente/Dorandi 2012, 25; De-Cesaris, "Aristotle's Account", 159f.; Palmieri, *La dottrine dell'anima*, 232.

[45] Michael Psellos, Συλλογαὶ διάφοροι καὶ ποικίλαι ("Various and diverse collections") 39, 21–25 O'Meara 1989. Cf. Arist. *de An.* I 2, 21–30 Förster (in Corcilius 2017) and F 85. Michael Psellos mentions the definition of the soul as self-moving number also in F 106 Isnardi Parente/Dorandi 2012 = Michael Psellos, ποῖον τὸ τέλος τῆς γεωμετρίας ("What is the goal of geometry") 163, 3–6 Boissonade 1838, without attributing it to Xenocrates yet.

[46] F 104 Isnardi Parente/Dorandi 2012 = Phlp. *In de An.* 81.25–30 Hayduck 1897, commentary on Arist. *de An.* I 2, 404b27–30 (F 85). Cf. Alexander in F 94 Isnardi Parente/Dorandi 2012 = Alex. Aphr. *In Top.* 493.21–494.16 Wallies 1891, commentary on Arist. *Top.* VI 14, 151b3, who also explains the definition by referencing the Pythagoreans. He does this in a very different way, however.

[47] ὡς Πυθαγόρειος. Translation van der Eijk 2005.

capacity for movement, since "among them" (κατ' αὐτοὺς)[48] what is self-moved (τὸ αὐτοκίνητον) was a/the principle of all movement.

It is unclear, why Philoponus introduces the Pythagoreans into his interpretation.[49] What is the connection between the number being an ἀρχή for all things and the soul's capacity for knowledge? One possible explanation is that he, like Michael Psellos, believed that some kind of *like is known by like* principle is at play here. Or Xenocrates is portrayed as a reconciler between Pythagorean and Platonic ideas of soul, maybe connecting the principle of everything, number, taken from the Pythagoreans, to the principle of motion (Plato), therefore making the principle of life a self-moved number.[50]

Philoponus, though, is a fickle interpreter, since he explains the definition in a different way in his commentary on Aristotle's rejection of Xenocrates's definition.[51] He provides the following comment on Aristotle's introduction to the refutation of this definition:[52]

Τὸ προκείμενον ἐλέγξαι τὴν Ξενοκράτους τοῦ Πλάτωνος διαδόχου περὶ ψυχῆς δόξαν, ὃς ἔλεγε τὴν ψυχὴν ἀριθμὸν εἶναι κινοῦντα ἑαυτόν. καὶ δῆλον ὅτι εἰ οὕτως ἔλεγε κατὰ τὸ φαινόμενον, εὐέλεγκτος ὁ λόγος. ἀλλ' ὅπερ καὶ ἐν τοῖς ἔμπροσθεν εἶπον, οὐκ ἄν τις οὐδ' ἄκρῳ δακτύλῳ τῶν μαθημάτων γευσάμενος τοιαῦτα ἂν εἴποι. ἔλεγεν οὖν ἀριθμὸν μὲν τὴν ψυχὴν διὰ τὸ πλήρωμα εἰδῶν εἶναι τὴν ψυχὴν καὶ λόγον ἐκ λόγων· πάντων γὰρ ἐν ἑαυτῇ τοὺς λόγους ἔχει, ὡς εἴπομεν. ἀριθμοὺς δὲ τὰ εἴδη ἐκάλουν, ὡς εἴρηται· καὶ αὐτὸς γοῦν ἐν τοῖς ἑξῆς φησιν 'καὶ εὖ δὴ οἱ λέγοντες τὴν ψυχὴν τόπον εἰδῶν'. ἀριθμὸν μὲν οὖν διὰ τοῦτο, κινοῦντα δὲ αὑτὸν διὰ τὸ αὐτοζῶν αὐτῆς· οὐ γὰρ ὑφ' ἑτέρου αὐτῇ τὸ ζῆν· αὐτοζωὴ γάρ ἐστιν. ὁ δὲ Ἀριστοτέλης, ὡς εἴωθεν, ἐλέγχει τὸ φαινόμενον τοῦ λόγου.

The next <task before him> is to refute the doctrine about the soul of Xenocrates, Plato's successor, who said that the soul is a number moving itself. And it is clear that if he said this when speaking at the level of what is manifest, the theory [is] easy to refute. But as I said above, even someone who has just tasted mathematics with the tip of his finger only, would not speak like that. He said, then, that the soul is a number because the soul is a fullness of forms and a λόγος ἐκ λόγων; for it has the λόγοι of all things within itself, as we have said. And they called the forms numbers, as has been said; and he [sc. Aristotle] himself, too, says in the sequel: 'Those who say that the soul is a place for forms, are correct' [(429a27–9)]. For these reasons he [sc. Xenocrates] calls it a number; and he says it is self-moving because of the autonomy of its life; for it does not derive its life from something else; it is an autonomous source of life. But Aristotle, as he is wont to, refutes the manifest [meaning] of the theory.[53]

---

48 The Greek is ambiguous. He is either referring to the Pythagoreans or to Xenocrates and his followers.

49 But cf. *supra* "The Soul as a Self-Moving Number: A Definition by Xenocrates".

50 Cf. Isnardi Parente/Dorandi 2012, 299.

51 Cf. Heinze 1892, 65.

52 F 117 Isnardi Parente/Dorandi 2012 = Phlp. *In de An.* 165.18–29 Hayduck 1897, commentary on Arist. *de An.* I 4, 408b32 (see F 112 *supra*).

53 Translation van der Eijk 2006, slightly modified.

John Philoponus says that Xenocrates does not mean this definition to be understood "at the level of what is manifest" (κατὰ τὸ φαινόμενον). He criticizes Aristotle and the following refutation.[54] Aristotle only refutes its literal meaning, taking soul to be a number made up from monads or similar. This, John Philoponus says, is not what Xenocrates had in mind by calling the soul a number moving itself, since anyone who had some knowledge of mathematics would know that it was easy to refute.[55] Instead, Xenocrates called the soul a number because it is a "fullness of forms" (τὸ πλήρωμα εἰδῶν) and a λόγος ἐκ λόγων. With the term λόγος Philoponus most likely means the numerical ratios from the first elements from which the soul according to the *Timaeus* consists.[56] But again we do not know how this leads to calling the soul a number precisely. Is the formulation "fullness of forms" an allusion to the *like is known by like* principle? Or does he call it a number because of the numerical ratios? Or does he combine both views? Finally, John Philoponus explains the soul's self-movement through its capacity to be its own source of life (αὐτοζῶν, αὐτοζωή)[57] and not getting its life from somewhere else.

John Philoponus, therefore, is an imprecise and most likely unreliable interpreter of Xenocrates's definition of the soul, offering two distinct interpretations in F 104 and F 117. He does not seem to know why Xenocrates defined the soul the way he did and keeps his explanations very general.

Thirdly, Aristotle's testimony in F 85 may also have been an inspiration for Nemesius of Emesa, for the latter highlights the soul's capacity for cognition in his explanation of Xenocrates's definition of the soul.[58] He first mentions the definition of the soul as self-moving number early in the second section of his work titled Περὶ ψυχῆς (*De natura hominis* 2, 68, p. 17, Morani 1987), where he attributes it to Pythagoras alone.[59] He later introduces Xenocrates as well:[60] Pythagoras, he says, likened God and everything else to numbers and defined the soul as a self-moving number. In this respect, Xenocrates followed him. Now this definition[61] did not result from the fact that the soul is a number,

---

[54] Cf. Isnardi Parente/Dorandi 2012, 306. Cf. Ps.-Simp. *In de An.* 62.10–17 Hayduck 1882.

[55] Cf. to this F 129 Isnardi Parente/Dorandi 2012 = Phlp. *In de An.* 171.17–20 Hayduck 1897, commentary on Arist. *de An.* I 4, 409a28 (F 112), where John Philoponus says, that Xenocrates can only have spoken about a number in analogy (κατὰ ἀναλογίαν).

[56] Cf. *infra* "Xenocrates and the *Timaeus* (F 108, F 109, F 179)".

[57] This is a formulation which we find in Neoplatonists and Aristotle, see Isnardi Parente/Dorandi 2012, 306. Cf. Aristotle in F 86 *supra* "Way of Proof (F 86)" and Arist. *Top.* V 8, 137b11 Brunschwig 2007.

[58] Cf. Isnardi Parente/Dorandi 2012, 303.

[59] See *supra* "The Soul as Self-Moving Number: A Definition by Xenocrates".

[60] F 110 Isnardi Parente/Dorandi 2012 = Nemesius of Emesa, *De natura hominis* 2, 102f. (p. 29f. Morani 1987). The following translations are by Sharples/van der Eijk 2008.

[61] It is not clear if the following paragraph is a reference to Pythagoras or Xenocrates, cf. Sharples/van der Eijk, 2008, 68 fn. 329.

but that, on the one hand, the soul is "among things that can be numbered and among things that are multiple"[62] and, on the other hand, that the soul "distinguishes things by assigning to each of them a shape and character"[63]. For it separates forms from forms, differentiates them through the otherness of the forms and the plentitude (τῷ πλήθει) of number "thereby making thinks numerable"[64]. This is why, according to Nemesius, they take part in number.[65] Without telling us whether he means Pythagoras or Xenocrates, Nemesius adds that "he" also gave testimony to the soul being αὐτοκινητόν. Nemesius then goes on to reject the idea that the soul could be a number.

It is hard to assess, then, what Aristotle wanted to say in F 85 precisely. Consequently, without further analysis this testimony does not help us to reconstruct Xenocrates's theory of the soul in any detail, but very generally ties it to cognition.

Xenocrates and the Timaeus *(F 108, F 109, F 179)*

Plutarch's account of Xenocrates's definition of the soul, however, provides greater insights for the reconstruction of the latter's theory of the soul. At the beginning of the *De animae procreatione in Timaeo*, Plutarch talks about different interpretations of Plato's *Timaeus* 35Af. He first paraphrases *Timaeus* 35Af. (1012Bf.):[66] Plato wrote that the demiurge took one part of the indivisible and the "ever invariable" (ἀεὶ κατὰ ταὐτὰ ἐχούσης) being and one part of the divisible being that "comes to pass in the case of bodies" (περὶ τὰ σώματα γιγνομένης). These he mixed together into a third kind of intermediate being (ἐν μέσῳ). Then "in regard to the nature of sameness again and that of difference he also in this way compounded it in the middle of the indivisible and what is indivisible among bodies" (τῆς τε ταὐτοῦ φύσεως αὖ πέρι καὶ τῆς τοῦ ἑτέρου· καὶ κατὰ ταῦτα συνέστησεν ἐν μέσῳ τοῦ τ' ἀμεροῦς αὐτὴν καὶ τοῦ κατὰ τὰ σώματα μεριστοῦ).[67] The demiurge takes these three[68] and blends them "all together into a single entity" (εἰς μίαν πάντα ἰδέαν) by force. From this

---

[62] ἐν τοῖς ἀριθμητοῖς ἐστι καὶ ἐν τοῖς πεπληθυσμένοις.

[63] ἡ διακρίνουοσα τὰ πράγματα τῷ μορφὰς καὶ τύπους ἑκάστοις ἐπιβάλλειν.

[64] διὰ τοῦτο ἀριθμητὰ ποιοῦσα τὰ πράγματα.

[65] ὅθεν οὐ παντάπασιν ἀπήλλακται τῆς κατὰ τοὺς ἀριθμοὺς κοινωνίας. – "For this reason things are not altogether divorced from kinship with numbers."

[66] The text deviates a bit from that of modern editions of the *Timaeus*. I follow the edition of Plutarch's text by Hubert 1954 with the critical remarks by Cherniss 1976, who prints the same text. Translations are by Cherniss 1976.

[67] There is a discussion as to how to understand this textually difficult passage in Plato; it is unclear, how many mixtures there are, cf. e.g. the discussion in Sonderegger, "Die Bildung der Seele". For interpretations in antiquity see Schwyzer, "Zu Plotins Interpretation"; Opsomer, "The Platonic Soul". For Xenocrates's interpretation see *infra*.

[68] What these three are depends on the interpretation of the passage.

"whole" (ὅλον) he takes parts and distributes them. Here Plutarch's report of the *Timaeus* stops.

In regard to Xenocrates, Plutarch gives the following account (1012D–F), adding that the discussion of Xenocrates (and Crantor) will be short:[69] Some of the most-esteemed men were won over by Xenocrates, "who declared the soul's essence to be number itself being moved by itself" (τῆς ψυχῆς τὴν οὐσίαν ἀριθμὸν αὐτὸν ὑφ' ἑαυτοῦ κινούμενον ἀποφηνάμενος). They believe that in the mixture of the Indivisible and Divisible the result is nothing but the generation of number, by identifying the Indivisible with the One (τὸ ἕν) and the Divisible with the Multiplicity (τὸ πλῆθος). The One limits the Mupltiplicity "and inserts a limit in infinitude" (τῇ ἀπειρίᾳ πέρας ἐντιθέντος), which they also call Indefinite Dyad (δυάδα [...] ἀόριστον). This number, they say according to Plutarch, is not yet soul, because it lacks "motivity and mobility" (τὸ [...] κινητικὸν καὶ τὸ κινητὸν). Once Sameness, the principle of motion and change, and Difference, the principle of rest, is blended in (the three elements therefore being number, Sameness, and Difference), the product is soul.

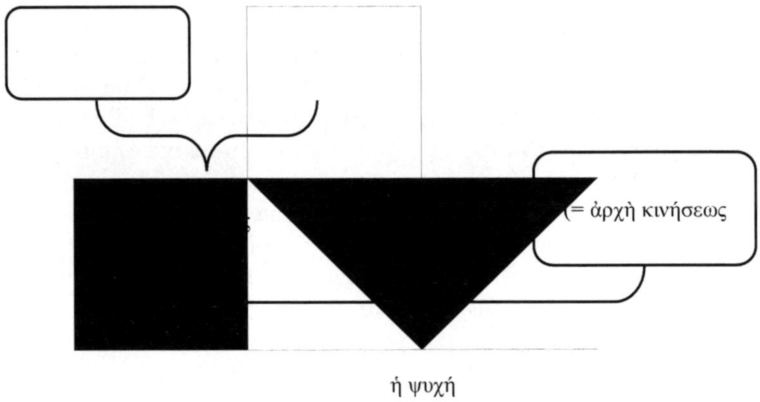

Fig. 1: Xenocrates's interpretation of Pl. *Ti.* 1012D-F according to Plutarch

[69] F 108 Isnardi Parente/Dorandi 2012 = Plutarch, *De procreatione animae in Timaeo* I, 1012D–1013B Hubert 1954. 1012D: ἔστι δὲ βραχὺς ὑπὲρ ἀμφοῖν ὁ λόγος. Because of this formulation, Cherniss 1976, 163, suggests "that what follows was taken not directly from Xenocrates and Crantor but from a report of their interpretations". Although this is possible, it is not necessarily so.

Soul, Plutarch says, is according to Xenocrates the potency (δύναμις) of "bringing to a stop and being at rest" (τοῦ ἱστάναι καὶ ἵστασθαι) and "of being in motion and setting in motion" (τοῦ κινεῖσθαι καὶ κινεῖν).[70]

This testimony is very important for two reasons: first, it is an explicit attribution of the definition to Xenocrates by a scholar who was familiar with at least the content of Xenocratean thought either through summaries or even from reading his works first hand.[71] Secondly, if we trust Plutarch's report of Xenocrates's interpretation of the *Timaeus*, we learn that Xenocrates established an exegesis of the *Timaeus* that fitted with his definition. In that exegesis, Xenocrates took the Divisible (which he equated with the Multiplicity, the Unlimited, and the Indefinite Dyad), and the Indivisible (which he equated with the One) as the principles of number. For it to become soul, Sameness (the principle of motion) and Difference (the principle of rest) must be added.[72] We cannot say why Xenocrates interpreted it in this way and whether this interpretation was in any way intended by Plato,[73] whom he knew personally, but we can surmise that he adds certain interpretations to the text. More importantly, we do not know if this interpretation of the text *motivated* his definition of the soul or if he interpreted the text in this way to *fit* his definition of the soul.

There is another passage in which Plutarch offers a rather obscure comment on the definition of soul as self-moving number, also in connection with the *Timaeus*. In his eighth question of the *Quaestiones Platonicae* Plutarch asks what Plato means in the *Timaeus* 42D4f. by saying that "the souls were sowed in earth and moon and all the rest of the instruments of time"[74]. In his discussion of this passage he starts to speak about what time (χρόνος) is (1006-1007).

---

[70] Cf. Macrobius's testimony in F 97 Isnardi Parente/Dorandi 2012 = Macrobius, *In Somnium Scipionis* I 6, 5 Armisen-Marchetti ^{2}2003, where Macrobius refers to the *Timaeus* as well. He ascribes the definition to Xenocrates in his doxographical report later in the text (F 96 Isnardi Parente/Dorandi 2012 = Macrobius, *In Somnium Scipionis* I 14, 19 Armisen-Marchetti ^{2}2003). It is most likely, that Macrobius's explanation is an interpretation of Arist. *de An.* I 2, 404b16–26 Förster (in Corcilius 2017) (the sentences before F 85) and the *Timaeus* 35Bf. On Macrobius's interpretation see also Armisen-Marchetti ^{2}2003, 146 fn. 93.

[71] See *supra* fn. 6.

[72] Apparently, Xenocrates thinks that Sameness and Difference are added without being mixed before, as is sometimes suggested today. Cf. Dillon, "The *Timaeus* in the Old Academy", 2003b = Dillon, "The *Timaeus* in the Old Academy", 2012b, note 15 on page 92; Dillon, *The Heirs of Plato*, 121f. Heinze 1892, 67, suggests that this solves an issue Plato had: if movement was connected with the ἄπειρον, forms should be able to move, too. Therefore, Xenocrates connected it only with the ἕτερον.

[73] Heinze 1892, 66, calls it an "completely unauthorized interpretation" ("sehr eigenmächtige Interpretation"), but cf. the critical remarks with further literature by Isnardi Parente/Dorandi 2012, 300f., and Krämer, "Die Ältere Akademie", 46.

[74] 1006C: Πῶς λέγει τὰς ψυχὰς ὁ Τίμαιος εἴς τε γῆν καὶ σελήνην καὶ τἄλλα ὅσα ὄργανα χρόνου σπαρῆναι; Translation by Cherniss 1976, 77.

Time, he says, was misinterpreted by Aristotle, Speusippus, and some of the Stoics; they (either all of them or the Stoics only) did not know time's essence (οὐσία) and its potency (δύναμις), but Pindar and Pythagoras seem to suspect (ὑπονοέω) it. Pythagoras, he says, said that time is the soul of everything (τοῦ ὅλου ψυχή). Plutarch goes on to describe time himself; he says that time is not an attribute or accident (πάθος οὐδὲ συμβεβηκὸς) of any chance motion, but it is

> cause and potency and principle of that which holds together all the things that come to be, of the symmetry and order in which the nature of the whole universe, being animate, is in motion; or rather, being motion and order itself and symmetry, it is called time, 'for all that mortal is, going his noiseless path, he guides aright' and for the ancients even held that the essence of soul is number itself moving itself.[75]

He then reports that Plato said that time came into being together with heaven, referring to *Timaeus* 30A and 52D–53A.

The reasoning in this passage is unclear, especially the reason for introducing the definition of the soul. If one takes the particle γάρ seriously, Plutarch seems to think that the *soul* being a number moving itself is a reason for understanding *time* as motion, order, or symmetry. Perhaps, we also have to understand it in the context of the quotation from Euripides: if time guides all mortals and all mortals have a soul, then the soul is in some way a number structured by time. Thirdly, Plutarch may refer back to Pythagoras's aforementioned definition of time being the soul of everything. If time is a soul and the soul is a number moving itself, then time is motion and order.

Notably, the definition is not ascribed to anyone in particular (in contrast to F 108), but to "the ancients" (παλαιοί). Cherniss 1976, 86f., suggests that Plutarch is vague on purpose: in F 108 Plutarch clarifies that Xenocrates misinterprets Plato's *Timaeus*, but here Plutarch uses the (in his view wrong) definition of the soul to support his own correct interpretation of time.

There are two later testimonies that show certain similarities to Plutarch's account in F 108, though for both it is less probable that they knew Xenocrates's writing as well as Plutarch.

The first testimony is by Proclus, who mentions Xenocrates in his commentary on *Timaeus* 35B1. The demiurge, he says, mixes Being (οὐσία), Sameness (τὸ ταὐτό) and Difference (τὸ θάτερον) into a single entity and

---

[75] F 92 Isnardi Parente/Dorandi 2012 = Plu. *Quaestiones Platonicae* 8, 1007Bf. Hubert 1954: οὐ γὰρ πάθος οὐδὲ συμβεβηκὸς ἧς ἔτυχε κινήσεως ὁ χρόνος ἐστίν, αἰτία δὲ καὶ δύναμις καὶ ἀρχὴ τῆς πάντα συνεχούσης τὰ γιγνόμενα συμμετρίας καὶ τάξεως, ἣν ἡ τοῦ ὅλου φύσις ἔμψυχος οὖσα κινεῖται· μᾶλλον δὲ κίνησις οὖσα καὶ τάξις αὐτὴ καὶ συμμετρία χρόνος καλεῖται· 'πάντα γὰρ δι' ἀψόφου βαίνων κελεύθου κατὰ δίκην τὰ θνήτ' ἄγει·' (E. *Tr*. 887f.) καὶ γὰρ ἡ ψυχῆς οὐσία κατὰ τοὺς παλαιοὺς 'ἀριθμὸς ἦν αὐτὸς ἑαυτὸν κινῶν'. Translation by Cherniss 1976, slightly modified.

divides it again.[76] Proclus interprets the division in the following way:[77] He thinks that the soul's "Being (οὐσία) is an intermediary between the Divisible and the Indivisible"[78]. The soul's Being is not one (μία) like the intellect's (νοῦς) Being, nor is it like the Being in the physical bodies that is divisible into infinity. Instead, the soul is neither of these "on account of the plurality of its parts"[79], because it is "still made numerically determinate"[80]. For in the division the god took one part, that remains one and indivisible, and, therefore, "the whole plurality"[81] is constituted of such indivisible parts, so that the whole plurality is not divisible into infinity.[82] Thus, the soul is both one and not one and it is contained in limits that are numerically determinate; in this way, he says, the soul can be called a number. Proclus goes on to explain that the soul, therefore, consists of a plurality of monads (τῶν μονάδων τὸ πλῆθος), which are neither mathematical (μαθηματική), insubstantial monads (ἀνούσιοι […] μονάδες) nor physical (φυσική) monads, but substantial (οὐσιώδης)[83] monads.[84] The soul consists of these indivisible monads "taking in the plurality of these monads in a uniform manner".[85]

In what follows Proclus supports his arguments by introducing the Indivisible and Divisible:[86] it is necessary that the soul is indivisible (it is one) and divisible (it is a plurality), for both the Indivisible and Divisible are part of it.

καὶ τοῦτ' ἦν, ὡς ἔοικεν, ὃ καὶ Ξενοκράτης ἀκούσας τοῦ καθηγεμόνος ᾐνίξατο λέγων κατ' ἀριθμὸν εἶναι τὴν ψυχὴν οὐσίαν, ἐξ οὐσιῶν μίαν πολλῶν αὐτὴν ὑπάρχειν δηλῶν κατ' οὐσίαν οὖσαν ἀριθμόν, ὅλην δι' ὅλης ἑαυτῆς μένουσαν, ἅμα μίαν καὶ διαιρουμένην εἰς πλῆθος μερῶν οὐσιωδῶν.

And it seems that it was this which Xenocrates heard from his teacher and put in a riddling manner when he said that the psychic essence is numerical (κατ' ἀριθμόν), showing that it exists as a single thing composed from many substances, being essentially (κατ' οὐσίαν) a

---

[76] To the problems concerning the interpretation of the *Timaeus*, see the footnotes to my discussion of Plutarch in F 108.

[77] Procl. *In Ti.* II 164f. Diehl 1904 = III 222–224 Van Riel 2012. I read the text by Van Riel 2012, the translations are by Baltzly 2009.

[78] ἡ οὐσία τῆς ψυχῆς μέση τῆς τε ἀμεροῦς ἐστι καὶ τῆς μεριστῆς.

[79] διὰ τὰ πλήθη τῶν μερῶν.

[80] ὡρισμένη δὲ κατ' ἀριθμόν.

[81] τὸ ὅλον πλῆθος.

[82] Cf. Baltzly 2009, 133 fn. 203.

[83] See 223, 21 Van Riel 2012: μονάδων […] οὐσιωδῶν.

[84] See Baltzly 2009, 133f. fn. 204 for the different kinds of monads.

[85] περιλαβοῦσα τὸ πλῆθος τούτων ἑνοειδῶς εἴη ἂν ἕν.

[86] F 109 Isnardi Parente/Dorandi 2012 = Procl. *In Ti.* II 165.3–12 Diehl 1904 = III 224.3–12 Van Riel 2012.

number; it remains a whole through the whole of itself, and it is simultaneously single and divided into a plurality of substantial parts.[87]

Xenocrates, he says, interpreted Plato in the *Timaeus* in the way Proclus described before: it is a number, for it consists of multiple parts but remains one.

I agree with those scholars who believe that Proclus only conjectures what Xenocrates's reasons were.[88] The closeness to Plutarch is coincidental only. Proclus's wording suggests that he does not know Xenocrates's reasons for calling the soul a self-moving number. He says "it seems" (ὡς ἔοικεν) and speaks of Xenocrates's "riddling manner" (ᾐνίξατο).[89] Notably, Proclus only talks of the soul as a number, not as a moving or self-moving number, and, therefore, shows considerable differences to Plutarch's report of Xenocrates's interpretation. This is also indicated by the many differences that a close reading of Proclus's and Plutarch's testimonies reveal: Plutarch on the one hand explains in great detail that Xenocrates and his followers identified the Indivisible with the One and the Divisible with the Multiplicity or Indefinite Dyad, whereas this is lacking from Proclus's account. Proclus on the other hand says that the soul is a plurality of monads, which might be inspired by Aristotle's critique,[90] which is absent from Plutarch's account.

The second testimony that shows resemblance to Plutarch's testimony in F 108 is by Themistius. He says in the introduction of his paraphrase concerning F 112[91] that Aristotle speaks of the definition of the soul by Xenocrates. Aristotle does not refute the definition "by contesting the term 'number', as Andronicus and Porphyry say, but by really inquiring into Xenocrates' meaning, as is clear from the latter's books *On Nature* where he would seem to make the soul a unit-like number"[92]. After this introduction Themistius paraphrases F 112 in full and then goes on to say that these were the problems

---

[87] Translation by Baltzly 2009, modified.

[88] Tarán, "Proclus and the Old Academy", 250–252, thinks that Proclus only conjectures why Xenocrates called the soul a number, but admits that he "may happen to be right up to a certain point, but it is not based on independent evidence, and it can hardly have been the main reason that prompted Xenocrates to hold this doctrine". Baltzly 2009, 134 fn. 206, is even more negative, saying that, because Proclus does not mention motion, it cannot come close to Aristotle's report of the soul as self-moving number.

[89] This might be the reason, why Heinze 1892, calls this testimony "irrelevant" ("unerheblich").

[90] Cf. Aristotle in F 112, *supra* "Non Constructive Testimonies".

[91] F 179 Isnardi Parente/Dorandi 2012 = Them. *In de An.* 31.1–6 Heinze 1899.

[92] Them. *In de An.* 31.1–5 Heinze 1899: Μετὰ δὲ ταῦτα διελέγχει τὸν Ξενοκράτους ὁρισμὸν τῆς ψυχῆς, οὐ πρὸς τοὔνομα τοῦ ἀριθμοῦ μαχόμενος, ὥς φησιν Ἀνδρόνικος καὶ Πορφύριος, ἀλλὰ καὶ πάνυ τὴν διάνοιαν ἐπιζητῶν τὴν Ξενοκράτους, ὡς δῆλόν ἐστιν ἐκ τῶν Περὶ φύσεως αὐτῷ γεγραμμένων, ἐν οἷς ἂν δόξειε μοναδικὸν ποιεῖν ἀριθμὸν τὴν ψυχὴν ὁ Ξενοκράτης. Translation by Todd 1996, 47.

raised by Aristotle with Xenocrates's definition of the soul.[93] It would take even more time, he adds, to discuss the problems raised by another unnamed philosopher[94] who called Aristotle's interpretation inconceivable (ἀδιανόητα). However, Themistius wants to contrast Aristotle's argument with Andronicus's explanation, which he finds "clearer and more plausible for the reconstruction of Xenocrates's theory"[95]. Andronicus, Themistius says, said that Xenocrates and his followers called the soul number because no animal derives from a simple body but from the primary elements mixed in a certain ratio and number (κατά τινας λόγους καὶ ἀριθμοὺς). In this way their theory was almost the same as the theory of those who made the soul a ἁρμονία, with the exception that Xenocrates's and his followers' definition was clearer (σαφέστερον) inasmuch as they added that soul was not any number, but only number moving itself as if they had defined it as ἁρμονία harmonizing itself. For soul as self-moving number, Andronicus says in Themistius's words, is the reason (αἰτία) for its blend, its ratio (λόγος) and its mixture from the primary elements. Themistius adds that Xenocrates's theory of the soul as self-moving number is best to be taken from the fifth book of his Περὶ φύσεως.

In this passage, Themistius contrasts Aristotle's refutation of Xenocrates's definition of the soul with Andronicus's explanation of it. Although, according to Themistius, Aristotle knew and understood the real significance of Xenocrates's definition and therefore refuted it in a constructive manner (and should not be criticized for it, as done by Porphyry and Andronicus), Andronicus's explanation, nonetheless, is in the eyes of Themistius helpful for understanding how Xenocrates came to this definition (πρὸς *σύστασιν* τοῦ λόγου). For Andronicus explains Xenocrates's definition by saying that he called it a number because it was mixed in a certain ratio and number from the primary elements just as those who posited that the soul was a ἁρμονία.[96] Xenocrates, though, added the reason as to why it could be mixed in that way, namely the soul's self-movement.

How trustworthy is Themistius's account? Although he mentions the precise book from which one could take the discussion of the soul, Themistius does not seem to have first-hand knowledge of Xenocrates.[97] He does not explain

---

[93] F 180 Isnardi Parente/Dorandi 2012 = Them. *In de An.* 32.19–34 Heinze 1899.

[94] This philosopher is generally assumed to be Porphyry as he was mentioned in F 179.

[95] ἀλλὰ χρὴ παραβάλλειν τὰ Ἀνδρονίκου πρὸς τὰ ἐκείνου, ὅσῳ καὶ σαφέστερα καὶ πιθανώτερα πρὸς σύστασιν τοῦ λόγου τοῦ Ξενοκράτους. Translation by Todd 1996, 49, modified. I take Themistius to mean by πρὸς τὰ ἐκείνου the explanations given by Aristotle (as do Isnardi Parente/Dorandi 2012, 195), rather than those given by the unnamed Porphyry (as Todd 1996, 49, suggests).

[96] See the critical remarks on this by Palmieri, *La dottrine dell'anima*, 261–266.

[97] See *supra* "The Soul as Self-Moving Number: A Definition by Xenocrates".

the definition himself, but paraphrases an explanation given by Andronicus,[98] which he might only have read second-hand through Porphyry.[99] He is very cautious with his phrasing in F 179, where he says that in the Περὶ φύσεως Xenocrates made the soul a unit-like number. He uses the optative, not the indicative for the word δοκέω: "where *he would seem* to make the soul a unit-like number"[100], and he does not refer to Xenocrates often.[101] Furthermore, there are also problems in terms of content: Aristotle, on the one hand, seems to understand that the soul is a number in a quite literal sense, being a 'sum-total of units'.[102] Andronicus, on the other hand, explains that the soul is a number because it is mixed in a certain ratio and number from the primary elements. How can Themistius consider both arguments to be correct?

Andronicus's testimony differs from Plutarch's testimony in important details. While Plutarch takes the soul to be a number because the mixture of the One and the Multitude is a number, Andronicus thinks that the soul is a number because it is mixed in a certain ratio and number. They also differ in the way they understand the soul's self-motion, but Andronicus's explanation according to which it was self-moved and is thus the reason for its mixture is not very clear.

The Soul as Intermediate Being (F 113)

One last interesting account in relation to the *Timaeus* is the explanation of Pseudo-Simplicius in the *In Aristotelis De anima*,[103] in a passage where he comments on F 85.[104] Although Pseudo-Simplicius does not seem to know Xenocrates's reason for calling the soul a self-moving number, his explanation is nevertheless plausible and worth considering. Pseudo-Simplicius places the soul in the middle of Xenocrates's ontological order of being. He first discusses the extremes (forms and informed objects) and then approaches the middle from both extremes, shifting in the discussion from the informed objects to the formative principles of the physical and the mathematical substances, and from the forms to the intellectual substance. I will discuss the text in three steps.

---

[98] Heinze 1892, 65; Palmieri, *La dottrine dell'anima*, 261f. Against this Cherniss, *Aristotle's Criticism*, 399f. fn. 325, and 567. Cf. Isnardi Parente/Dorandi 2012, 333.

[99] Moraux, *Der Aristotelismus bei den Griechen*, 132.

[100] ἐν οἷς ἂν δόξειε μοναδικὸν ποιεῖν ἀριθμὸν τὴν ψυχὴν ὁ Ξενοκράτης. Translation by Todd 1996, 47.

[101] In the collection of Isnardi Parente/Dorandi 2012, there is, besides F 179 and F 180, only one further testimony by Themistius (F 61).

[102] See *supra* "Non-Constructive Testimonies".

[103] This work is ascribed either to Simplicius or Priscianus, see Goulet, "Simplicius de Cilicie", and Sorabji in Urmson/Lautner, *Simplicius*, 1f.

[104] F 113 Isnardi Parente/Dorandi 2012 = Ps.-Simp. *In de An.* 30.4–24 Hayduck 1882. I thank Andreas Kindler and Klaus Corcilius for the fruitful discussions concerning this testimony.

Ξενοκράτους ὁ τῆς ψυχῆς οὗτος λόγος βουλομένου τὴν μεσότητα αὐτῆς τῶν τε εἰδῶν καὶ τῶν εἰδοποιουμένων ἅμα καὶ τὸ ἴδιον αὐτῆς ἐνδείξασθαι· ὁ γὰρ ἀριθμὸς τὸ εἶδος, τὸ δὲ κινητὸν τοῖς εἰδοποιουμένοις προσήκει. ἐκ τῶν ἄκρων οὖν ὂν δῆλον ὅτι οὔτε[105] ἀριθμὸς ἁπλῶς ἔσται οὔτε κινητόν· τοῦ μὲν γὰρ ὑφεῖται, ᾗ τοῦ ἀμερίστου ἐκβέβληται, τοῦ δέ ἐστι κρείττων, ᾗ τοῦ μεριστοῦ ὑπερέχει. τὸ συναμφότερον οὖν ἄν πως εἴη ὡς ἀμφοτέροις κοινωνοῦσα, ἀριθμὸς κινητός.

1) This account of the soul is that of Xenocrates, who wished to exhibit its mean position between forms and the informed and at the same time also its special [character] (ἴδιον). For the number is form, while being in motion is characteristic of the informed. It is clear that, being between the extremes, the soul is neither simply number nor something in motion. For it is inferior to the former, since it has lost its undivided character, but superior to the latter, since it is superior to the divided. So it should be somehow both together, since it takes part in both, a number in motion.[106]

Pseudo-Simplicius says that Xenocrates had two reasons to call the soul a self-moving number. First, it is called a moving number because the soul is both form and informed, being neither completely undivided nor completely divided. In which way, one might ask, can it be neither undivided nor divided? We do not know, but Pseudo-Simplicius implies that he does not know the precise way either, since he says, that the soul "should be somehow" (ἄν πως εἴη) both number and in motion.

κατὰ δὲ τὸ οἰκεῖον τῆς μεσότητος ὑφ' ἑαυτοῦ κινητὸς λέγεται, ὅτι οὐχ ὡς διαστατική ἐστι μέση ἡ ψυχή, οἷος ὁ φυσικὸς λόγος καὶ πρὸ τούτου κατὰ τοὺς ἄνδρας ἡ μαθηματικὴ οὐσία, οὐδὲ οἷα κατὰ τὸ προϊὸν ἀπὸ νοῦ φῶς οὐσία νοερὰ μὲν ἔτι μένουσα, τῷ δὲ εἰς τὸ φανὸν καὶ σύμμετρον τοῖς ὑπὸ νοῦ καταλαμπομένοις προέρχεσθαι ἐξαγγέλλουσα τὸ μόνιμον καὶ κρύφιον τῆς νοερᾶς φύσεως, ἀλλὰ κατ' αὐτὴν τὴν ζωτικὴν ἰδιότητα ἔγερσιν καὶ ζέσιν τινὰ πάσης δηλούσης ζωῆς, ἀμέριστον μὲν καὶ ἐν ἑαυτῇ μένουσαν τῆς νοερᾶς, περὶ δὲ τὰ σώματα μεριζομένην καὶ ἑτέρωθεν εἰς ἕτερα ὑφιζάνουσαν τῆς σωματοειδοῦς, τῆς δὲ ψυχικῆς τὴν ἀφ' ἑαυτῆς εἰς ἑαυτὴν ἀνέλιξιν καὶ ἐκ διαστάσεως ἅμα συναγωγήν.[107]

2) But, appropriately to its mean position, it is said to be self-moved. For the soul is not an intermediate as [something] extending (διαστατική)[108] a) as is the formative principle of the

---

[105] ἐκ τῶν ἄκρων οὖν ὂν δῆλον ὅτι οὔτε is an emendation by Torstrik for ἐκ μὲν οὖν τῶν ἄκρων μονονοὺ † δηλοῖ τὸ οὔτε, which I accept.

[106] Translation by Urmson/Lautner 1995, modified.

[107] τὴν ἀφ' ἑαυτῆς εἰς ἑαυτὴν ἀνέλιξιν καὶ ἐκ διαστάσεως ἅμα συναγωγήν is an emendation by Torstrik for τὴν ἀφ' ἑαυτῆς εἰς † ἀνέλιξιν καὶ εἰς διάστασιν ἅμα συναγωγήν, which I accept.

[108] διαστατικός traditionally means "dissolving, separating, extending" whereas διαστατός means "divisible, extended". Urmson/Lautner 1995, 48, translates διαστατική with "extended" in reference to Baltes 1972, 165, but Baltes himself writes "spaltend, dehnend" which means "separating, extending". According to the TLG, Plotinus, Porphyry, Proclus, Iamblichus and John Philoponus do not use διαστατικός but only διαστατός. Ps.-Simplicius uses διαστατικός on two other occasions in *In de An.*: in 215.16–18 Hayduck 1882 (ἐπειδὴ μετὰ διαστάσεως καὶ μορφῆς αἱ φανταστικαὶ ἐνέργειαι, αἱ δὲ τοῦ καθαροῦ λόγου καὶ ἔτι μᾶλλον αἱ τοῦ νοῦ τοῦ διαστατικοῦ καὶ μορφωτικοῦ ὑπερέχουσι μερισμοῦ.), where I would read "extending and form

physical (φυσικὸς λόγος)[109], and before that, as these men said, the mathematical substance; b) nor is it like light proceeding from the intellect, an intellective substance ever at rest, which, by proceeding into the apparent on a level with/fitting to (σύμμετρον) the things irradiated by intellect, it proclaims the enduring and hidden [character] of the intellective nature. c) But [sc. the soul is an intermediate] because of its peculiarity that is characteristic of its life, since every life shows some kind of awaking and effervescence: i) the intellectual [life shows an awaking and effervescence which is] partless and stays the same in itself, ii) the bodily life [shows an awaking and effervescence which is] divided among the bodies and sinking from here to there, iii) [and] the psychic [life shows an awaking and effervescence which is] an unfolding from itself into itself and at the same time a contraction from being extended.[110]

Pseudo-Simplicius explains why the soul is called self-moved, but unfortunately the text is intricate, both in syntax and meaning. He explains, I believe, that the soul is an intermediate,[111] but not as the formative principle of the physical and the mathematical substance on the one hand (a), nor as the

---

giving division" rather than "extended and formed division" (Blumenthal 2000, 75, translates rather loosely "the division of extension and shape"); in 305.32–35 (τὸ πῦρ […] κατ' αὐτὴν δὲ τὴν διαστατικὴν πορείαν ὠθούμενον οὐ βιαίως οὐδὲ ταύτην, ἀλλ' οἷον ἑκουσίως, ἐκτεινόμενον δὲ ὅμως Hayduck 1882), it is possible that it either means "extending course", thought of the fire as being in motion and thus extending its course, or "extended course", thought of as "dimensional course" (Steel 2013, 115). In comparison, διαστατός is used twice in Ps.-Simp. *In de An.*: 42.26 and 252.33 Hayduck 1882 where in both cases it means "extended". Simplicius uses διαστατικός only in two places in his extant work: several times in a completely different sense in *Commentarius in Epicteti enchiridion* 37.30–74 Hadot 1996, where he uses διαστατικός and συναγωγός as technical terms (Brennan/Brittain 2002, translate "disassociative" and "associative") to explain different kinds of relations (σχέσις) or coordinations (σύνταξις). And in *In Aristotelis Physica commentaria* 249.2–5 Diels 1882, Simplicius uses διαστατικός once (ἀναλογεῖν δ' ἂν μητρὶ λέγοις καὶ καθόσον διαστατικὴ καὶ διαιρετικὴ τῶν εἰδῶν ἐστιν ἡ ὕλη, ὥσπερ τῶν πατρικῶν σπερμάτων αἱ μητέρες καὶ τῶν βρεφῶν τρέφουσαι καὶ αὔξουσαι αὐτὰ εἰς μείζονα ὄγκον.), in relation to ὕλη, which "provides extension and division for forms, just as mothers provide extension and division for the father's seeds and offspring and nourish them and cause them to grow to a greater size" (Translation Baltussen/Share/Mueller 2012). Here the active act of extending and dividing (just as nourishing and causing them to grow) seems to be in focus. For all these reasons, I believe that in the present case διαστατική means "extending", which is most likely also the understanding of Isnardi Parente/Dorandi 2012, who translates "ha una funzione separante" (p. 157). I do admit, though, that "extended" could be possible as well.

[109] Cf. for this translation of φυσικὸς λόγος Ps.-Simp. *In de An.* 312, 20 Hayduck 1882.

[110] Translation of a)–b) is by Urmson/Lautner 1995, modified, c) is my own translation; the division of the text a)–c) is also mine.

[111] The middle status is also stressed later in the text, see F 115 Isnardi Parente/Dorandi 2012 = Ps.-Simp. *In de An.* 65.37–66.3 Hayduck 1882, commentary on Arist. *de An.* I 5, 409a31 (part of F 112).

intellective substance on the other hand (b).[112] These three objects have an extending effect and are in the middle, but in different ways, which are not explicit in the text. I suggest the following:

a) The formative principle of the physical has an extending effect, since it is the principle for objects that are extended in space, and it is in between forms and informed objects, being the formative principle for physical objects, but not itself a physical object. The interpretation of the mathematical substance is more challenging. It is unclear how precisely the mathematical substance has an "extend*ing*" effect. Pseudo-Simplicius is most likely thinking of geometrical objects that have extension. It is, as mathematical substance is for Platonists, in between forms and informed objects, and ontologically "before" the formative principle of the physical.

b) The intellective substance does not expand in space, but it expands intellectually, i.e. it thinks. It is in the middle between forms and informed objects, because it bridges the gap between informed objects and their forms, finding the intellective nature of the latter hidden in the former.

I think we must surmise *ex negativo* that the soul does not expand in space, as physical or mathematical substance do, nor does it expand intellectually, as intellectual substance does.

The soul, instead, is an intermediate that has an extending effect in a different way, which is described in more detail in c). Now Pseudo-Simplicius shifts his attention to different types of lives: the intellectual, the corporeal, and the psychic life. The psychic life is in between the intellectual and the corporeal life:

i) The intellectual life shows a liveliness that is indivisible and stays the same.

ii) The corporeal life shows a liveliness that is divisible and "sinks from here to there", i.e. it moves only passively.

iii) The psychic life, instead, is divisible and indivisible, and it does not stay the same like the intellective life, but unfolds (i.e. moves) like corporeal life. But unlike corporeal life it contracts and extends actively *from itself* and *in itself*[113] just as the intellective life stays in itself.

---

[112] The Greek text is ambiguous. I think that what Pseudo-Simplicius is trying to say is that the formative principle of the physical, the mathematical essence, and the intellective substance are all extending and in the middle. An alternative interpretation might be that only the formative principle of the physical and the mathematical, but not the intellective substance are extending.

[113] This latter part depends on Torstrik's emendation, but is most certainly the meaning of the text.

Up to this point, Pseudo-Simplicius clearly refers to the *Timaeus* 34A–35A for his explanation,[114] but then goes on to develop it further. The soul in terms of number is 'almost' a form, not completely divisible and remaining in itself, but in terms of movement it is 'almost' informed, to a certain degree divisible, and moved, but moved by and in itself.[115] Although this interpretation is different from Plutarch's account in F 108, it explains the soul's definition from another angle. While Plutarch explains how Xenocrates's definition fits with the *Timaeus*, Pseudo-Simplicius gives us reasons why Xenocrates developed this definition. We do not know, however, how close this interpretation is to Xenocrates's actual reasons for defining the soul as self-moving number.[116]

διὰ ταῦτα μὲν οὖν ὁ Ξενοκράτης ἀριθμὸν αὐτὸν ἑαυτὸν κινοῦντα τὴν ψυχὴν ἀπεφήνατο. ὁ δὲ Ἀριστοτέλης τὸν ἀριθμὸν ὁριστικὸν προειπὼν καὶ τῶν γνωστῶν καὶ τῶν γνωστικῶν, ἐπὶ τῆς ψυχῆς εὐλόγως ὡς γνωστικὸν εἰρῆσθαι ἀκούει, καὶ διὰ τοῦτο τοὺς εἰπόντας τὴν ψυχὴν ἀριθμὸν αὐτὸν ἑαυτὸν κινοῦντα συμπλέξαι ἔφη τὸ κινητικὸν καὶ τὸν γνωστικόν.

3) For these reasons, then, Xenocrates declared that the soul was a self-moving number. Aristotle, who has said before that the number is defining both for what knows and what is known, correctly understands it to be the soul that is called the knower. And this is why he said that those who call the soul a self-moving number plaited it together, it being capable of motion and cognition.[117]

Until now, Pseudo-Simplicius had explained why Xenocrates called soul a self-moving number. Now he proceeds to explaining the Aristotelean text he is actually commenting upon, namely why Aristotle said that Xenocrates plaited the capacity of motion and cognition together and thus came to call the soul a self-moving number. In this context, Pseudo-Simplicius refers to another definition by Aristotle, who uses 'number' "in two senses: that which is counted or countable, and that by which we count, see *Physics* 4, 219b5–8, 223a24–8. [...] The

[114] In the *Timaeus*, the soul is put in the middle (34B) and mixed together from a Being that is partless and always staying the same (35A1f. Burnet 1902: τῆς ἀμερίστου καὶ ἀεὶ κατὰ ταὐτὰ ἐχούσης οὐσίας cf. to ἀμέριστον μὲν καὶ ἐν ἑαυτῇ μένουσαν τῆς νοερᾶς in F 113) and from a Being that is divisible and comes to be among the bodies (35A2f. Burnet 1902: τῆς αὖ περὶ τά σώματα γιγνομένης μεριστῆς cf. to περὶ δὲ τὰ σώματα μεριζομένην in F 113).

[115] This interpretation (1–2) is repeated in a shorter version in Pseudo-Simplicius's commentary on F 112, see F 114 Isnardi Parente/Dorandi 2012 = Ps.-Simp. *In de An.* 61.23–62.11 Hayduck, 1882, on *An.* I 4, 408b32 (part of F 112): the soul is in the middle between indivisible form and divisible objects in motion (τὸ [...] κινούμενον), because it "descended as a whole into division" (τὸ ὅλον τοῦτο εἰς μερισμὸν ὑποβάν, translation by Urmson/Lautner 1995, 87), but is neither completely divided nor staying form, but "somehow slackening and loosening the indivisible unification" (τῷ χαλάσαι καὶ ἐκλῦσαί πως τὴν ἀμέριστον ἕνωσιν, translation by Urmson/Lautner 1995, modified). We may again note the vague expression πως as if Pseudo-Simplicius, too, was unsure what this meant. He adds again that it is not called moving, but self-moving because it does slack, but is not torn from itself (ἀποσπασθείσης).

[116] Heinze 1892, 65, and Isnardi Parente/Dorandi 2012, 305f., are rather sceptical.

[117] Translation by Urmson/Lautner 1995, 48, modified.

commentator transforms this relation"; as the counted is to that by which we count, so too is "the known (countable number) to the knower (counting soul)".[118] This last part of the testimony explains the Aristotelean text in a completely different way than other authors.[119] The testimony holds that it was not Xenocrates who said that the soul is a number because it recognizes, but rather that Aristotle interpreted it in this way because of one of his own definitions. We know neither if this was really what Aristotle wanted to say, nor if there is some truth to it with regard to Xenocrates.

Assessment of the Constructive Testimonies

The constructive testimonies can be divided roughly into two types of explanation: the first one explains the soul as self-moving number because of its capacity for cognition and movement, a position most prominently taken by Aristotle, though without a precise explanation as to what this means. The testimonies differ in the way they understand Aristotle's text: Michael Psellos explains it through the *like is known by like* principle, similarly to Nemesius of Emesa who says it is because the soul can make things countable; John Philoponus maybe agrees with them or traces the definition back to the Pythagoreans, and Pseudo-Simplicius interprets Aristotle by refering to his *Physics*. We do not have any independent sources that could affirm these interpretations.

The second type of explanation covers various interpretations of the *Timaeus*. Plutarch explains in great detail how Xenocrates interpreted the *Timaeus* in a way that fitted his definition. Later authors also refer to the *Timaeus* in their interpretations: Proclus supports his own interpretation of the *Timaeus* by citing Xenocrates; Andronicus (through Themistius) explains that the soul is a number, because it is mixed in a certain ratio and number from the primary elements, comparing it to the ἁρμονία theory; finally, Pseudo-Simplicius is at least inspired by the *Timaeus* in his explanation of Xenocrates's definition of the soul.

To these two patterns we must add as a third helpful account Aristotle's remark on Xenocrates's definition, where he connects the definition with the fact that the soul is explanatory of its own being alive, although the connection is not clear.

In general, we do not know how close these interpretations are to Xenocrates's actual reasons for calling the soul a self-moving number. In summary, the most insightful testimonies for the definition seem to be the following: 1) Aristotle's testimony, in which he connects the definition with the soul's capacity for being explanatory of its own being alive (F 86), most

[118] Urmson/Lautner 1995, 168 fn. 143.

[119] Cf. the interpretations mentioned *supra* "Cognition and Movement (F 85)".

likely reports genuine Xenocratean thought, although we do not know precisely how the soul as a self-moving number accounts for being explanatory of its own being alive. In particular, we can gather more reliable information for the definition of the soul from F 86 than from F 85. In F 85 Aristotle says that the soul was called self-moving because of its capacity of knowledge and motion (F 85), but this connection is unclear and was understood differently even in antiquity. 2) Plutarch's testimony, in which he explains how Xenocrates interpreted the *Timaeus* (F 108). This detailed account is by a scholar who seems to have known Xenocrates's writings first- or second-hand. It might be supported by Andronicus's testimony in Themistius (F 179). Yet we do not know whether Xenocrates called the soul a self-moving number because of that interpretation or interpreted the *Timaeus* in this way to fit his definition. 3) Pseudo-Simplicius's explanation of the soul's definition is a plausible, detailed interpretation that clarifies how the soul fits into Xenocrates's ontology (F 113). It is not clear, however, if this interpretation is based on any Xenocratean text.

5. Summary

Why did Xenocrates call the soul a self-moving number? The analysis of the ancient testimonies on Xenocrates's definition of the soul shows that even in antiquity the reason is far from clear. The testimonies give different answers and differ considerably in quality and quantity. On the one hand, we have testimonies that do not help us to understand the definition itself but illuminate how the definition was viewed and criticized by his contemporaries (Aristotle) and philosophers who lived after him (e.g. Alexander of Aphrodisias). On the other hand, there are testimonies that explain the definition, but in different ways, either connecting the definition with the soul's capacity to be explanatory of its own being alive (Aristotle), with its capacity for cognition (starting with Aristotle), or with Plato's *Timaeus* (most prominently Plutarch and Pseudo-Simplicius). An important result of the analysis, however, is that although the testimonies can be loosely grouped into these three categories, they differ substantially in the details of their interpretation, and most likely only few authors actually knew Xenocrates's original thought. The testimonies, therefore, offer several possible answers to the question as to why Xenocrates called the soul a self-moving number. It is hard to assess which (if any) of these answers is correct.[120]

Nonetheless, they offer us various plausible options that are worth considering. We can assume – although this is not stated explicitly in the

[120] With this assessment, I am somewhat more optimistic than Heinze 1892, 65, who says that there is nothing to gain from Aristotle or his commentators.

testimonies – that Xenocrates adopted the soul's self-movement from Plato. Plato already stressed its intermediate status between the formed and the informed world and made it the source for movement in the informed world.[121] If we trust Aristotle (F 86), the self-movement amounts to the soul being explanatory for its own being alive. But why is the soul a number?

1. Xenocrates might have been influenced by the Pythagoreans, although further analysis of the similarities between their ontology and Xenocrates's ontology would be necessary to paint a clearer picture of the way in which he was influenced. The testimonies on the soul analyzed in this contribution do not give us any clear indication.

2. Xenocrates was most likely influenced by the *Timaeus*. a) From Plutarch (F 108) we learn that Xenocrates interpreted the *Timaeus* in a way that fitted his definition. There, the mixture of the One and the Mutiplicity is number, and once Sameness and Difference is added, the result is the soul. We do not know, however, why he interpreted the *Timaeus* in this way. Further study on the significance of the One and the Multiplicity as well as number in Xenocrates might illuminate this. b) This might be connected to the idea that the soul is a number, because according to the *Timaeus* it consists of different elements in certain ratios (as is suggested by Philoponus in F 117, Proclus in F 109, and Andronicus/Themistius in F 179).

3. According to Aristotle, Xenocrates proposed his definition due to the soul's capacity for cognition. a) There might be a *like is known by like* principle at play here (as suggested by Michael Psellos) if Xenocrates really thought that forms are numbers; however, further analysis of Xenocrates's ontology would be necessary to confirm this. b) Alternatively, Aristotle had different reasons for saying that the capability of cognition implied it being a number. Maybe Aristotle said this because according to him the soul is able to distinguish and count (as suggested by Nemesius in F 110 and Pseudo-Simplicius in F 113).

4. The soul might be a number, as suggested by Pseudo-Simplicius in F 113, because it stands in the middle between forms and informed objects. Again, a closer study of Xenocrates's ontology might shed further light on how plausible this interpretation is.

6. List of Testimonies on the Soul, Arranged by Author

– Aetius: F 90, F 125
– Alexander of Aphrodisias: F 93–95
– Aristotle: F 85–89, F 112

---

[121] The soul's movement is especially prominent in Pl. *Lg.* 893B–898C. Cf. Pl. *Phdr.* 245C–246A, and Pl. *Ti.* 34Af., 40Af. Cf. Brinker, "Seele (Psychê)"; Heinze 1892, 66; Thiel, *Die Philosophie des Xenokrates*, 331; Palmieri, *La dottrine dell'anima*, 237–242.

– Cicero: F 119–121
– Damascius: F 131
– Iamblichus: F 98
– Lactantius: F 127
– Ps.-Lucianus, *Encomium Demosthenis*: F 132
– Macrobius: F 96–97
– Meletius: F 111
– Michael Psellos: F 106, Συλλογαὶ διάφοροι καὶ ποικίλαι ("Various and diverse collections") 35, 23f., and 39, 21–25 O'Meara 1989
– Nemesius of Emesa: *De natura hominis* 2, 68 (p. 17 Morani 1987), F 110, F 123
– Philoponus: F 101–104, F 117–118, F 129
– Ps.-Philoponus, *In Aristotelis Analytica posteriora*: F 105
– Plutarch: F 92, F 108
– Proclus: F 109
– Ps.-Simplicius, *In Aristotelis de Anima*: F 100, 113–116
– *Scholia in Dionysium Thracem*: F 107
– Tertullian: F 122, F 124, F 128
– Themistius: F 99, *In de An.* 12, 28–33 Heinze 1899, F 179, F 180
– Theodoretus: F 91, F 126, F 130

Bibliography

Ancient authors are abbreviated according to the LSJ.

Armisen-Marchetti, Mireille (ed.), *Macrobe. Commentaire au songe de Scipion. Texte établi, traduit et commenté. Tome I: Livre 1* (Collection Des Universités de France), Paris ²2003.

Baltes, Matthias, *Timaios Lokros. Über die Natur des Kosmos und der Seele*, Leiden 1972.

Baltussen, Han/Share, Michael/Mueller, Ian (eds.), *Simplicius: On Aristotle Physics 1.5–9*, (Ancient Commentators on Aristotle), London / New Delhi / New York / Sydney 2012.

Baltzly, Dirk (ed.), *Proclus. Commentary on Plato's Timaeus. Translated with an Introduction and Notes. Volume IV: Book 3, Part II: Proclus on the World Soul*, Cambridge / New York / Melbourne / New Delhi / Singapore 2009.

Barnes, Jonathan (ed.), *Aristotle. Posterior Analytics. Translated with a Commentary*, (Clarendon Aristotle Series), Oxford ²1993.

Blumenthal, Henry J. (ed.), *'Simplicius': On Aristotle On the Soul 3.1–5* (Ancient Commentators on Aristotle), London / New Delhi / New York / Sydney 2000.

Boissonade, Jean François (ed.), *Ψελλος. Michael Psellus. De operatione daemonum cum notis Gaulmini curante Jo. Fr. Boissonade. Accedunt inedita opsucula Pselli*, Nürnberg 1838.

Bonitz, Hermann, *Index Aristotelicus*, Berlin 1870.

Brennan, Tad/Brittain, Charles (eds.), *Simplicius: On Epictetus Handbook 27–53*, (Ancient Commentators on Aristotle), London / New Delhi / New York / Sydney 2002.

Brinker, Wolfram, "Seele (Psychê)", in: Christian Schäfer (ed.), *Platon-Lexikon. Begriffswörterbuch zu Platon und der platonischen Tradition*, Darmstadt ²2013.

Brunschwig, Jacques (ed.), *Aristote. Topiques. Tome I: Livres I-IV*, (Collection des universités de France poubliée sous le patronage de l'association Guillaume Budé), Paris 1967.

– (ed.), *Aristote. Topiques. Tome II: Livres V-VIII*, (Collection des universités de France poubliée sous le patronage de l'association Guillaume Budé), Paris 2007.

Burkert, Walter, *Lore and Science in Ancient Pythagoreanism. Translated by Edwin L. Minar*, Cambridge/Massachussetts 1972 (English edition, translated with revisions from Walter, Burkert, *Weisheit und Wissenschaft: Studien zu Pythagoras, Philolaos und Platon*, Nürnberg 1962).

Burnet, Ioannes (ed.), *Platonis opera. Recognovit brevique adnotatione critica instruxit. Vol. IV: Tetralogiam VIII continens*, (Scriptorum Classicorum Bibliotheca Oxoniensis), Oxford 1902 (Reprint of Oxford 1901).

Carter, Jason W., *Aristotle on Earlier Greek Psychology. The Science of Soul*, Cambridge / New York / Melbourne / New Delhi / Sydney 2019.

Charles, David, *Aristotle on Meaning and Essence*, (Oxford Aristotle Studies), Oxford 2000.

Cherniss, Harold, *Aristotle's Criticism of Plato and the Academy. Vol. 1*, Baltimore 1944.

– (ed.), *Plutarch's Moralia in Seventeen Volumes. Vol. XIII, Part I: 999c–1032f*, (The Loeb Classical Library), Cambridge / Massachusetts / London 1976.

Corcilius, Klaus (ed.), *Aristoteles. Über die Seele. De anima. Griechisch – Deutsch. Übersetzt, mit einer Einleitung und Anmerkungen*, (Philosophische Bibliothek 681), Hamburg 2017.

Cramer, John A. (ed.), *Anecdota Graeca e codd. manuscriptis bibliothecarum Oxoniensium descripsit. Vol. III*, Amsterdam 1963.

De-Cesaris, Giulia, "Aristotle's Account of Speusippus' and Xenocrates' Metaphysical and Epistemological Theories", Durham 2020. http://etheses.dur.ac.uk/13441/ (accessed on 01.10.2024).

Detel, Wolfang (ed.), *Aristoteles. Analytica Posteriora. Übersetzt und erläutert. Zweiter Halbband*, (Aristoteles. Werke in deutscher Übersetzung, Band 3, Teil II), Berlin 1993.

Diehl, Ernestus (ed.), *Procli Diadochi in Platonis Timaeum commentaria. Vol. II*, Leipzig 1904.

Diels, Hermannus (ed.), *Simplicii in Aristotelis Physicorum libros quattuor priores commentaria*, (Commentaria in Aristotelem Graeca IX), Berlin 1882.

Dillon, John, "Plutarch's Debt to Xenocrates", in: Aurelio Pérez Jiménez/José García López/Rosa María Aguilar (eds.), *Plutarco, Platón y Aristóteles: Actas del V congreso internacional de la I.P.S. (Madrid-Cuenca, 4-7 de Mayo de 1999)*, Madrid 1999, 305–311.

–, *The Heirs of Plato: A Study of the Old Academy, 374-274 BC*, Oxford/New York 2003a.

–, "The Timaeus in the Old Academy", in: Gretchen. J. Reydams-Schils (ed.), *Plato's Timaeus as Cultural Icon*, Notre Dame 2003b, 80–94.

–, "Plutarch's Debt to Xenocrates", *The Platonic Heritage. Further Studies in the History of Platonism and Early Christianity*, London / New York 2012a, X.

–, "The Timaeus in the Old Academy", *The Platonic Heritage. Further Studies in the History of Platonism and Early Christianity*, London / New York 2012b, III.

Dorandi, Tiziano, *Diogenes Laertius. Lives of eminent philosophers. Edited with introduction*, (Cambridge Classical Texts and Commentaries 50), Cambridge / New York / Melbourne / Madrid / Cape Town / Singapore / São Paulo / Delhi / Mexico City 2013.

Eijk, Philip J. van der (ed.), *Philoponus: On Aristotle On the Soul 1.1–2*, (Ancient Commentators on Aristotle), London / New Delhi / New York / Sydney 2005.

– (ed.), *Philoponus: On Aristotle On the Soul 1.3–35*, (Ancient Commentators on Aristotle), London / New Delhi / New York / Sydney 2006.

Finamore, John F./Dillon, John (eds.), *Iamblichus De anima. Text, translation, and commentary*, (Philosophia Antiqua. A Series of Studies on Ancient Philosophy XCII), Leiden / Boston / Köln 2002.

Giusta, Michelangelus (ed.), *Tusculanae disputationes*, Turin 1984.

Goldin, Owen (ed.), *Philoponus (?). On Aristotle Posterior Analytics 2*, London / New Delhi / New York / Sydney 2009.

Goulet, Richard, "Simplicius de Cilicie. Œuvres. (3) Commentaire Sur Le De Anima d' Aristote", *Dictionnaire des philosophes antiques*, 2016, VI: 356–3361.

Hadot, Ilsetraut (ed.), *Simplicius. Commentaire sur le Manuel d'Épictète. Introduction et édition critique du texte grec*, (Philosophia Antiqua. A Series of Studies on Ancient Philosophy LXVI), Leiden / New York / Köln 1996.

Hayduck, Michael (ed.), *Simplicii in libros Aristotelis De anima commentaria*, (Commentaria in Aristotelem Graeca XI), Berlin 1882.

–, *Ioannis Philoponi in Aristotelis De anima libros commentaria*, (Commentaria in Aristotelem Graeca XV), Berlin 1897.

Heinze, Richard (ed.), *Xenokrates. Darstellung der Lehre und Sammlung der Fragmente*, Leipzig 1892.

– (ed.), *Themistii in libros Aristotelis De anima paraphrasis*, (Commentaria in Aristotelem Graeca V. Pars III), Berlin 1899.

Hicks, Robert D. (ed.), *Aristotle. De anima. With translation, introduction and notes*, Amsterdam 1965 (reprint of Hicks, Robert D. *Aristotle. De anima. With translation, introduction and notes*, 1907, Cambridge)

Hilgard, Alfredus (ed.), *Scholia in Dionysii Thracis artem Grammaticam. Recensuit et apparatum criticum indicesque adiecit*, (Grammatici Graeci pars tertia), Leipzig 1901.

Hubert, C. (ed.), *Plutarchi Moralia. Recensuit et emendavit. Vol. VI. Fasc. 1*, Leipzig / Berlin 1954.

Isnardi Parente, Margherita (ed.), *Senocrate – Ermodoro. Frammenti. Edizione, traduzione e commento*, (Istituto italiano per gli studi filosofici. La scuola di Platone, collezione di testi diretta da Marcello Gigante volume terzo), Napoli 1982.

Isnardi Parente, Margherita/Dorandi, Tiziano (eds.), *Senocrate e Ermodoro. Testimonianze e frammenti. Edizione, traduzione e commento a cura di Margherita Isnardi Parente. Edizione rivista e aggiornata a cura di Tiziano Dorandi*, (Testi e Commenti), Pisa 2012.

Krämer, Hans Joachim, "Die Ältere Akademie", in: Hellmut Flashar (ed.), *Die Philosophie der Antike. Band 3: Ältere Akademie. Aristoteles. Peripatos*, (Grundriss der Geschichte der Philosophie, begründet von Friedrich Ueberweg), Basel ²2004, 1–165.

Mansfeld, Jaap/Runia, David T. (eds.), *Aëtiana. Vol. V: An edition of the reconstructed text of the Placita with a commentary and a collection of related texts, Part 3: Book 4 text and commentary. Book 5 text and commentary*, (Philosophia Antiqua. A Series of Monographs on Ancient Philosophy 153/3), Leiden / Boston 2020.

Morani, Moreno (ed.), *Nemesii Emeseni. De natura hominis*, (Bibliotheca Scriptorum Graecorum et Romanorum Teubneriana), Leipzig 1987.

Moraux, Paul, *Der Aristotelismus bei den Griechen. Von Andronikos bis Alexander von Aphrodisias. Vol. I: Die Renaissance des Aristotelismus im 1. Jh. v. Chr.*, (Peripatoi 5), Berlin / New York 1973.

Neuerburg, Fabia/Tsiampokalos, Theofanis/Wozniczka, Piotr, "Einleitung", in: Fabia Neuerburg/ Theofanis Tsiampokalos/Piotr Wozniczka (eds.), *Fragmente einer fragmentierten Welt. Zur Problematik des Umgangs mit Fragmenten in der gegenwärtigen klassisch-*

philologischen Forschung, (Transmissions. Studies on conditions, processes and dynamics of textual transmission Volume 11), Berlin / Boston 2024, 1–22.

O'Meara, Dominic J. (ed.), *Michaelis Pselli Philosophica minora. Vol. II: Opuscula psychologica, theologica, daemonologica*, (Bibliotheca scriptorum graecorum et romanorum Teubneriana), Leipzig 1989.

Opsomer, Jan, "The Platonic Soul, from the Early Academy to the First Century Ce", in: Brad Inwood/James Warren (eds.), *Body and Soul in Hellenistic Philosophy*, Cambridge / New York / Melbourne / New Delhi / Singapore 2020, 171–198.

Palmieri, Flavia, *La dottrine dell'anima nell'Accademia antica. Speusippo e Senocrate*, (Doxai. Testi e Studi Di Filosofia Antica), Roma 2025.

Polansky, Ronald (ed.), *Aristotle's De anima*, Cambridge / New York / Melbourne / Madrid / Cape Town / Singapore / São Paulo 2007.

Reinhardt, Tobias (ed.), *M. Tulli Ciceronis. Academicus primus. Fragmenta et testimonia academicorum librorum. Lucullus. Quae recognovit brevique adnotatione critica instruxit*, (Oxford Classical Texts), Oxford 2023.

Riedweg, Christoph, *Pythagoras. Leben, Lehre, Nachwirkung. Eine Einführung*, München 2002.

Rodier, Georges (ed.), *Aristote. Traité de l'âme. Traduit et annoté. Tome I: Texte et traduction*, Paris 1900.

Ross, David, *Aristotle's prior and posterior Analytics. A revised text with introduction and commentary*, Oxford 1957 (Reprinted lithographically from corrected sheets of the first edition 1949).

–, *Aristotle. De anima. Edited, with Introduction and Commentary*, Oxford 1961.

Scholten, Clemens, *Theodoret. De Graecarum affectionum curatione. Heilung der griechischen Krankheiten. Übersetzt, eingeleitet und mit Anmerkungen versehen*, (Supplements to Vigiliae Christianae. Texts and Studies of Early Christian Life and Language 126), Leiden / Boston 2015.

Schwyzer, Hans-Rudolf, "Zu Plotins Interpretation von Platons Timaeus 35A", *Rheinisches Museum Für Philologie. Neue Folge* 84, 4 (1935): 360–368.

Sharples, R. W./Eijk, P. J. van der, *Nemesius. On the Nature of Man. Translated with an introduction and notes*, (Translated Texts for Historians 49), Liverpool 2008.

Shields, Christopher (ed.), *Aristotle. De anima. Translated with an Introduction and Commentary*, (Clarendon Aristotle Series), Oxford 2016.

Siwek, Paulus (ed.), *Aristotelis tractatus de anima graece et latine. Edidit, versione latina auxit, commentario illustravit*, Roma 1965.

Sonderegger, Erwin, "Die Bildung Der Seele in Platons Timaios 35a1–b3", *Museum Helveticum* 54.4 (1997): 211–218.

Steel, Carlos (ed.), *'Simplicius': On Aristotle On the Soul 3.6–13. Translated by Carlos Steel in Collaboration with Arnis Ritups*, (Ancient Commentators on Aristotle), London / New Delhi / New York / Sydney 2013.

Tarán, Leonardo, "Proclus and the Old Academy", in: Jean Pépin/Henri Dominique Saffrey (eds.), *Proclus Lecteur et Interprète Des Anciens. Actes Du Colloque International Du CNRS, Paris (2–4 Octobre 1985)*, Paris 1987, 227–276.

Thiel, Detlef, *Die Philosophie des Xenokrates im Kontext der Alten Akademie*, (Beiträge Zur Altertumskunde 231), München / Leipzig 2006.

Todd, Robert, *Themistius: On Aristotle On the Soul*, (Ancient Commentators on Aristotle), London / New York 1996.

–, "Themistios", in: Hubert Cancik/Helmuth Schneider/Manfred Landfester (eds.), *Der Neue Pauly*, 2006. http://dx.doi.org/10.1163/1574-9347_dnp_e1207580.

Torstrik, Adolfus, *Aristoteles De aninma libir III*, Berlin 1862. http://archive.org/details/bub_gb_R1U-AAAAcAAJ.

Urmson, J. O./Lautner, Peter (eds.), *Simplicius: On Aristotle On the Soul 1.1–2.4. Translated by J. O. Urmson. Notes by Peter Lautner*, (Ancient Commentators on Aristotle), London / New Delhi / New York / Sydney 1995.

Van Riel, Gerd (ed.), *Procli Diadochi In Platonis Timaeum commentaria. Recognovit brevique adnotatione critica instruxit. Liber tertium*, Oxford 2012.

Wallies, Maximilianus (ed.), *Alexandri Aphrodisiensis in Aristotelis Topicorum libros octo commentaria*, (Commentaria in Aristotelem Graeca II. Pars II), Berlin 1891.

– (ed.), *Themistii Analyticorum posteriorum paraphrasis*, (Commentaria in Aristotelem Graeca V. Pars I), Berlin 1900.

– (ed.), *Ioannis Philoponi In Aristotelis Analytica posteriora commentaria cum anonymo in librum II*, (Commentaria in Aristotelem Graeca Voluminis XIII. Pars III), Berlin 1909.

Zum Konzept der Seele in der Alten Akademie
Ein Vergleich

Christoph Poetsch

Die Seele war, als Individualseele und Weltseele, ein zentraler Diskursgegenstand innerhalb der Alten Akademie. Der vorliegende Beitrag möchte anhand punktueller Einzelanalysen einen vergleichenden Blick auf die Seelenkonzeptionen der Alten Akademie, insbesondere in Bezug auf die Prinzipienphilosophie und das Konzept der Weltseele, werfen.[1] Dies ist, in der Wechselwirkung, für das Seelenkonzept Platons ebenso erhellend, wie für das seiner beiden Schüler Xenokrates und Speusipp, mittelbar womöglich auch für Aristoteles.

Die tentative These, die mit diesem Vorhaben verbunden ist, lautet, dass die altakademischen Positionen, trotz aller Unterschiede, doch einige auffällige systematische Ähnlichkeiten bieten, wobei eine markante – und m.W. bislang wenig beachtete – Beziehung der Weltseele zum Urprinzip bei allen analysierten Positionen besonders auffällig ist. Keineswegs bestritten wird damit wohlgemerkt, dass diese auch weiterhin klare systematische Unterschiede aufweisen. Es geht also um ein graduelles ‚Mehr' an Gemeinsamkeiten, nicht um schlichte Koinzidenz oder gewaltsame Vereinheitlichung. Gleichwohl vermag die Analyse jedoch anzudeuten, dass der altakademische Seelendiskurs, gerade mit Blick auf das Philosophem der Weltseele, augenscheinlich einem einheitlichen Rahmen folgte, innerhalb dessen sich die einzelnen Akademiker verschiedentlich positionierten. *Vice versa* mag dieser diskursive Gesamtrahmen auch die Einzelpositionen zu erhellen – zumal uns diese Positionen im Falle von Speusipp und Xenokrates nur sehr bruchstückhaft überliefert sind.

Der Vergleich wird anhand einer begrenzten Anzahl von Analysen zu zentralen Textpassagen durchgeführt. Dies sind nacheinander: 1) Aristoteles' Auseinandersetzung mit Platons Seelenkonzeption in *De anima* I 2, 2) Xenokrates'

[1] Der Beitrag ist damit im Forschungsfeld zur Alten Akademie, aber auch zu Platons innerakademischen, mündlichen Lehren angesiedelt. Wichtige Impulse haben diese Fragen zuletzt durch den grundlegenden Aufsatz von Primavesi, „Platonische Zwei-Elementen-Lehre" erfahren, der durch eine akribische philologische Analyse zentralster Textpassagen nicht nur den Zeugniswert des Aristoteles einmal mehr gegen die überholten Angriffe von H. F. Cherniss verteidigt (vgl. dazu auch das Zitat von Sir W. D. Ross als Motto des Aufsatzes), sondern auch die von Aristoteles unabhängige Berichtslinie über Speusipp und Theophrast entscheidend stärkt (a.a.O., bes. 42–45).

Konzept der Weltseele ausgehend von Frg. 188 (Isnardi Parente)[2] sowie 3) Speusipps Lokalisierung des Seelischen als dritte Wirklichkeitsstufe in Frg. 29a (Tarán)[3]. Kontrastfolie für die Analysen der drei wichtigsten Platon-Schüler ist durchgängig Platons eigene Seelenkonzeption, wie sie im vorliegenden Band Thema ist.

1. Aristoteles, *De anima* I 2 (404b16–27)

Auch wenn Platons eigene Seelenkonzeption hier nicht im Zentrum steht, sei mit Aristoteles' vieldiskutierter Passage in *De anima* (404b16–27)[4] begonnen; vor allem, weil sie mittelbar ein aufschlussreiches Licht auf den breiteren altakademischen Kontext wirft und zusätzliche Kontur für die anschließende Besprechung von Xenokrates und Speusipp bietet.

Kurz zum Kontext der fraglichen Passage, der für das Verständnis durchaus relevant ist: Aristoteles beginnt im zweiten Kapitel des ersten Buches bekanntlich das Referat der Seelenkonzeptionen seiner Vorgänger. Dabei unterteilt er die bisherigen Ansätze nach zwei Hauptmerkmalen, und zwar gemäß dessen, was die Seele im Wesentlichen, κατὰ φύσιν (*An.* 403b25), ausmacht: die *kinetischen* und die *kognitiven* Kapazitäten, also die Fähigkeit zu Bewegung und Selbstbewegung einerseits sowie zu Wahrnehmung und Erkennen andererseits.[5] Zu den Vertretern der ersten Gruppe zählen die Atomisten Demokrit und Leukipp (*An.* 403b31–404a16) sowie einige anonyme Pythagoreer (*An.* 404a16–21)[6] und – in einer Art Zwitterposition[7] – auch Anaxagoras (*An.* 404a25–b7). Zur zweiten Gruppe zählt Aristoteles namentlich Empedokles (*An.* 404b11) und Platon (*An.* 404b16). Auch die Beschreibung dieser zweiten Gruppe endet mit einer Zwitterposition, die im Text zwar anonym bleibt (*An.* 404b27–30), gemeinhin aber Xenokrates zugesprochen wird – wir werden auf die Einordnung dieser Position zurückkommen. Die Anlage der Passage im

---

[2] Für die Zählung der Xenokrates-Fragmente folge ich der – nach meiner Wahrnehmung – immer noch gängigeren Zählung nach Isnardi Parente, *Frammenti*. Inhaltliche Änderungen ergeben sich, soweit ich sehen kann, für das vorliegende Argument durch Isnardi Parente/Dorandi, *Testimonianze e frammenti* nicht.

[3] Die Speusipp-Fragmente werden nach der Ausgabe von Tarán, *Speusippus* zitiert.

[4] Der griechische Text von *De anima* folgt A. Förster nach Corcilius, *Aristoteles. Über die Seele*.

[5] κινήσει τε καὶ τῷ αἰσθάνεσθαι (*An.* 403b26–27); Letzteres ist nicht auf die Sinneswahrnehmung begrenzt: τὸ γινώσκειν καὶ τὸ αἰσθάνεσθαι (*An.* 404b9).

[6] Den Pythagoreern wendet sich Aristoteles in *De anima* I 4 nochmals ausführlicher zu (407b27–408a18).

[7] Als Zwitterposition ist die Position des Anaxagoras deshalb zu charakterisieren, weil er einerseits νοῦς und Seele als *Bewegungs*prinzip fasst (*An.* 404a25–26), andererseits aber mit dem νοῦς eindeutig eine *kognitive* Kapazität als eben dieses Bewegungsprinzip benennt.

Ganzen ist also von einer deutlichen Analogie durchzogen,[8] was nicht zuletzt für die Einordnung der letzten, anonymen Position von Relevanz sein dürfte.

Der Grundgedanke, der die beiden Positionen der kognitiven Gruppe zusammenhält, ist das bekannte Prinzip, dass Gleiches nur Gleiches zu erkennen vermag (*An.* 404b17–18). Die Seele muss demzufolge aus den gleichen Elementarprinzipien bestehen wie die Dinge, die von der Seele erkannt werden. Die Implementierung dieses Prinzips verläuft bei Empedokles und Platon jedoch unterschiedlich: Bei Empedokles, der eine Vielzahl von körperlichen Elementarprinzipien annimmt, ist jedes dieser Elementarprinzipien selbst Seele und diese ist entsprechend in der Lage, die Elemente und die aus ihnen bestehenden Dinge zu erkennen (*An.* 404b11–15).

Bei Platon ist die Lage komplexer und das Referat des Aristoteles ist deutlich schwerer zu rekonstruieren. Der Kern der Implementierung des epistemologischen Prinzips ‚Gleiches erkennt Gleiches' scheint dabei nicht, wie bei Empedokles, in einer direkten Engführung von Seele und Dingen zu liegen, sondern in einer *indirekten* Beziehung und der Rückführung beider Seiten auf einen *gemeinsamen* Ursprung. Die Seele kann die Dinge also genau deshalb erkennen, weil Seele wie Dinge auf denselben Ursprung zurückzuführen sind und in diesem Sinne gleich sind. Die Pointe der platonischen Argumentation, die Aristoteles hier, v.a. unter Berufung auf *Peri Philosophias*,[9] referiert, liegt genauer gesagt darin, dass die Seele und die Erkenntnisgegenstände beide eine

---

[8] Folgt man der Prämisse, dass mit der zahlenhaften Harmonie bei den Pythgoreern eine deutlich amaterialistische, gewissermaßen ‚idealistische' Tendenz gegeben ist, dann tritt im Gesamtaufbau von *De anima* I 2 schemenhaft, aber doch erkennbar eine Kombinatorik von a) materialistischer und b) amaterialistischer Variante der 1) kinetischen und der 2) kognitiven Seelenkapazität zu Tage, wobei jeweils eine ‚Zwitterposition' eingeschoben wird: 1a) kinetisch-materialistisch (Demokrit/Leukipp); 1b) kinetisch–amaterialistisch (Pythagoreer); Zwitterposition mit Schwerpunkt auf Bewegungsaspekt (Anaxagoras); 2a) kognitiv–materialistisch (Empedokles); 2b) kognitiv–amaterialistisch (Platon); Zwitterposition mit Schwerpunkt auf Kognitionsaspekt (anonym; *communis opinio*: Xenokrates).

[9] Die Zuordnung dessen, was hier mit καὶ ἐν τοῖς περὶ φιλοσοφίας λεγομένοις bezeichnet ist, wurde vielfach diskutiert; vgl. etwa die Ausgangspunkte im 20. Jh. bei Cherniss, *Aristotle's Criticism*, 565–580; Cherniss, *The Riddle*, 14–15; de Vogel, „Problems", 304–305; Ross, *Theory of Ideas*, 146; 209–215; Saffrey, *ΠΕΡΙ ΦΙΛΟΣΟΦΙΑΣ*. Für Positionen des 19. Jh. vgl. Saffrey, *ΠΕΡΙ ΦΙΛΟΣΟΦΙΑΣ*, 1. Zu unterscheiden sind zwei Aspekte: Erstens, auf welches Werk (im weitesten Sinne – wenn man etwa eine Referenz auf eine mündliche Vorlesung in Betracht zieht), d.h. auf welchen *Aussageort*, bezieht sich περὶ φιλοσοφίας? Und zweitens, wem ist die dort ausgesagte – und im Zuge von *An.* 404b18–27 paraphrasierte – *Position* zuzuordnen? Nach den Argumenten bei Ross, *Theory of Ideas*, 209–215; Saffrey, *ΠΕΡΙ ΦΙΛΟΣΟΦΙΑΣ*; Gaiser, „Quellenkritische Probleme", 49–63 scheint mir, bzgl. der zweiten Frage, eine Zuordnung der referierten Position zu Platon sicher (vgl. auch Phys. 194a36 sowie Ross, *Theory of Ideas*, 146; Shields, *De anima*, 110) und, bzgl. der ersten Frage, eine Verortung im zweiten Buch von Aristoteles' Dialog *Peri philosophias* am plausibelsten. Ross, *Theory of Ideas*, 210 bemerkt zu Recht, dass die zweite Frage die wichtigere ist.

Zahlstruktur aufweisen, die ihrerseits durch das platonische Prinzipienpaar hervorgebracht wird. Im Einzelnen finden wir in Aristoteles' *Peri Philosophias*-Referat nacheinander folgende Aussagen:[10]

[1] Das ‚Lebewesen selbst' besteht aus der Idee des Einen selbst und der ersten Länge, Breite und Tiefe.
[2] Die anderen [sc. die Sinnendinge (?)] bestehen auf ähnliche Weise [wie das ‚Lebewesen selbst'].

Darüber hinaus aber auch auf andere Weise:[11]

[3] *nous* ist das Eine, *epistēme* ist die Zwei (denn sie geht einfachhin auf Eines), *doxa* ist die Zahl der Fläche [sc. die Drei] und *aisthēsis* ist die Zahl des (dreidimensionalen) Körpers [sc. die Vier].

Denn:

[4] Die Zahlen sind die *eidē* selbst und die *archai.*[12]
[5] Die Zahlen sind [sc. entstehen] aus den *stoicheia.*[13]
[6] Die *pragmata* werden teils durch *nous*, teils durch *epistēme*, teils durch *doxa* und teils durch *aisthēsis* beurteilt [sc. erkannt].
[7] Diese Zahlen sind *eidē* der *pragmata.*[14]

Das referierte Argument konzentriert sich in der ersten Hälfte ([1]–[2]) auf die Seite der Erkenntnisgegenstände, während es in der zweiten Hälfte ([3]–[7]) zusätzlich stärker die Seite des Erkenntnissubjektes, also die Seele, mit in den Blick nimmt.[15] Das *tertium comparationis*, das beide Seiten im Sinne des Prinzips ‚Gleiches erkennt Gleiches' zusammenführt, ist die schon genannte Zahlstruktur, genauer ihre Engführung mit der vierstelligen Dimensionsfolge –

---

[10] In der Übersetzung direkt in Aussageform gebracht; der griechische Text (inkl. der *Timaios*-Passage, die im Anschluss besprochen wird): τὸν αὐτὸν δὲ τρόπον καὶ ὁ Πλάτων ἐν τῷ Τιμαίῳ τὴν ψυχὴν ἐκ τῶν στοιχείων ποιεῖ· γινώσκεσθαι γὰρ τῷ ὁμοίῳ τὸ ὅμοιον, τὰ δὲ πράγματα ἐκ τῶν ἀρχῶν εἶναι. ὁμοίως δὲ καὶ ἐν τοῖς περὶ φιλοσοφίας λεγομένοις διωρίσθη, [1] αὐτὸ μὲν τὸ ζῷον ἐξ αὐτῆς τῆς τοῦ ἑνὸς ἰδέας καὶ τοῦ πρώτου μήκους καὶ πλάτους καὶ βάθους, [2] τὰ δ' ἄλλα ὁμοιοτρόπως· ἔτι δὲ καὶ ἄλλως, [3] νοῦν μὲν τὸ ἕν, ἐπιστήμην δὲ τὰ δύο, μοναχῶς γὰρ ἐφ' ἕν, τὸν δὲ τοῦ ἐπιπέδου ἀριθμὸν δόξαν, αἴσθησιν δὲ τὸν τοῦ στερεοῦ· [4] οἱ μὲν γὰρ ἀριθμοὶ τὰ εἴδη αὐτὰ καὶ αἱ ἀρχαὶ ἐλέγοντο, [5] εἰσὶ δ' ἐκ τῶν στοιχείων, [6] κρίνεται δὲ τὰ πράγματα τὰ μὲν νῷ, τὰ δ' ἐπιστήμῃ, τὰ δὲ δόξῃ, τὰ δ' αἰσθήσει, [7] εἴδη δ' οἱ ἀριθμοὶ οὗτοι τῶν πραγμάτων. (*An.* 404b16–27 = Test Plat 25A Gaiser)

[11] Vgl. unten Anm. 15.

[12] Alternativ: Die Ideen selbst sind die Zahlen und die *archai.*

[13] Alternativ: Die Ideen selbst sind aus den *stoicheia.* (Falls man der Alternative aus Anm. 12 folgt.)

[14] Alternativ: Diese Zahlen der *pragmata* sind Ideen.

[15] Gaiser, „Quellenkritische Probleme", 52 und Szlezák, *Platon*, 519 ergänzen in der Wendung ἔτι δὲ καὶ ἄλλως gedanklich „dasselbe" (sc. „darüber hinaus *dasselbe* auch auf andere Weise"). Dies scheint mir dem Aufbau des Arguments jedoch eher entgegenzustehen.

wenngleich das Argument in der referierten, knappen Form ohne Zweifel nicht über eine bloße Analogisierung hinausgeht.[16]

Beginnen wir mit der ersten Hälfte. Aussage [1] formuliert eine protodimensionale Struktur des „Lebewesens selbst". Hierunter ist, zumal nach dem Aufruf des *Timaios* kurz zuvor, nach der Mehrheit der Interpretationen – und meines Erachtens zu Recht – der Ideenkosmos zu verstehen.[17] Er entwickelt sich der Aussage zufolge aus der „Idee des Einen selbst" und einer ersten dimensionalen Diastatik – wobei Letztere in meinen Augen als Auswirkung des zweiten Prinzips zu deuten ist.[18] In Aussage [2] scheint es naheliegend und plausibel, τὰ ἄλλα entsprechend auf die physischen Sinnendinge zu beziehen.[19] Für deren Entstehen ist die Dimensionsfolge auch in Platons Dialogen in Ansätzen greifbar, in den *Nomoi* etwa und auch in der *Politeia*.[20] Die erste Hälfte des rekonstruierten Arguments formuliert also, dass Ideenwelt und Sinnenwelt in ihrer Grundstruktur durch eine mathematische Dimensionalität ausgezeichnet sind. Diese Dimensionalität ist durch die vierstufige Dimensionsfolge gegeben, welche auf den Zahlen der pythagoreischen Tetraktys aufbaut und die beiden Grundbereiche der Wirklichkeit je einzeln, in der Analogie aber auch in ihrer übergreifenden Gesamtheit strukturiert und eint.[21]

---

[16] Ziel ist im Vorliegenden wohlgemerkt nur, den – ohnehin schon kryptischen und verknappten – Gedankengang zu rekonstruieren und zu verstehen; nicht aber zu eruieren, ob eine solche Form der Analogisierung in irgendeiner Weise sachliche Richtigkeit oder argumentative Durchschlagskraft für sich beanspruchen kann.

[17] Zur Übersicht der Deutungsoptionen und -positionen vgl. Gaiser, „Quellenkritische Probleme", 50–51. Neben der von K. Gaiser angeführten Alternativoption, unter αὐτὸ τὸ ζῷον die Gattungsidee des Lebewesens zu verstehen (vertreten u.a. von Cherniss, *Aristotle's Criticism*, 575–578), wäre grundsätzlich auch denkbar, dass sich αὐτὸ τὸ ζῷον auf die Weltseele bezieht. Letztere Option ist im Kontext der *De anima*-Stelle – Idee ist ja: das Erkenntnissubjekt besteht aus denselben Elementarprinzipien wie das Erkenntnisobjekt – nicht grundsätzlich auszuschließen, wurde jedoch, soweit ich sehe, bislang nicht vertreten.

[18] So auch Szlezák, *Platon*, 520.

[19] *Prima facie* denkbar wäre auch ein Verständnis der Passage, wonach τὰ ἄλλα hier einfach weitere Ideen meint, die auf ähnliche bzw. gleiche Weise entstehen. Ein solches Verständnis wird m.E. allerdings der – auch im *Timaios* – herausgehobenen Position des αὐτὸ τὸ ζῷον kaum gerecht, da es dieses dann zu einer gleichsam nur exemplarischen Idee unter vielen herabstufen würde.

[20] Vgl. *Lg.* 894a1–8 sowie *R.* 587b12–588a10 (zur Dimensionsfolge als Hintergrund der Tyrannenzahl vgl. Poetsch, „Dimensions of Pleasure"). Auch das Liniengleichnis weist letztlich Anklänge an die Dimensionsfolge auf, vgl. Poetsch, *Philosophie des Bildes*, 92–98.

[21] Zu bedenken ist also, dass Platon augenscheinlich eine vierstellige dimensionale Strukturierung der Gesamtwirklichkeit (bestehend aus physischer Welt *und* Ideenwelt) und ebenso – etwa vor dem Hintergrund von *Ti.* 39e7–40a2 – eine *interne* vierstellige Gliederung dieser beiden Bereiche *je für sich* ansetzen kann. Vom Grundgedanken her entspricht dies der Linieneinteilung in der *Politeia*, wenn dort die Binnenteilungen zur Gesamtteilung analog sind (*R.* 509d6–8).

Ziel der zweiten Hälfte ist nun augenscheinlich, dieselbe Struktur auch für die Seite der erkennenden Seele aufzuweisen; wobei die verschiedenen Erkenntnisleistungen der Seele – für Platon typisch – im ständigen Bezug auf ihre je spezifischen Erkenntnisgegenstände angeführt werden.[22] Hier ist Aussage [3] offenbar als Konklusion zu verstehen, da die nachfolgende(n) Aussage(n) als Begründung (γὰρ *An.* 404b24) aufgeführt werden. Aussage [3] ordnet den einzelnen Erkenntnisvermögen – die wir ähnlich im *Timaios* (28a1–4; 37b6–c3) und der Sache nach wohl auch in der *Politeia* finden[23] – die vier ersten Zahlen im Sinne einer dimensionalen Entfaltung zu. Die „Zahl der Fläche" ist hierbei die Drei, da es mindestens drei Punkte braucht, um eine Fläche zu definieren; die Zahl des dreidimensionalen Körpers ist entsprechend die Vier. Kern dieser Aussage ist also die zahlhafte Strukturierung der seelischen Erkenntnisvermögen, abermals in enger Bindung an die Dimensionsfolge – was recht genau das Komplement zur den Erkenntnisgegenständen in den Aussagen [1] und [2] bildet. Damit ist die ‚Beweisführung' im Sinne des Prinzips ‚Gleiches erkennt Gleiches' im Grunde bereits abgeschlossen:[24] sowohl die Erkenntnisgegenstände, als auch die erkennende Seele weisen die auf der Tetraktys-Zahlstruktur aufruhende, dimensionale Stufenfolge auf; folglich ist ‚Gleiches erkennt Gleiches' gegeben.

Gleichwohl werden diese Aussagen weiter begründet. Hierzu greift das Argument in [4]–[7] auf die Zahlstruktur der Ideen, genauer die Ideenzahllehre,[25] zurück. Aussage [4] führt hierzu Zahlen und Ideen sowie den ἀρχή-Begriff eng, während Aussage [5] deren Herkunft aus den στοιχεία erklärt. Beide Aussagen finden eine fast wörtliche Entsprechung im Platon-Referat von *Metaphysik* A 6, noch dazu ebenfalls unter Verwendung des στοιχεῖον-Begriffs.[26] Damit

---

[22] *Locus classicus* für dieses Vorgehen ist zweifelsohne die Linienanalogie der *Politeia*.

[23] Vgl. Poetsch, *Philosophie des Bildes*, 74–78.

[24] Diese Bündigkeit, in der das Beweisziel bereits kurz nach dem Anfang erreicht ist, erinnert entfernt an das aristotelische Vorgehen in *Metaphysik* IV 4; vgl. hierzu den grundlegenden Aufsatz von Rapp, „Satz vom Widerspruch".

[25] Unter „Ideenzahlen" bzw. „Ideenzahllehre" verstehe ich die Auffassung, dass die (platonischen) Ideen selbst Zahlen, und zwar sogenannte „eidetische Zahlen" (εἰδητικοὶ ἀριθμοί) sind. Unter „Idealzahlen" verstehe ich Ideen von Zahlen (z.B. die Idee der Zwei). Von beidem zu unterscheiden ist die besondere Rolle der ersten zehn Zahlen, der Dekas, denen innerhalb der Ideenzahllehre eine besondere Stellung zukam, augenscheinlich (auch) durch die in [1] formulierte Begründung des Ideenbereichs im Ganzen. Vgl. zur Terminologie Krämer, *Arete*, 245; Primavesi, „Platonische Zwei-Elementen-Lehre", 8 Anm. 29.

[26] ἐπεὶ δ' αἴτια τὰ εἴδη τοῖς ἄλλοις, τἀκείνων στοιχεῖα πάντων ᾠήθη τῶν ὄντων εἶναι στοιχεῖα. ὡς μὲν οὖν ὕλην τὸ μέγα καὶ τὸ μικρὸν εἶναι ἀρχάς, ὡς δ' οὐσίαν τὸ ἕν· ἐξ ἐκείνων γὰρ κατὰ μέθεξιν τοῦ ἑνὸς τὰ εἴδη εἶναι καὶ τοὺς ἀριθμούς. (*Metaph.* 987b18–22). Das καὶ in 987b22 folgt Primavesi, „Platonische Zwei-Elementen-Lehre", bes. 21–23 und der bei Asklepios überlieferten Variante. Das Argument, dass Aristoteles hier ein so wichtiges und schwieriges Philosophem wie die Ideenzahllehre nicht einfach *en passant* in einem Halbsatz erstmals innerhalb von *Metaphysik* A einführt (a.a.O., 9–10), ist sehr gewichtig.

sind mit den στοιχεία in Aussage [5] sehr wahrscheinlich die beiden platonischen Elementarprinzipien gemeint.[27] So besteht der wesentliche Wert der Aussagen [4] und [5] für das vorliegende Argument offenkundig darin, die Ideen, welche die ἀρχαί der Dinge sind, als Zahlen auszuweisen und diese wiederum aus den beiden Elementarprinzipien abzuleiten. Diese Ideenzahllehre findet sich bekanntlich im Sinne der εἰδητικοὶ ἀριθμοί auch in *Metaphysik* M und N wiederholt für Platon.[28]

Aussage [6] formuliert nun, dass die Erkenntnisgegenstände, die πράγματα, durch vier unterschiedliche Erkenntnisweisen erkannt werden. Entscheidend ist in Aussage [6] allerdings, dass hier auch πράγματα durch νοῦς und ἐπιστήμη erkannt werden. Das ist insbesondere deshalb merkwürdig, weil hierdurch mit den πράγματα nicht nur die physischen Sinnendinge, auf die sich δόξα und αἴσθησις richten, gemeint scheinen – und auf die man den Terminus πράγματα gemeinhin beziehen würde –, sondern *auch* die Ideen, die durch νοῦς und ἐπιστήμη erkannt werden.[29] Angesichts dieses Befunds sind zwei Optionen möglich: Entweder (a) man liest πράγματα in [6] unter *Einschluss* der Ideenwelt oder (b) man bezieht die πράγματα in [6] einzig auf die Sinnendinge, unter *Ausschluss* der Ideen. Folgt man Option (a), dann ist in der Folge Aussage [7] so zu verstehen, dass die Zahlen die εἴδη – also die ‚Gestalten' im Sinne ihrer Erkennbarkeit und Fassbarkeit[30] – *aller* πράγματα, d.h. der Sinnendinge *und* der Ideen, sind. Erkennbarkeit ist damit, für Ideen wie für Sinnendinge, wesentlich an Zahlhaftigkeit, an mathematische Strukturiertheit und Kodierung geknüpft. Nach Option (b) hingegen versteht man [7] als Aussage darüber, dass die Zahlen die Ideen der Sinnendinge sind; dass also die zahlhaften Ideen die

---

[27] Ich nutze hier die Übersetzung „Elementarprinzip" für den griechische Terminus στοιχεῖον, der gemeinhin mit „Element" übersetzt wird. O. Primavesi hat zu Recht darauf hingewiesen, dass man im Ausgang vom στοιχεῖον-Begriff statt von Platons „Prinzipienlehre" ebenso auch von dessen „Elementenlehre" sprechen könne (vgl. Primavesi, „Platonische Zwei-Elementen-Lehre", 1). Dennoch scheint mir im vorliegenden Kontext eine allzu scharfe Trennung nicht notwendig. Dies ergibt sich insbesondere daraus, dass Aristoteles die beiden Ausdrücke zwar nicht synonym, aber immer wieder doch in so großer Nähe nutzt, dass sie zwei Aspekte derselben Sache (nämlich der Prinzipienfunktion) beschreiben; entsprechend scheint mir „Elementarprinzip" für στοιχεῖον am treffendsten. Vgl. bei Aristotles etwa: ἐπεὶ δ᾽ αἴτια τὰ εἴδη τοῖς ἄλλοις, τἀκείνων στοιχεῖα πάντων ᾠήθη τῶν ὄντων εἶναι στοιχεῖα. ὡς μὲν οὖν ὕλην τὸ μέγα καὶ τὸ μικρὸν εἶναι ἀρχάς, ὡς δ᾽ οὐσίαν τὸ ἕν· (*Metaph.* 987b18–21); οἱ λέγοντες τὸ ἓν ἀρχὴν εἶναι καὶ οὐσίαν καὶ στοιχεῖον πάντων, καὶ ἐκ τούτου καὶ ἄλλου τινὸς εἶναι τὸν ἀριθμόν (*Metaph.* 1080b6–7); οἱ τὸ ἓν μὲν ὁμολογοῦντες ἀρχὴν εἶναι πρώτην καὶ στοιχεῖον, τοῦ ἀριθμοῦ δὲ τοῦ μαθηματικοῦ (*Metaph.* 1091b23–24).

[28] Vgl. *Metaph.* 1080b11–14.1086a4–5.1086a11–13.1090b32–33.

[29] Strenggenommen müsste man, im Sinne der Linienanalogie, auch noch mathematische Entitäten als Gegenstände der διάνοια bzw. ἐπιστήμη hinzunehmen; um der Übersichtlichkeit willen sei im Vorliegenden nur von den Ideen als nicht-empirischen Gegenständen gesprochen.

[30] Vgl. zum sachlichen Verständnis dieses Ansatzes die Ausführungen weiter unten, im Anschluss an J. Stenzel.

Prinzipien der physischen Dinge sind. Das würde dann nochmals explizit machen, was in Aussage [4] über den ἀρχαί-Ausdruck nur angedeutet, bei Platon aber bekannt und unproblematisch ist: dass nämlich die Ideen die Prinzipien ihrer Ideate, der materiellen Sinnendinge, sind.

Nun sprechen jedoch mehrere Gründe gegen Option (b). Zum einen ist die Aussage in [6] letztlich eindeutig: die πράγματα schließen die Ideen als Gegenstände von νοῦς und ἐπιστήμη mit ein; auch wenn dies dem gängigen Verständnis des Terminus πράγματα zu widersprechen scheint.[31] Option (b) kann dann nur annehmen, dass zwischen [6] und [7] der Ausdruck πράγματα seine Bedeutung ändert – was schon unter allgemeinen hermeneutischen Gesichtspunkten wenig erfolgversprechend ist. Zuletzt ist jedoch von besonderer Wichtigkeit, dass sich erst durch ein Verständnis im Sinne von Option (a) eine Motivation für Aussage [5] ergibt, die andernfalls merkwürdig in der Luft hängt. Denn nur unter Zugrundelegung von Option (a) wird durch Aussage [7] sinnvoll mit Blick auf Aussage [5] eingeholt, dass auch die Ideen zahlenhaft

---

[31] Eine mögliche Parallelstelle für diese umfassende Auffassung der πράγματα findet sich abermals im Platon-Referat von *Metaphysik* A 6: ἔτι δὲ παρὰ τὰ αἰσθητὰ καὶ τὰ εἴδη τὰ μαθηματικὰ τῶν πραγμάτων εἶναί φησι μεταξύ (*Metaph.* 987b14–16). Auch hier könnten mit den πράγματα die Sinnendinge *und* die Ideen gemeint sein (so auch Lattmann, *Mathematische Modellierung*, 311 Anm. 58). Primavesi, „Platonische Zwei-Elementen-Lehre", 13–16 hat dafür argumentiert, dass hier eine brachylogische Verwendung von μεταξύ + gen. vorliegt, bei der nur eines der beiden Extreme (hier: τὰ πράγματα) bezeichnet wird, während das andere (hier: τὰ εἴδη) sachlich zu ergänzen ist. Angesichts der von ihm angeführten Argumente und Belege ist die brachylogische Verwendung für Aristoteles in jedem Fall gesichert. Mit Blick auf die Folgestelle 987b27–29 (καὶ ἔτι ὁ [sc. ὁ Πλάτων] μὲν τοὺς ἀριθμοὺς παρὰ τὰ αἰσθητά, οἱ [sc. οἱ Πυθαγόρειοι] δ' ἀριθμοὺς εἶναί φασιν αὐτὰ τὰ πράγματα, καὶ τὰ μαθηματικὰ μεταξὺ τούτων οὐ τιθέασιν.), die definitiv auf 987b14–16 Bezug nimmt, scheint jedoch weiterhin zumindest ein Stück weit fraglich, ob diese brachylogische Verwendung (dem formelhaften Verweissinn, nicht der tatsächlichen Konstruktion nach – die ja bei nur einem Relat bei den Pythagoreern ausgeschlossen ist) auch in 987b14–16 vorliegt. O. Primavesi zitiert diese Stelle als Beleg für seine Deutung: „Da es nun aber bei den Pythagoreern keine ‚Ideen' gibt, können jedenfalls in dieser Wiederaufnahme der μεταξύ-Formel [sc. 987b28–29] mit den πράγματα nur die sinnlich wahrnehmbaren Dinge gemeint sein. Dann aber spricht alles dafür, τῶν πραγμάτων an unserer Stelle [sc. 987b15–16] ebenso zu verstehen." (a.a.O., 15–16). Denkbar wäre jedoch auch, dass mit τὰ πράγματα als Sammelbegriff alle *von der jeweiligen Position* als seiende angesehene Entitäten bezeichnet werden. Das wären bei den Pythagoreern in der Tat nur die sinnlich-physischen Entitäten, aber dies würde dann nicht automatisch heißen, dass auch für Platon τὰ πράγματα nur die Sinnendinge meint. Dafür könnte zum einen das bestärkende αὐτὰ sprechen, vor allem aber ist auffällig, dass für Platon im μέν-Teil zuvor gerade *nicht* der Terminus πράγματα, sondern eben αἰσθητά gewählt wird! – wenngleich, zugegeben, der Folgesatz (987b30: παρὰ τὰ πράγματα für „neben den Sinnendingen" bei Platon) wiederum für O. Primavesis Deutung spricht. Wie immer man hier entscheidet: Für die vorliegende Analyse ist das Detailverständnis von *Metaph.* 987b14–16 von sekundärer Bedeutung, gleichwohl mag die Synopse von *Metaph.* 987b14–16 mit Aussage [6] in *An.* 404b25–27 möglicherweise erhellend sein.

strukturiert sind; und zwar aufgrund ihrer Herkunft aus den Urprinzipien – gerade wenn man Aussage [1] als Parallele hinzuzieht.[32]

Rekonstruiert man das Argument also im Sinne von Option (a), ist allerdings als implizite Zusatzprämisse anzunehmen, dass *auch* die Seele letztlich aus den στοιχεῖα, also den Urprinzipien, entsteht. Dies ist jedoch unproblematisch: denn zwar wird dies im *Peri Philosophia*-Referat nicht explizit gesagt, gleichwohl aber referiert Aristoteles dies gleich zu Beginn im *Timaios*-Referat.[33] Die entscheidende Pointe der Gesamtargumentation ist damit also: Die Seele und alle Erkenntnisgegenstände – Sinnendinge *und* Ideen – entstehen letztlich aus den beiden Urprinzipien ἕν und ἀόριστος δυάς und damit ist das Prinzip ‚Gleiches erkennt Gleiches' für *alle* Erkenntnisgegenstände, Sinnendinge wie Ideen, gewahrt; wobei sich diese Gleichheit von Erkennendem und Erkanntem im Kern über die Zahlhaftigkeit von Seele und Erkenntnisgegenständen manifestiert. Die Information, die in [4]–[7] gegenüber [1]–[3] also noch hinzutritt, besteht darin, dass die zahlenhafte Dimensionsstruktur, die in [1]–[3] bereits das Beweisziel ‚Gleiches erkennt Gleiches' sicherstellt, *ihrerseits* noch einmal in den beiden platonischen Urprinzipien begründet wird, welche damit den letztendlichen Fluchtpunkt von ‚Gleiches erkennt Gleiches' darstellen. Im eigentlichen Sinne erkannt werden dabei immer zahlhafte Gestalten (εἴδη) durch die ebenfalls zahlenhaft organisierte Seele, wobei beide Seiten letztlich auf die Urprinzipien zurückzuführen sind.

Rein sachlich schließt hier natürlich die Anschlussfrage an, wie eine solche Erkennbarkeit qua Zahlhaftigkeit genauer zu interpretieren ist. Hierfür können bis heute die Untersuchungen von J. Stenzel mit großem Gewinn hinzugezogen werden. J. Stenzel hat im Detail gezeigt, wie nicht nur die für die griechische Mathematik so typische, größere Nähe von arithmetischer Zahlenlehre und geometrischer Größenlehre Licht zu werfen vermag auf Philosopheme wie etwa die Dimensionsfolge und -entfaltung;[34] sondern auch, wie gerade im Zahlbegriff Exaktheit und damit epistemische Fassbarkeit paradigmatisch verwirklicht sind[35] – während zugleich die Folge der natürlichen Zahlen mit je einer Einheit von (zunehmend mehr, aber neuen) Einheiten die Grundfigur einer aus zwei Urprinzipien – Einheit und unbestimmte Zweiheit – entstehenden Menge ist.[36] Entscheidend ist in diesem Kontext auch der antike Logos-Begriff, der als ‚Verhältnis' und ‚Verhältniseinheit' gerade die *Beziehung* von zahlhaften Einheiten zueinander zu fassen vermag und darin immense epistemologische

---

[32] Bestärkend kommt hinzu, dass auch in [1] und [2] *beide* Prinzipiat-Bereiche angesprochen werden.

[33] Πλάτων ἐν τῷ Τιμαίῳ τὴν ψυχὴν ἐκ τῶν στοιχείων ποιεῖ (*An.* 404b16–17).

[34] Vgl. Stenzel, *Zahl und Gestalt*, 61–89 sowie a.a.O., 94–97 zu *An.* 404b16–27.

[35] Bes. Stenzel, *Zahl und Gestalt*, 49–50.

[36] Vgl. Stenzel, *Zahl und Gestalt*, bes. 30–33.46–47.

Bedeutung hat.[37] Dass diese zahlhafte, vom Logos geprägte Gestalthaftigkeit auch noch für die Sinneswahrnehmung gelten kann, zeigt eine bemerkenswerte – und hier eventuell altakademisch (mit)geprägte – Auffassung bei Theophrast.[38]

Ausgehend von der angeführten Rekonstruktion der Argumentation ergeben sich weiterhin (mindestens) vier Folgefragen. Zuerst ist hierfür der Befund zu nennen, dass Aristoteles die Position Platons aus zwei Quellen referiert – nämlich neben *Peri Philosophias* auch aus dem *Timaios* (*An.* 404b16–18), was bislang ausgespart wurde. Zu fragen ist deshalb erstens, ob diese beiden Quellen letztlich auf ein und denselben Gedankengang verweisen. Diese Frage ist in meinen Augen aus zwei Gründen zu bejahen: Zum einen leitet Aristoteles die zweite Darlegung, also jene aus *Peri Philosophias*, mit ὁμοίως (*An.* 404b18), sprich: „auf gleiche Weise“, „auf ähnliche Weise“, ein und legt damit eine sachliche Äquivalenz nahe. Zum anderen laufen die Beschreibungen beider Quellen letztlich auf dasselbe Prinzip ‚Gleiches erkennt Gleiches‘ hinaus, was eine Bejahung der ersten Frage ebenfalls nahelegt. Die *Timaios*-Passage liefert zudem die wichtige Aussage, dass (auch) die Seele aus den Elementarprinzipien entsteht – was, wie gezeigt, im *Peri Philosophias*-Abschnitt bereits als Prämisse bzw. als bekannt vorausgesetzt wird. Nicht ganz vollständig aufzulösen scheinen allerdings gewisse terminologische Spannungen zwischen den beiden Abschnitten.[39]

---

[37] Von größtem Wert sind hierzu bis heute Toeplitz, „Mathematik und Ideenlehre“; Stenzel, *Zahl und Gestalt*, 35–36.40–43.162–174.

[38] πῶς οὖν ὁ λόγος τῆς αἰσθήσεως αἴτιος; ὁ γὰρ λόγος ἐν τῆι τῶν πλειόνων μίξει καὶ ἐν τῆι πρὸς ἄλληλα σχέσει. (Frg. 282 Fortenbaugh et al.; zit. nach Primavesi, „Platonische Zwei-Elementen-Lehre“, 40).

[39] Betrachtet man die beiden Abschnitte zum *Timaios* und zu *Peri philosophias* bzgl. der drei zentralen Termini στοιχεία, πράγματα und ἀρχαί, so ergibt sich folgendes Bild: Der Terminus στοιχεία ist unproblematisch, er kann in beiden Referaten auf die höchsten „Elementarprinzipien“ verweisen. Die beiden anderen Ausdrücke finden sich in der abschließenden Aussage γινώσκεσθαι γὰρ τῷ ὁμοίῳ τὸ ὅμοιον, τὰ δὲ πράγματα ἐκ τῶν ἀρχῶν εἶναι (*An.* 404b17–18). Der letzte Halbsatz kann nun auf zwei Weisen verstanden werden: (i) die Sinnendinge sind aus den Prinzipien (sc. den Ideen) oder (ii) alle Dinge (sc. Ideen und Sinnendinge) sind aus den Prinzipien (sc. den Urprinzipien). Variante (i) läuft parallel zu Aussage [4], sie kann den ἀρχαί-Begriff mit Blick auf den nachfolgenden *Peri Philosophias*-Abschnitt semantisch konstant halten, muss aber πράγματα dann alleine auf die Sinnendinge beziehen und steht damit in Spannung zum *Peri Philosophias*-Abschnitt (wenn dieser, wie gezeigt, nach Option (b) gelesen wird). Variante (ii) hält den πράγματα-Begriff konstant, hat aber zwei andere Hypotheken: zum einen muss der ἀρχαί-Begriff gegenüber Aussage [4] von den Ideen auf die Urprinzipien übergehen; zum anderen besteht die Schwierigkeit, dass ein Entstehen von Sinnendingen *und* Ideen aus den Urprinzipien im *Timaios* nicht behandelt wird. Beide Hypotheken sind aber m.E. einlösbar. Denn einerseits arbeitet Aristoteles gerade mit dem ἀρχαί-Begriff durchaus variabel (vgl. oben Anm. 27). Und andererseits ist es denkbar, dass der fragliche Halbsatz von Aristoteles spezifisch an seine bereits vorgebildete Hörerschaft gerichtet ist, für

Bejaht man die erste Frage zur sachlichen Deckung von *Timaios*- und *Peri Philosophias*-Abschnitt, so schließt sich eine zweite Folgefrage an: Wo genau findet Aristoteles die anhand von *Peri Philosophia* deutlicher greifbare Argumentation im *Timaios* – denn auf der Hand liegt dies keineswegs, eher vermag diese Sicht auf den *Timaios* auf den ersten Blick zu verwundern (wir werden bei Xenokrates darauf zurückkommen). Bei genauerer Betrachtung finden sich jedoch in der Tat Versatzstücke im *Timaios*, die mit den Momenten aus dem *Peri Philosophia*-Referat in Deckung zu bringen sind. Grundsätzlich bringt natürlich zum einen insbesondere *Ti.* 37a2–c7 Ausführungen, die zum Prinzip ‚Gleiches erkennt Gleiches' passen. Daneben findet sich jedoch eine Reihe an weiteren wichtigen Aspekten: 1) Die Vierzahl der Dimensionen des „Lebenswesens selbst" ist, wenn man unter diesem Lebewesen den Ideenkosmos versteht, tatsächlich auch im *Timaios* angedeutet: dort findet sich, vermittelt durch die Vierzahl der Gattungen an Lebewesen im physischen Kosmos, die Vierzahl auch als Grundfigur der Ideenwelt ausgesagt (*Ti.* 39e7–40a2). 2) Eine mit der Seele enggeführte Dimensionsfolge – von Zahl, Linie, Fläche, Körper – findet sich auch im *Timaios*, in der Passage zur Seelenmischung, anschaulich umgesetzt: Zuerst wird das Seelenmaterial als primär zahlhafter Verhältniskomplex beschrieben (*Ti.* 35b1–b5; vgl. 37a4), bevor dieser der Länge nach ausgewalzt wird (*Ti.* 35b5–7), dann in der Form eines ‚Chi' in die zwei Dimension ausgefaltet wird (*Ti.* 35b8), bevor durch das Zusammenführen der Enden die dritte Dimension sphärisch erschlossen wird (*Ti.* 35bc1) und zuletzt auch noch die Bewegung mit hinzukommt (*Ti.* 36d2–d7). Auch der *Timaios* hält also eine auffällig ähnliche dimensionale Strukturierung der (Welt)seele parat,[40] was sich weitreichend auch mit der Dimensionspassage im 10. Buch der *Nomoi* deckt (*Lg.* 894a1–8), wo ebenfalls, genau passend, die Seele bzw. Weltseele den entscheidenden Kontext bildet. Und auch die Passage zur Tyrannenzahl in der *Politeia* bietet einen direkt vergleichbaren Hintergrund.[41] 3) Zuletzt ist auch zu bedenken, dass der Zahlkomplex in der Weltseelenmischung ja zugleich eine Form von Sein darstellt (*Ti.* 35a1–4) – die zahlenhafte Strukturierung des Seins ist also auch durch das ‚Material' der Seelenmischung latent angedeutet.

Zieht man die Argumentation aus *Peri Philosophias* und die Darstellung im *Timaios* auf die skizzierte Weise zusammen, dann ergibt sich als dritte

---

die eine Herkunft aller Dinge aus den Urprinzipien (vgl. *Metaph.* 987b19–20) schon mit einer verkürzten Wendung wie τὰ δὲ πράγματα ἐκ τῶν ἀρχῶν einsichtig war – im *Timaios* werden die Urprinzipien zumindest erwähnt, wenn auch zugleich ausgespart (vgl. Anm. 42). Zu bedenken ist zudem, dass auch im Timaios die Seele (ganz im Sinne von Aussage [6]) nicht nur Sinnendinge, sondern auch Ideen erkennt (*Ti.* 28a1–2.37a5–b1.37c1–5); rein sachlich ist also auch hier Variante (ii) angemessener.

[40] Auch *Ti.* 53c5–d7 deutet einen dimensionstheoretischen Aufstieg an.

[41] *R.* 587b11–588a10. Vgl. für den Nachweis des dimensionstheoretischen Hintergrunds der Passage Poetsch, „Dimensions of Pleasure".

Folgefrage, wo genau im *Timaios* Aristoteles die Aussage findet, dass die Seele aus den Elementarprinzipien, den στοιχεῖα, entsteht? Denn dass im *Timaios* die Seele aus den Urprinzipien erstellt oder entstehen würde, scheint im Text so nicht wirklich auszumachen.[42] Die Frage mag für den Moment hier noch offenbleiben. Festzuhalten ist jedoch, dass zumindest die Möglichkeit besteht, dass Aristoteles im *Timaios* eine Entstehung der Seele aus den Prinzipien selbst formuliert sieht – wenngleich sie für uns im Text kaum direkt auszumachen ist. Wir werden bei Xenokrates darauf zurückkommen.

Zuletzt ist noch der Einwand einer vierten Folgefrage zu bedenken: Ist die aus *Peri Philosophias* referierte Position überhaupt auf Platon zu beziehen? Meines Erachtens sprechen (mindestens) drei Argumente für eine affirmative Antwort auf diese Frage. Erstens ist zu bedenken, dass Platon die einzige Position ist, die in der gesamten Passage namentlich genannt wird.[43] Es ist also nur folgerichtig, das Gesagte auf ihn zu beziehen; zumal das ὁμοίως (*An.* 404b18) dies ebenfalls nahelegt. Zweitens ist festzuhalten, dass erst der ab-schließende Satz zur „sich selbst bewegenden Zahl" – und nur dieser – rein inhaltlich einen klaren Bezug auf Xenokrates bietet. Deshalb nun den *vorangegangenen* Abschnitt vor *An.* 404b27 auch auf Xenokrates zu übertragen, übersieht jedoch Entscheidendes: Der *Peri Philosophias*-Abschnitt fokussiert eindeutig und ausschließlich auf die *kognitiven* Kapazitäten, während der Satz zur selbstbewegten Zahl gerade auf die kognitiven *und* die kinetischen Kapazitäten der Seele eingeht – hier wird also eindeutig eine neue, *andere* Position aufgerufen,[44] die, wie schon gesagt, eine Art Zwitter zwischen den beiden bis dato in *De anima* I 2 diskutierten Grundkonzeptionen der Seele darstellt. Statt das Vorangegangene für Xenokrates zu reklamieren, scheint es sogar von den Textbefunden eher angebracht, die selbstbewegte Zahl – zumindest der Sache nach – auch für Platon, neben Xenokrates, mit in Anspruch zu nehmen.[45] In jedem Fall ist der Gesamtaufbau von *De anima* I 2 für die korrekte Zuordnung

---

[42] Allenfalls ist dies dann der Fall, wenn man die Bestandteile der Weltseelenmischung (*Ti.* 35a1–8) als Derivate der Prinzipien versteht und *Ti.* 37a2–c3 hinzuzieht (so Gaiser, „Quellenkritische Probleme", 50; ähnlich auch Shields, *De anima*, 110–111). Das ist nicht prinzipiell ausgeschlossen, gleichwohl ist zu bedenken, dass die Untersuchung der höchsten ἀρχαί, der ἀρχὴ bzw. ἀρχαὶ ἁπάντων, im *Timaios* aufgrund der aktuellen Darstellungsform explizit ausgespart bleibt (*Ti.* 48c2–d4).

[43] So schon Gaiser, „Quellenkritische Probleme", 55–56.

[44] Die Übersetzung von Shields, *De anima* setzt diesen Satz deshalb zu Recht vom Vorherigen ab.

[45] *Phdr.* 245c5–246a2 etwa fasst die Seele nicht über ihre kognitiven Kapazitäten, sondern zweifelsohne als Bewegungsprinzip; der zahlenhafte Charakter wird z.B. in der Weltseelenmischung deutlich. Die griffige Kurzformel von der „selbstbewegten Zahl" ist damit schlussendlich der Sache nach im Grunde gut platonisch – zumal auch Xenokrates unter „Zahl" hier sicher nicht eine Einzelzahl, sondern einen Zahlenkomplex verstanden haben wird; vgl. auch Halfwassen, *Aufstieg zum Einen*, 225 mit Anm. 97.

der Positionen von Bedeutung. Und drittens ist zuletzt, wie bereits gezeigt, die Nähe zwischen dem *Peri Philosophia*-Referat und dem *Timaios* auch inhaltlich gegeben.

2. Xenokrates, Frg. 188 (Isnardi Parente)

Für Platons zweiten Nachfolger, Xenokrates, werde ich mich, gemäß der vorliegenden Grundthese, weniger auf seine notorische Formel von der Seele als „sich selbst bewegende Zahl“ konzentrieren, als vielmehr auf die Stellung der Seele im systematischen Gesamtgefüge und ihre Beziehung zu den Urprinzipien. Beginnen wir deshalb mit einem für sein Seelenkonzept zentralen Fragment[46] aus dem Kommentar des Plutarch zur Weltseelenmischung im *Timaios*, das einen wichtigen Hinweis für die Auffassung liefert, dass Xenokrates die Weltseele als genuines Prinzipiat der beiden Urprinzipien aufgefasst hat:

Da aber von den angesehensten Männern Xenokrates einige für sich gewann, der ja das Wesen der Seele als sich selbst bewegende Zahl auffasste, andere (von ihnen) aber Krantor von Soloi zuneigten, der die Seele aus der noetischen und der auf Ebene der Sinnendinge beurteilbaren Wesensnatur mischte, glaube ich, dass die Aufklärung (dieser beiden Positionen) in der Enthüllung uns gleichsam eine Art Einleitung bieten wird. Der Logos [hier etwa: die Aussage, Position] von beiden ist kurz und bündig. Die einen [sc. Xenokrates und Anhänger] glauben nämlich, dass mit der Mischung des unteilbaren und des geteilten Seins nichts anderes zum Ausdruck gebracht wird als die Entstehung der Zahl – denn das Eine ist unteilbar, die Vielheit aber ist teilbar, und aus diesen (beiden) entsteht die Zahl indem die Vielheit durch das Eine bestimmend definiert wird und der Unbegrenztheit, die sie auch „unbestimmte Zweiheit“ nennen, Grenze auferlegt wird. (Auch Zaratas, der Lehrer des Pythagoras, nannte diese die ‚Mutter‘ der Zahl, das Eine aber de(re)n ‚Vater‘, weshalb auch die Zahlen besser seien, die der Monade ähneln [sc. die ungeraden]). Aber diese Zahl hielten sie noch nicht für (die) Seele, da ihr das Bewegende und die Bewegung fehle. Aber nach der Beimischung des Identischen und des Verschiedenen – von denen das eine das Prinzip der Bewegung und Veränderung ist, das andere aber (das Prinzip) der Ruhe – sei die Seele entstanden, wobei die Seele um nichts weniger ein Vermögen zum Stillstellen und In-Ruhe-Sein ist, wie eines zum In-Bewegung-Sein und zum Bewegen.[47]

---

[46] Wenn hier und im Folgenden von ‚Fragment‘ die Rede ist, so folge ich damit der eher weitgefassten Nutzen dieses Terminus in den einschlägigen Sammlungen für die behandelten Altakademiker. Mit Fragmenten – also: wörtlichen Versatzstücken, dem wörtlichen Originallaut – haben wir es dabei in den seltensten Fällen zu tun. Folglich wäre oftmals eher von ‚Testimonien‘ zu sprechen.

[47] ἐπεὶ δὲ τῶν δοκιμωτάτων ἀνδρῶν τοὺς μὲν Ξενοκράτης προσηγάγετο, τῆς ψυχῆς τὴν οὐσίαν ἀριθμὸν αὐτὸν ὑφ᾽ ἑαυτοῦ κινούμενον ἀποφηνάμενος οἱ δὲ Κράντορι τῷ Σολεῖ προσέθεντο, μιγνύντι τὴν ψυχὴν ἔκ τε τῆς νοητῆς καὶ τῆς περὶ τὰ αἰσθητὰ δοξαστῆς φύσεως· οἶμαί τι τὴν τούτων ἀνακαλυφθέντων σαφήνειαν ὥσπερ ἐνδόσιμον ἡμῖν παρέξειν. ἔστι δὲ βραχὺς ὑπὲρ ἀμφοῖν ὁ λόγος. οἱ μὲν γὰρ οὐδὲν ἢ γένεσιν ἀριθμοῦ δηλοῦσθαι νομίζουσι τῇ μίξει τῆς ἀμερίστου καὶ μεριστῆς οὐσίας· ἀμέριστον μὲν γὰρ εἶναι τὸ ἓν μεριστὸν δὲ τὸ πλῆθος, ἐκ

Xenokrates hat diesem Bericht von Plutarch zufolge in der Weltseelenmischung also im ersten Schritt, in der Mischung der zwei Arten von οὐσία, eine Entstehung der seelischen, zahlhaften und vorerst noch bewegungslosen Grundsubstanz aus den beiden Urprinzipien gesehen, wobei diese Urprinzipien hier als das Eine und die unbestimmte Zweiheit bzw. als Vielheit auftreten. Für Xenokrates scheint somit hinter der Weltseelen-Mischung im *Timaios* letztlich Platons Prinzipienpaar zu stehen – was er in seiner eigenen, gegenüber Platon modifizierten[48] Konzeption aus Nus-Monas und Vielheitsprinzip aufnimmt. Die Weltseele Platons stammt in der xenokratischen Sicht demnach, in augenscheinlich sehr direkter Weise, von den Urprinzipien her. So wenig dies auf den ersten Blick am Text des *Timaios* greifbar ist, so fügt es sich doch überraschend genau zur Aussage des Aristoteles, der sein *Timaios*-Referat in *De anima*, wie schon angesprochen, mit eben genau dieser Aussage einleitet: dass nämlich Platon im *Timaios* die Seele aus den στοιχεῖα bestehen lasse (Πλάτων ἐν τῷ Τιμαίῳ τὴν ψυχὴν ἐκ τῶν στοιχείων ποιεῖ *An.* 404b16–17). Xenokrates und Aristoteles treffen sich also genau darin, dass sie die Weltseele des *Timaios* auf das platonische Prinzipienpaar als direkten Ursprung zurückführen.

Das vermag durchaus zu verwundern. Denn unmittelbar ist in der Schaffung der Weltseele nur von verschiedenen Arten des Seins, des Identischen und des Verschiedenen die Rede. Das lässt sich, etwa im Sinne des Xenokrates, zwar einigermaßen plausibel auf das Prinzipienpaar in analoger Weise abbilden, aber es setzt doch augenscheinlich weitere Informationen und Kenntnisse voraus – und ist ohne diese kaum dem Text direkt zu entnehmen.

Von besonderer Wichtigkeit ist deshalb ein weiterer textueller Befund. Denn in der Tat findet sich im *Timaios* an anderer Stelle eine Aussage, die dem Verständnis von Xenokrates und Aristoteles erstaunlich nahekommt. Und zwar sagt Timaios an etwas späterer Stelle über die Weltseele, sie sei „geschaffen vom Besten der Noetischen[49] und immer Seienden als das beste Gewordene der

---

δὲ τούτων γίγνεσθαι τὸν ἀριθμὸν τοῦ ἑνὸς ὁρίζοντος τὸ πλῆθος καὶ τῇ ἀπειρίᾳ πέρας ἐπιτιθέντος, ἣν καὶ δυάδα καλοῦσιν ἀόριστον. (καὶ Ζαράτας ὁ Πυθαγόρου διδάσκαλος ταύτην μὲν ἐκάλει τοῦ ἀριθμοῦ μητέρα τὸ δ᾽ ἓν πατέρα· διὸ καὶ βελτίονας εἶναι τῶν ἀριθμῶν ὅσοι τῇ μονάδι προσεοίκασι), τοῦτον δὲ μήπω ψυχὴν τὸν ἀριθμὸν εἶναι· τὸ γὰρ κινητικὸν καὶ τὸ κινητὸν ἐνδεῖν αὐτῷ. τοῦ δὲ ταὐτοῦ καὶ τοῦ ἑτέρου συμμιγέντων, ὧν τὸ μέν ἐστι κινήσεως ἀρχὴ καὶ μεταβολῆς τὸ δὲ μονῆς, ψυχὴν γεγονέναι, μηδὲν ἧττον τοῦ ἱστάναι καὶ ἵστασθαι δύναμιν ἢ τοῦ κινεῖσθαι καὶ κινεῖν οὖσαν. (Plutarch, *De procr. an. in Ti.* 1, 1012D–1013A = Frg. 188 Isnardi Parente; Übers. CP).

48 Wichtigster Unterschied ist die Setzung des ersten Prinzips als νοῦς, während Platons erstes Prinzip ἔτι ἐπέκεινα τῆς οὐσίας liegt (*R.* 509b9). Zu diesen beiden Grundkonzeptionen in der Alten Akademie vgl. auch das wichtige Zeugnis zu Aristoteles' Περὶ εὐχῆς bei Simplikios: σαφῶς εἰπὼν [sc. ὁ Ἀριστοτέλης] ὅτι ὁ θεὸς ἢ νοῦς ἐστὶν ἢ ἐπέκεινά τι τοῦ νοῦ (Frg. 1 Ross).

49 Der Plural ist hier bemerkenswert, gerade im Hinblick auf die Stellung des *einen*, einzigen Besten über den *vielen* untergeordneten Entitäten.

Gewordenen“ (τῶν νοητῶν ἀεί τε ὄντων ὑπὸ τοῦ ἀρίστου ἀρίστη γενομένη τῶν γεννηθέντων *Ti.* 37a1–2). Diese Aussage hat ein entscheidendes Pendant im Sonnengleichnis der *Politeia*. Dort heißt es von der Sonne, sie sei der „Sprößling des Guten, den das Gute analog zu sich selbst gezeugt“ habe (τὸν τοῦ ἀγαθοῦ ἔκγονον, ὃν τἀγαθὸν ἐγέννησεν ἀνάλογον ἑαυτῷ *R.* 508b12–13; vgl. *R.* 509d1–3.517c3–4). Von diesem Guten wird weniger später, im VII. Buch – und in praktisch wörtlicher Entsprechung zum *Timaios* – gesagt, es sei ἄριστον ἐν τοῖς οὖσι (*R.* 532c5–6). Beide Äußerungen sind vor dem Hintergrund der diskreten geometrischen Analogie, derer sich Platon häufig bedient,[50] strukturell folglich deckungsgleich: Beide benennen die analoge Stellung zweier höchster Instanzen über zwei ihnen untergeordneten, pluralen Entitäten, dem Ideenkosmos bzw. dem physischen Kosmos (A steht über B; C steht über D);[51] und beide benennen die höhere dieser beiden oberen Instanzen als Prinzip der untergeordneten (A ist Prinzip von C).

Streng genommen bedarf es zweier Zusatzprämissen, um diese beiden Aussagen aus dem *Timaios* und der *Politeia* vollständig parallelisieren zu können: zum einen die Assoziierung von Zeus und Weltseele; und zum anderen die Auffassung der Sonne als sichtbares Werkzeug der Weltseele bei der Ordnung des Kosmos. Beide Prämissen sind jedoch am platonischen Dialogwerk gut ausweisbar: Die Assoziierung von Zeus und Weltseele findet sich im *Philebos*, aber auch im *Kratylos* und im *Phaidros*.[52] Und die enge Bindung der Sonne an die Weltseele als deren sichtbares Ordnungsorgan findet sich wiederum wörtlich im *Theaitetos*, im Rahmen der Auslegung des homerischen goldenen Seils (*Il.* 8.17–27) und unter Voraussetzung eben jener Engführung von Zeus und Weltseele.[53]

Das heißt aber, im Rückbezug auf Xenokrates und Aristoteles sowie für die altakademische Diskussion der Seele bzw. Weltseele insgesamt: Die bei beiden Schülern zu findende – und auf den ersten Blick sicher kontraintuitive Sichtweise –, dass Platon die Weltseele in direkter Abkunft von seinem Prinzipienpaar konzipiert habe, findet, zumindest mit Blick auf das erste Prinzip,[54] seinen Widerklang im platonischen Dialogwerk. Dies hat zwar Konsequenzen, die im Verhältnis zur altakademischen *Timaios*-Interpretation nicht ohne Spannung

---

[50] Vgl. zur Analogie bei Platon grundlegend u.a. Bärthlein, *Analogiebegriff*; Gerlach, „Fügung der Welt“; Schölles, *Vieles und nicht nur Eines*, 48–57; Fronterotta, „ΑΝΑΛΟΓΙΑ“.

[51] Vgl. auch: δύο αὐτὼ εἶναι, καὶ βασιλεύειν τὸ μὲν νοητοῦ γένους τε καὶ τόπου, τὸ δ' αὖ ὁρατοῦ (*R.* 509d1–2).

[52] *Phlb.* 30d1–4; *Cra.* 396a7–b2; *Phdr.* 246e3–6 – zu Letzterem vgl. Xenokrates Frg. 213 und Dillon, *Heirs of Plato*, 102 Anm. 44. Vgl. zum Komplex von Zeus, Sonne und Weltseele ausführlicher Poetsch, „Logoi der Sonnenanalogie“, 243–245.

[53] *Tht.* 153c9–d3. Vgl. hierzu im Detail Poetsch, „Logoi der Sonnenanalogie“, 244.

[54] Dass das zweite Prinzip im *Timaios* noch nicht angesprochen ist, könnte (auch) damit zusammenhängen, dass im ersten Anlauf des Timaios die χώρα (als Erscheinungsform des zweiten Prinzips) noch nicht zum Tragen kommt.

sind,[55] aber mit Blick auf die Diskussion des Seelenkonzepts in der Alten Akademie zeigt es doch eine überraschende Konstanz und Konsistenz.

Gegen die skizzierte Interpretation der angeführten Platon-Passagen in *Politeia* (508b12–13) und *Timaios* (37a1–2) ließe sich freilich einwenden, dass durch die Einfügung der Weltseele insbesondere in die Verhältnisgleichung der Sonnenanalogie die Dinge unnötig verkompliziert werden. Schließlich besteht der zentrale Zweck dieser Analogie darin, Unbekanntes (das Verhältnis des Guten zu den Ideen) durch *Bekanntes* (das anschauliche Verhältnis der Sonne zur Welt des Werdens) zu erläutern. Hier nun aufseiten der Sonne das obskure Philosophem der Weltseele einzuführen, verunklärt die Sachlage eher, es unterminiert die didaktische Anschaulichkeit und läuft letztlich Gefahr, *obscurum per obscurius* zu erklären.[56] Unbestritten ist, dass durch die Hinzunahme der Weltseele die Dinge in der ersten Konsequenz zweifelsohne nicht einfacher werden. Zu begegnen ist dem Einwand aber mit drei Argumenten:[57] Erstens ist zu bemerken, dass das durchgängig anschauliche Verhältnis von Sonne und Werdewelt durch die Hinzunahme der Weltseele keineswegs annulliert oder ersetzt werden soll; vielmehr ist die obige Interpretation im Sinne eines *zusätzlichen* Verhältnisses zu verstehen. Die rein anschauliche Ebene von Sonne und Werdewelt bleibt also als solche gewahrt, es finden sich hinter ihr jedoch im Anschluss mehrere unanschauliche Verhältnisse und Ebenen. Zweitens ist zu bedenken, dass durch das Verhältnis von (an höchster Stelle weltimmanenter) Sonne und (relativ welttranszendenter) Weltseele ein textueller Befund in der *Politeia* erklärbar wird, der andernfalls größere Interpretationsprobleme mit sich bringt: Das zusätzliche Verhältnis ermöglicht es, das zweipolige Changieren zwischen einer Verortung der Idee des Guten als höchste ideen*immanente* Idee und als ideen*transzendentes* Prinzip gleichungsanalogisch zu motivieren.[58] Und drittens erlaubt erst die zusätzliche Einführung der Weltseele in die Sonnenanalogie eine ebenso zwanglose wie vollständige – und im Text der *Politeia* eindeutig geforderte (*R.* 517a8–b4) – Koordinierung der drei großen *Politeia*-Gleichnisse, insbesondere was die Ausdeutung des Höhlenfeuers und der vorbeigetragenen Statuetten betrifft.[59]

---

[55] Spannungsreich wird die Sachlage dadurch, dass unter den Deutungs- und Identifikationsoptionen des Demiurgen für gewöhnlich nur der nushafte Ideenkosmos und die Weltseele auftauchen (so man ihn nicht als gänzlich eigene Instanz begreift), nicht aber das Gute selbst. Diese Option verdient jedoch, bei Lichte betrachtet, ernsthafte und ausführlichere Betrachtung. Vgl. hierzu auch Szlezák, *Platon*, 453–456.

[56] Ich danke K. Corcilius für diesen Einwand und die daran anschließenden Diskussionen – nicht nur zu diesem Punkt, sondern zu vielen weiteren Aspekten des vorliegenden Beitrags.

[57] Die nachfolgenden Ausführungen sind stark gerafft, für eine ausführlichere Formulierung der Argumente sei auf Poetsch, „Logoi der Sonnenanalogie" verwiesen.

[58] Für Details und textuelle Nachweise vgl. Poetsch, „Logoi der Sonnenanalogie", 251–256.

[59] Vgl. im Detail Poetsch, „Logoi der Sonnenanalogie", 261–262.

Im Ganzen betrachtet scheint es nach Frg. 188 folglich so, dass Xenokrates die Weltseele als prominente Systemstelle nach den beiden Prinzipien, als deren ebenso genuines wie prominentes Prinzipiat aufgefasst hat.[60] Dies hat, wie gezeigt, durchaus Rückhalte im platonischen Dialogwerk, wenngleich es dort nur in Andeutungen vorliegt. Dabei ist durchaus bemerkenswert, dass damit nicht nur die Gesamtheit der Ideen Ergebnis des Zusammenwirkens der beiden Prinzipien ist (wie etwa der Bericht von Aristoteles in *Metaphysik* I 6 für Platon nahelegt), sondern auch die nächstniedrigere Instanz, die Weltseele. Dies würde sich – die große Nähe von Seelischem und Mathematischem bei Platon vorausgesetzt[61] – zumal mit dem von O. Primavesi neu konstituierten Text von *Metaph.* 987b22 bemerkenswert gut decken.[62]

Zuletzt sei für Xenokrates noch ein weiteres Zeugnis, Frg. 213, hinzugezogen, das für die vorliegende Fragestellung einschlägig ist, in systematischer wie philologischer Perspektive aber einige Fragen aufwirft. Der Text von Aetios beschreibt das xenokratische Prinzipienpaar, Monas und Dyas, in Bezug auf die Weltseele. Der fragliche Abschnitt lautet wie folgt:

> Xenokrates, Sohn des Agathenor, aus Chalcedon sieht die Monas und die Dyas als Götter an. Erstere [sc. die Monas] (gilt ihm dabei) als männlich, den Rang des Vaters innehabend, im Himmel als König herrschend; er spricht sie [sc. Monas] an als ‚Zeus', ‚ungerade' und ‚Geist', welcher ihm der erste Gott ist. Letztere [sc. die Dyas] (gilt ihm) als weiblich, Mutter der Götter, dem Los nach herrschend über den Bereich unterhalb des Himmels – sie [sc. die Dyas] ist für ihn die Weltseele. Aber auch der Himmel ist ihm ein Gott und die Sterne feurige olympische Götter.[63]

Das Testimonium liefert offenkundig einen hierarchischen, absteigenden Aufriss der Theologie des Xenokrates, innerhalb derer auch die Weltseele firmiert. Allerdings ist der Text in seiner zitierten Form nicht unumstritten. Während etwa M. Baltes und D. Thiel den Text in seiner erhaltenen Form für korrekt

---

[60] Anhand der Vermittlung von Einheit und Vielheit in der Seele wird dieser Befund auch durch Frg. 189 (Isnardi Parente) erhärtet.

[61] Ausführliche Analysen und Argumente hierzu bei Merlan, *Platonism to Neoplatonism*, bes. 11–33 und Gaiser, *Platons ungeschriebene Lehre*, bes. 41–66.

[62] Vgl. oben Anm. 26. Die Deckung ergibt sich vor dem Hintergrund der genannten Prämisse, nach der Seele und mathematische Entitäten bei Platon aufs Engste verwandt und möglicherweise deckungsgleich sind. In der Folge wäre in *Metaph.* 987b19–22 dann nicht nur das Entstehen der Ideen aus den Urprinzipien, sondern auch die Genese des Seelisch-Mathematischen ausgesprochen.

[63] Ξενοκράτης Ἀγαθήνορος Καλχηδόνιος τὴν μονάδα καὶ τὴν δυάδα θεούς, τὴν μὲν ὡς ἄρρενα πατρὸς ἔχουσαν τάξιν ἐν οὐρανῷ βασιλεύουσαν, ἥντινα προσαγορεύει καὶ Ζῆνα καὶ περιττὸν καὶ νοῦν, ὅστις ἐστὶν αὐτῷ πρῶτος θεός· τὴν δ' ὡς θήλειαν, μητρὸς θεῶν δίκην, τῆς ὑπὸ τὸν οὐρανὸν λήξεως ἡγουμένην, ἥτις ἐστὶν αὐτῷ ψυχὴ τοῦ παντός. θεὸν δ' εἶναι καὶ τὸν οὐρανὸν καὶ τοὺς ἀστέρας πυρώδεις ὀλυμπίους θεούς (Aetios, *Plac.* 1.7.30 = Frg. 213 Isnardi Parent = 1.7 §21 Mansfeld/Runia)

halten,[64] hat insbesondere J. Dillon mehrfach dafür plädiert, dass im Text eine Lacuna, und zwar im Bereich von μητρὸς θεῶν δίκην, also in der Beschreibung des zweiten Prinzips, vorliegt.[65] Hauptgrund für die Annahme eine Lacuna ist bei J. Dillon die sich aus dem Text in seiner gegenwärtigen Fassung ergebende Gleichsetzung von Dyas und Weltseele[66] – eine Gleichsetzung, die auch Jaap Mansfeld und D. T. Runia in ihrer Aetios-Edition für schwierig halten.[67]

Für Position (a), die Korrektheit des erhaltenen Textes, sprechen v.a. folgende Argumente: (1) Der Text ist grammatisch intakt, eine Änderung ist deshalb erst einmal nicht angezeigt – in jedem Fall liegt die Beweislast klar aufseiten eines Texteingriffs. (2) Die Aussagen speziell zum ersten Gott lassen sich gut mit Platons *Timaios* in Einklang bringen, also jenem Dialog, der für Xenokrates besonders zentral war.[68] (3) δίκην muss an der fraglichen Stelle nicht als Eigenname aufgefasst werden.[69] Für Position (b), die Annahme besagter Lacuna, sprechen v.a. die nachfolgenden Argumente: (1) Eine Identifikation des zweiten Prinzips mit der Weltseele ist vor dem Hintergrund alles Sonstigen, das wir über die altakademischen Systeme kennen, fürs Erste zumindest merkwürdig.[70] (2) Betrachtet man den Text nur für sich, so kann man sich bei unvoreingenommener Betrachtung zumindest des Eindrucks nicht erwehren, dass die Aufzählung der Attribute für den ersten Gott (‚Zeus', ‚ungerade', ‚Geist') nach einer komplementären Liste für die Dyas verlangt – eine

---

[64] Vgl. Baltes, „Theologie des Xenokrates"; Thiel, *Philosophie des Xenokrates*, 265–288.

[65] Dillon, *Middle Platonists*, 26; Dillon „Xenocrates' Metaphysics", 49; Dillon, *Heirs of Plato*, 102–107 (mit der Modifikation ebd., 102, dass wohl schon die Vorlage von Aetios verderbt gewesen sein könnte). J. Dillon schlägt folgende Ergänzung vor: „Letztere [sc. die Dyas] (gilt ihm) als weiblich, <den Rang der Mutter der Götter innehabend, welche er ‚Rhea', ‚gerade' und ‚Materie' nennt; und als deren Sprössling postuliert er> Dikê, herrschend über den Bereich unterhalb des Himmels, welche für ihn die Weltseele ist." Übersetzung ins Deutsche durch CP; im englischen Original: „the other, as female, <holding the rank of Mother of the Gods, which he terms 'Rhea' and 'even' (*artios*) and 'matter' (*hyle*); and as offspring of these he postulates> Dikê, ruling over the realm below the heavens …" (Dillon, *Heirs of Plato*, 103).

[66] „[…] to portray the secondary dyadic principle as itself ‚the Soul of the universe' is a gross distortion of Xenocrates' metaphysical system" (Dillon, *Heirs of Plato*, 103).

[67] „The identification of the Dyad with the World Soul is difficult to explain." (Mansfeld/Runia, *Aëtiana*, 400). Die Ergänzung von J. Dillon zitieren Mansfeld/Runia, ohne sie jedoch zu übernehmen.

[68] Vgl. hierzu v.a. Baltes, „Theologie des Xenokrates", 193–197.

[69] So Baltes, „Theologie des Xenokrates", 192 gegen den Vorschlag von P. Boyancé.

[70] M. Baltes schreibt hierzu: „Mit noch größerem Recht kann die Weltseele als ‚Dyas' bezeichnet werden, da sie nach dem Tim[aios] deutlich eine dyadische Struktur hat, sofern sie aus zwei ‚Kreisen' besteht, dem sog. Umlauf des Selben und dem des Anderen […]." (Baltes, „Theologie des Xenokrates", 195; vgl. auch Thiel, *Philosophie des Xenokrates*, 285–286). Den Bezug der Weltseele auf den klar prinzipientheoretisch besetzten Begriff ‚Dyas' einzig auf die zwei Kreise der Weltseele (deren einer zudem weiter aufgeteilt wird!) zu stützen, ist in meinen Augen bei Weitem keine zufriedenstellende Begründung für diese unbestreitbare Merkwürdigkeit.

Einschätzung, die selbst M. Baltes als Vertreter von Position (a) teilt.[71] (3) In der überlieferten Form steht Frg. 213 mit seiner klaren Identifikation von Dyas und Weltseele in jedem Fall in deutlichem Widerspruch zu Frg. 188-189, wo, wie gezeigt, die Weltseele zwar in spezifischem, prominentem Bezug zu den Prinzipien steht, aber doch deren *Produkt* ist; und nicht – wie in Frg. 213 nach Position (a) – mit einem dieser beiden Prinzipien identifiziert wird.[72] Eine klare sachliche Spannung zwischen den überlieferten, zentralen Berichten liegt dann in jedem Fall vor. (4) Zu bemerken ist zuletzt auch, dass der Text des Aetios auch in nachfolgenden Abschnitten Lacunae aufweist;[73] eine Lacuna im fraglichen Abschnitt erhält dadurch zumindest zusätzliche Wahrscheinlichkeit.

Im Ganzen betrachtet sind, wenngleich die Beweislast zweifelsohne bei (b) liegt, in meinen Augen die Argumente für Position (b) die stärkeren. Folgt man dieser Sicht, dann bietet auch Frg. 213 eine weitere Bestätigung des obigen Befunds, wonach bei Xenokrates eine spezifische Beziehung der Weltseele zu den Prinzipien gegeben ist. Als oberstes Prinzip des sinnlichen Kosmos ist die Weltseele demnach gleichsam eine Art ‚Statthalter' der Prinzipien, insbesondere des ersten Prinzips, und zugleich deren prominentestes Prinzipiat. Doch selbst wenn man in der obigen Gegenüberstellung Position (a) folgt, so kann Frg. 213 doch, im Sinne der angeführten Fragestellung, ebenfalls eine starke Beziehung der Weltseele zu den Urprinzipien bei Xenokrates belegen – in diesem Fall sogar die direkte Identifikation der Weltseele mit dem zweiten Prinzip. Folgt man jedoch Position (a), so sind in der Folge die Widersprüche zwi-schen Frg. 213 und Frg. 188 (wie auch Frg. 189) eigens zu erklären.

3. Speusipp, Frg. 29a (Tarán)

Ähnlich wie schon die Seelendefinition des Xenokrates lässt sich auch Speusipps definitorische Kurzfassung systematisch sinnvoll und erkennbar an die platonische Seelenkonzeption anschließen. Seine Aussage, dass die Seele die ἰδέα τοῦ πάντῃ διαστατοῦ sei (Frg. 54 Tarán), kann offensichtlich an Aussagen des *Timaios* anschließen, wo zweimal explizit davon die Rede ist, dass die Weltseele den kosmischen Raum – und damit alles dreidimensional Ausgedehnte – durchdringe und von außen umfasse.[74] Auch bei Platon ist die Seele in diesem Sinne die ‚Gestalt' alles Dreidimensionalen. Im Vorliegenden soll es aber gemäß der Eingangsthese weniger um diese knappe Seelenformel

[71] Vgl. Baltes, „Theologie des Xenokrates", 192.

[72] Vgl. auch Dillon, *Heirs of Plato*, 103.

[73] Vgl. in den Zeilen 101 und 102 bei Mansfeld/Runia, *Aëtiana*, 374 (= 1.7 §21).

[74] Vgl. *Ti.* 34b3–4: διὰ παντός τε ἔτεινεν καὶ ἔτι ἔξωθεν τὸ σῶμα αὐτῇ περιεκάλυψεν, *Ti.* 36e2: πάντῃ.

Speusipps gehen, sondern vielmehr um die systematische Stellung der Seele in der Gesamtordnung des Seins, zumal in Beziehung zu den Prinzipien.

Hilfreich ist hierfür zuerst Frg. 29a (Tarán), in welchem Aristoteles die oberen Ebenen von Speusipps System in Abgrenzung von der dreigliedrigen Seinstaxonomie Platons referiert:

> Es scheint manchen, dass die Grenzen der Körper – wie Oberfläche, Linie, Punkt und Einheit – Seinsarten[75] sind, und dies in höherem Maße als Körperliches und Dreidimensionales. Neben den Sinnendingen gibt es ferner, so glauben die einen, nichts Derartiges, wohingegen die anderen glauben, dass es mehr und in höherem Maße seiende ewige Dinge gebe – wie etwa Platon die Ideen und die mathematischen Entitäten als zwei Seinsarten ansieht, als dritte aber die Seinsart der sinnlich wahrnehmbaren Körper. Speusipp hingegen glaubt, dass es, vom Einen her beginnend, noch mehr Seinsarten gibt und dass es Prinzipien einer jeder einzelnen Seinsart gibt, ein (Prinzip) der Zahlen, ein anderes (Prinzip) für die Größen, und dann (ein anderes Prinzip) der Seele. Und auf diese Weise zog er die (Zahl der) Seinsarten weiter in die Länge.[76]

Für die vorliegende Analyse sind in diesem Referat besonders zwei Dinge relevant: zum einen die spezifische Verortung der Seele auf der dritten Stufe, nach den Zahlen und den geometrischen Größen. Zum anderen scheint Aristoteles mit der Wendung ἀπὸ τοῦ ἑνὸς ἀρξάμενος anzudeuten, dass das Eine in dieser Stratifikation als übergeordnetes Prinzip, jedoch nicht als eigene οὐσία fungiert, sondern paradigmatisch für die einzelnen regionalen Formprinzipien steht.[77] Hierfür spricht unter anderem, dass Aristoteles in *Metaphysik* Λ, in einer Passage, die offenkundig Speusipps ‚episodisches Alls' aufs Korn nimmt, die mathematische Zahl als das Erste, also als erste Seinsstufe, anspricht.[78] Mit Blick auf die systematische Position der Seele ist in jedem Fall deren Stellung auf der dritten Ebene, *nach* der arithmetischen und der geometrischen Seinsart, festzuhalten.

---

[75] Möglich auch die Übersetzung „Substanzen", dann jedoch im Sinne von Substanz*arten*, nicht im Sinne von Einzelinstanzen einer Substanz.

[76] δοκεῖ δέ τισι τὰ τοῦ σώματος πέρατα, οἷον ἐπιφάνεια καὶ γραμμὴ καὶ στιγμὴ καὶ μονάς, εἶναι οὐσίαι, καὶ μᾶλλον ἢ τὸ σῶμα καὶ τὸ στερεόν. ἔτι παρὰ τὰ αἰσθητὰ οἱ μὲν οὐκ οἴονται εἶναι οὐδὲν τοιοῦτον, οἱ δὲ πλείω καὶ μᾶλλον ὄντα ἀΐδια, ὥσπερ Πλάτων τά τε εἴδη καὶ τὰ μαθηματικὰ δύο οὐσίας, τρίτην δὲ τὴν τῶν αἰσθητῶν σωμάτων οὐσίαν, Σπεύσιππος δὲ καὶ πλείους οὐσίας ἀπὸ τοῦ ἑνὸς ἀρξάμενος, καὶ ἀρχὰς ἑκάστης οὐσίας, ἄλλην μὲν ἀριθμῶν ἄλλην δὲ μεγεθῶν, ἔπειτα ψυχῆς· καὶ τοῦτον δὴ τὸν τρόπον ἐπεκτείνει τὰς οὐσίας. (*Metaph.* 1028b16–24 = Frg. 29a Tarán)

[77] Dillon, *Heirs of Plato*, 51 (vgl. auch a.a.O., 54–55) zufolge sind demnach bei Speusipp wohl drei ‚Eine' zu unterscheiden; und zwar a) das Eine als erstes Prinzip von allem, b) das Eine als Regionalprinzip der Zahlen, c) die Eins als erste Zahl unter den Zahlen.

[78] οἱ δὲ λέγοντες τὸν ἀριθμὸν πρῶτον τὸν μαθηματικὸν καὶ οὕτως ἀεὶ ἄλλην ἐχομένην οὐσίαν καὶ ἀρχὰς ἑκάστης ἄλλας, ἐπεισοδιώδη τὴν τοῦ παντὸς οὐσίαν ποιοῦσιν (οὐδὲν γὰρ ἡ ἑτέρα τῇ ἑτέρᾳ συμβάλλεται οὖσα ἢ μὴ οὖσα) καὶ ἀρχὰς πολλάς· τὰ δὲ ὄντα οὐ βούλεται πολιτεύεσθαι κακῶς. "οὐκ ἀγαθὸν πολυκοιρανίη· εἷς κοίρανος ἔστω." (*Metaph.* 1075b37–1076a4).

Aufschlussreich ist für diesen Befund nun in meinen Augen zudem das Speusipp-Fragment aus dem vierten Kapitel von Jamblichs *De communi mathmatica scientia*, auch wenn es seinerseits eine Reihe an weiteren Fragen, nicht zuletzt die der Zuschreibung, mit sich bringt. Letztere kann ich im Vorliegenden nicht eigens zum Gegenstand machen, schließe mich aber der Position J. Dillons an,[79] wonach hier im Kern ein Referat, teils eine sich augenscheinlich recht nahe am Originaltext entlangbewegende Paraphrase von Speusipp vorliegt. Die für die hiesige Fragestellung relevante Passage aus Jamblich lautet wie folgt:

> Die Elementarprinzipien aber, aus denen die Zahlen sind, sind nicht einmal, weder schön noch gut. Aus der Zusammensetzung des Einen und der Materialursache der Vielheit aber hypostasiert die Zahl, und erst in diesen (Zahlen) erscheint das Seiende und Schönes. Aus den Elementarprinzipien der Linien folgt die geometrische Seins(art), in welcher ebenso das Seiende und das Schöne ist, in der aber (auch) weder Verwerfliches noch Schlechtes ist. Zuletzt aber, in den (Entitäten), die auf vierter und fünfter (Stufe) von den letzten Elementarprinzipien zusammengesetzt sind, entsteht erstmals und ohne Absicht Schlechtigkeit, aufgrund des Herausfallens und weil (sie) nicht nichts von dem, was gemäß der Wesensnatur ist, beherrschen.[80]

Mit Blick auf die oberen beiden Seinsstufen, die arithmetische und die geometrische, sowie deren Herkunft aus den Prinzipien decken sich die Angaben bei Jamblich gut mit den zuvor zitierten Ausführungen von Aristoteles in Frg. 29a. Die Nennung der Vielheit als Materialprinzip fehlt bei Letzterem, was aber einer Parallelisierung der beiden Passagen nicht im Wege steht, da die Annahme eines Materialprinzips bei Speusipp als solche unstrittig ist. Wichtig ist weiterhin, dass uns der Text bei Jamblich darüber informiert, dass Speusipp augenscheinlich im Ganzen *genau fünf* Seinsstufen angenommen hat. Außerdem ist aufschlussreich, dass Speusipp augenscheinlich eine Kontrastierung zwischen den ersten beiden Seinsstufen einerseits und den letzten beiden Seinsstufen andererseits im Blick hatte. Und zwar insofern die beiden oberen Stufen Sein und Schönheit aufweisen, jedoch frei von Schlechtigkeit und Hässlichkeit sind, während die beiden unteren Stufen eben diese negativen Attribute (auch? oder ausschließlich?) aufweisen. Die folgenden Passagen bei Jamblich legen zudem nahe, dass hier ein Kontrast zwischen unkörperlichem und körperlichem Sein vorliegt – was durchaus an die ontologische Grundunter-

---

[79] Vgl. hierzu Dillon, „Speusippus in Iamblichus“.

[80] τὰ δὲ στοιχεῖα, ἐξ ὧν οἱ ἀριθμοί, οὐδέπω ὑπάρχει οὔτε καλὰ οὔτε ἀγαθά· ἐκ δὲ τῆς συνθέσεως τοῦ ἑνὸς καὶ τῆς τοῦ πλήθους αἰτίας ὕλης ὑφίσταται μὲν ὁ ἀριθμός, πρώτοις δὲ ἐν τούτοις τὸ ὂν φαίνεται καὶ κάλλος, ἐφεξῆς ἐκ τῶν στοιχείων τῶν γραμμῶν τῆς γεωμετρικῆς οὐσίας φανείσης, ἐν ᾗ ὡσαύτως τὸ ὂν καὶ τὸ καλόν, ἐν οἷς [οὔτε] οὐδὲν οὔτε αἰσχρόν ἐστιν οὔτε κακόν· ἐπ' ἐσχάτῳ δὲ ἐν τοῖς τετάρτοις καὶ πέμπτοις τοῖς συντιθεμένοις ἀπὸ τῶν στοιχείων τῶν τελευταίων κακίαν γενέσθαι οὐ προηγουμένως, ἐκ δὲ τοῦ ἐκπίπτειν καὶ μὴ κατακρατεῖν τινα τοῦ κατὰ φύσιν. (Jamblich, *De comm. math. sc.* 18,1–12 Festa)

scheidung bei Platon erinnert, wenngleich Speusipp, der die Ideenlehre bekanntlich verworfen hat, an deren Stelle die mathematischen Zahlen setzte.

Besonders wichtig ist jedoch für die vorliegende Fragestellung das merkwürdige Fehlen der dritten Seinsstufe in der Aufzählung bei Jamblich. Es scheint mir nun naheliegend, diese dritte Stufe vor dem Hintergrund der Ausführungen bei Aristoteles (Frg. 29a) mit der Seele zu identifizieren. Wenn diese Annahme richtig ist, dann ergibt sich gerade durch die Aussparung der dritten Stufe in der Gegenüberstellung der Seinsstufen bei Jamblich eine markante Korrelation zwischen der Seele auf der dritten Stufe und dem Urprinzip des Einen oberhalb der ersten Stufe; und zwar insofern beide ihren jeweiligen Bereichen übergeordnet sind, wobei der Seelenstufe zugleich eine Art Scharnierposition zwischen dem Unkörperlichen und dem Körperlichem zukommt.

Diese spezifische Beziehung der Seele und des ersten Prinzips lässt sich tatsächlich noch durch ein weiteres Indiz erhärten; und zwar durch einen Rückbezug auf eine zentrale Textpassage bei Platon: das Sonnen- und das Liniengleichnis. Notwendig für diesen Bezug ist allerdings die bereits erwähnte Beziehung der Sonne zur Weltseele.[81] Erst diese erlaubt es zu erkennen, dass gemäß der in der Sonnenanalogie ausgesagten, direkten Beziehung des ersten Prinzips zur Sonne/Weltseele (*R.* 508b12–13), die Weltseele letztlich als beherrschendes Prinzip des physischen Kosmos[82] genau zwischen dem zweiten und dem dritten Abschnitt der Linie zu stehen kommt; wenngleich sie im Liniengleichnis nicht als eigener Bereich behandelt wird. Hierfür ist insbesondere zu bedenken, dass der zweitunterste Bereich der Linie durch den zentralen Terminus τά περὶ ἡμᾶς ζῷα (*R.* 510a5) spezifisch auf die verkörperte Einzelseele verweist und sich die Mittelstellung des Seelischen in der vieldiskutierten – und vielgescholtenen – Gleichheit der beiden mittleren Liniensegmente widerspiegelt.[83] Zu bedenken ist zudem, dass die Reihe der mathematischen Wissenschaften im VII. Buch der *Politeia* sich dadurch im Sinne der Dimensionsfolge auf die Linien analog abbilden lässt und vor allem die beiden obersten Bereiche – Arithmetik und Geometrie – genau mit den beiden oberen Seinsstufen Speusipps korrelieren. Dementsprechend würde sich hinter dem fünfstufigen Universum Speusipps in der Tat Platons Linienanalogie – erweitert um das dort nur angedeutete Scharnierelement der Seele – als mögliches systematisches Vorbild schemenhaft abzeichnen. Wenn diese Überlegungen und diese ausgezogenen Parallelen zu Platon richtig sind, dann wären auch die vierte und die fünfte Seinstufe tentativ zuzuordnen: die vierte

[81] Vgl. zuvor, im Abschnitt zu Xenokrates.

[82] Vgl. hierzu auch die beiden Könige in der Sonnenanalogie der *Politeia* (*R.* 509d2–3); zur Auslegung der Sonne in dieser Analogie vgl. im Detail Poetsch, „Logoi der Sonnenanalogie".

[83] Diese Interpretationen beruhen auf ausführlichen Analysen der Linienanalogie, deren Ergebnisse ich hier nur als solche nennen kann. Vgl. im Detail Poetsch, *Philosophie des Bildes*, 61–98; Poetsch, „Logoi der Sonnenanalogie"; Poetsch, „Fin de la Ligne".

Seinsstufe in Speusipps System würde demnach die verkörperten Einzelseelen umfassen, während die fünfte Stufe alles Körperlich-Physische als solches umfassen würde.[84] Beides würde dem Auftreten des Bösen auf diesen Stufen, das im Text Jamblichs explizit vermerkt ist, durchaus entsprechen.

Kein Zweifel: eine solche Interpretation der Jamblich-Passage wird sich mangels weiterer Quellen zu diesem Punkt nicht letztgültig beweisen lassen. Die kryptische Passage zur vierten und fünften Stufe fügt sich aber, so scheint mir, auffällig gut in eine Reihe an Befunden, die alle auf den altakademischen Diskurs zur systematischen Stellung der Weltseele zurückzuführen sind. Zu nennen sind hier zum einen die Stellung der Weltseele als Dreh- und Angelpunkt zwischen den beiden ontologischen Grundebenen des Unkörperlichen und des Körperlichen. Und zum anderen vor allem die markante und direkte Beziehung der Weltseele zum ersten Prinzip, die uns schon bei Xenokrates, in der *De anima*-Passage bei Aristoteles und auch bei Platon selbst begegnet ist. All das weist auf einen differenzierten und regen Diskurs in der Alten Akademie zum Seelenbegriff, von dem wir Spuren und Schemen bei den einzelnen Vertretern dieser Institution in bemerkenswert passgenauer Form in den erhaltenen Texten finden.[85]

Bibliographie

Bärthlein, Karl, *Der Analogiebegriff bei den griechischen Mathematikern und bei Platon*, Würzburg 1996 [Dissertation 1957].

Baltes, Matthias, „Zur Theologie des Xenokrates“ [1988], in: ders., *ΔΙΑΝΟΗΜΑΤΑ. Kleine Schriften zu Platon und zum Platonismus*, Stuttgart / Leipzig 1999, 191–222.

Cherniss, Harold Fredrik, *Aristotle's Criticism of Plato and the Academy*, Baltimore 1944.

–, *The Riddle of the Early Academy*, Berkeley et al. 1945.

Corcilius, Klaus, *Aristoteles. Über die Seele. De anima. Griechisch – Deutsch*, Hamburg 2017.

de Vogel, Cornelia Johanna, „Problems Concerning Later Platonism II“, *Mnemosyne* 2 (1949), 299–318.

Dillon, John, *The Middle Platonists. A study of Platonism. 80 B.C. to A.D. 220*, London 1977.

[84] Mein Argument trifft sich damit im Ergebnis mit dem Vorschlag J. Dillons („I would suggest that the distinction here being made [sc. zwischen der vierten und fünften Ebene bei Speusipp] is between animate and inanimate physical beings.“ Dillon, *Heirs of Plato*, 55), wenngleich ich über eine andere Interpretationslinie dorthin gelange und – anders als J. Dillon – das Körperliche noch stärker auf den fünften Bereich konzentrieren würde. Zum Einwand, dass im Liniengleichnis die *beiden* unteren Bereiche als körperlich und sichtbar apostrophiert werden, vgl. im Detail Poetsch, *Philosophie des Bildes*, 73–74.

[85] Für die Einladung wie auch die äußerst gelungene Ausrichtung der Tübinger Platon-Tage mit zahlreichen guten Diskussionen (die den vorliegenden Beitrag maßgeblich bereichert haben), möchte ich Irmgard Männlein, Klaus Corcilius und Samuel Meister ganz herzlich danken.

–, „Speusippus in Iamblichus“, *Phronesis* 29 (1984), 325–332.

–, „Xenocrates’ Metaphysics. Frg. 15 (Heinze) Re-examined“, *Ancient Philosophy* 5 (1986), 47–52.

–, *The Heirs of Plato. A study of the Old Academy, 347–274 B.C.*, Oxford 2003.

Fronterotta, Francesco, „ΑΝΑΛΟΓΙΑ in Platone. Occorrenze e significato“, *Archivio di Filosofia* 84 (2016), 49–64.

Gaiser, Konrad, *Platons ungeschriebene Lehre. Studien zur systematischen und geschichtlichen Begründung der Wissenschaften in der Platonischen Schule*, Stuttgart [3]1998 [1963].

–, „Quellenkritische Probleme der indirekten Platonüberlieferung“, in: Hans-Georg Gadamer (Hg.), *Idee und Zahl. Studien zur platonischen Philosophie*, Heidelberg 1968, 31–83.

Gerlach, Stefan, „Die Fügung der Welt. Mathematik und Ontologie der Proportionenlehre im platonischen Timaios“, *Philosophisches Jahrbuch* 115 (2008), 21–43.

Halfwassen, Jens, *Der Aufstieg zum Einen. Untersuchungen zu Platon und Plotin*, München / Leipzig [2]2006 [1992].

Isnardi Parente, Margherita, *Senocrate. Ermodoro. Frammenti*, Neapel 1982.

Isnardi Parente, Margherita/Dorandi, Tiziano, *Senocrate. Ermodoro. Testimonianze e frammenti*, Pisa 2012.

Krämer, Hans Joachim, *Arete bei Platon und Aristoteles. Zum Wesen und zur Geschichte der platonischen Ontologie*, Heidelberg 1959.

Lattmann, Claas, *Mathematische Modellierung bei Platon zwischen Thales und Euklid*, Berlin / Boston 2019.

Mansfeld, Jaap/Runia, David Theunis, *Aëtiana V. Part 1: General Introduction. Book 1. Text and Commentary*, Leiden 2020.

Merlan, Philip, *From Platonism to Neoplatonism*, Den Haag [2]1960 [1953].

Poetsch, Christoph, *Platons Philosophie des Bildes. Systematische Untersuchungen zur platonischen Metaphysik*, Frankfurt/M. 2019.

–, „Die Logoi der platonischen Sonnenanalogie“, *Zeitschrift für philosophische Forschung* 75 (2021), 235–273.

–, „Dimensions of Pleasure. A first Detailed Reconstruction of Plato’s ‘Tyrant Number’“, *Apeiron* 55 (2022), 391–416.

–, „La fin de la Ligne. Quelque remarques sur la Ligne et la critique de l’art dans la *République*“ in: Anca Vasiliu / Elsa Grasso (Hg.), *Platon et la pensée de l’image*, Paris 2023, 105–128.

Primavesi, Oliver, „Aristoteles und Speusipp über die Platonische Zwei-Elementen-Lehre: Metaph. A 6 und die Kommentatoren Asklepios, Proklos und Aspasios“, in: Christian Brockmann / Daniel Deckers / Stefano Valente (Hg.), *Aristoteles-Kommentare und ihre Überlieferung. Wichtige Etappen von der Antike bis in die frühe Neuzeit*, Berlin / Boston 2024, 1–100.

Rapp, Christof, „Aristoteles über die Rechtfertigung des Satzes vom Widerspruch“, *Zeitschrift für philosophische Forschung* 47 (1993), 521–541.

Ross, William David, *Plato’s Theory of Ideas*, Oxford 1951.

Saffrey, Henri-Dominique, *Le ΠΕΡΙ ΦΙΛΟΣΟΦΙΑΣ d’Aristote et la théorie platonicienne des idées nombres*, Leiden [2]1971 [1955].

Schölles, Manuel, *Warum gibt es überhaupt Vieles und nicht nur Eines? Archytas und die Pluralität des Seins*, Heidelberg 2015.

Shields, Christopher. *Aristotle. De anima*. Oxford 2016.

Stenzel, Julius, *Zahl und Gestalt bei Platon und Aristoteles*, Darmstadt [3]1959 [1924].

Szlezák, Thomas Alexander, *Platon. Meisterdenker der Antike*, München 2021.
Tarán, Leonardo, *Speusippus of Athens. A critical study with a collection of the related texts and commentary*, Leiden 1981.
Thiel, Detlef, *Die Philosophie des Xenokrates im Kontext der Alten Akademie*, München / Leipzig 2006.
Toeplitz, Otto, „Das Verhältnis von Mathematik und Ideenlehre bei Plato“, *Quellen und Studien zur Geschichte der Mathematik, Astronomie und Physik* 1 (1929), 3–33.

List of Contributors

Riccardo Chiaradonna
Professor of ancient philosophy at the University of Roma Tre

Klaus Corcilius
Professor of ancient philosophy at the University of Tübingen

Andrea Falcon
Emeritus Professor at Concordia University, Montréal
and Guest Professor at the University of Tübingen

Mary Louise Gill
Professor of classics and philosophy at Brown University, Providence

Tomas K. Johansen
Professor of philosophy at the University of Oslo

Susanna Kinzig
Doctoral Student at the University of Tübingen

Fiona Leigh
Professor of ancient philosophy at University College London

Béatrice Lienemann
Professor of ancient philosophy at the University of Fribourg

Samuel Meister
Assistant Professor of ancient philosophy at the University of Geneva

Georgia Mouroutsou
Associate Professor of philosophy at Western University, Canada

Peter Oxenknecht
M.A. (University of Tübingen)

Christoph Poetsch
Dr. Phil. (Ruprecht-Karls-University of Heidelberg)

Jan Szaif
Professor of ancient philosophy at the University of California, Davis

Index of References

Tübingen Platon-Tage

This series publishes selected papers of conference proceedings, papers held as lectures during the biennial international *Tübinger Platon-Tage.* Held in Tübingen, which has a long tradition of studying Plato, the aim of this symposium is to stimulate interest in Plato by providing the findings from recent Plato studies. The conferences focus on central questions of Plato's dialogues and philosophy, including the reception of Plato in the imperial period, late antiquity and Renaissance. The authors of the articles are distinguished scholars from Germany and abroad as well as promising young scholars.

ISSN: 2629-3978
Suggested citation: TüPlaTa

All available volumes can be found at *www.mohrsiebeck.com/tueplata*

Mohr Siebeck
www.mohrsiebeck.com